Persons—What Philosophers Say About You

2nd Edition

Warren Bourgeois

Wilfrid Laurier University Press

WLU

We acknowledge the financial support of the Government of Canada through the Book Publishing Industry Development Program for our publishing activities.

National Library of Canada Cataloguing in Publication Data

Bourgeois, Verne Warren, 1947-

Persons : what philosophers say about you

2nd ed.
Includes bibliographical references and index.
ISBN 978-0-88920-379-2 (paper)
ISBN 978-0-88920-946-6 (e-book)

1. Persons—History. 2. Persons. I. Title.

BD450.B68 2003 128 C2001-903200-5

Waterloo, Ontario, Canada N2L 3C5
www.wlupress.wlu.ca

This printing: 2011

Cover design by Jane Grossett of Mindpage Design,
based on Giorgio de Chirico's *The Melancholy and Mystery of a Street*, 1914.

Printed in Canada

Contents

Acknowledgments

I am grateful to Kwantlen College for awarding me educational leave in 1989-90, during which the first draft of this book was written. I am also grateful to the University of British Columbia for making me a research associate in the Department of Philosophy during my leave. I have benefited greatly from discussions with members of the philosophy department, in particular, professors Richard Sikora, Samuel Coval, Michael Phillips, and Donald Brown. Jonathan Katz at Kwantlen University College, Leonard Angel at Douglas College, Michael Stack at the University of Manitoba, and Ray Jennings at Simon Fraser University offered insightful suggestions about persons. Papers adumbrating the theory developed here were read to two colloquia of the departments of philosophy of the University of British Columbia and Simon Fraser University. Sandra Woolfrey's many comments made this a much more accessible book, and I benefited from the criticisms of unnamed reviewers. I would like to have responded to all my colleagues' questions, but I have come to appreciate the saying that one never completes a book but just stops writing. In any case, I have reached the natural limits of the second edition of my first volume on this subject.

The first edition of this book was published with the help of a grant from the Canada Council.

INTRODUCTION

Where I Am Coming From

Daphne's tragedy: Radical, personal change

My topics—the nature of persons and personal identity—are for Daphne shot through with significance. Daphne is not the real name of the person who inspired this book but a name I will use here. I choose the name since Daphne in Greek mythology suffers a somewhat parallel tragedy. Daphne was a brilliant philosopher teaching at the University of British Columbia where I was on a post-doctoral fellowship. We became inseparable. In the next five years, we came to know each other's hearts and minds so well that we could often dispense with spoken communication. We were married in August of 1985. In October of that year, Daphne suffered a massive attack of multiple sclerosis. After nearly a year of attacks and remissions, in August 1986, Daphne passed for the last time beneath the dark archway that separates those who can intelligibly express their wishes from those who cannot.

What people are and what changes a person can survive had long been metaphysical concerns of mine. They suddenly appeared to me as practical questions of great moral import. Here, I offer all-too-brief expositions of some of the great philosophers of the Western philosophical tradition, including some of our contemporaries, to reveal some of the sources of our cultural heritage for dealing with what I witnessed and what Daphne suffered. No attempt is made here, however, to deal with the rich traditions of the Orient. My own answers to the questions that forced themselves so roughly to the forefront of my philosophical thought are rooted in the past, but, I hope, grow beyond it to become applicable to our current deeds.

Through my theory of persons, it is at least possible that one might suffer radical change and still be a person—although not the same person one once was. It is also possible that one might be still a human being but no longer a person at all. Before I work through others' theories of persons, and my own, however, I will explain in further detail what happened to Daphne. This is what I am trying, through my thought, to absorb into my life.

Multiple sclerosis is a disease that can take many forms. Some suffer attacks infrequently with long periods of remission. At another extreme, some steadily and quickly worsen, losing physical or mental abilities, perhaps both. At first it was not clear how Daphne's case would progress. From the start, however, she was very different from the way she had been just prior to that massive attack in October 1985.

Initially, peculiar bodily changes and total exhaustion beset Daphne. She was unable to carry on her life in a normal way. At the beginning, however, neither she nor I could quite believe that this condition would continue. Even though she had already lost the pitch of her intellectual abilities, we assumed that she would return to what for her was normal and for most of us would be an exceptional mental clarity. I would say of Daphne at the onset of her illness, "She is not herself today," in the faith that tomorrow would see the familiar traits return. Intelligence, energy, curiosity, hope, and their allies, I supposed, would surely revive in full measure. They did not.

The disease gave Daphne very strange sensations. The myelin sheath, a protective covering on the nerves, was being attacked in Daphne's body by her own immune system. She spoke of inappropriate sensations from familiar stimuli, as, for instance, a warm shower feeling normal on half her body and cold on the other half. Half her tongue was numb. Strange tingling and buzzing sensations came from no observable stimulus at all. With quite good justification but, very uncharacteristically, Daphne became highly irritable, fearful, and depressed. The thought that her body would always undergo such intensely strange sensations was literally driving her mad.

Eventually, after the first massive attack was in remission, hope did return to Daphne, in a muted form. She began to think that she might have periods of being like her old self. In the past she had worked with great enthusiasm at every task, from putting down inlay in a hardwood floor to the most abstract of intellectual investigations. She was as clever at crafting physical objects as at constructing theories. Although she suspected that she would never regain her former impressive ability to craft material things—since she knew that her eyesight and physical dexterity were permanently impaired—she nonetheless hoped to return to her philosophical work as an outlet for her immense creative impulse. A flame still flickered in those eyes that had burned with a zeal for philosophical understanding. For the time being, however, all our energies were directed at improving Daphne's health. During the period I describe, there was no time for reflection. The struggle with the disease consumed us.

Daphne had had a keen, incisive mind and a powerful memory. Her mind was immediately somewhat dulled and her memory, in the short term, was less certain. I remember her lying down with some philosophical books gathered around her, making a valiant effort to be what she had been. Not only did she realize that she could not understand the text she was reading, but her own marginalia explicating the text had become incomprehensible. This was not the first time since becoming ill that she had tried unsuccessfully to work. She picked up something else while I turned to a task that distracted me for a moment. What she had picked up fell from her hands. I looked up. It was her own doctoral thesis. She could not understand a word of it. In this moment, the realization rushed upon her that she would not recover the abilities in which she had invested so much of her life. She looked up at me as if from a great depth.

In the past she had worked with blazing intensity. She had needed to be reminded to eat and sleep when she became engrossed in philosophical work. Now she could neither concentrate nor work at all and, after many attempts, had come to believe she never would work again. Are we what we are able to do? Daphne was inconsolable. For a while she seemed convinced that she had observed her own death.

It is impossible to convey in a few paragraphs, or really at any length, the long droning suffering punctuated by such dramatic events as Daphne's realization that she could no longer do the work by which she had defined herself. The day to day was not dramatic; rather, Daphne's quotidian was a terrible tedium of struggle against an unseen enemy, which dragged her by infinitesimal degrees into a dark pit.

The disease had caused massive scarring of her brain resulting in dementia. Daphne, who had been capable of deep philosophical thought and discussion, after the onset of dementia, would at her most vocal repeat things by rote. She would sing with me a few words of simple songs she had known in her girlhood. With heavy-handed irony, fate had written a script in which the only things Daphne could say without prompting were I don't know, Yeah, No, and OK. She would repeat such phrases as many as fifty times in a row as she lay smiling in her hospital bed. Now even this limited verbal ability is gone; Daphne can only sit and stare, unresponsively.

Daphne would have agreed that merely to live through tragedy, to learn nothing from it, and to pass nothing on is to compound the tragedy. In Daphne's own opinion, which she expressed before becoming ill, people in her present circumstances should be counted as the same sentient beings but not the same persons they once were in the crucial sense of "person." Daphne, I believe, can no longer learn from her decline, but we can.

There was no way to measure clearly the downward slide. While some characteristics that had seemed necessary to Daphne—her passionate intellectual intensity, her great critical acumen, her immense intelligence—were waning, others seemed to remain unscathed. Daphne, even in such desperate straits, was more concerned for others than for herself and extremely sensitive to the suffering of any being, whether or not that being could think. Ironically, she had, at times, cursed the intensity of her passion for philosophy that drove her like a whip. She had longed on occasion to be an unthinking sentient being like our pet cats on which she lavished affection. This sort of choking irony doubtlessly inspired the proverb, "The gods grant the wishes of those whom they wish to condemn." In any case, under stress that might have embittered her, Daphne retained love, empathic understanding, and pity. It was only much later—when she was like one possessed—that the deeply ingrained sweetness of her character was, at least temporarily, displaced.

After a deep depression about the loss of her mental abilities—a depression which lasted through some attacks and remissions—Daphne began to have trouble remembering her passion for philosophy. I remember distinctly, in a year replete with poignancy, the moment when she first said aloud that she no longer felt horror at losing her ability as a philosopher. Why, she asked, could she not be happy as a homemaker without the strange need to ask immense questions? Of course I encouraged this line of thought, but the strangeness of its coming from Daphne chilled me deeply. Who was saying such things to me?

Although formerly unthinkable changes had taken place in Daphne, it still seemed to me that she had to some degree survived these changes. Until she became completely demented, there was usually enough of Daphne's former character to make her recognizable as a continuation of her former self—the person whom I thought I knew so well. The changes were quite varied. While some characteristics flew away, others remained as always. Some things about Daphne seemed not so much lost as muted or redirected. She had been served well as a theorist by an extraordinary independence of mind and pertinacity in the pursuit of ideas. Her defence of her considered views sometimes bordered on intellectual ferocity. Once she was unable to understand philosophy, her love of theorizing was directed at surveying the literature on the causes of multiple sclerosis and seeking to discover the nature of the demon with which she struggled. Without the critical ability she once had, she fell prey to many false hopes and tried, partly through desperation, a number of "cures" which she would have dismissed had she had her former abilities and had she lacked a motive so strong that it crushed reason. Daphne's pertinacity and independence now served her less ably than they had in her earlier life. The purely intellectual passion became a passion to escape from a terrible fate. The horror of the roller-coaster ride downward redirected her energy and creativity into fantasies about curing her ailment and into delusions about the abilities and motives of the neurologists who delivered the ever-worsening news.

Just prior to Daphne's final descent into dementia, I had to ask myself to what extent paternalism was justified in my care of Daphne. This was a question that would have made no sense prior to her illness. Then, she always knew what she was doing and clearly had the right to decide for herself what actions she would take. I could hardly argue when I heard her say in response to my doubts about some particularly irrational and harmful sort of putative cure, But my brain is being eaten away! On the other hand, I had to protect her from making her condition worse. There was still some chance of remission of the disease if she could be protected from other serious harms. The immense respect which Daphne had earned had to be tempered with the knowledge that she was, in some important sense, no longer herself, no longer the person who had earned complete autonomy. In the past I would never have treated Daphne as a child; now, sometimes being forced to do just that made me very ill at ease. Fortunately, by that time, she did not seem to be aware that I was distracting her from some of her ill-considered attempts at curing the disease.

To describe her as Plato might have done, Daphne was a very spirited person, but one in whom reason clearly ruled. As reason weakened, spirit took the upper hand, with some disastrous consequences. Whatever the physical mechanisms in terms of loss of cells in the nervous system, the results of multiple sclerosis in her case can be accurately described as the loss of the inhibiting force of reason and the release of violent emotions with a consequent marked change in personality. Those to whom Daphne had always been forbearing felt the full brunt of an anger that she had formerly reserved for those she had good reason to believe to be unjust. Once the disease had an insuperable grip on her mind, she lost the power to distinguish a crime from a minor fault and the blast of her anger blew at random. What before would have been seen as a change from greatness of heart to meanness, could not be seen that way when Daphne's mind was unravelling. Perhaps to speak of personality changes or character changes makes no sense when the mind is so embattled.

In any case, everything remaining that was familiar to me in Daphne's character began to fade in and out. As the ability to reason and communicate—whether verbally or by other signs—diminished, the things I thought of as character or personality traits became harder to assess. When, eventually, she became unable to walk as well as demented, the opportunity for self-expression was as limited as it is for a baby. This is not to deny that an infant may have and display a personality, but to point out how severely limited such a personality was in comparison with the dizzyingly complex personality that Daphne once had. Even that infantile personality is gone now.

Some traits may survive even such dread changes as a total loss of intelligence. Sweetness of temper, for instance, is a trait which we could for years attribute to Daphne with very minimal action on her part. One can also have such sweetness as an underlying characteristic and yet be a fierce debater on the side of what is just, as Daphne was before her illness. Daphne had a fine sense of humour as well; it did not leave her while she could still respond. The wide range of things which formerly amused her narrowed to the humour of the pit, but still she could laugh in the face of an unimaginably wretched fate. Long after she had lost the ability to speak at all, she sometimes smiled, although it was apparently the tone of voice rather than the content of what was said that amused her. Now she does not respond at all. Week to week I hardly noticed the changes but, as I reflect on longer periods, I see the gradual ebbing away of even what little was left to Daphne. The complex personality which included such traits as considered gentleness, subtle whimsicality, intellectual pertinacity, and highly developed empathic understanding could not survive the simplifying effects of the loss of all reasoning ability.

Daphne suffered a diabolical torture in going into and out of episodes of some lucidity before she descended finally and utterly into dementia. In lucid moments she begged for euthanasia; she was too weak to take her own life. This wish to die seemed to be the considered and rational wish of someone who did not want her body to live on after the death of her mind and personality. It was, however, uncertain whether remissions might not still occur and give Daphne a life worth living. Once she had passed beyond the horror of watching her mind ebb away, once she could no longer understand what was happening to her, her foremost source of misery had ceased. Should Daphne's wishes to die still have been considered for this new Daphne who seemed like a sometimes-happy infant? Was this really Daphne or rather a human being only as closely related to her as a mentally challenged daughter would have been? Now that she shows not even emotional responses, has she crossed some significant divide between persons and non-persons? When she was competent what rights did Daphne have to specify what was to be done with her body when her mind had gone? The questions spring up like weeds. Answers are rare, delicate blossoms to be carefully cultivated.

Now that Daphne does not respond verbally at all, one unfamiliar with the neurological diagnosis and her history might think she is somewhat like those who suffer from locked-in syndrome—able to think normally but unable to express herself by word or gesture. This is clearly not the case. While she was still able to speak she gradually lost her intellect and spoke more and more as one who was becoming demented. Magnetic resonance imagery (MRI) showed the plaques on the brain that explained this dementia. There is a wealth of evidence that the dementia is real, deep, and permanent. The person we knew cannot return.

In spite of the terrible inspiration for this book, it is not a book cloaked in mourning. Mourning is something I have come through. My tone at times may even seem flippant to those who think philosophers must never smile. Philosophical ideas are not forbidding things: they are meant to be lived. I refuse to dress them in widower's weeds.

How to read this book

The intended audience

This is a broad survey, not a book for professional philosophers specializing in the area of concepts of a person. I have tried to make it accessible to anyone who cares deeply about people and is willing to think hard. My aim is to provide a map of a large and strange territory. Professional philosophers usually take some part of that territory and explore it very thoroughly, but there is not space for such intense investigation in a work of this scope. This book covers a huge range of ideas about persons and points out many pathways that may invite further exploration. There are numerous sketches of historical developments concerning the concepts of a person. For the lay reader or philosophy student, these sketches provide choices between varied philosophical traditions within Western philosophy. At the end there is a quick look at where my own explorations have led me. Readers may wonder, though, as they view the sweep of Western thought on persons, how to compare the many adumbrated views.

A framework for comparing views about persons

The views we will consider are in the category of conceptual analysis. Each is an attempt to say what a person is, in general. This is not social history or psychology, so there is no claim made here about societal activity or causes of individual behaviour. Instead we are looking at the history of what we have believed ourselves to be and of the changes we have believed we could survive. We will analyze various concepts of a person to see what follows from adopting each one.

One question to keep in mind is how these views are related to common sense about persons. Philosophers are fond of the old saying that common sense is not all that common and seldom sensible, but I am more sanguine about common sense and believe it is a good way to categorize views on persons. Some of the philosophers mentioned in these pages are, indeed, partly the source of today's common sense as what was once philosophical invention has filtered down. Of course these are Western philosophers, and it is a culturally relative Western common sense that I use. As long as we apply the concept with this in mind, common sense can help. Even without any analysis of common sense, for instance, one can recognize that a philosopher whose theory implies that each human body is associated with a series of about a dozen different persons, or one who says there are no persons at all, is departing considerably from common sense. Since a concept of a person is fundamental to much of our thinking, it would be nice to stick as close to common sense as we can.

To elaborate, it is necessary to anticipate somewhat the second-to-last chapter of this book to say a little about some common ideas about persons in the history of Western philosophy and to prepare for these ideas as they crop up between here and the distant end of this book. Here, then, are some beliefs that many of us have about ourselves. To begin with, we are *complex* creatures. Any view that characterizes persons as so simple as to have no parts or internal divisions would not be about us. On the other hand, we are *not reducible* simply to a set of parts in a certain configuration. One cannot take a person apart and put her back together in the way that one can, say, a computer. Each of us is, moreover, a unique *individual*. People seem to be, as well, *continuous* during the life of their bodies with more or less *determinate* beginnings and endings. In some sense, a person is an *indivisible* whole. Persons as individuals—and perhaps even as a class—*cannot be defined*. Finally, persons have *freedom* of the will.

The picture of persons I have just drawn is one that many philosophers reject in one or more of its aspects. The sources of these ideas emerge as I set out the history of the concepts of a person, and can be useful as ways to compare views. I will eventually defend some form of each in what I present as a defence of common sense.

Philosophers tend to divide their conceptual analyses into three main areas: metaphysics, epistemology, and axiology. In metaphysics we ask questions about reality and existence. Most of the recent philosophical work on persons is of this sort. The questions of whether we are complex, irreducible, individual, continuous, determinate, and free can be seen as metaphysical questions about what we are really like. Of course these metaphysical questions raise epistemological questions about what we can know about these matters, for instance, the question of our definability. Axiology covers questions of value such as those raised in ethics and aesthetics. Here I frame questions and answers in metaphysical, epistemological, and ethical terms.

Another way to compare views is to look at their applications to one's life. Daphne's story comes up again and again, as I ask what various philosophers would say about it. You may have stories of your own to which these theories can be applied. Ask of each philosopher's theory: is it speaking of real people, and what difference would the theory make to your life if you believed it? If you find something which strikes you, you will at least know who to read to follow it up in more detail than I can present in this brief survey.

Questions and arguments

At the end of each chapter are questions to help readers check their mastery of the content of the chapter. The book's glossary can help to clarify the questions and their answers. Arguments on the topics in each chapter are also provided. These may help readers debate with themselves to become clearer about their own views on questions we all must answer if we are to reflect on what we are. The arguments are intended to inspire objections. I am told that H.L. Mencken said that to every complex question there is an answer that is simple, clear, and wrong. I hope that the questions and arguments here can help readers avoid oversimplification about fundamentals.

Content questions

1. What is meant by each of the following terms as they apply to persons?
   (a) complex, (b) irreducible, (c) individual, (d) continuous, (e) determinate, (f) indivisible, (g) indefinable, (h) free
2. Briefly characterize the following fields of study within philosophy: metaphysics, epistemology, and axiology.

Part 1

Philosophical Background

CHAPTER 1

The Nature of Persons

What is philosophy?

Philosophy is an activity in which philosophers engage in debate on such big questions as the one we hear in the popular press, What is the meaning of life? Philosophers look at such a question and ask about its presuppositions, the things that must be true for the question to make sense. In this case, the question presupposes that there are persons, purposes, and purposes of persons. Say that ten times fast. I rephrase this question as What is the purpose of persons? Other questions that might make it into the category of big questions include: What is truth? Is there a God? What is reality? What is beauty? What makes actions morally right? What is love? What is justice? Questions of this nature, fall into three main categories of inquiry, which correspond to three extra-large questions: What matters? What is real? What can be known? Philosophers tend to understand these questions as having "if anything" attached at the end and do not start an inquiry assuming that something matters or is real or can be known.

What matters? is a question about values. The general area dealing with this is the theory of value or axiology, but those terms are rarely used in philosophy. Instead, philosophers talk about two special

---

Notes to chapter 1 are on pp. 475-76.

areas within axiology: ethics, the study of moral concepts, judgments and codes, and aesthetics, the study of artistic value and beauty. What is real? is a question of metaphysics, the theory of reality. Philosophers consider what can exist or what existence is in this field. What can be known? is a question of epistemology, the theory of knowledge. In this area, philosophers look into the nature of knowledge, methods of acquiring knowledge, and the limits of knowledge. Often, a single big question will be dealt with in all three areas within philosophy. Many of the great philosophers have been systematic thinkers who tried to find a way to answer all three of our extra-large questions in one unified theory referred to as a worldview.

Philosophical answers and irritants

Anyone who has had any dealings with philosophers is probably aware of their devilish habit of giving out questions in response to questions. Contrary to an opinion popular among students who have done poorly on their first exam, this philosophical questioning of the question is not usually motivated by a desire to be irritating and evasive. What philosophers generally try to do is to find out precisely what a question is before they attempt an answer. Philosophers, whenever they undertake to answer a question, are acutely aware that what the question really means depends on the context in which it is asked.

Here we are asking maddeningly difficult questions: What are persons? What makes this person now identical to that person in the past? and What marks the beginning and the end of a person? Of course we have to be very careful about what we are asking. That depends in part on whom we ask. If, for instance, we ask a lawyer what persons are, she will probably say that they are individuals, corporations, or other organizations satisfying a certain list of juridical requirements. If we do not stop her there, she will probably rattle off that list. While we may be vitally interested in what the law says about persons, we have some prior work to do on the concept of a person to answer some of the questions that arise when someone undergoes radical change.

Another example of contextual dependency shows us that we might get sidetracked regarding the related question, What makes this person identified in one way identical to that person identified in another way? Suppose that I inquire at a government office whether

Fay and Kay McLeod are two persons, identical twins perhaps, or just one person with two names. A clerk tells me that they must be one person because they have the same social insurance number. Fay and Kay show up later, looking as alike as two peas in a pod, to gently dispute the clerk's opinion. The clerk refuses to revise her opinion. Fay and Kay then have a not-unheard-of bureaucratic headache, but that has nothing to do with the question I was asking. Seeing them together, I can see that they are not the same person. They are identical for the clerk's bureaucratic purposes until they get their records revised, but we should not let this quaint bureaucratic stubbornness discourage us from treating them as different persons.

This example of Fay and Kay underlines our tendency to accept a difference of bodies, however similar, as a knock-down, drag-out argument in favour of the conclusion that there is a difference between two persons. As was pointed out above, this difference of bodies is rather limiting as a criterion of difference. It seems to work at a given time but not over time. None of us has the same body that we had when we were rocked in our mother's arms. It will become evident that much of the puzzling we do about persons depends on prior assumptions about time. We will have to stop and ask in some of the debates about who's who whether we are talking about persons through complete lifetimes, persons through a large segment of a life, or persons in a brief period of time. One may have no difficulty thinking one is the same person who began this paragraph, but is one the same person one was when one was two years old? Will one be the same person if one becomes senile in later life? For those who say, Yes, is some sort of continuity other than the mere continuity of the body the underlying reason? See what your answers are as you read critically the answers of the philosophers in the discussion here. First, I issue some warnings about our methods.

Words for persons

In the miasma of unclear intellectual discussion, the oft-heard cry of the great bull philosopher, Define your terms! reverberates like a foghorn. Sometimes, trying to define a term makes little sense. It may be perfectly well understood in a context of use. It may be poorly understood, but the resources for a precise definition may not be at hand. In some cases, it may not even be in principle definable, though its meaning is understood. For instance, Moore pointed out that we know what "pleasure" means but cannot define it.[1] Similarly, Strawson treats "person" as a primitive term, that is, as a term at the base of our vocabulary, a term which is used to define others but is not itself definable in a non-circular way.[2] He is treating the term "person" as Moore treats "pleasure." Perhaps there are some contexts in which it is reasonable to treat the word "person" in this fashion, but there are others where definition is worthwhile.

Amelie Rorty's list of person candidates

Considering a list of terms sometimes used in place of the word "person" can be enlightening. Consider these terms from literature offered by the philosopher Amelie Rorty: "'Heroes,' 'characters,' 'protagonists,' 'actors,' 'agents,' 'persons,' 'souls,' 'selves,' 'figures,' 'individuals' are all distinguishable. Each inhabits a different space in fiction and in society."[3] With the possible exceptions of "heroes," "protagonists," and "figures," these terms all function in some contexts outside of literary criticism as synonyms of "person." Note the strangeness, however, of debating the possibility of most of these terms to describe a fetus, a corporation, or God. As soon as one notices the variety of concepts of a person, many of the debates about which beings fall within the category of a person become harder to understand.

The history of the term "person"

Concerning oneself with various definitions of the term "person" may seem to be an ivory-tower pursuit to those who think that they know well enough what persons are. That it is not so is evident from the weight people put on the term in debates concerning abortion and euthanasia. Nor is this seriousness about definition a new phenomenon. The definition of "person" was a matter of life and death as long ago as, for instance, the late Middle Ages. Servetus, a mediaeval physician and polemicist, wrote an essay on the mistakes in the doctrine of the Trinity, the puzzling Christian doctrine that God is three persons in one. Servetus used one of the possible derivations of *persona*, the Latin term for "person." He was assuming that *persona* came from words referring to an actor's mask. This suggested to him that "person" in this religious context meant "role" like the role that the actor would play. He then gave the very reasonable explanation of the Trinity that there is only one God, but God plays three roles or performs three functions. Servetus was burned to death at the stake as a heretic on Calvin's accusation.[4] Define your terms, but carefully.

Much of the difference between the pro-life and pro-choice groups in the abortion issue hinges on the question of whether all human beings, including fetuses, are persons. Although people on both sides talk as if they would like to burn their opponents at the stake, the more likely causes of death of human beings are from abortion itself, and from radical pro-life groups blowing up abortion clinics or shooting abortion providers. Murder is the unjustifiable taking of the life of a person. Using an abortion for, say, birth control, would be murder if a fetus were a person. Pro-choice groups deny that the fetus is a person. Neither side denies that the fetus is a human being. This may seem strange to someone who thinks that all and only human beings are persons, a standard assumption among pro-lifers. What the pro-choice groups are saying, though, is that it is wrong to think of all human beings as persons. Obviously, we are badly in need of some definitions from both sides to begin to clarify the heated debate between them.

Why can we not just look at a dictionary and find out who is right? For one thing, you will find many definitions of "person" in any good dictionary, some on one side of the issue, some on the other, some favouring neither, and some irrelevant. It turns out that our selection of a meaning for "person" in such contexts as the abortion debate is a moral one. On this selection hang important decisions about what we should do.

One response, then, to the problems we are having with the concept of a person and the definition of "person" is to decide what we should do, and then choose the concept of a person that suits that decision. This is in effect what often happens in debates about abortion and euthanasia. But while there are philosophers who would agree with this policy, there are many who think that reflection on the concept of a person should be a precursor to or at least a concomitant of the ethical decisions. In fact, our contemporary concepts of a person include some that developed as innovations in ethics.

Legal problems

As I was writing the first draft of this book, the Parliament of Canada was attempting to put a new law concerning abortion into the Criminal Code. The Supreme Court of this country is still wrestling with the definition of "person" as it has done in the past. As the legal proverb goes, hard cases make bad law and, I would add, intractable concepts do as well. Fortunately, Canadians currently have no law on abortion.

According to the polls reported on the news, a large majority of people in this country side with the pro-choice movement. This is some indication that the majority's attitudes to the fetus are consistent with the idea that a fetus is not a person in the sense that confers rights and duties. Some philosophers hold that the fundamental right is the right to be treated as a person and that all other rights flow from this.[5] It makes, for them, a huge difference what you count as a person. If, for example, a fetus is not a person but merely a potential person, then it may have something like what lawyers call a "future interest" in life and in becoming a person—which is a much weaker entitlement than a full-fledged right. This is a concept I will try to clarify in chapter 17 after looking at the history of the concept of a person.

Trendelenberg goes so far as to say that the development of the concept of a person as an end is an indication of moral progress in a society.[6] The distinctly moral use of the concept is, however, a relatively recent invention in our culture. The watershed in this development is Kant, who tells us, "Rational beings are called persons because their nature distinguishes them as an end unto themselves; that is, as something that may not be used simply as a means, and consequently in so far limits all caprice and is an object of esteem."[7] This introduces the idea that persons cannot, like tools or animals, be treated simply as a way of achieving some result and also the idea that rationality is a necessary feature of persons. The special place this conception accords to persons has been the foundation of much of our thinking about rights and duties that are conceived of as applying only to persons. Recently this has been challenged by animal rights activists, who accuse the traditional ethicists of speciesism. Perhaps animals do have rights, but I would argue that persons' rights are stronger. We should treat both animals and people better than we do.

The concept of persons as ends, not means, as those for whom things are done rather than that which is used to accomplish purposes, is linked to rationality. Rationality is itself a contested concept, but it is often taken to include not merely the capacity for logical thought but also the capacity to express thought in language. Rational beings of any sort are worthy of esteem, on this view, but, as it happens, the only beings we know of who are indisputably rational are human beings. Other beings may behave as if they understand reasons for doing things, but we are the only beings who can boast about it. Now some would claim that some chimpanzees such as Washoe, who has learned many signs in the American Sign Language for the Deaf, have demonstrated that non-human beings are rational. There is also much speculation of late that the ancient dream of machines that can really think will be realized. Does this make them worthy of the esteem we accord to persons? Perhaps rationality is irrelevant, as Bentham thought, and merely the ability to suffer and feel pleasure is what should give us cause for concern about a being "The question is not Can they reason? nor Can they talk? but Can they suffer?"[8] There is, then, a debate about whether being a person as defined in terms of rationality or mere sentience is the mark of a member of a moral community.

If we accept the term "person" into our moral vocabulary, either as a defined term or a primitive one, the question remains whether it is descriptive of something that is the source of moral value or is merely honorific. Do we first value something and then confer on it the title of person? To some extent this is what is happening when environmentalists use talk appropriate to persons to speak of ecosystems or the whole planet. They have not suddenly turned into animists, but are trying to persuade us to value and treat well the planet on which we live. If we say that the earth has rights or that she is our mother, these are honorific, extended uses of terms. They are evocative and poetic. A use of "person" applied to the fetus may be similar. We want our society to be especially careful of the future interests of fetuses, and we achieve this by speaking of their rights. This talk is almost totally indistinguishable from the differently motivated claims that there are genuine rights of the fetus and that the fetus is a person in more than this extended sense. If fetuses are to be classed as genuine persons with full rights, then clearly the sense of "person" being used is not the sense discussed earlier that requires developed rationality. To avoid taking the seemingly irrelevant criterion of mere species membership as determining whether a being is a person, we might look at an idea of ancient origin, that of the soul.

Those who believe that a soul inhabits the body at conception and that this soul is the source of the esteem in which we hold the person, or that this soul just is the person, would say literally the things that others might say as a figure of speech in speaking of the fetus. To call it an unborn person is to make a strong claim. The debate over how to best use this term is a fight over the tools of moral persuasion.

Whatever one may think of the religiously inspired sense of the term, "person" is a powerfully evocative moral term. Consider, for instance, its importance in the feminist movement. The group that can persuade others to adopt its usage is the group that will sway hearts and minds to its moral position. We will, then, have to examine closely the concept of a person and the cluster of such related concepts as rationality, soul, self, and rights. Before we proceed, another warning is in order: there are some philosophers who would nip this investigation in the bud. They do not believe we can ask or answer any sensible questions about persons at all.

Pseudo-questions

One philosophical tack to take when one sails into a troublesome question is to dismiss the question as not a real question at all, but to consider it as a pseudo-question. The question What is a person? or the question What makes this person identical to that person? may be said to ask nothing at all. One reason which might be given is that the general criteria sought are not to be had. What answers the question will get will always be relative to the particular usage and context. They are real questions when limited to such contexts, but as general questions are meaningless.

On the other hand, some might think there is a generally accepted use of "person" but no answer to the question merely because the term is primitive. Other terms of importance such as "duty" or "moral" are to be defined in terms of "person." In this case, to ask What is a person? is not to ask a genuine question for there can be no answer. The only answer would be a definition, and that is just what cannot be given if the term is genuinely primitive.

The term "person" may be said to be so ambiguous that the question of personal identity and survival, unqualified, is no question at all. This, in fact, is my view, but rather than merely dismiss the question I want to qualify it in various ways to transform it into various clearer questions. I do not want to say that the term must be used to name mere fictions and phantasms.

Paradoxes of conflicting intuitions

When I see Daphne lying in a hospital bed, recognizable as the woman with whom I spent years prior to her illness, I may say to myself that this is the person I knew, but she is much changed in personality and abilities. It seems equally intuitively plausible to say that the person whom I once knew could not survive such changes. There is so little psychological continuity, and so much of the brain of this woman has been destroyed, that by the psychological or bodily criteria of sameness of persons, this woman is a different person from the one I knew. Dictionaries reflect the different uses of "person" that correspond to these conflicting intuitions about what a person is. Outward resemblance and some kind of continuity of body are, however, the most weighty considerations in our society. The police would have no hesitation, for example, in identifying this woman as my wife and the same person who, in far better health, was a brilliant philosopher and teacher. The strength of this outward resemblance criterion is probably dependent on our religious heritage—on the doctrine of the immortal soul entering the body at conception and, whatever the changes to the mind, leaving the body only at death.

Even in a largely secular society, we retain the doctrine of the soul, or some vestige of it through the outward resemblance doctrine of the person, as a safety. We do not want to give up on people too soon. Whenever anything can be done to revive them we must try. Such doctrines help us to make incredible efforts to preserve life and health in others. If we see them as persons—indeed as the same persons they were—after a catastrophe, then we will treat them very differently than we would if we were to see them as mere bodies from whom the person has fled or as new persons in familiar bodies. We are more likely to honour promises made to the person prior to the catastrophe. We are able to steel ourselves, with the help of gratitude, to the task of seeing to their medical care and comfort.

It seems a good idea then, as a social insurance policy, to think of people as the same even after a mental catastrophe. Sometimes, however, it leads to unreasonable expectations of those who have directly suffered the catastrophe and of those who care for them. We may, when things get bad enough, wish to adopt the view that calling someone who remains after such a catastrophe the "same person" may be a fiction that has outlived its usefulness. Nonetheless, it is often difficult to do so. The power of our conflicting intuitions on this score can pull us apart. For this reason alone, it is best to look for whatever clarity we can muster.

Puzzles concerning related concepts

When we ask about the nature of persons or, for many purposes the same question, about what makes a person the same through change, ancient puzzles about identity and time raise their grizzled heads. Many philosophers are in rough agreement about how to define identity, but we should be aware of the complications that arise from the roughness. Here is a standard way of defining identity called Leibniz's law: "Whatever x and y are, x is identical to y if and only if x and y have all their properties in common." To say that x and y have all their properties in common means that they are totally alike. In other words, it means that x is red if and only if y is red, and x is shorter than the Eiffel Tower if and only if y is as well, and so on for anything you might want to say about these things x and y. Now Leibniz's law has two parts, one controversial and one not much disputed. I will begin, however, with the controversial part, which is called the identity of indiscernibles, and goes roughly like this: if x and y are totally alike, they are identical. Being indiscernible means being totally alike.

Could there be two people who are totally alike? I am not talking about mere similarity of the sort one gets with "identical" twins. Could there be two people who were alike in *every* respect? To answer that question we have to know whether a radially symmetric universe described by Max Black is possible, and that is a very long story.[9] To make the story short, I once held that, on the interesting interpretations of Leibniz's law, it is logically possible for there to be two people at one time who are indiscernible, totally alike.[10] Such people would exist on opposite sides of a point of symmetry in the centre of a radially symmetric universe. (Now I doubt this, as discussed in the Arguments for analysis at the end of chapter 3.) Such considerations are, however, interesting as limits on possibility, not my major concern here. I am concerned now with the survival of persons over time in possible worlds like our own in their major physical aspects.

To understand this next point, it is important to understand the phrase "if and only if" as used in contexts where precision is needed. For any two sentences, A and B, "A if and only if B" means "if A then B, and if B then A." Given this usage we can see that Leibniz's law has two parts: the indiscernibility of identicals—if x is identical to y then x and y are indiscernible—and, secondly, the identity of indiscernibles—if x and y are indiscernible, then x and y are identical.

The relatively uncontroversial part of Leibniz's law is the indiscernibility of identicals. This works, of course, for a person, or anything else, at a given time. No one expects to be exactly the same in ten years' time as she is now. Indeed, everyone changes in some respects second by second.. If x is a person from birth to death, the whole life, and y is too, then again we will have no trouble with applying the indiscernibility of identicals. If x really is y, all of the events in x's life will be in y's life. The problem with the principle is in its application to one person at different times of her life.

Identity over time

Since what primarily interests me is the survival of persons through changes, I need to know a little about identity of individuals (persons or not) over time. While both parts of Leibniz's law are false if x and y are one individual at different times, some restricted version of one or both parts of Leibniz's law might be true in such cases. To see that they are false if unrestricted, we just have to notice that we change properties as we live; so we do not have all the properties we once had. My hair is longer than it was yesterday, so I am not totally like myself yesterday. A naive application of Leibniz's law assures me that I am not the same person as I was yesterday. The reply that jumps to many a philosopher's lips is: Properties like hair length are not essential to the person. Now we see how we might restrict our principles, namely, to talk not of having all properties in common but of having the essential properties in common.

What on earth is an essential property? The idea is that it is a property a thing has to have to exist. If you take an ordinary chair and remove its back and legs, it is no longer a chair but a disconnected collection of chair parts. Are there any properties that persons must have to be persons in general, or are there properties that certain persons must have to be themselves? Suppose that a person permanently loses consciousness. Does that person cease to exist? The body and, perhaps, the subconscious remain. This is, for many of us, one of those kinds of case where we want to say both Yes and No. Similarly, a brilliant person such as Daphne who becomes demented provides us with a difficult example. The only kind of answer which will be adequate to our intuitions is likely to be that for some purposes we say the person remains and for others we do not. There are, it appears, various concepts of a person.

Other relations called "identity" by the hoi polloi

Another way of approaching the problem which harks back to the business of pseudo-questions is to claim that identity is a concept that does not apply to persons. Persons are changeable things. The number two is identical to the sum of one plus one, but these are unchanging abstract objects. A person at one time is never identical to a person at another time, it may be claimed, since there are always changes over time. What the hoi polloi take to be identity is only similarity. This claim is something of an irritant. We know perfectly well that we are, in some important sense, identical with ourselves in earlier periods of our personal histories. I am not just like the person who started writing this book; I am that person. To get rid of the irritant, we will have to find a way to speak about identity of objects over time in ways that preserve more than mere similarity of the various stages of the objects.

Objects

The problems with identity are exacerbated by our tendency to treat as primary such examples of identity as involve unchanging objects or objects that change relatively little in comparison to persons. Almost none of us doubt that the number two today will still be the number two a thousand years from now. One might explain this in a way congenial to Plato and friends by saying that two is an unchanging abstract object. The moon is also going to be the same moon it was, despite minor changes. We generally accept as objects things that do not change or that do not change in ways that are very noticeable or pertinent to our practical concerns. Persons, however, change from moment to moment and, whether or not they appear stable to their friends and loved ones, over the years they change their bodies and many of the characteristics by which we know them. The young lovers who gazed at the moon become the old persons who, I hope, still gaze at the apparently unchanging moon. Perhaps their love survives (oh fortunates!) and they say that they are still the people they knew back then on a warm summer night. But even their love is very different now. Persons sometimes seem to be much more like the things we call "processes" than like the things we tend to call "objects," much more like a sunrise than like the relatively stable moon, though they are importantly unlike either sort of thing. On the other hand, when we think of persons as souls or selves unchanging within the body and mind, persons seem more like objects and less like processes.

Processes

Processes are notoriously hard to deal with simply because they are a stream of changes. Heraclitus' old saying—"You could not step twice in the same river; for other and yet other waters are ever flowing on"[11]—is an ancient expression of the puzzles afforded by the identity of processes. Of course, if we consider the matter carefully, we see that, if Heraclitus is right about rivers, we must admit that one cannot step on the same rock twice. Some properties of the rock will have changed from one moment to the next. In fact, though, we want to answer Heraclitus by saying that being totally unchanging is not necessary for remaining. Rocks, rivers, and persons retain their identity through change. For practical purposes, outward similarity is sufficient to guarantee that we have the same ones from moment to moment. When the rock is worn down by the river over time or the person ages, we lose similarity between the beginning and end of the process, but neighbouring stages of the process are similar, and that is enough for us to count the rock or the person as a single thing.

If Bryce has a brother, Victor, who goes away on a long journey and comes home remarkably changed in appearance and character, Bryce might not admit that Victor is the same person at first. If the newcomer shows Bryce that he knows where a pet cat was buried dozens of years ago and comes up with enough similar detail about their earlier lives together, Bryce may accept him, guardedly, as Victor. It would not be so difficult to accept if Bryce had seen Victor go through the changes day by day. As it is, Bryce uses memory as an assurance that such a process took place. Memory as a criterion of personal identity comes in for a lot of discussion by philosophers. We shall have occasion, if I remember, to talk much of memory later on.

Generally speaking, we are fairly confident about how to decide whether brother Victor is one with this apparent stranger who comes to Bryce's door. We are prepared for great change when it happens over time and at a distance. What is harder to deal with is great change that comes suddenly and does not fit the expected or hoped-for pattern of life. Daphne's change from a brilliant scholar, a complex personality, and a physically strong person to someone who is physically and mentally infantile came about within ten months. A part of the pattern of life—accepted at the beginning or the end—is suddenly forced upon the middle period. The process does not take its expected course, much as a river is forced by some cataclysm beyond its banks and into another bed. Is it the same river? Our understanding of sameness, objects, and processes will be stretched as we look at what philosophers have to say on these topics.

Reduction

Another way to deal with the difficulty of the concept of a person is to trade it in on something more tractable. "Reductionism" is the term for theories which reduce a concept to some other, more manageable concept; the concept of a person can be reduced, for instance, to the concept of a repertoire of behaviour or to that of a brain. From the behaviourist point of view, the highly skilled woman who becomes demented has simply lost a complex repertoire of behaviour, much of it linguistic. To say that she is a new person is to say that certain stimuli no longer elicit the former responses. To say that the woman is a different person from the one formerly inhabiting that body is just quaint shorthand, according to the behaviourist, for talking of this complex change in stimulus-response patterns. For those who accept the motto, same-brain/same-person, the woman would be the same person given that the brain has remained largely unchanged. But in cases of dementia from organic causes the brain may change radically; hence by the brain criterion the person may be a different one. Behaviour, in any case, does not determine identity according to the same-brain/same-person theorist. Evidently, then, reductionism is a broad category into which we can fit various conflicting theories about persons. The main thing reductionists have in common is that they attempt to boil persons down to something they think they can understand.

Reductionism, especially for a rich concept like that of a person, seems to rely on the principle of the drunkard's search as told by Kaplan: "There is the story of a drunkard searching under a street lamp for his house key, which he had dropped some distance away. Asked why he didn't look where he had dropped it, he replied, 'It's lighter here!'"[12] Reductionists tend to restrict attention to whatever is well lit by our understanding; thus, they may ignore in this case that which really makes up persons. Not all are so motivated, but those who look at one aspect of persons—such as their brains, their psychological continuity, or their behaviour—are illuminating their investigation without due regard for the likely location of the solution to problems concerning concepts of a person.

Thought experiments

Philosophers frequently dream up weird examples to test their understanding of concepts. With respect to persons, they talk about machines that can duplicate human behaviour and appearance, brain transplants, mind interchanges, teletransportation, and various other supposedly logically possible kinds of event which need not be medically or even physically possible. This tends to alienate people in other fields who wonder what philosophers have been smoking. The justification given is usually that philosophers are torturing the concepts to see just what they are made of. Just as the metallurgist stretches metals until they break to find their tensile strength, philosophers try out our ordinary concepts in situations designed to see what their limits are. Unlike the tensile strength of a metal, however, the limits of a concept are not definite and quantifiable. The testing procedure is by consequence not singular, clear, or rule governed.

For example, a philosopher may speculate on what we would want to say about personal identity if we had a machine that could record all the data in a person's body and duplicate the person.[13] No sooner has this speculation been put forth than another philosopher will say that it is not even clearly a logically possible example until we are shown in detail the background assumptions concerning this process of replication. Wilkes, for example, would argue that we have no reason to take this example seriously since it is not clear that there could, even in principle, be an exact replica produced.[14] Lots of things seem possible when we have not spelled out the details.

Another kind of attack on such thought experiments comes from a philosopher who objects to the presupposition of materialism. The duplication is, by hypothesis, a duplication of the structure of the matter of the original person. There is no guarantee, the non-materialist would argue, that such a duplication produces a person at all. It is, moreover, bound to be an imperfect replica since selves, or souls or whatever the non-materialist thinks we are in addition to bodies, are not replicable.

While reductionism is very popular in philosophy now—especially the materialist kind of reductionism—it is often put forward with insufficient attention to the kinds of objections revealed here.

A grand system to ground the question

One of the ways to avoid having our philosophical theory nipped in the bud is to be systematic. If, instead of just focusing on the concept of a person in isolation, we develop a unified theory of existence, knowledge, and morality in which our concept of a person fits, then we are better prepared for the slings and arrows that outraged objectors are likely to call down upon our heads. There are three main kinds of metaphysical views—that is views about existence in general—which are used in the discussion of the concepts of a person.

Materialism: Never mind

Materialism is the view that everything that exists is matter. No minds or souls or spirits or selves are non-material persons or parts of persons. This is considered by its defenders to be a no-nonsense, what-you-see-is-what-you-get sort of theory. They may even say that it would be nice if all this romantic bull about spirits were true, but sorry Virginia, there is no Santa Claus. Their opponents accuse them of feigning anaesthesia.[15]

Dualism: Mind and matter

Dualism is the view that both material and non-material things exist. Non-material things such as thoughts and minds are every bit as real as material things such as brains and electrochemical impulses at the neuron-synaptic connections. Most non-philosophers whom I have questioned about this are dualists. They believe, for instance, that their memories are different in kind from whatever physical things are going on in their heads when they have these memories. Their opponents ask them, with a smirk, how the material and non-material worlds interact.

Idealism: No matter

Idealism is the view that there is no matter, just minds, ideas, and perhaps other things such as spirit combining to give rise to the illusion of a material world. Millions of people in India think this is common sense but, on this side of the world, people tend to take a step away if you spout this view. Their opponents accuse them of ignoring the obvious.

Neutral monism: Never mind; it doesn't matter

Some philosophers, such as Bertrand Russell, have held that there is only one kind of stuff that dreams and rocks are made of. Mind and matter are built from the same building blocks. This view is called "neutral monism." Materialists think the neutral monists are closet idealists, while idealists think they are closet materialists. Dualists think they are missing something.

This metaphysical starting point concerning what kind of stuff there is usually influences our views about how we know things about this stuff. Ethical views tend to be influenced as well. Dualists and idealists can make a place for spirit, for example, which generally carries with it views about human dignity and worth. These views are harder to defend on the other metaphysical ground.

Wittgensteinian ladder heaving

There are philosophers who abhor systems of the sort just discussed. For the early Wittgenstein, his own system—a noteworthy example of system abhorrence—was a mere ladder to be climbed to a better understanding of the world.[16] Once one had this understanding, the ladder could be heaved away. His system, then, is not the truth, but a mere means to seeing the truth. He seems to conclude that the truth about persons is that there are none. In his account of persons, the concept of a self or person pretty well disappears.[17]

Reaction to philosophical interpretation

After this day-trip through the territories of philosophy, many readers may have some strong reactions. To be fair, none of the views or methods mentioned above has really been given a run for its money. Still, you may as well know what some of the anti-philosophic reaction is. Like Wittgenstein's reaction, above, this other reaction is more likely than not to be absorbed into philosophy where it can be taken seriously by philosophers. Intelligent anti-philosophy is often a kind of philosophy.

Irritation with the exaltation of language

One of the strong contemporary winds on the borderlands of philosophy is great irritation with the philosopher's exaltation of language. The twentieth-century philosophical trend to reduce questions about persons, existence, morals, or whatever to questions about language was itself once a reaction to what was seen as an excess of ungrounded speculation. The pendulum swings. Now we are exhorted to talk about persons rather than merely about the word "persons." It seems to me for reasons already given that we cannot talk about persons without examining the language we use to do so. If I am right, we are talking about many different things. This does not mean that we should merely speak about things having to do with usage. This is properly the realm of the scientific linguist. Maybe philosophers should share their work. Ultimately we have to get down to the questions about what there is, how we know it, and what to do. If philosophers get hung up in the linguist's enterprise and never get to these questions, then we have abdicated our ancient role as philosophers. Some are quite willing to give it up as a bad job. I am not.

Rejecting the vocabulary and method of analytic philosophy

Readers should be aware that philosophers in the West are roughly divided into the Analytic and Continental schools which are separated by a grand gulf of method. British and North American philosophers comprise most of the Analytic school, as they are generally fond of fine detailed analysis of concepts with a heavy concentration on the insights to be gained by examining language. Continental philosophers, by contrast, are fonder of large system building and larger pictures in general. They consider the Analytic school to be lacking profundity. The Analytic philosophers sometimes deride what they see as imprecision or vacuity on the part of the Continentals, as Berlinski did when he spoke of the great soupy volumes that pour off the European presses with the inevitability of death.[18] There are, however, other good philosophers on both sides of this wide methodological gulf who find work to value on the farther shore.

As the Analytic school is the place where I was brought up, I will try to analyze the concepts of a person and perhaps add to those concepts. The continental style of philosophizing, which tends to be systematic and more poetic than I am used to, has influenced me. But one can only study so much. The influence of the continentals on what you read here is mainly indirect, through philosophers who write in a way that is accessible to the analytically minded.

Survival is what counts

While I have some larger systematic opinions, I will not always be working from the top down. Trying to settle on the most general philosophical views without at the same time working on the middle and lower levels makes for the danger of becoming separated from life and bound within the walls of a coherent but inapplicable system. This approach from all levels at once sometimes makes for a spaghetti of ideas, from which I hope a larger pattern will emerge. If not then, may you enjoy the sauce.

What is crucial to me in keeping the connection with life is that puzzles about, for example, duplication of persons, not lead us too far astray from the real work at hand. We have only academic concerns about duplication at this stage in our technical history, but we have some very real and present worries about what constitutes survival of a person. That is my focus.

The way the answers miss the point

Our new-world version of Western European culture is in the throes of giving birth. Birth may have its beauty, but it is not a sight for the faint of heart. The infant, if it survives, will be a new and coherent view of what we are as individual persons and how we fit into our world and society. We desperately need some answers. The old religious world order is no longer capable of motivating the majority. The answers that are offered by pundits of the present are necessarily anachronistic. Either they cling to a dead order or they wait for a new one in which they might inhere.

I will not try to avoid anachronism. What emerges here is a series of proposals for a way to think and, as a consequence, a way to live. I may advise living to some extent in the past, to some extent in the future. What I will try to avoid is the giving of answers that miss the point of such questions about personal identity as are asked by those in the front lines. The couple contemplating abortion or the family wondering whether to commit a beloved parent to an institution wants to know where persons begin and end. They are hearing answers—such as, All and only human beings are persons—which do not address their difficulties. That answer may underlie one concept of a person, but it is not one that helps them to make a decision. If it is forced into that role, as it frequently is, then it creates only a hollow illusion of a solution. Instead of this, I intend to explore the many concepts of a person to see how they are motivated and what, if anything, each can do to help us live and make choices.

Content questions

1. What kinds of questions are we asking about persons? How is each categorized as metaphysical, epistemological, or ethical?
2. What is a primitive term?
3. What is a philosophical pseudo-question?
4. Explain in a general way how context gives meaning to questions. Include how some philosophical questions become meaningless if their context is not specified.
5. What are the most weighty considerations in our society for survival of persons?
6. State Leibniz's law. Which part of it is controversial?
7. How does a naive application of Leibniz's law make survival of any change in a person impossible?
8. Why do persons seem to be more like processes than like objects?
9. Define "reductionism" as applied to persons.
10. Give two objections to the use of the duplication of persons through thought experiments.
11. Distinguish the following metaphysical theses: materialism, dualism, idealism, and neutral monism.

Arguments for analysis

The arguments, sequences of arguments, or deductions at the end of each chapter are for students to learn to analyze deductive arguments in philosophy. Most philosophical arguments are deductive; that is, they attempt to establish their conclusions with certainty given that the premises are true. The contrast is an inductive argument that attempts to establish its conclusion with a degree of probability given that the premises are true.

There are two features of deductive arguments that we seek. The first is validity, a kind of minimal test that arguments should pass before being taken seriously as deductive. An argument is deductively valid if and only if it is not possible for the conclusion to be false if the premises are true. No matter what the facts are, the truth of the conclusion of a valid argument is guaranteed by the premises. Here is a simple example: All persons have minds. Seymour is a person. Therefore, Seymour has a mind. This is a deductively valid argument in which the first two sentences are the premises and the third sentence is the conclusion. The conclusion follows from the premises. Of course we have no assurance that the premises are true, so until they are established, we should not accept the conclusion on the basis of this argument.

This leads us to a second desirable feature of deductive arguments, that they have true premises. When arguments both have both validity and true premises, they are sound. Sound arguments are the ones we want in philosophy.

Consider, now, in terms of validity and soundness, how we may challenge the arguments offered at the end of each chapter in this book. First we should ask if each argument is valid. Until this minimal test is passed, there is no sense in investigating the premises on which the argument is based. If the conclusion does, indeed, follow from the premises, then it is worth checking for the remaining part of soundness by investigating each premise. Do not bother checking the premises until you know the argument is valid. None of these arguments should be accepted as it stands. They start debates but do not end them.

Argument 1: System building

Here I will present an argument with three parts corresponding to metaphysics, epistemology, and axiology. It is designed to show that these three areas are closely linked in their application to the concepts of a person. It is, therefore, advisable to consider all three main subdisciplines of philosophy when we try to understand any one of them in this context.

Axiology requires metaphysics and epistemology

This is the easy bit. If we are to understand values, we must have a view about whether they are real and we must decide what we can know about them. Values that are neither real nor knowable are not clearly of use in answering questions about art or morality. Even if we decide that unreal or non-knowable values will be of use, that decision will involve considerable and unavoidable use of both metaphysics and epistemology. An example may help. Suppose we want to discover the morally right ways of treating persons. We are presupposing that there are such things as persons, that there are standards for determining what is right, and that we can know these things. Readers who are thinking, Don't be silly; of course there are persons, may be surprised by how hard it is to explain and argue for that apparently obvious metaphysical claim. It may already be clear to many readers that there is a considerable debate about moral standards and the ways we come to *know* them. In any case, epistemological questions are bound to crop up too.

Metaphysics requires axiology and epistemology

This is a more controversial claim. It seems to many philosophers that we can consider questions of existence and knowledge independently of questions of value. Plato would have disagreed (as discussed in chapter 3); he thought that the same things that explained what exists and can be known explain what is valuable. At least we can say that, once we decide what we think existence of persons comes to, then we will have an idea of what we think can be known about persons, and these things will greatly influence our thoughts on value.

Consider, for example, the metaphysical claim that persons are merely convenient fictions for organizing our talk about events. Given this view it would seem, on the face of it, silly to say we know who someone really is or that we morally owe that person special treatment. At least we would have to understand such talk in the way we understand talk about such fictional characters as Sherlock Holmes who lives on Baker Street. Yet when I say that I know my mother very well and owe her more than I can tell, I am reluctant to think of this as similar to talk about Sherlock Holmes.

Epistemology requires metaphysics and axiology

This too is a bit of a stretch and depends on large systematic considerations. Nonetheless, it is plausible to claim that some epistemological claims have important consequences for metaphysical and ethical ones. For example, suppose that it is possible to know what persons will do in the future. This epistemological claim about foreknowledge may have the metaphysical consequence that freedom of the will does not exist. If we can know what people do before they do it, then, apparently, they cannot freely choose to do things. After all, their actions must be determined by what happened earlier if we can know what they will do in the sense of having a justified, true belief that they will act thus. I may think that I choose freely to give to charity, but it is already true beforehand that I will choose to do so. My choice is predetermined. How can I be morally valued for something I cannot help doing? The metaphysical question of existence of free will and the ethical question of our merit for our choices seem to be closely linked to the epistemological question concerning foreknowledge.

Conclusion

It appears, therefore, that, at least when we are trying to understand persons, we must consider metaphysical, epistemological, and ethical questions together. Questions of any one sort lead to questions of the other two kinds. It should be noted, however, that some philosophers who do not agree with this conclusion and who have spent considerable time ignoring it would find flaws in the above argument. If you think the big questions about persons are important, then you should ask yourself if you agree with the argument. Try giving objections to parts of it. Always think critically about claims for which I argue and about the arguments that lead to them.

Argument 2: Leibniz's law

This argument is designed to show that we must restrict Leibniz's law, as expressed in this chapter in order to prevent it from being obviously false.

Suppose, for the sake of argument, that this law is true for any properties whatever at any time whatever. Now let us consider a person, Max at 5 p.m. on Tuesday, January 3, 200X. Let us consider whether Max is the same person the next day at the same time. Since he has by this time had his hair cut, Max does not have all the same properties that he did at 5 p.m. the previous day. We cannot, therefore, say that Max on Tuesday is the same as Max on Wednesday. But this is absurd. Merely having a haircut is not enough to change who Max is. We should, of course, reject our initial assumption that led to this absurdity. We reject the view that Leibniz's law is true without restriction.

The above argument is a *reductio ad absurdum* (or just *reductio*). That means it makes an assumption, reduces that assumption to absurdity by showing that something absurd follows from that assumption, and then rejects that assumption. The assumption is only made in the first place to show how it goes wrong.

In this case, the argument gives us a reason to reject Leibniz's law in an unrestricted form. We might restrict it to things considered at the same time. If we want to consider things through time, we would have to specify the sort of properties that are relevant. For persons, we might want to look at the properties that are *essential.* These would be properties that a person must retain to be the same person. Hair length, clearly not one of these, is an *accidental* property—the kind of property a thing can acquire or lose without changing into another thing. What is it about you that makes you who you are? Whatever those things are, they are your essential properties, the way you must be to be you.

CHAPTER 2

So Who Cares?

What really matters about people?

What matters about people seems relative to cultures, countries, or individuals. There is, nonetheless, a degree of objectivity, even cross-cultural objectivity, in assessments of what matters.[1] With respect to the cultural relativity of values, Asch points out that we do not conclude that standards for shelter are relative merely because one society builds a temporary shelter of ice while another makes a thatched hut. Similarly we should not conclude that moral values vary simply because social practices differ from one society to another. He considers as an example a son killing his parents: "In the society that follows this practice there prevails the belief that people continue to lead in the next world the same existence as in the present and that they maintain forever the condition of health and vigor they had at the time of death. It is therefore a filial duty of the son to dispatch his parents, an act that has the full endorsement of the parent and the community."[2] Not just the deed but the meaning it has to the doer is an indicator of values. People everywhere tend to care about people, in my assessment. That does not mean we all think of people in the same way. Who or what is counted as a person may vary from place to place and time to time, with perspectives in one culture

Notes to chapter 2 are on pp. 476-77.

or period that another considers abominable. Sometimes individuals or even large groups seem to care deeply about things which, from other points of view, it is irrational to care about. Hitler's caring about astrology but not about millions of lives is a paradigm of an irrational scheme of what matters—no less an evil for being absurd. While there is always debate on what matters, there is also widespread agreement within cultures on particular cases.

Often when there is disagreement, as between a Nazi and almost everyone else, the disagreement is not over principles. Almost everyone in the West admits that we ought to respect persons. The disagreement is over what a person is. The absurd idea that only Aryans are real persons, once the Nazi takes it to heart, allows the Nazi to commit horrific atrocities with less emotional trauma and fewer moral qualms than could be managed with the admission that Jews, Slavs, and the other victims are persons. In general, we agree on what matters, but we disagree about the facts or wilfully ignore some of the facts where persons are concerned.

What matters about people includes, moreover, much that goes beyond whatever moral principles we may adopt. Few of us are exclusively concerned with morality. Frankfurt even claims that those of us who take morality seriously may still not, in some circumstances, find moral considerations pre-emptive.[3] This seems to me to be false. Frankfurt's example is of someone who finds it too costly to explore various alternatives to find the best one: "he might plausibly judge it more important to himself to reserve for other uses the time and the effort which a conscientious exploration of the relevant moral features of his situation would require."[4] In this kind of case, one is right to forgo the investigation only if the moral obligation to seek the knowledge is weak enough. If people's lives depend on the investigation, and I fail to investigate on the grounds that it might bankrupt me, I will remain culpably ignorant of the best thing to do. If it is a small matter of which of two actions might be more fair, and I fail to investigate on the grounds that it might bankrupt me, I would remain ignorant of the best thing to do—but not culpably so. I have a moral justification or at least a morally valid excuse for not investigating. It seems to me that, although there are many other things that matter about people, the ones which matter from a moral point of view must always be given first consideration. Only when there is a morally sufficient reason for leaving aside further moral considerations can we go on to the other things—practical, aesthetic, or whatever they may be—that move us.

We have to be wary about oversimplifying the point of the preemptive strength of our moral attitudes toward persons. We should not permit, for example, the sort of slavish adherence to principle evident in the following example. To a Nazi who knocks at my door looking for Anne Frank in order to send her to a concentration camp, I say, I cannot tell a lie. She's in the closet. This is mindless adherence to the principle that we should be honest, if there is no reason to tell the truth in this case other than honesty. Sometimes we are morally obligated to lie. Not only the facts of the situation but our decisions concerning what matters about people will strongly influence our application of principles of morality. The process of carefully weighing and balancing principles, facts, and what matters to us is one that taxes even a saint. There is no simple way to decide how to treat other persons. It could, however, help if we could agree on what counts as a person.

There was once, in our culture, a somewhat easier answer to the question of what matters. The idea that what matters to me might not matter to another was accepted for a limited number of cases. People could disagree on matters of taste, but there was a central core of religious values that mattered to almost everyone. Many societies of the past believed that what ultimately mattered was what mattered to God. Even then, it wasn't so easy, as there were many differences of opinion about what mattered to God or the gods within a given religion, and more differences across religions. One could, however, look to the religious leadership of a society to get a fairly definite answer concerning what mattered. In Europe, Britain, and North America now, this leadership no longer holds sway. We are cast upon secular devices to get congruence of opinion on what matters.

After the question, What matters about people? we can ask, To whom? The answer, To God, will no longer win the day. Many think that, in Nietzsche's famous phrase, God is dead. Some think He is just resting. In any case, if something matters to God, then He must have a good reason for caring about it. The religious believer will only be able to persuade the non-believer that something matters by appealing to those reasons. "Many and mysterious are the ways of the Lord," is not a reply likely to impress those who think there is no Lord to have any ways.

The question, Matters to whom? can, however, often be answered, To you, or To your group. That will usually elicit, Show me. If, for example, I say to Bernice, You ought to care about the people in the Third World, she may find my remark foolish until I can prove to her that their suffering can lead to harm to her country and herself. Bernice might be persuaded, for instance, that her country's consumption of the forests of the Third World will ultimately have deleterious effects on her own country's environment by threatening the earth's atmosphere. Or, I might even be fortunate enough to persuade her that people should matter to her even if their suffering does not impinge on the well being of herself and her country. A person's suffering matters, no matter who, no matter when, no matter where. This latter principle, however, is so fundamental to most Western moral systems, that it is one from which other principles are deduced rather than itself admitting of deduction.

God substitutes

This brings us to the standards by which we judge what matters. These include our own proclivities, but they also include moral standards we have accepted for whatever reason. The religious believer will say there is nothing like the real thing and cite God's will. The whole idea of substituting something for God in the discussion is upsetting for the believer. The idea of including God is equally anathema for the non-believer. If they are going to talk to each other, they will have to consider what matters to them about people independently, to some extent, of why it matters. Various creeds other than the religious ones bear examination.

For example, Judith Shklar defines liberals as persons for whom "cruelty is the worst thing they do."[5] It is unlikely that Bernice adopts such a standard but, if she does, we need merely persuade her that many of our actions are thoughtlessly cruel to people in the Third World whose lives are made grim by our consumption of their resources. This grim tenure of life is crucially important on the liberal standard since that standard makes what matters about people their capacity to be cruel and to suffer cruelty. The dictates of liberalism were, in the past, founded on religious dogma. The abolition of slavery by Europeans and North Americans depended largely on the Judeo-Christian tradition. Liberalism remains, while the source of it is secularized.

Having such a standard as Shklar's liberalism is not necessarily a matter of believing that the standard is, or is grounded in, some absolute. Rorty invites us to adopt it even though he admits that there are no absolutes, but he is careful not to defend this liberalism as if there were standards for its defence to which he could appeal.[6] This would be to expose liberalism to the doubts to which those standards are bound to be subject. If we simply choose to affirm liberalism without deriving it from anything, we are, by an act of will, caring about people. Rorty's method is radical; he tries to change the vocabulary in which we speak of liberalism and thereby to support liberalism through making its opponents' vocabulary look bad. Rorty's rhetorical persuasiveness notwithstanding, his choice of liberalism cannot escape criticism merely by avoiding absolutes or making the vocabulary in which these absolutes are expressed look bad.[7] The refusal to accept absolute standards does not entail that any standard is acceptable.

Secular absolute moral standards

Most of us want to say that there are, relative to a given context, things it is rational to care about and others it is not proper to be concerned about. If I choose to care deeply and exclusively about the pattern on my wallpaper, I will probably end up in a padded cell. Those of us who choose liberalism would, moreover, be willing to criticize Bernice if she chose to be concerned only about people in her own country. Whether or not they are absolute, we will use our standards to criticize choices of what to care about. Even if we believe there is no God to back up our choices and even if we admit that they are unfounded—chosen with an absurdist's belief that there can be no foundation, we tend to act as if God were on our side. What our side is morally depends, usually, on the context in which we find ourselves and, in Western societies, on our concepts of a person.

The relationship between the concept of a person and morality is a vexed one in contemporary philosophy. Findlay claims that separateness of persons is the basic fact for morals.[8] Williams denies this utterly: "The category of person, though a lot has been made of it in some moral philosophy, is a poor foundation for ethical thought, in particular because it looks like a sortal or classificatory notion while in fact it signals characteristics that almost all come in degrees—responsibility, self-consciousness, capacity for reflection, and so on."[9] It becomes clear enough that philosophers are working with a number of different concepts of a person. We will look at a slate of these to see which might help us with our problems, moral and other kinds. An initial taxonomy of concepts of a person will emerge.

Aesthetic standards

Even more than moral standards, aesthetic standards are contentious. Curiously, even more than moral standards, aesthetic standards tend to be treated as God-given. Judging people's choices by aesthetic standards is, moreover, in my experience, even more likely to arouse hostile reaction than is doing so on moral grounds. It seems that we tend to forgive others if they are morally sincere in their differences with us, but let them not be what we consider low in taste! Dear reader, admit that you can respect the cannibal who sincerely believes it is his moral duty to feast on human flesh, but that you have more trouble respecting those whose choice of interior decor makes you nauseous. No? Well, you are probably a rare one.

The moot nature of aesthetic standards and our intolerance of difference in these may cause us no direct ill effects in trying to ascertain what a person is. An aesthetics of theory, of course, might affect us if there were any possibility of achieving an elegant theory about the nature of persons. We seem so far from such a blissful state of theorizing that I believe these aesthetic standards ought to come into play hardly at all in our choice of concepts. Here, we do not have the luxury of choosing a pretty idea: we need one that works, even if it is as ugly as homemade sin.

Where aesthetic standards may be relevant is in the general battery of tests we have for being a person. One might suppose that having some kind of aesthetic sense is a distinguishing quality of persons. Other animals and some machines may be rational, but only persons have the capacity for aesthetic awareness, it may be claimed. This is at least an interesting claim. There is, however, a considerable debate about what it is to have some kind of aesthetic sense. Still, some take solace in believing that, while God is dead, art lives. From their point of view, what matters about people is their ability to have the aesthetic experience.

Most of us, however, put aesthetic judgments lower on the mattering list, second at least to moral judgments. It is not unheard of, however, that an artist be out of step with the majority on this point. Artists have been known to put art above, for example, human and animal suffering—not just their own. It is in fact part of the traditional role of the artist to challenge the values of society and this, together with the elevation of aesthetics to the pinnacle of what matters, may bring about moral monstrosities, including a profound disrespect for persons. Ironically, the use of the aesthetic sense as the defining characteristic of persons may lead to the undermining of the worth of persons.

For the majority, in any case, there is another sense in which aesthetics typically comes into what matters about persons. We are attracted to those we consider beautiful, sometimes in spite of their lack of moral character. We are attracted also to those who produce beauty around them or who can reveal it to us in nature. It seems, then, useful to reflect on the aesthetic experience in order to see a little more clearly what it is we care about in people. According to W.D. Ross, aesthetic enjoyment is "a blend of pleasure with insight into the nature of the object which inspires it."[10] This view explains why it is easier to appreciate the appearance of beautiful people than of non-representational works of art. As persons we have insights into people ready-made. Art, however, requires an understanding which does not come free. The necessary insight is hard won.

There seems, in addition, to be another explanatory feature of Ross's view of art. Since the aesthetic experience includes pleasure, those who can evoke or help to evoke this experience would naturally be valued. One never has to seek an explanation for people caring about pleasure. I, for one, have never stopped in the middle of an orgasm to ask whether it is worthwhile. Nor are more subtle pleasurable experiences usually questioned except when they are bought at great cost morally or financially. Then we question not the goodness of the experience in itself but the means to achieving it. People, therefore, who can bring out the aesthetic experience through their personal appearance or their work are people we tend to care about. In general, the capacity of persons to evoke and experience the aesthetic is a large though often unrecognized part of what matters about them. Aesthetic value is one of the commonest but least recognized sources of absolutes in a society that no longer relies on religion to supply those absolutes.

Solidarity of persons

God's death, moreover, makes people huddle together. Without someone to protect us and to want us to get along, we are all we've got. That may make us value one another more. One who misguidedly thinks himself the instrument of God's wrath can push the button to start a nuclear conflagration. So the world ends in fire; well isn't that what it is supposed to do? This world is not what counts. When that fire-and-brimstone attitude dies, the importance of the here and now and those who populate it becomes paramount. The vitality of the Shklar/Rorty liberalism alluded to earlier is, perhaps, an effect of the secularization of the world for all that it had its original source in religion. The liberal can take no joy in seeing herself as the avenging angel armed with the fiery sword.

This liberalism is a close relative of a movement that has been steadily gaining ground since such nineteenth-century authors as Butler, Mill, and Bentham clarified it, some would say created it. I refer to utilitarianism, the doctrine that what we ought morally to do is to create the greatest pleasure and least suffering for the greatest number of people. In short, we ought to maximize pleasure. Bentham would prefer to maximize the pleasure of all sentient beings though, not just people. Some versions of utilitarianism are apparently able to dispense with the concept of a person as morally fundamental. Instead of saying, We persons are all we have got, a utilitarian might say, We sentient beings are all we have got.

This move to sentient beings, however, does not obviate the moral difficulties that we have already seen can be entangled with the concept of a person. As soon as one defends a doctrine in which the interests of sentient beings other than persons might supersede those of persons, the problems emerge in another form. Perhaps the best way to maximize pleasure on this planet would be to eliminate persons. After all, people are destroying the planet. That there could be a justification for killing everyone—say, by creating and releasing an incurable viral ailment specific to human beings—seems to be an odd result at best in what purports to be a moral theory. To stop it, one would have to argue that there is more pleasure to be had by keeping us persons around. To do that, one might argue that persons are capable of more pleasure than mere sentient beings; so the pleasure of the person having an aesthetic experience through listening to music should not be equated with the pleasure of the mosquito taking a sip of a person.

Of course this business of weighing our pleasures against those of other sentient beings brings us back to the problem of what we are and why we should care so much about us. The general answer in terms of solidarity of persons is that we are all we have. Animal welfare activists and environmentalists will blanch at this claim. They think too much emphasis has been placed on this new god of human solidarity. By elevating people to a position of ultimate value, we may ignore the other inhabitants of the earth and the earth itself. Not only people, they would say, but other animals—indeed, whole ecosystems—are all we have.

I, for one, am not about to make the world safe for mosquitoes by killing off persons, no matter how numerous mosquitoes and their little pleasures might be. Almost all utilitarians would agree with me on this point. It may nonetheless be true that we do care too much about persons and too little about other sentient beings. Perhaps we should care more about the planet on which we live. However we may change our attitudes in these respects, we ought not to return to caring too little about people. The ideal is to expand the circle of solidarity to include non-persons and their interests in our consideration of what we ought to do.

Spirituality

Not all who want to give up the idea of a deity want to give up the idea of spirituality. Some maintain that this is the essential characteristic of persons. Saying just what spirit might be, however, is not at all easy to do. Spirit is often held to be ineffable or expressible only indirectly as, for example, through the poetry of the Romantics. Nonetheless, some have attempted definitions. For example, Steven G. Smith, after an interesting historical survey of definitions of the term "spirit" defines it as "the intentional togetherness of beings who are for themselves 'I' and for others 'You,' that is, other to each other."[11] Now a fetus cannot make the distinction between I and You and cannot participate in intentional togetherness. Nor it seems can some severely brain-damaged adults. But these are only the most extreme cases. There are many whose minds are terribly limited who would be able to join in this intentional togetherness. Thus the resulting concept of person, when we take persons to be those beings with spirit, takes the emphasis off mind and intellect, thereby including many more human beings as persons. Nonetheless, it still distinguishes the babe in arms from the two-year-old, since the babe under this definition does not have spirit.

Many competing notions of spirit, of course, would not have the consequences just noted. In any case, thinking of persons in terms of spirit gives us a set of definitions of "person" corresponding to those of "spirit." This particular example from Smith serves to show that taking spirit as a God-substitute may have important consequences for the distinction of some human beings from persons. Furthermore, doctrines of spirit bring with them views about what matters; often spirit itself is at the top of a hierarchy of what matters where God used to be. What matters about people, from this view, is their spirit.

Love

Love is everything, sums up what some people care most about, namely the foremost kind of caring. Although romantic love is the first kind of love that springs to mind, the love of the parent for the child, love of friends, of country, of humanity, of natural objects, and of artifacts are all familiar. When love is a God-substitute and so is placed at the top of the hierarchy of mattering, we may be glorifying any or all of these kinds of love. People may matter on this kind of view since they are the objects of love or since they are the ones who love. The capacity to love at least has a chance of being a capacity that picks out persons while merely being an object of love does not. It seems, then, that being able to love is what matters about people when love is a God-substitute.

Definitions of love are passing rare, but this is one of the better ones: "Mutual love seems to be a blend of virtuous disposition of two minds towards each other, with the knowledge which each has of the character and disposition of the other, and with the pleasure which arises from such disposition and knowledge."[12] Notice that the kind of love here defined is person-to-person love, and the conception of a person necessary to support such love is quite complex. While an expectant mother could love a fetus, that would not be mutual love as here defined. Only highly developed human beings could be the sort of persons to have the emotional and intellectual means to experience this kind of love. Even very young children and adults with the intellectual or emotional maturity of young children cannot love in this way, though they may well love in other ways.

If capacity to love is, as I have speculated, one of the things that matter about persons, then we ought to look closely at love. As reflection on Ross's definition reveals, there are various things in this category of love that we might have in mind when we think of the capacity to love. The capacity for what Ross calls "mutual love" is, I believe, a defining characteristic of persons in a narrow but very important sense. It is, in fact, part of a common ideal. When we consider what persons should be, we include this capacity. When we praise someone as "a real *Mensch*" (a real person), for example, a large part of what matters so much to us about this person is the capacity for engaging with others in mutual love.

Assuming what?

When we ask what matters about people, we have to consider—as for all questions—the background assumptions. One such assumption is that there is something that matters. Pity the person who does not share this minimal assumption. Another is that something about people in particular matters. Most of us, save the very depressed, have few doubts on either score. We are assuming, though, that nihilism with respect to values has been defeated. It is never completely defeated, but raises its ugly head from time to time. We put it down largely by an act of pure will. We create our own values, not in the sense that we dream them up but that we ally ourselves to standards and views about what matters which tend to be shared by most people.

There are, unfortunately, persons for whom other persons do not matter. Some of these are egoists. For an egoist, only she herself matters. Some are concerned not so much with themselves as with things outside the realm of persons. The scientist, for instance, is often praised for being cold, dispassionate, and fascinated with items quite beyond the personal. I think of this praise as an evil. The world is becoming uninhabitable for persons, and scientists need to be passionately involved with people to help overcome this tragedy. I am no more enamoured of the totally dispassionate scientist than of the artist who elevates aesthetics above persons. In any case, in contradistinction to those who reject this basic assumption, I—and I hope you are with me—am assuming that somehow people matter.

One more assumption that only a philosopher is likely to consider is whether there are persons in the world at all. Perhaps all of the concepts of person that we use are defective. In that case, there might be no such things. Once we thought there was phlogiston—a mysterious substance that was thought to be transferred from one object to another when heat was transferred. Now we think that supposition was based on a misconception of what heat is. What if all of our informative and value-laden conceptions of person turn out like that? Certainly I am assuming that there is something to talk about under the general heading of "persons." The proof is in the pudding. If, at the end of this investigation, we find that we have no clearer conception, then perhaps we will be willing to take a leaf from Rorty's book and to try to develop a vocabulary in which we no longer have terms like "person."[13] This would overcome by evasion the intractable questions of our current enterprise. Sidestepping is not such a bad thing if it gets us out of a blind alley and into one that leads somewhere. We must, however, explore this alley thoroughly before taking that option. I think we will find the alley is not blind after all.

Mystical and religious importance

Mystics, religious believers, Platonists, and many others think that what is important about any person is the immortal part. Trapped within our physical being or temporarily residing voluntarily in, on, or through us in this mortal coil is the real person. This is a very strange idea when it is thought through. Consider the ever-popular transmigration of souls doctrine, for instance. If Alvaro were a buccaneer in a former life but now has nothing in common with that buccaneer—that he can remember—in what sense was that Alvaro? If one becomes totally demented, at least there is the continuation of a body connecting the earlier and later selves. If we imagine being buccaneers in earlier lives, do we imagine being continuous Egos who are conscious in now one body, now another, with no memory of what happened in earlier bodies? With continuity like that, who needs discontinuity? This bare Ego that flits from body to body may not really be something we can consistently work into a plausible theory of persons. It is worth a try, though. Undeniably, the bare Ego has a strong intuitive appeal as the popularity of the transmigration myth testifies.

Problems such as the identification of featureless Egos or souls led Aristotle and St. Thomas Aquinas to demand that the body go along with the soul as an inseparable unit, the soul being the form of the body. Although the relationship between the soul and the body is more complex, one can think of their inseparability as comparable to the inseparability of a body and its health. It would no more make sense to speak of the soul leaving the body and yet still existing than it would to speak of the health leaving the body behind and still existing out there somewhere: I've lost my health but it's around here somewhere. Much less does a doctrine of transmigration stand up under the light of Aristotle's concept of the self or soul;[14] so that one might say, Jean lost her health. Now my brother Harry has Jean's health. Of course we can talk sensibly of people having the same *type* of health but not have the very same *token* of health.

By the way, the Christian doctrine of the resurrection was necessitated by this Aristotelian view of the soul. If a Christian cannot go to heaven without her body, it will have to be reconstituted when that trumpet sounds. While this doctrine is a little less problematic than that of the featureless soul able to transmigrate, it has its problems.

For instance, which body should be resurrected on that day, your two-year-old body, your body in its prime, or your then-current remains? We have had occasion to remark that the body is a process. Different stages of this process may be more different than two different bodies at the same time. If the soul is the form of the body, it too must be a continuing process. All the difficulties of identifying persons through time that arise when we focus on our mortal changing bodies will arise for this kind of soul. One wants something unchanging, incorruptible, and immortal to serve as an identifier through the changes of all the other parts of the person. This soul doctrine does not, at first glance, look promising. Suspend judgment on it, though, until we have given it a good run.

Being yourself (who else?)

It is not only the philosophers and mystics who claim to be aware of some continuing soul, self, Ego, or inner person which underlies the changes in the visible person. Most of us have been exhorted to "be ourselves," for instance by parents who did not want us to run with the gang and be moved by stronger personalities or groups to do what is not true to ourselves. Well, who else can one be but oneself? Sartre's message in the play *Huis Clos* is that one is what one does, not what one says or imagines oneself to be but the sum total of one's actions. But then who is performing these actions, a series of subtotals? Most of us think that, when we choose to act in a certain way, consistently with our character—or even in efforts to pull ourselves up by our bootstraps to change our character—*we* choose. There is a choosing self which precedes and survives the choice. Such is the dictate of common sense. We have to ask whether this common view is really sensible. Some of the philosophers discussed below challenge it, though I myself am rather partial to common sense.

Promises and the question of who's who?

If you are lucky enough to have a friend whom you would describe with such well-worn phrases as steady as a rock, then you seem to have some concept of a dependable person. Such a person does not say, when one invokes her promises, That was then and this is now. One knows what to expect from her. This is not necessarily the kind of persistence through change sought by those who put forward ideas of an immortal soul, but this continuity of personality and character is much of what we normally refer to when we use the words "the same person."

If remembering and living up to promises made, not under duress, is an example of the sort of thing we can ideally expect when we are met with the same person over time, then how far can this expectation be disappointed without damaging that sameness? Even posing this question will seem to some to conflate metaphysical and ethical issues, but many of the most useful concepts of a person are not easily confined within the boundaries of one philosophical field. We have terms such as "psychopath" to single out those at one extreme with respect to what can be expected, given their promises. At this extreme, there is genuine doubt about classifying human beings who are truly psychopathic as persons. At least there is the tendency to classify them as incomplete persons since they are mentally deformed. The total lack of the moral dimension is just as serious as the total loss of the intellectual capacity when it comes to being a person. A woman who, when confronted with a promise, is always content to answer, That was then and this is now, might as well answer, That was her, this is me. Or is that far too strong? The connectedness of the parts of a person's life is, at least partly, a moral matter. We will have to look into the extent to which abiding by certain moral rules is necessary to being a unified person throughout the life of the body of that person.

Loneliness and person surrogates

Being alone is being without the company of persons. On the proverbial desert island, one may have the company of coconuts and wild pigs, but neither can play chess or music, discuss philosophy, or sympathize. Reflecting on what would make me feel less alone on a desert island, I discover some of the features of persons that I value, not all of which are inseparable from persons. Chess-playing ability, for example, can be hived off and assigned to a machine, but it is a poor substitute for playing with a person. It is the total package that makes the difference. Playing whatever you play with what some silicon worshipper has called "liveware" (namely, a person) introduces important changes that are hard to name. Playing music with a band and playing all the parts oneself on a sequencer are very different experiences. Part of the difference comes out in a remark of Pascal's concerning not such cooperative activities as these but hostility of a sort. He notes that the universe can easily crush a man, but "of the advantage which the universe possesses over him the universe knows nothing. Thus all our dignity consists in thought. It is that upon which we must take our stand, not upon space and duration. Let us, then, labor to think well; that is the principle of morals."[15] A person's thought, unlike a machine's processing, is grounded in self-knowledge.

Many would suppose that the chess-playing computer does know that it possesses an advantage over me when it beeps hideously and flashes "Checkmate!" on the screen with unnecessary repetition. In an impoverished behavioural sense of "know" it may be said to know of its advantage, but Pascal would be unlikely to accept this as knowledge of the sort he has in mind. When a real person says, without beeping or flashing, "Check and mate," she conveys so much more to me than does the computer. She really knows she has won. There is a mystery to be penetrated in distinguishing the sense in which persons know, feel, and even detect things from the sense in which, to date, computers, their peripheral devices, and their programs can know, feel, or detect things.

Do not suppose that I am setting up the barricades in such a way as to defend carbon-chemistry chauvinism, the view that persons must be housed in flesh and blood. It is not clear to me that computers could not possibly be persons in some useful sense. They are a long way from being so now. Not to put too fine a point on it, they mimic some specific tasks of persons very well, but are narrow to the point of being laughable compared with even a limited person. It is unlikely that we will ever value them much as we do persons unless they can be made to look somewhat like and act and feel very like us. One should not suppose, however, that a huggable body is, in general, necessary to being a valuable person. Consider Joseph Merrick, the Elephant Man, a famous example of a grossly deformed human being who was a person of merit.

Certainly as we explore the idea that machines might be person surrogates—or even persons plain and simple—we will see that, as with persons and morality, the concepts of a person and the concepts of a computer when rubbed together generate much heat and little light. On one side are contemporary philosophers such as Dennett who see the difference between computers and persons, or persons and thermostats for that matter, as a difference in degree, at least with regard to belief attribution.[16] Opposed to this view are those who would agree with Thomas Nagel's prediction, that: "Eventually, I believe, current attempts to understand the mind by analogy with man-made computers that can perform superbly some of the same external tasks as conscious beings will be recognized as a gigantic waste of time."[17] Here, too, there arises the question of the limit on the variety of concepts of a person. The usefulness of the computer model in conjunction with some concepts of a person may contrast sharply with its usefulness with others.

Continuity of an individual's projects

Can you imagine Einstein giving up physics to become a janitor? Some people become so identified with their projects that we can just barely envisage them in other projects. Some people sacrifice their lives for the continuation of something they have worked for: democracy, the family, the progress of science, the health of the environment, or a country. Many are even more willing to sacrifice the lives of others. Whatever matters about people, it is not always taken to be pre-emptive. Consideration for the individual person may become submerged in the pursuit of a goal even when this goal has to do with the betterment of people generally.

Indeed, there is an opinion which still has some currency in this age of individualism that persons count not so much as individuals but as parts of the whole. It is the ongoing history of the species, the striving for perfection of the human race, which gives meaning and purpose to the individual project, and hence, to the individual person. Yet the artist in a prison cell whose works are never seen is a tragic figure just for being cut off from the people who might appreciate her art. There is no art in isolation. On this view, projects have meaning only in so far as they are at least potentially connected to the great fabric of interpersonal connection. What matters about persons is that they are the warp and woof of this fabric. This wide view of what matters has had tragic effects in the hands of, for instance, the Nazis, some of whom may really have believed in a utopian goal to which they sacrificed individuals.

Continuity of the species' projects

Adopting this wide view of what matters, in which the value of the individual depends on that of the species, we come quickly to the question, Well what matters about the species then? Is there some huge, overarching project of the species which gives meaning to our beetling little efforts as individuals? One way back to individuals is through the suggested perfection of individual persons through the striving of the species. Each contributes something to the wisdom of the whole, which is then passed on until persons evolve who are as good as they can be within the limits of the flux of the quotidian. This hope usually rides under some such banner as the perfectibility of humankind.

There are some unattractive features of this sort of species project. It crushes incentives provided by our Western individualism. Most Western religions have provided for the survival of the individual person in their theology: it is you yourself who will get to heaven if you do what the religious leaders tell you. Working selflessly for some species perfection is less than attractive for most people. Another wrinkle is that the species has not been getting clearly better. A candid look at history does not encourage the adoption of this perfectibility view. Nonetheless, there is some truth in it. Part of what we usually think is important about people is their connection to the great ongoing river of persons through time. Few of us can conceive of our work as important in itself without that connection. The unattractive features of thinking in terms of large projects are not far to seek. Consider the humane goal of Marxism to make all people cooperative and its outcome in Stalinism. Our understanding of persons should, ideally, help to balance the projects of individual persons with the grand projects in aid of all humanity. Only then can the continuity of some grand project truly help us to improve what matters at the level of individuals.

Persons for persons' sake

The individualist's response to finding what matters in grand projects is partly to value persons for their own sake as intrinsically worthwhile. Persons just matter. They do not have to be part of something bigger. Often the debate between the individualist and the promoter of the species is pursued at the level of mottoes. No man is an island, says one. Nothing of value was ever achieved by a committee is the response. This is the strategy recommended by Rorty[18]—of making the opponent's vocabulary look bad. Perhaps it would be better to admit, as an individualist, the importance of our connections to the whole while striving to understand what it is about the concept of a person that serves as a moral barrier to the excesses of Stalin and of the Nazis. Often, however, rather than justification of a satisfying sort, we simply hear the motto that persons are intrinsically valuable.

There is another facet to this move away from justification of our valuing persons by saying they just matter. This facet has to do with the apparent absurdity of the lives of persons. Nagel speaks of "the collision between the seriousness with which we take our lives and the perpetual possibility of regarding everything about which we are serious as arbitrary, or open to doubt."[19] If we are always creating our own values, including our valuing of other persons, we are always in danger of seeing the whole of our lives from a point of view outside that system of values. Our ability to take such points of view may be part of some of the important concepts of a person. This ability, however, lets us pull the rug out from under our own feet. If we accept Nagel's view, we see that we simply choose to value persons, not because of some reason or absolute moral standard but just because we choose. What matters about persons, as what matters about anything, is up for grabs.

To pursue this and other leads discovered in this chapter, we need to try to develop some of the various concepts of a person which have begun to emerge as we tried to notice why people matter to us. The kind of mattering may correspond to the kind of concept of a person that is a background condition of the mattering. The first place to look for enlightenment concerning all the questions that have been raised is in the record of what great minds have produced on this topic. The history of the concepts of a person collects for us the wisdom of our culture with respect to persons. Within this history are the contributions of the great philosophers, to whom I now turn.

Content questions

1. Why would the answer, These are God's values not be enough to escape giving reasons for having those values?
2. How does Judith Shklar define "liberals"?
3. How does Ross define "aesthetic enjoyment"?
4. What is utilitarianism?
5. What difference does it make to our values to say, We sentient beings are all we've got, instead of, We persons are all we've got?
6. How does Ross define "mutual love"?
7. What is an egoist?
8. Why did Aquinas insist that the body go along with the soul to heaven?
9. What does Sartre say you are?
10. Who said that all our dignity consists in thought? Why did he say that?
11. What does Nagel see as the source of the absurdity of the lives of persons?

Arguments for analysis

Argument 1: Moral considerations are pre-emptive

Consider what follows from taking moral considerations seriously. If we believe we are morally obligated to perform an action, then, I will argue, we could not excuse ourselves from performing that action by appeal to some non-moral consideration. Whatever we appeal to either will be insufficient to morally justify ignoring our obligation, or will be sufficient. If it is sufficient, then it is a moral consideration. Suppose it is insufficient. If we accept such considerations as pre-emptive, then we are putting morality in second place at best. Morally right actions would just be the ones we do if there is nothing more important to us than morality to move us. Surely this is not taking morality seriously, for morality requires us to follow its dictates and to find out if we are in accord with them or not. Ignorance of a moral duty is no excuse when it is morally culpable ignorance. Unless morality is pre-emptive, it is not taken seriously.

Take Frankfurt's example at the beginning of chapter 2 as an illustration. Let's say that it is Zeke who finds it too costly to explore moral alternatives. This could, itself, be a moral consideration strong enough to justify ignoring the exploration of moral alternatives. Suppose Zeke would face bankruptcy in order to find out what is the fair thing to do with respect to an accounting error. The accounts are extremely complex. The amount of money that may or may not be owing to someone is, say, five dollars. It would be absurd to put his firm into bankruptcy to explore the alternatives in such a case. Zeke is not morally obligated to investigate in such a case. Moral considerations are pre-emptive, but there are higher considerations than the ones, such as apparent fairness, that Zeke justifiably fails to take into account.

On the other hand, perhaps Zeke is obligated to investigate in a much more important case. Zeke is a factory owner. He wonders whether he is doing his duty to protect the lives of the workers in his fireworks factory. In this case, Zeke is morally obligated to investigate to reassure himself that he is doing his moral duty to his workers. He is morally obligated even if it would bankrupt him to do so. He would not be taking morality seriously if he said to himself, I ought to investigate to see if I'm doing my moral duty, but it is too expensive since the factory is losing money and is located half-way around the world from here. If the duty is important enough, morally then one must investigate, get someone trustworthy to do it, find some other morally acceptable solution, or give up on morality. In this case, peoples' lives, not five-dollar debts, are at issue.

Of course there will be borderline cases. In these cases it will be a very difficult judgment to make whether to investigate some moral concern. Taking morality seriously would require that we think very hard about whether we are morally obligated to investigate moral concerns in such cases. Making our best judgment about whether we should investigate a moral concern is itself a moral concern.

Argument 2: Standards

Here I will argue that standards of rationality, morality, aesthetics or anything else must ultimately depend on absurd choices. Whatever standards we appeal to, we must base them on more fundamental standards or accept them unjustified. Choices of standards that are based on nothing are absurd. Therefore, all of our standards depend, ultimately, on absurd choices. I will illustrate this with rationality. We in the West accept certain standards as rational. For example, we would consider anyone who believed an explicit logical contradiction to be irrational. At some point, however, we run out of justifications for such standards. Suppose Camilla says to me, Convince me to be rational. If I offer a rational argument for being rational, Camilla might say, I would believe that if I were rational, but you have to convince me first to be rational before I will believe you. Suppose I say, Be rational or I will hit you. Camilla might respond, I really don't want to get hit, and, if I were rational, I would do as you say to avoid a beating, but I am not yet rational. We cannot have reasons for becoming rational, we just choose to be rational.

Part 2

Ancient Philosophers' Views on Persons

CHAPTER 3

Persons in Ancient Greece and Rome

This you call great thought? Sources of the obvious

Philosophical insights of yesteryear are the commonplaces of today. Over the centuries, the novelty of thinking in a way that was once a great discovery wears off. What we now take for granted was once controversial. Take, for example, the idea that it is inconsistent with the dignity and worth of persons that any person be made a slave. While this idea is of ancient origin, the concept of the person did not, in ancient times, include all human beings. Aristotle, for example, thought some human beings were slaves by nature.[1] The success of contrary opinions is relatively recent and sometimes seems to have a tenuous grip on the minds of our contemporaries. Although it is widely regarded as common sense now, prior to the Civil War in America, there were frequent public denunciations of the more inclusive notion of persons. Many of us believe, that the claim that no human being ought to be made a slave is self-evidently true, but it is an impression that has been established recently with much bloodshed. Many of the philosophical contributions we look at in the following quick tour of history will have this feature of being yesterday's controversy and today's common sense.

Notes to chapter 3 are on pp. 477-78.

Recycling

Another thing that is strange about philosophical investigation as opposed to most other fields is the reissuing of former systems. Kathleen Wilkes at Oxford, for example, is a defender of Aristotle's views about human beings, although she does not defend slavery.[2] Old ideas in a new historical context become new ideas. It is not that there is no progress, but that the progress in philosophy is not linear. In the enormous spaghetti of ideas presented through philosophy, one may follow a single noodle—such as the concepts of a person—through many twists and turns. The structure of the whole may appear elusive in such an investigation. Nonetheless, there is an overall structure and development to the discipline that makes the dish palatable to those with a taste for strong spice. As in cuisine, there are many kinds and measures of progress in philosophy. Ideas are sometimes lost and recovered or recreated. The old and the new mingle in surprising ways. Some thoughts of the great philosophers of the past may seem odd to us now or too obvious, but what we now think often depends on their work—sometimes in subtle ways.

The ancients

To spark ideas about persons, I will give an impressionistic tour through the history of Western philosophy from the ancient Greeks to the present on the topic of persons. I accept in advance the penalty for offering opinions on the thought of the great philosophers—some aficionados of each philosopher will say I have got that philosopher wrong. The issue is even more complicated than interpretation usually is since the word from which our word "person" is derived, the Greek *prosopon* is not used in any of our senses of "person" until the Stoics.[3] The things I say about Plato's and Aristotle's views on persons will consequently be deemed by some to be anachronistic. I maintain that they were talking about persons in some of our senses of "persons" whatever words they used. However I may be pilloried or praised by those who differ with my views on the history of language and ideas, I will be satisfied if this survey proves to be a useful heuristic in our coming to understand the many concepts of a person now current.

Prior to the invention of persons

Trendelenberg begins a scholarly treatise on the history of the word "person" by speaking of a Kantian sense of "person," in which persons are rational decision makers who are ends unto themselves. That is, they may not rightly be used as a mere means to achieve some purpose. Then he tells us:

> We would be at a loss to translate this concept back into Greek, the noble mother of our scientific ethical terms. Plato and Aristotle have no adequate expression for it. They talked about the man, not the person, when they wished to designate what was peculiar to man. A concept like that of Kant cannot develop where there are slaves, at any rate not out of the general moral consciousness. It denotes progress in scientific concepts when a later period is able to define such a concept as person.[4]

Slaves are used as tools or as beasts of burden. This is an unthinkable thing to do to a person or, as we would say today, it is contrary to *human* rights or the rights of *man*. The Greeks of that day had no word for person in the very narrow sense of which Trendelenberg speaks, but there are concepts of a person that we now use which are of course translatable. In almost any English dictionary one can find, for instance, "human being" as one of the synonyms of "person." The Sophists, moreover, challenged the institution of slavery and Aristotle considered arguments that it was an unjust institution.[5] Although they didn't have a word with the sense Trendelenberg is using, it seems safe to say that they probably had some of the concepts of person which we use today. The way to understand what Trendelenberg is saying or ought to say, then, is that the concept of a person as an end but never simply a means and, thereby, as fundamental to morals was not among the concepts of a person that were popular enough to generate jargon in ancient Greece.

To go this far with Trendelenberg does not mean, of course, admitting that the problems we have noticed thus far in our investigation have not come in for comment by the Hellenic philosophers of antiquity. One might say, nonetheless, that there tends to be a light emphasis on the personal in the philosophy of that time. Those philosophers saw puzzles about persons as merely a special case of more general problems to do with the cosmos or at least the state. Prior to the time when Socrates and the Sophists debated ethical matters at length, most of the philosophical inquiry had to do with the nature of things, human beings among them. The Pythagoreans developed a concept of form or limit as a means of differentiating matter into separate entities.[6] Persons, like other things, were considered to be matter together with form. This prefigures later concepts of the person as body plus soul, which was originally body plus form.

Before we try to make sense of the notion of form—which was so important in the development of Western civilization—we should, while dallying with the pre-Socratics, consider some other concepts and problems that have influenced the evolution of the concepts of a person.

Heraclitus: Identity through change—the same river

Heraclitus is often quoted as having said that you cannot step twice into the same river, drawing our attention to the problem of identity through change.[7] Heraclitus was interested in the general concept of the identity of a process. Just as a single river is a constantly evolving process, all things are in a similar state of change. A river constantly changes its waters, its banks, and its bed. What makes the river the same one through all the changes? Heraclitus did, after all, admit that there was a sense in which the river is the same even though it is continually renewed by a change of waters, for he also said: "In the same rivers we step and we do not step. We are and are not."[8] One can make many things of such a paradoxical fragment preserved by chance through the centuries. I read it as saying that we should attend to different kinds of identity for both rivers and people. A person, a river, or any process is made up of many temporal segments or stages. If one seeks an unchanging person, one finds nothing: we are not. If one looks at the whole process, one finds something to identify: we are. There is one process, but each stage of it is different from every other stage. Heraclitus also said: "The sun is new every day."[9]

What stays the same through change, according to Heraclitus, is that which underlies all existing things. He called this "Fire." It is anachronistic, but gives contemporary readers a fair idea of his thought, to say that he envisaged a kind of matter/energy out of which all things are formed and which is conserved through change: "all things are an exchange for Fire, and Fire for all things."[10]

It would be, however, too great an anachronism to attribute to the ancient Greeks a distinction between mind or soul and matter. Souls, minds, and spirits were conceived as simply a more rarefied version of the stuff of which all things are made.[11] Heraclitus, like those who followed in this period, did not think of a continually existing soul or mind as preserving the unity of the person. Like any existing thing, a person to Heraclitus was just a quantity of Fire, an individual blaze within the great conflagration of the universe which burned for a time and then went out. There are those today who think of persons as a particular system of matter/energy that develops through a part of the space-time continuum before entropy sets in. This kind of physicalist account—although it can provide much more detail than the theory Heraclitus put forth in 504-501 BC—can claim that ancient speculation as its granddad.[12]

Although both Heraclitus' speculation and current physicalist theories are suggestive of a way of understanding persistence through change, neither tells us what we mean by a person. We need to know how to distinguish persons as blazes from the whole big Fire and persons from such other little blazes as trees, cows, and computers. Since those who subscribe to physicalist accounts do not permit themselves the explanatory uses of soul, mind, or spirit, they will have to say how to get along without them. In the end, they may wish to delete such categories as that of persons but, if so, they would have a lot of explaining to do which talk of little blazes or localized systems of matter/energy does not accomplish.

Although back in those days the non-materialist options did not appear in the explanation of what we are, there was a move in that direction sparked by a concern with what we should do. Socrates and the Sophists gave rise to Plato.

Man as the measure: Protagoras versus Socrates

Socrates is the model of the philosopher for most people who have any conception of what a philosopher is. Once one gets into a philosophy department at a college or university, one finds that, while

Socrates is admired, he is hardly the current model. It is hard to follow someone who thought we ought not to write books. The Socratic method of leading questions works as a teaching tool and a heuristic, but that is not where most of us want to stop. Unlike Socrates, we cannot influence our society by going down to the marketplace to discuss the true and the good with our fellow citizens. Just try getting a philosophical discussion going in your local supermarket or at the stock exchange. I suppose that shopping malls have some possibilities, but be careful.[13] Socrates was put to death for practicing philosophy in public. As for me, I will write books and discuss philosophy in colleges and universities for now. Space in the mall is too expensive.

Socrates spent a lot of his time in ancient Athens in intellectual combat with some intellectuals of the day called Sophists, men who taught practical logic and rhetoric but who also purveyed a philosophy of relativism and skepticism. Knowledge, truth, and value were thought by these teachers to be either unattainable or fictions. Socrates studied with some Sophists at the rather informal equivalent of today's university and then turned their skills to the pursuit of absolute knowledge, value, and truth.

The foremost of the Sophists, Protagoras, said: "man is the measure of all things, of the things that are, that they are, and of the things that are not, that they are not."[14] In other words, what is real is relative to the observer. On the one hand Protagoras is putting people at the centre of the universe and making them the rulers of reality. On the other hand, the universe shrinks to the size of the individual.

Maintaining a kind of dignity of persons in the face of this relativism, Socrates sought to find a route for them through this observer-dependent reality to something more real beyond the reality we make up. Even at this early stage in philosophical discussion, however, there appears the tension between relativist views, which tend to devalue persons, and absolutist views, which exalt them. Naturally the absolutist views tended to be more popular from that day to the near past. Ultimately, they were a bit hard to believe in the face of the evidence of contemporary anthropology to the effect that what is taken as absolute varies from culture to culture. In our own age, relativism has been a driving force and, in academic circles, the winner—though not the clear winner—of this ancient debate. To see how absolutism won back then and for most of the intervening history of Western culture, we should start with Plato's views about what we are.

Plato: Participating in the form of person

Plato's solution to Heraclitus' problem of unity in diversity and Plato's response to Protagoras' relativism come by way of a development of the Pythagorean concept of Form. By the time Plato wrote the *Republic*[15] he had fully developed a unified theory of reality, knowledge, and value—the theory of the Forms. Like all the theories we will look at in this quick trip through philosophical history, we will see the theory mainly in its application to understanding what we are, though that was not its primary focus. According to this theory, persons—like all things in the flux of the quotidian—had a degree of reality, knowability, and value according to the degree to which they participated in certain Forms that were beyond, in a realm of absolute and unchanging reality, knowability, and value.

A red ball was red and round, according to Plato, because it participated in the Forms of redness and roundness. The more it participated, the redder and rounder it got. One can get a very rough grasp of what this participation is by thinking of copying of or imitating a pattern. I imitate a role model, perhaps, and so become a pale imitation of that model. If that model were perfect, even a pale imitation might not be so bad at all.

Persons participated in Forms. A good person was one who participated in the Form of goodness. In fact, anything that existed did so by participating in the Form of goodness; so everything was to some degree good. Our current saying that there is a little goodness in everyone was thought by Plato to be necessarily true. Being evil was being spiritually deformed, but a total loss of Form was a loss of existence. A person could not be totally bad any more than a statue could be totally shapeless or a musical composition totally unstructured. It is tempting to think of the Forms as abstract universals, like some contemporary conceptions of redness, roundness, goodness, and the like, but it is not clear that the distinction of the abstract from the concrete was the same in Plato's mind as it commonly is in ours today. Like the distinction of the material from the non-material world, this is probably a distinction that evolved from later reflection on Plato's theories. In any case, the Forms were postulated to provide an explanation of why things are the way they are. A person endured through change, moreover, because an unchanging and eternal part of the person maintained some Form. This self or soul had been, prior to being born in chains of mortality, directly acquainted with that other world, the realm of Forms. In this way, Plato answered both Heraclitus' question about change and Protagoras' question about value.

The good qualities that a person had were a reflection of these eternal Forms in that person's soul. Bad qualities were to be thought of as mere deprivations of such a reflection. Forms were wholly positive in value. The well-ordered soul, the soul of the just person, was a soul in which the three main parts—Reason, Spirit, and Appetite—were in their appropriate roles. The just person was one in whom Reason ruled both Spirit and Appetite. Spirit was that part of the person from which courage and anger, for instance, sprang. Appetite can be thought of as a collection of such drives as those to seek shelter, comfort, food, and the bodily pleasures, especially sexual satisfaction. Reason was to direct us as to the priority of Spirit and Appetite. Courage might lead us, for instance, to try to cross a desert, while Appetite would try to keep us nearer comfort and sustenance. Reason would rule in favour of Appetite if there was good evidence that crossing the desert would be fatal and to no great purpose. Appetite, on the other hand, might keep us away from battle when Courage would draw us in. Reason would give courage the nod if doing battle was necessary to preserve the city-state which made one's life worthwhile. The ideal person, then, to put it in somewhat modern terms, would not be immune to the tug of emotions and drives, but would think through the best course of action rather than simply submitting to emotions or drives. The ability to see what is best, moreover, corresponds to the ability to see the Forms.

I have not gone into Plato's reasons for believing in the Forms or the tripartite soul composed of Reason, Spirit, and Appetite. Ultimately his reason for adopting both is that they give us a coherent picture of the world and our place in it. I will not argue further for the theory of Forms here but I would like to put forward one of Plato's arguments for the tripartite soul. This soul or self which directs the body is rather unlike the Christian idea of soul or the Cartesian notion of the self, to which we come later. These later kinds of soul or self are simple things, not divided into parts. Plato, however, sees a need for complexity in persons simply because persons are themselves often divided concerning what to do. If I am extremely thirsty, but I have reason to think that the water hole I have crawled up to is poisoned, I am drawn to drink and repulsed from drinking at the same time. Plato reasons that one, simple, indivisible thing could not be in two opposite states at the same time. There must, therefore, be at least two things within me, one attracted to the water and one repulsed from it. The self must be complex, not simple.

This idea that there are different decision-making faculties within us is not hard to accept today because of the blanketing influence of Freud. It has not always been so. A divisible self or soul may still sound strange to some contemporary ears. On the other hand, we still have such expressions as "sounds strange to my ears," which hark back to the era of Plato and earlier. The heroes of Homer's *Iliad* speak as if their hands, feet, hearts, minds, and various other bits are all decision makers. A person was thought of as a complex collection of things, a committee of decision makers.[16] The triadic structure which Plato gives to this collection is reflected in Freud's division of our selves into the Ego, the Super Ego, and the Id.[17] Readers who think of their inner self as one, single, continuing, indivisible thing must come up with some other explanation of the phenomenon of the divided self at the poisoned water hole. Plato's explanation, which was a natural in the ancient world, will not suit you at all. The many thinkers who have argued for the simplicity of the soul will appeal to you more. As usual, I wish to consider that there may be two different concepts of a person here rather than a disagreement about the characteristics of a single thing. Alternatively, we may be looking at different parts of a person under the single title of "soul" or of "self." Perhaps we have an indivisible self as well as a committee of decision makers within.

The conception which we often meet today of a person as an essentially social being is very much a part of Plato's theory. It is an anti-individualist stance that Plato takes, since he believes that the Form of goodness is a clear and perfect guide that should be followed despite individual ideas about what is good. The perfect state is one that has the same Form as the perfect person. Reason rules. This means that a class of those who are themselves ruled by Reason in their own souls, whom Plato referred to as Guardians, should have complete autocratic control of the society. Below them, Plato called a military and policing group Assistants, whom Spirit ruled. The base of society he viewed as formed by Craftsmen, those who produced goods and services and had personal souls driven mainly by Appetite. Plato would think our own societies in Western democracies where Craftsmen are allowed to rule as wicked because they are ill formed. Similarly, he considered military dictatorships to be evil in so far as the dictator or oligarchy is from the class of Assistants. To be a truly capable ruler is to be a truly capable person, physically, morally, and intellectually at the height of human ability. A state that participates in the Form of goodness is one whose rulers do as well. The ideas of the individual and individual freedoms must be severely limited, according to Plato, in order to enforce the participation of the state in goodness.

At the beginning of this all too brief exploration of Plato's theory I intimated that persons were not the main focus of that theory. The reason is that, with respect to valuing persons as individuals, Plato stands midway between Christ and the Buddha. Buddha teaches that the ultimate attainment for an individual person is the annihilation of individuality, absorption into the cosmos, getting off the wheel of becoming. Christ, on the other hand, teaches that individuals will be rewarded for their merit by eternal life. The individual is not merely absorbed but survives to enjoy the fruits of moral rectitude in this vale of tears. Following Aristotle, who comes up next in this historical jaunt, Christians before Protestantism believed the soul to be the form of the body, so that even the body had to survive by resurrection. Plato, however, offered us a very limited form of survival, in which, of a being governed by Reason, Spirit, and Appetite, it is clear that Appetite and perhaps Spirit are left behind with the body. Only the intellectual component—perhaps conceived of as some rarefied, airy matter—is released at death. The distinction between the full-bodied survival that Christ offered and the absorption that Buddha welcomed is blurred. It is unlikely that the survival of our immortal souls, as understood by Plato, would appeal to any of our contemporaries who are concerned with survival of bodily death.

Such a brief presentation of bits of Plato without much defence must make Plato sound rather quaint. If we think about the way we talk and think about things today, though, we may find that Plato's influence is everywhere in our own worldview. We speak of Platonic relationships, meaning a relationship that is the result of Spirit governed by Reason and not driven by sexual desire from that part of ourselves called Appetite. And one who knows something is in*formed*. The intervening centuries have not prevented us from thinking often in terms of something like Forms. The enormous appeal of a world of Forms where things are as they ought to be—a world of which our own is a pale imitation, a world that can be attained by a struggle of the soul to perfect itself in morals and intellect—is an appeal that will not let Plato's Forms go the way of phlogiston and other quaint conceptual antiques. There are serious criticisms of the theory, some brought by Plato himself,[18] so we must proceed cautiously with anything we gain from it.

What about Daphne?

What does the theory of Forms do to help us with our topic? Consider Daphne, whom I spoke of in the introduction. She has lost most of the physical and mental abilities by which I knew her, but her body remains, to outward appearance, much as it was. Daphne can be seen from Plato's vantage point as someone who has changed Form. She no longer participates in the Forms to the degree she once did. This deformation of the self is an evil, a privation of the Form of the Good, which eradicates the natural gifts that Daphne had, thereby placing her in a different position in society. Once she had a soul in which Reason was foremost, governing Spirit and Appetite. Plato would have considered Daphne an example of the sort of person fit to be among the rulers of the state, someone who could see the Forms.

But how are we to think of Daphne's survival, and how should we act toward her? In Plato's time, Daphne could not have stayed alive as she does now with heroic medical care. Probably Plato would have considered Daphne a deformed instance of the same person as the former Daphne, but whoever survives in a deformed state survives only to a degree. Then how are we to act toward such people? Justice, for Plato, is achieved by giving each person in society the role to which that person is suited by natural gifts, and there is no longer any role for Daphne in Plato's scheme of things. There is no further guidance to be had from Plato in such cases, but it would be anachronistic to expect it. All Plato can do is to underline the extremity of the tragedy of such a complete deformation of a soul so finely wrought.

For others, however, who are not in Daphne's state, Plato's conception of the person as an inner self composed of Reason, Spirit, and Appetite may have some appeal. To order one's soul well with Reason ruling, Spirit second, and Appetite firmly under their control is a task well worth undertaking whether one understands it literally or figuratively. Rather than giving us a view about what persons, in general, are, Plato has given us an ideal. He tells us what, given certain natural gifts, we should be.

What I like about Plato

Plato tells us something of the inner complexity of people: the way we fight with ourselves is picturesquely captured in the doctrine of the tripartite soul. He also holds up an ideal of personal development toward greater goodness, greater participation in the Form of the Good. It seems like a good idea to subjugate one's spirit and appetite to one's reason. Whether or not we swallow the theory of Forms holus bolus, we can still adopt the concept of an ideal toward which human beings must strive to become the best persons whom their natural gifts allow. He reminds us as well that people achieve their development in the context of a society, not as totally independent agents. Some of these themes are carried on in the work of Plato's most famous student, Aristotle.

Aristotle: Down-to-earth souls

Aristotle gives us a lot to think about with respect to persons just as his teacher did. There are many differences in their views, but perhaps the main one is that Aristotle concentrates on the here and now, on what we would think of as the real world. Plato thought our world was an illusion, low in value, knowability, and reality, the muck of change and hence of corruption. Aristotle, by contrast, shows no desire to escape from this world to a world of Forms; instead, he brings the Forms back to this world and reduces their godlike stature. For him, form, or structure, loses its capital F.

Even less than for Plato is there any ground for making a distinction of material from non-material things in Aristotle's worldview. Form and matter are not really separable. We have already seen that, in Aristotle's down to-earth approach, the soul is the form of the body. You cannot have one without the other. This seems to simplify the problem of re-identifying people over time. To see if the same person is there, one might think one merely has to see if the same body is there, for the person is an embodied soul in the sense of materialized form or formed matter.

There are some difficult cases of identification of bodies of living organisms just as there are difficult cases for any thing. The difference between a wax statue and a puddle of melted wax is clear enough, but there are some stages in the melting process where it is hard to say if the statue is gone yet or not. A statue's form is just its shape. With more complex forms, such as the soul of a person, identification becomes even more difficult. As if that were not enough, persons' souls are special, because they include the capacity for reason. This means that, after all, even when we can apparently identify a body as the same, if the abilities have changed enough, the person is gone. Aristotle would not count a body as the same body if the person could no longer reason. The person, the embodied soul, is a substance in which properties such as being able to reason inhere. If the soul itself is changed, then something necessary to the existence of the person, the essence, is changed rather than just an accidental property such as having black hair. For Aristotle, one still exists when one's hair turns grey but not when one becomes totally senile. To see, given Aristotle's views, how we might test for sameness of a person, let us look a bit more closely at the Aristotelian notion of a soul.[19]

Psuche was Aristotle's term for soul, self, or organizing principle of a living organism. It was not what the soul became in later Christian thought but, rather, a group of capacities. The *psuchai*, or souls of living things, constituted an ordered hierarchy from the *psuchai* of the simplest vegetables through those of the various animals up to the *psuchai* of persons at the top.[20] Just as the capacity for locomotion distinguishes animals from plants, the capacity for rational thought distinguishes human beings from lower animals. This capacity is a part of a person's *psuche* but so is the capacity to eat.[21] In fact, the *psuche* has an indefinite number of parts.[22] This is much more complex and interesting than the tripartite soul Plato proposed. To understand a person, in Aristotle's way of looking at things, you need to understand her biology as well as her psychology. That is not all.

As with Plato, the social and political aspects of a person's life are crucial. Aristotle looks at the whole universe the way we would look at a person. If we want to know why a person does something, we ask about that person's intentions. If one wants to know why an acorn is made the way it is, from an Aristotelian view, one looks for an explanation in terms of what it intends to become or what its purpose is. One looks at adult specimens of any organism to see what the end or purpose of their earlier developmental stages were. Since the end of human social development is a state, people are political animals.[23] Somewhat as acorns were meant to produce oaks, people were meant to produce societies. A hermit, I suppose, is malformed, missing something in the *psuche*.

Just as Aristotle saw the soul as a more complex entity than it was in Plato's theory, so the state is not just divided into three classes of person. Our varied *psuchai* allow for many types of persons. He holds, nonetheless, to Plato's idea that a good state is one made up of good people. The rules for being good, hence the rules for politics, are not so limited for Aristotle. Nonetheless, within a community it was important for everyone to abide by the same laws to prevent discord. An olive tree by nature bears fruit, but the tree may not bear fruit if conditions are poor. People are by nature sociable and people may be unsociable unless the state is carefully regulated. With people, as with everything in nature, the antecedent purpose determines the eventual outcome, *given the right conditions*.[24] As Voltaire said much later in *Candide*: "We must cultivate our garden."

Because all of Aristotle's explanations are couched ultimately in terms of the purpose things have by nature (their *telos* or end), he is concerned with the way things turn out in the end. A fetus or a child is not yet a full person but merely a potential person. The fully and normally developed adult is the model we must look at to understand his conception of a person as an embodied soul. This is often what we do in contemporary debates when we think about what persons are. But we may forget this normal adult model when we try to apply our results to children or adults who have lost certain essential capacities. For some of our purposes, children are full persons, not just potential persons, but saying this requires a different concept of a person to the one Aristotle is employing; such a different concept entails a very different sort of moral view to Aristotle's. To get an appreciation for Aristotle's view we must look at his notion of a person's soul.

The core idea in the notion of the *psuche* or soul is that of ability. Once one loses the essential abilities, which one must have to be a certain kind of substance, then one no longer is in the same class of substances. Take a simple case first. Suppose I use an oblong piece of sandstone as my door step in front of my house. It weathers and crumbles. It is now not a deformed door step, it is not a door step at all. It is just a heap of rubble. Similarly, Aristotle, seeing that a human being has lost the capacity to reason—which he takes as the crucial capacity for separating persons from animals with lower orders of *psuchai*—would not count this human being as the same person nor as a person at all.

Aristotle had, because of his emphasis on ability, what would seem to us today to be a rather harsh moral and political outlook. He was happy with viewing some human beings as slaves by nature and with keeping women totally out of politics. He failed to take up Plato's view—unbelievably radical for its time—that women could be in any position for which they had the ability, even Guardianship of the Republic.[25] While Aristotle has much to say to us that may be useful, we probably will not be able to make do with his concept of a person on its own.

What about Daphne?

Given the theory I have adumbrated here, Aristotle would have thought that Daphne had gone out of existence. Something of the matter that made up Daphne remains but with a different form. The woman we now call "Daphne" is not a person in the sense that Daphne of old was, for rationality, the foremost part of her *psuche*, is gone.

What I like about Aristotle

What is particularly useful in Aristotle's conception is the great complexity which he sees in the soul or self, its inseparability from the body, and the integration of people into a taxonomy of living things.

People are part of nature. The concept of a soul as something to be found, only in the world, and not as something that is out of this world, is a concept which merits further investigation. The *psuche*, soul, or self can only be had by "a natural body of a particular kind, viz. one having *in itself* the power of setting itself in movement and arresting itself."[26] The difference between animals and people on this account is not in having a soul but in its degree of complexity. We are all part of one fabric.

It may well be objected, for reasons alluded to earlier, that the use of the words "soul" or "person" in our discussion of Aristotle is anachronistic. Certainly, whatever he was talking about, he was not talking exactly about what most speakers of English have in mind when they use these terms. There is reason to think, however, that his remarks are pertinent to our present concerns about our souls, selves, or persons. For now, we will see what the ancients following Aristotle had to say.

Rome and the invention of persons

In an exceptionally Teutonic offering in the *Monist* in 1910, "A Contribution to the History of the Word Person: A Posthumous Treatise by Adolf Trendelenberg," one finds some clues as to current dictionary definitions and philosophical predilections. A person may be thought of as a role or a part played, and this is associated with the possible origins of the word "person" in the Latin *persona*, meaning "an actor's mask."[27] What is behind the mask? Perhaps the human being puts on this role and, since one may have different roles from time to time, there may be different people associated with a single human being. Playing one's role well and consistently was the ethical desideratum of the Stoics, so even this minimal sense of "person" has a moral use. This use of the term flows into that in Roman law where the legal drama had its *dramatis personae*, and *persona* indicates those who bear characteristic legal relations, such as the plaintiff and defendant.[28] It is also related to such uses as first person in grammar.[29] Trendelenberg believes that the grammatical and legal uses "helped each other along in the course of the generalization in which finally *persona* and *homo* became synonymous."[30] In early Roman law, all human beings, even slaves, were distinguished from mere things and included among persons.[31] The ideas that persons are necessarily human and that they have moral and legal importance are part of the early evolution of the concept of a person. Philosophers who call this carbon-chemistry chauvinism and see no moral import in the concept of a person fly in the face of Western European common sense. That is the philosopher's job, to some extent, but gadflies can sting themselves.

In Justinian's time, relatively late in the history of ancient Rome, slaves began to be conceived as mere things, not persons, because the concept of freedom became closely linked with that of a person. Freedom, in this body of law, was the "natural power to do what you please unless you are prevented by force or law."[32] This, too, it seems to me, is clearly related to the dignity of persons which sometimes gets glossed over, passed off, ignored, or denied in the contemporary debate on personal identity. We do not want to mess up our metaphysics with such messy, fuzzy stuff as freedom.

To be careful, however, we should note that the law concerns itself with granting political freedom from such things as slavery to those who already have the title *persona*. I think, nonetheless, that it makes no sense to concern oneself with political freedom for those who do not already have metaphysical freedom. We must have the free will needed to exercise our political freedom or we are all enslaved to forces visible or invisible. The debate between the proponents of free will and determinists who think we have none is only prefigured roughly by these developments in Roman law.

One must not, in any case, get too carried away with the advent of the word *persona*. I have been speaking of the views of philosophers in classical antiquity on persons. Even following the introduction of *persona*, however, they did not have a word with all the connotations of "person" that we find in contemporary European languages. The words and phrases the Greeks were using could be translated by "human being" or, in political contexts, possibly even "free, adult, male human being." Slaves and women were only considered persons by the enlightened few. The heritage of our word "person" does, however, reach back to classical antiquity where it even has some moral force. Much of its current moral force, however, dates back only to Kant in the eighteenth century.

The equivalent of the word *persona* in Latin is the Greek *prosopon*. These words both refer to the mask that actors wore on stage. The mask became associated with the role the actor played. We still use person in the sense of "role" sometimes in English. This sense of the role or character played is a very important one, morally, for the ancient philosophers in Greece and Rome known as Stoics.[33]

Stoicism

The Stoics thought that what we ought to do is to play the person or role we have been given by providence. This role is totally beyond our control to choose. In the grand theatre of the universe, we should accept our parts and play them well. That is the only scope for human choice and self-betterment. One can choose to rankle at the person one must play or one can accept this role and play it well. In a world where everything is determined by providence, it is odd that we nonetheless have, on this deterministic Stoic view, the freedom to choose to accept or rail against our roles.[34] We are, in any case, determined to play those roles however we choose to feel about them.

This Stoic philosophy was already established in the third century BC and still going strong when Epictetus wrote in the first century AD:

> Remember that you are an actor in a play, the character of which is determined by the Playwright: if he wishes the play to be short, it is short; if long, it is long; if he wishes you to play the part of a beggar, remember to act even this role adroitly; and so if your role be that of a cripple, an official, or a layman. For this is your business, to play admirably the role assigned you; but the selection of that role is Anothers.[35]

This limited view of what a person is stifles the striving to change one's conditions. It is, consequently, a means of maintaining the status quo. People bear pain and injustice stoically because it is their lot in life to act as good sufferers. In this case, however, the interest of the individual is not, as with Plato and Aristotle, subjugated to the interests of the state. The focus, at least, has shifted to concern about individual lives. The Stoics, however, assume that individual lives are best served by the recognition that we are only acting out roles given to us by providence. This is the way to happiness. If one is a miserably treated slave, one becomes happy with being just that. Like the Epicureans before them, the Stoics thought not of satisfying desires for power or pleasure but of overcoming desires. In this subjugation of desire there is a superficial resemblance to Buddhism but, unlike the Oriental views in which the individual is ideally absorbed into something larger, the Stoic philosophy puts the individual in the spotlight.

While the Stoics gave us a rather limited concept of a person—the person as a role—they did develop the concept of a person beyond mere species membership. The satisfaction, moreover, in the quiet life of acceptance which they promoted was personal satisfaction, not satisfaction in serving the state. Personal freedom, though limited by Stoicism to the choice between acting one's role or railing against it, was also tied at this early stage of its development to the concept of a person.

What about Daphne?

The Stoic's idea that it is part of the nature of persons that persons have the ability to choose and are responsible for the way they feel about their lot in life is one which, however limited the freedom, rules out a severely mentally handicapped human being as a person. Daphne cannot choose to accept or reject her role, as far as we can tell. When she was last able to choose, she utterly rejected her approaching role as a demented cripple and chose death, demanding euthanasia. The Stoic development of the concept of a person does not help us with the questions raised earlier about respecting the choices of a person when those choices were made prior to radical changes. Some may find comfort in Stoicism as a means of bearing their own suffering, but it gives us too limited a concept of a person to rule on our conflicting intuitions where Daphne is concerned. We can only say that Daphne is not a person in the sense of the term introduced by the Stoics who invented, if not the concept, the word.

Plotinus and later Roman developments

While its limitations for our present purposes are evident, Stoic forbearance was much admired in ages which followed the classical period of Greece and Rome. The idea that we should obediently play whatever role we discover is our lot in life was to be modified, however, to permit a kind of striving for self-improvement within the role. The religious thinking that dominated the Middle Ages was responsible for the movement away from the limited concept of a person which the Stoics had bequeathed. The Christian concepts of persons, moreover, were presaged in Roman times by Plotinus' revision of Plato.[36]

Consider first the development of the concept of a person in the law. The courtroom was seen, by the Romans, as a kind of drama and the roles in this play, for instance of the plaintiff and the defendant, were naturally called *persona*, persons. As only human beings can have legal rights and stand in juridical relation to one another, this legal usage moved the term in the direction of being synonymous with "human being."[37] Assuming that the use of language has a lot, though not everything, to do with concept formation, the concept of a person which is our heritage from the Stoics—person as character or role—was being enriched to include our juridical relations and our humanity. At the same time, spiritual dimensions were being thrown into the mix.

The spiritual input came from a dramatic revision of Plato by the Roman philosopher Plotinus. Plotinus revived the notion of an immortal soul as the crucial part of the person but he moved this concept more in the direction of the non-material. Throughout ancient Greek philosophy, spirit was thought of in terms of some material but rarefied thing, like breath. The immortal soul that Plotinus sees as the true reality, as opposed to our bodily, earthly, existence, resembles fairly closely the Christian notion of a soul which is of a different order entirely from the body. The soul is responsible for its actions, although Plotinus, like the Stoics, paradoxically maintained as well that all events are determined. This soul then seeks to perfect itself morally and intellectually, thereby achieving a mystical union with God.[38]

This sort of view is radically different from that of the Stoics in that it gives the person the chance for self-improvement. Unfortunately, it reverts to the otherworldly conception of reality. The healthy here-and-now emphasis of Aristotle and his successors is lost. This has the decidedly unfortunate effect of making the world and persons' bodies merely disposable packaging. As the events of the Middle Ages show, such a view of the person can lead to incredible atrocities. It is not an evil to torture heretics into recanting their heresy then to kill them quickly once they have confessed, as their souls can then go to heaven in a state of grace. If the here and now is of no value, human suffering in this temporal world can always be justified by an appeal to the eternal bliss to come.

Respect for persons becomes respect for their immortal souls, and the devil take their poor, suffering bodies. Although it is misleading in many respects, and well out of fashion with historians, there are reasons for the epithet the "dark ages." Respect for the whole person is kept in abeyance while concepts of the non-material side are developed. While people are expected to accept their suffering stoically and play the roles they have been given, they are expected to perfect themselves spiritually. The intellectual perfection that Plotinus strove for is sometimes dropped from the picture as a hindrance to faith. The mortification of the intellect and the flesh in favour of the spirit is a new twist. Another concept of a person emerged in the Middle Ages. We see how this comes about through a look at some major figures in the philosophy of those wonderful and terrible times.

What about Daphne?

To think of Daphne not as the body so lacking in normal abilities but as an immaterial soul is to think of her as surviving still. Plotinus' move away from the Greek notion of a breath-like, physical thing as the soul makes the soul mainly a mystery. It is hard to see, however, how Daphne could develop spiritually or intellectually even if we can make sense of a soul of the sort Plotinus describes. Such a soul cannot act or think through a body like Daphne's, for that body is entirely passive. As Daphne herself wondered when she felt her mind ebbing along with her body, what could we possibly mean by a disembodied mind or soul?

The Roman idea of persons under law has been developed in such a way that we now treat Daphne as a person for juridical purposes, though as one who must be in the guardianship of others. This reflects a concern for persons in some sense broader than that which we have seen developing in ancient Rome. Certainly it goes beyond the picture of persons as beings struggling for their betterment through spiritual development. Perhaps the subjugation of the intellect to faith has had a beneficial side effect in making us realize the worth of features of persons that are outside of the realm of reason.

Intellectual ability had been the primary distinguishing feature of persons according to Aristotle. The Stoics, Roman law, and Plotinus helped to broaden the concept so that a person could have legal or spiritual worth of importance equal to or greater than intellectual ability. The battle to distinguish persons from the cosmos or the state—a battle against absorption in larger units—was also vigorously engaged in Roman times. We see this struggle continue in the Middle Ages.

Content questions

1. Use the example of slavery to show how the commonplaces of today were great insights of days gone by.
2. What is the Kantian use of "person" to which Trendelenberg refers?
3. Why does Heraclitus say that you cannot step twice into the same river?
4. What does Protagoras mean by saying that man is the measure of all things?
5. Why can a person not be totally bad according to Plato?
6. Put Plato's argument for the complexity of the soul in your own words. Can you think of an objection?
7. Briefly say what the Form of the Good is and how Plato uses it.
8. Give some examples of the influences of Plato's theory of the Forms on contemporary language.
9. Why would Plato be opposed to contemporary advice to follow our hearts?
10. Why does a soul without a body make no sense to Aristotle?
11. Briefly describe Aristotle's hierarchy of souls.
12. Why would Aristotle think the capacity to reason must be retained by any human being who remains a person?
13. What is the significance of the derivation of the word "person" from the word meaning "an actor's mask"?
14. Why is it strange according to the Stoics to say that you ought to strive to better your place in society?
15. Why would Plotinus not think physical illness important to the concept of a person?

Arguments for analysis

Argument 1: Two kinds of identity

Here I will argue that Heraclitus uses two senses of "same," and that only one of these is relevant to personal identity. Heraclitus says that you cannot step into the same river twice because new water is always flowing.[39] The sense of "same" or "identical" that is used here is sometimes called "qualitative" because it depends on something *x* having all the qualities or properties of some thing *y*. Once there is any qualitative difference, we say *x* and *y* are not the same. The river today is not the same as the river tomorrow because of slightly different qualities and volume of the water in it. Of course you are not qualitatively identical to the person you were yesterday but that does not make you a different person. Having exactly the same qualities or properties that you had yesterday is not what we mean when we say you are the same person. Numerically identical persons might not be qualitatively identical. Of course Heraclitus admits that there is another sense in which we are the same: "We are and are not."[40] We are identical to our former selves but not qualitatively identical. This sense of identity in which we are identical with our former selves is sometimes called "numerical identity" as opposed to "qualitative identity." The fragments from Heraclitus do not tell us how we survive some changes through time or how we succumb to other changes and cease to be, but his metaphor of a river is a useful one. A river may change many qualities and still be called the same river. If the change is great enough, however, we might not accept this. If, for example, an earthquake radically changed the course and type of river, then we might be reluctant to say that the river now is identical with the river before the earthquake. Grisly Gulch Creek might replace the Happy Valley River. The type of identity that allows us to say that the Happy Valley River survived for a period of time and then was replaced is the type of identity that we need when we are talking about sameness of persons.

Argument 2: Qualitative but not numerical identity

First we consider an argument based on Max Black's famous radially symmetric universe example (mentioned in chapter 1). This argument is intended to show that two qualitatively identical persons could be numerically different. After this will come a counter-argument. A radially symmetric universe is symmetric through a central point. Each existent thing in the universe is duplicated on the other side of the universe. Radians drawn from any point on an object through the point meet a completely similar point on a duplicate object. Every quality that one of the members of such a pair has is matched by a quality—including relations to other objects—had by its double. This is true unless we assume an absolute space-time grid and treat spatio-temporal location as a quality. Let us take space as relationally defined or deny that spatio-temporal location is among the qualities of a thing. Now we have a possible universe in which any person has an exact double. Anything one says or does, the other says or does. Their brains are in the same state at any given time. Presumably, therefore, they would have the same thoughts. It appears, then, that we could have two individuals who are qualitatively identical but numerically distinct persons.

Argument 3: Objections to argument 2

Here we give several reasons for thinking that argument 2 does not establish its conclusion that it is possible to have numerically distinct persons who are qualitatively identical. The main reason to doubt this argument by example is that it is not clearly the right sort of example. We could describe Black's universe as one in which one person has two bodies totally synchronized with one another. There is no reason to think that the universe described has two qualitatively identical persons in it. A further objection is that it is not clear that such a universe is physically possible. If it is not, then there is no possibility of having persons with physical bodies in such a universe. This universe may be a physically unrealizable mathematical model. The appearance that it is physically possible rests on the background assumptions about the physical laws in this universe being left unspecified. It is not at all clear that, given new physical laws that make the model realizable, we would have anything that we would accept as persons in that model. Given these objections, we should conclude that it is still debatable whether two distinct persons could be qualitatively identical.

CHAPTER 4

The Mediaevals

The soul and the intellect

St. Augustine adopted a worldview similar to that of Plotinus, making it the standard view of the Middle Ages. The world was arranged in a hierarchical form with God at the top, somewhat like the Form of goodness in Plato's system. In this worldview, love of God and faith are substituted for knowledge. God, of course, is mysterious and unknowable. Although Augustine strives to make Christianity intellectually acceptable, reason is not given the first place among human abilities. Nonetheless, persons gain a new importance with the advent of Christianity since they are made in the image of God and are closer to God than other things in creation except angels. Plotinus had bequeathed a hierarchy with God at the top and unanimated matter at the bottom.[1] Augustine adds human dignity to the picture. Each person is worthy of the love of others unless, by choice, that person makes herself less than worthy by being insufficiently loving.

Love and dignity of persons

Augustine assures us that God cares about us as individuals. That love is the source of our worth, and he assures us that we can strive as indi-

---

Notes to chapter 4 are on pp. 478-79.

viduals to be worthy of love. Still, a person cannot achieve a state of grace by effort alone, but only by God's gift of grace. We can be damned on our own steam but we need God's help to be saved. This gives some scope, at least, for freedom of the will as an important feature of persons.

The ability of persons to love is, however, the most notable feature that is given new importance in Augustine's conception of a person. We inevitably love, and we may love things, other people, and ourselves. When we expect too much from the object of our love, our love is disordered; hence we become restless and miserable. Of course, Augustine claims that our ultimate spiritual need can be satisfied only by love of God.[2] Love of God, according to Augustine, makes us a member of a society, the City of God, which is at war with the City of the World. The latter is composed of those who love themselves and the world.[3] What or whom we love and how we love turn out to be the most important features of persons. In spite of the heavy apparent debt to the classical period, Augustine ushers in a new way of thinking about persons and a new importance for them in the old hierarchy. Persons still do not count because they are ends in themselves, but they have dignity and value since God has a purpose for them and cares about them.

Unfortunately, the enlightenment of some of Augustine's views does not carry through in practice. He was writing as the Roman Empire was in its death throes and with it goes much of the civilization necessary to provide a context for the humane pursuit of Augustinian ideas. Instead of the emphasis on individuals as exalted by God's love and worthy of love, one sees in this period the idea of the hierarchy burned into human society. In imitation of the divine hierarchy, there is a feudal social hierarchy in which the Monarch is at the top, with the nobles arranged in a subordinate hierarchy of their own, followed by the free men at the next level, and the poor suffering serfs are at the bottom, near the position of inanimate matter. Rigidity of the social structure prevents the pursuit of justice as Augustine conceived of it, justice based on mutual love.[4] The serfs were told by religious leaders to stay in their social place and wait for the reward in the next life.

Augustine may have said that justice is the habit of the soul which imparts to every man the dignity due him,[5] but that habit would not be in anything remotely approaching general circulation until the repressive economic and cultural forces of the Middle Ages relented. Neither Christian doctrine nor the religious philosophers such as Augustine or Plotinus gave credence to the politically expedient view of persons as immortal souls in largely expendable packaging. The mortification of the flesh is not required by those teachings but only by repressive political forces.

In aid of inclusivity

The nod in the direction of gender equality which we saw in Plato's *Republic*[6] is certainly nowhere to be seen in this period. In a strictly hierarchical society in which persons get varying degrees of respect, women are in a relatively poor position with respect to men. The queen is less than the king. The noblewoman is less than the nobleman. So it goes until one finds at the bottom of the hierarchy the female child of a serf. On the plus side, some women in feudal society, such as the queen and religious sisters were treated with great respect for their persons.

Other groups who are slowly gaining the status of persons in our society have, perhaps, benefited from the changes wrought by Augustine. Those who are handicapped, mentally or physically, provide an example. Although the Augustinian contribution to the concept of a person is dependent on the acceptance of a particular brand of theism, in which the worth of individuals is conferred by a loving God, the influence of this view on secular opinion is considerable. One does not have to be a religious thinker in our times to accept the general principle that persons have worth and dignity independently of their abilities and usefulness to society. In particular, intellectual ability is not the essence of persons. At least while our times remain less harsh, in Europe and North America, than Augustine's era, we find room to value people who require the support of society but do not have the wherewithal to continue to contribute to society. In extreme cases, the very defencelessness of the person is taken as a ground for special protection as a member of the class of persons rather than as a ground for ejection from that class.

Another feature of Augustine's work on our topic is the increase in individualism. The Oriental ideal of absorption of the individual into the state or the cosmos is fended off with the doctrine of individual excellence through the striving to be worthy of God's love. This emphasis on the person as opposed to a larger entity is continued by some of the subsequent major figures in philosophy during the Middle Ages.

What about Daphne?

Augustine's emphasis on love is interesting from two vantage points. On the one hand, taking the capacity for mutual love as a defining ability of persons may count against treating Daphne as a full person. Daphne's capacity for mutual love is very much diminished, if it remains at all. One must have some sense of self and other for love. One must be able to remember other people to some degree. On the other hand, since Augustine makes the dignity and value of persons dependent simply on their being loved by God, rather than on their possession of abilities, Daphne would be a person to whom we have strong moral obligations, although she could not be a person in the sense of one who bears responsibilities.

What I like about Augustine

The emphasis on mutual love and on worth being independent of ability are strong strains in secular humanist as well as religious thinking. Perhaps they need not strain against one another as long as we characterize the capacity for mutual love as a defining capacity of persons while being loved or at least being an appropriate object of love as a moral feature of human beings whether persons or not. Appropriately secularized, the idea that being a person is partly an affair of the heart (as we would say today) is an idea with great appeal.

The Arab-Christian dispute over individualism

While Plato, through Augustine, exerted a strong influence on the thought of the early Middle Ages, the works of Aristotle were temporarily lost to scholars of that time. Through Arabian philosophical communities, however, where Aristotle's works were still read, came some of the opposition to Plato that we have already noticed. Avicenna, a Persian writing in the tenth and eleventh centuries, was hotly discussed in Europe. His view of persons was like that of Aristotle. Persons were formed matter, the soul being the form of the body. Avicenna, however, threw in a dash of Plato in that the soul, or some intellectual part of it, somehow survived the death of the body to be absorbed into a kind of mass soul or mind.

Absorption in the Agent Intellect

As with the Greeks generally, intellect was considered by Avicenna to be the most important feature of the person. It included perception of objects external to the person, memory, and the power to discover the essence of things through abstraction, although the ability to abstract was not a human ability but something done for us from the outside by the somewhat mysterious Agent Intellect. This idea of an Agent Intellect—somewhat like a super-conscious mind—disturbed St. Bonaventura for it "threatened the notion of the discrete individuality of each soul, since each returned to its source, the Agent Intellect."[7] Maimonides, the great Jewish philosopher of the fourteenth century, developed a similar view to Avicenna's.[8] Here we have again the Oriental idea of absorption of the individual into a mass soul.

It is interesting that it is Christianity that seriously opposes this absorption doctrine while retaining the idea of a reality beyond this world. After all, the otherworldly aspect of Christianity is used during those times for political purposes inimical to individualism. Conceptually, however, Christianity drew to itself all that was useful in promoting the importance of the individual soul. The older Greek ideas that gave less importance than Christianity to the individual, although they gave more to the intellect, succeeded only in eventually improving the reputation of the intellect. St. Anselm, for instance, thought that reason together with faith and divine guidance would reveal rational proofs of articles of faith. But no major Christian thinker in the Middle Ages returned to the idea of the absorption of souls into something larger without personal distinctions in each soul remaining. Individualism was here to stay as long as Christianity was. The dogma that supported the worth of individual souls eventually supported the political power of the individual—but only in later ages long after the evolution of the concept of a person.

Another philosopher from the Arabic world was the Spaniard Averroës, writing in the then-Moslem culture of Cordova in the twelfth century. In his famous commentaries on Aristotle, his version of the Aristotelian doctrine about persons was true to the original. The soul was the form of the body and was itself material; hence, the soul died with the body.[9] This down-to-earth secular philosophy could not have survived in the parts of Europe controlled by Christians. Opposition to the Platonic doctrine of the immortal soul was, of course, anathema to Christianity. Even more than Avicenna, Averroës undermined the separateness of individual intellects, putting all of our intellectual abilities at the doorstep of the Agent Intellect, that impersonal rational force in the universe. While this secularizing force had its impact diverted by the great thinkers of Christian Europe, they benefited from and adapted the Aristotelianism of Averroës. In particular, the greatest systematic philosopher of the Middle Ages, St. Thomas Aquinas, found a place for Aristotle at the heart of Catholicism.

St. Thomas Aquinas

By the thirteenth century when Aquinas was writing, the influence of Aristotle was rising and threatening the philosophical ground on which Christianity had taken its stand. It is easy to maintain a doctrine of the immortality of the soul against the backdrop of Platonic metaphysics since Plato himself had put forth such a doctrine of the soul. Mind you, we have seen that the soul which Plato conceived was a rather wispy thing by comparison with the full-blooded person that was needed to make Christian doctrine work. If I were to be concerned about my personal survival in an afterlife, I would not be motivated to follow a religion which promised me that only some intellectual part of me would survive. It is not just my reasoning capacity that I would want to defeat death.

The body: You can take it with you

Here then is the dilemma which inspired so much of the subtle metaphysics of Aquinas' era: immortality of the soul requires something unchanging and incorruptible as the soul, while full-blooded personal survival requires that we take along our corruptible, changeable old bodies. Recall that the soul Aristotle conceives of is a part of the person which dies with the body, as his concept of the soul is the form of the body. Survival without the body makes no sense, for the body is an essential part of the person.

Intellect is, for Aquinas as for Plato, Aristotle, and the Aristotelians of Aquinas' day, the distinguishing characteristic of human beings. We need intellect to come to know God and thereby to come to love God.[10] The idea that to know Him is to love Him is reminiscent of Plato's view that to know the Form of Goodness is to do good things since Goodness is irresistible to the soul that sees it. Aquinas, however, emphasizes another feature of persons which is not clearly compatible with such a doctrine of irresistibility, namely that we are free to choose sin or devotion.

Within the restrictions of theology, Aquinas was very creative in fashioning a system which, while it emphasized Aristotle, did not leave Plato behind. Since Aristotle had designed his own system to supplant Plato's this proved to be a task which Aquinas, for all his skill, did not quite manage. In the process of his magnificent failure, however, he had a profound influence on what we think we are. Since theology demands that persons be able to commune with God, Aquinas was driven to try to retain the otherworldly features of the soul while not overthrowing Aristotle's insight that our bodies are essential to us. But how can the corruptible, changeable, and finite commune with the incorruptible, unchangeable, and infinite? Plato's answer, that the immortal part of us escapes from the body, is not compatible with Aristotle's insight.

Aquinas asserts, then, that our incorruptible, free, intelligent, individual souls are not merely housed in our bodies but must be unified with those bodies if we are to be whole persons. He does not, of course, accept Aristotle's claim that such a soul cannot exist without the body. The soul, however, is radically incomplete without the body. Most people in Christian cultures, when they think of themselves going to heaven, do not imagine that the decrepit body from the grave gets dragged along. Neither do they imagine that a disembodied intellect without memory or attachment to the earthly body is absorbed into another reality. Most Christians probably imagine that it is their body in the adult stage of life—made perfectly healthy and beautified, free of pain and all the defects to which matter is prone—that soars into the blue. For this image, we can thank Aquinas. Aquinas merely extends the Platonic conception of rarefied matter, which was the Platonic soul, to include not just some essence akin to breath but the whole body in a reformed, purified, glorified state. Just as the soul, purified of the evil that was in it, is renewed, so the body is made better than it ever was with this renovated form to structure and limit it properly. According to this doctrine, in our life on earth we are always to some degree malformed, but our bodies will be perfectly formed in the hereafter.

An uneasy marriage of Plato and Aristotle

Aquinas is often thought of as replacing the Platonic metaphysics, by and large, with Aristotelian metaphysics within the church. While this is true in some sense, it can be misleading if we overlook the victory of Plato in the fundamental areas of the doctrine of the immortality of the soul and the existence of a greater, better reality beyond this vale of tears. Aristotle told us that what you see is what you get. It is, furthermore, wrong to see in Aquinas a return to Aristotelian materialism and a retreat from Platonic dualism. It is wrong because the distinction between materialism—the view that all is matter—and dualism—the view that both material and non-material things exist—cannot be foisted on the ancient world without anachronism. Plato, like Aristotle, thought in terms of one kind of stuff out of which both souls and bodies are made. Souls were much more subtle, as breath is more subtle than flesh. Our current dualism with respect to persons had still not clearly developed in Aquinas' time. He was simply extending the Platonic doctrine of the soul to include more of what makes up the person on earth.

This view has its dissenters such as this one from Stevenson: "It is a common and recurrent misinterpretation of Christian doctrine that it asserts a dualism between the material body and an immaterial soul or mind. Such a dualism is a Greek idea."[11] I would say, rather, that the Christian doctrine through a large part of its history incorporates the Greek monistic view that there is just one kind of thing. For persons, in particular, there is not a distinction to be made between material and non-material parts of ourselves. In the many streams of current Christianity, of course, there are factions that support dualism. This dualism is, however, the outcome of a long process of evolution of ideas through Plato and Aquinas to Descartes, and it does not become a robust part of Christianity until the seventeenth century. Aquinas' philosophy is even today the theoretical underpinning of a major player in the Roman Catholic Christian community.

Contention between dualists and monists (who believe that there is just one kind of stuff) still goes on within Christian communities. Aquinas contributed to this debate the claim that we can have immortality and keep our bodies, which are reconstituted at Judgment Day.

As with any have-your-cake-and-eat-it-too theory, Aquinas' runs into some difficulties. From an Aristotelian vantage point and from many modern viewpoints concerning persons, some of Aquinas' problems seem quaint. For example, Aquinas has trouble with cannibalism. When two human bodies are intermingled in this grisly way, what gets resurrected and how?[12] Although there is a certain black comedy in these concerns, the theory that makes them important to Aquinas has been enormously influential in our conception of ourselves. After all, Aquinas gets himself into these fixes by insisting on both Aristotle's idea that we are one, single, unified body and soul, while wanting to claim that we are more than the corruptible temporal stuff of this life.

Most of us believe that we are something more than intricately organized chunks of matter capable of locomotion. Those who accept and those who deny this belief both get into difficulties that are reminiscent of the debate between Aquinas and his Aristotelian contemporaries. We need to know how to identify and re-identify bodies, we need to know what else there is to us, and we need to know how to identify and re-identify that something else. We need to know whether our personalities can be expressed through different bodies or in other ways. Aquinas' problem of survival of the person in the afterlife is very similar to many of our contemporary concerns about survival within this life. Many of the questions we might ask have answers in Aquinas' adaptation of the classical Greek literature on persons.

A fetus, for example, is not a person by these lights, no more than an acorn is an oak. As Aristotle would have it, the fetus is merely a potential, not an actual, person. For Aquinas, after some weeks of development, the fetus has an immortal soul, but not from conception onward. Both the soul and the body develop and change. What keeps them the same through change is the underlying substance which remains through all changes of properties to that substance. There are both necessary properties that the substance cannot lose while remaining in existence, and accidental properties that it may change.

While the person is the fully formed adult, there is a continuity of substance through the changes from the potential person to the person. The soul, or form of the body, becomes more fully actualized over time, but is never perfectly actualized in this life. The soul that chooses evil over good deforms itself and loses the chance of perfect actualization in the next life. Nonetheless, to make sure the right person is rewarded or punished in the next life, we must have a way of seeing this deformed person or this glorified person as the same person who walked this earth. The substance is the same. That is why, for Aquinas and for Catholics today, the body had to be resurrected—not some ghostly apparition of the body but the real thing from the grave. This gruesome solution to the problem of survival of persons is the strange result of trying to wed incompatible systems, Plato's and Aristotle's. Aristotelians would say that one cannot separate the form and the matter temporarily prior to resurrection in the way in which Aquinas was forced to do. Formless matter is not a particular thing, and matterless form cannot exist.

Essentialism, potential persons, and survival

Whether or not one takes the problems surrounding resurrection seriously, the idea that there is an essential me which exists through all my changes is one which appeals to *me*. What this underlying substance is that remains through the changes is to be found, according to Aristotle and Aquinas, by looking for my necessary or essential properties. What is there about me which could not change while I remain in existence? Notice, however, that their answers have to do with my existence as a human being rather than as a person. The person is not actualized at the beginning of the life of the human being. The underlying substance does not initially have, for instance, the personality which is unique to the later person. The question naturally arises for Aquinas, as it does for many of us, whether different persons could be in one body. After all, if the Aristotelian inseparability of body and soul is denied, how do we keep our physical and spiritual parts properly paired up? Aquinas can always appeal to God's benevolence to overcome such problems. A benevolent and omnipotent God would not allow and could prevent mix-ups.

Other difficult questions arise in the context of Aquinas' theories. When does the potential person develop enough to be the actual person? The adult human being in the prime of life is the person by Aristotle's lights. But for both Aristotle and Aquinas, there is the problem of what the person is through change. Since the distinction between person and human being is only nascent in the works of Aristotle, like the distinction between material and non-material, it would be anachronistic to pull out too definite an answer to such questions. By Aquinas' time, however, the problem of the three persons of the Trinity (discussed later) had placed the question of the concept of a person at front and centre. The particular part of that problem, though, which arises for Aquinas is that someone who chooses a personality through training to respond in certain situations with a certain kind of action is deliberately changing some personal properties. For instance, a timid mother who decides to face any future danger to her child may become courageous by choice. While these may be accidental properties of the human being, they appear to be necessary properties of the individual person, at least if a particular personality is essential to being an individual person. On this view, the timid person cannot be identical to the courageous person.

In Aquinas survival through radical change becomes particularly difficult, since the beatified soul and body make up a person who is vastly different from the earthly original. Even within our earthly lives, however, we may change from sinners to saints. To say that one remains the same substance, or the same human being, while changing the personality only points to further difficulties. What is the continuing person who is responsible for the old sinful acts, for the new saintly ones, and, indeed, for changing from a sinner to a saint? What is essential to the person if one can go through such radical change? These sorts of questions are left largely for later philosophers to explore.

What about Daphne?

The notion of radical change brings us to Daphne's case, to the case of a fully developed adult who becomes severely demented. From Aquinas' perspective, as long as it is possible to be a person when the intellect and control of the body are destroyed, Daphne would still remain in the class of persons and merit the treatment due all persons.

This does not, in and of itself, entail that the person with whom we are confronted after the radical changes is the same person whom we once knew. Survival requires that the special characteristics which singled her out within the class of persons are also sufficiently represented after the change. The problem for Aquinas is to say how the soul, now devoid of intellect and character necessary for being responsible for actions, is the same soul that was once well-formed or deformed depending on the choice of good or of evil that Daphne might have made. Daphne can no longer, for example, exercise the good character she developed. She cannot prove her merit by responding to situations. Perhaps Aquinas would say that the soul in such a demented human being is like the soul in one who is dead. On resurrection of the body it will resume its abilities. One wonders, however, what the soul is, over and above the intellect and its abilities.

What I like about Aquinas

With all its problems, the picture of the person that emerges in the work of Aquinas reinforces the conception that we are individuals. The intellectual part of us which survives bodily death and awaits reunion with the perfected body is distinct from other intellects. No super-conscious mind absorbs the individual.[13] Intellect is crucial in distinguishing us from the other animals. From this point of view, the demented human being is, perhaps, no longer a person in the same way that a fetus or an infant is not yet a person. Unlike the Aristotelian system, that of Aquinas does not make a great deal of the value of persons depend on intellect. Those who are intellectually impoverished in this world, as long as they choose, within their limited capacity, good over evil, will be reformed and able to know God in the next world. Nonetheless, there is enough of an emphasis on intellect and its capacity to distinguish us as individuals to disturb some of those who followed Aquinas. The mystic and anti-intellectual tendency within Christianity is still at war with Aquinas' intellectual faction within Christianity.

In any case, Aquinas' adaptation of Greek thought importantly advances individualism and the conception of persons as free and self-determining. We move further in the Western tradition away from the fatalistic and anti-individualistic doctrines associated with the Orient. The idea of personality becomes crucial as well. Our intellect and freedom are properly used to choose certain habits that can guide us through sticky patches in our moral lives. In the course of development as persons then, we perform this paradoxical self-creation—making ourselves the persons we eventually become. The person—perhaps even the potential person—chooses a personality or set of habits that will make the future person what she becomes. The guide is not some Aristotelian *telos* (end or purpose) which makes this development inevitable. We are our own guides. I must train myself to automatically do the right thing when the occasion of a sin arises.[14]

In some ways, the contemporary view of Sartre—that existence precedes essence, that we first exist and later create what is necessary to our being the persons we are—is anticipated in Aquinas' view of persons. This doctrine of self-creation that has us pull ourselves up by our boot straps and the denial of a limiting, pre-existing nature of persons is also to be found in the humanists, especially in Pico Della Mirandola's *Oration on the Dignity of Man.*[15] All of these authors need to grapple with the distinction between two questions: What must something be like to be a person? and In what does the survival of an individual person consist? The individual would have to keep the general characteristics necessary to be a person at all, and retain as well certain characteristics which made that person different from other persons. A class essence and an individual essence are both needed for survival.

In philosophy, we have to see where we have been to see where we are going. I hope that it is evident by now that contemporary secular concerns about persons are guided in part by Aquinas' hand. In any case, I am going to look at some other mediaeval religious developments which carry the concepts of a person forward into the later Middle Ages. They do so with great drama.

Philosophy as the handmaiden of religion

In the Middle Ages, philosophy played second fiddle to religion. Since religion was such a powerful part of the culture, second fiddle was a pretty good position. Then, the doctrine of the Trinity, and theology generally, coloured the concepts of person. One astonishing example of questions concerning persons caused an immense stir in AD 362 when a church council was held solely for the purpose of investigating and determining the meaning of the word "person."[16] Imagine what was required to draw bishops from around the Christian world to Alexandria when travel was arduous and dangerous for a meeting with one item on the agenda. Only a topic of the utmost importance could provoke such a remarkable meeting.

Three persons, one God

The religious doctrine which required this philosophical discussion at the highest levels of the church was the doctrine of the Holy Trinity. According to this doctrine, there is but one God in three persons: the Father, the Son, and the Holy Ghost. The meaning of "persons" which the bishops went to such enormous trouble to decide was crucial because it determined the orthodox interpretation of the doctrine of the Trinity. Since people in the Middle Ages could be put to death by the church for being unorthodox (that is, heretical), religious leaders took the definition of the concept of a person to be a matter of life and death—much as today when extremist pro-lifers use the rhetoric of civil war to condone the shooting of doctors. In AD 1532 it was no different. Recall from chapter 2 that because Servetus declared that the three persons in the Godhead were three functions, in the same sense as three roles, he was burned at the stake. It was his bad luck that the bishops did not agree on what they meant by the term "person" back in AD 362.

At the meeting in Alexandria there were three positions. The Greek bishops thought that God had three hypostases (substances) but one essence. The Roman bishops thought this concept would lead them away from monotheism; they demanded that the word "person" be used instead of the word "hypostasis." A third group thought the whole debate was a quibble over words. All agreed that the three persons of God were not merely roles that God was playing. The third group seems ultimately to have carried the day since the words "hypostasis" and "person" became synonyms in the theology of the Middle Ages. Genuine philosophical differences, however, were patched up by this linguistic plaster of diplomatic synonymy.[17]

The position of the Greek church seems incoherent in terms of the Aristotelian philosophy from which it sprang. If God is three substances or hypostases, then God cannot have one essence, since individual substances are defined by and inseparable from their essences. The concepts of a person which had been in use up to the time of the bishops' council did not help. They did not want to use "person" to mean "role" or "human being." They could not use it in such a way as to imply that God was not really one being, but they could not use it so as to say that it was a mere manner of speaking to say that he was three of something. History had boxed them into loading onto the concept of a person the full weight of a mysterious doctrine. Anyone who, like Servetus, tried to take a perfectly legitimate meaning of the word "person" and demystify the doctrine of the Trinity was likely to pay the highest price for such perfidy.

This outcome is not a propitious turn of events for the discussion of a concept or concepts. Things got worse before they got better. Even such civility as Aquinas had accorded to intellectual knowledge was viewed with suspicion by some later religious leaders. Mysticism was seen as a safer road to knowledge of God, since reason tended to unseat faith rather than to shore it up. On the other hand, out of the theological wrangling came the use of the Latin term *persona* to mean "an individual, intransmissible (incommunicable), rational essence which is self-existent." A thing is self-existent if and only if it is not a part, nor a quality of another thing.[18] This moves the concept of a person from that of a mere role which cloaks the living human body to something independent of the body and, perhaps, something of greater dignity and moral significance. A general warming trend in the political life of Europe coinciding with a waning of the power of the churches was still needed before the public, philosophical discussion of persons could be undertaken without grave danger. This thaw began in the late Middle Ages and was accelerated in the Renaissance.

Content questions

1. Describe one way in which Augustine's worldview is similar to that of Plotinus and Plato.
2. What is the most notable feature given new importance in Augustine's concept of a person?
3. How is Augustine's view helpful to the handicapped?

4. How did Averroës and Avicenna undermine the concept of persons as individuals?
5. Explain one aspect in which Aquinas mirrors Plato and Aristotle where distinguishing features of human beings are concerned?
6. How does Aquinas meet difficulties in trying to combine Platonic and Aristotelian ideas of persons?
7. Why does the substance of a person have to be preserved in the afterlife according to Aquinas?
8. Give two examples of the way that Aquinas' adaptation of Greek thought advances individualism.
9. What is it to be self-existent? How does this figure in the conception of a person that emerged from the theological wrangling of the Middle Ages?

Arguments for analysis

Argument 1: Self-existence rules out virtual human beings as possible persons

In reflecting on what we believe ourselves to be and what we believe is possible in the popular media (*Star Trek*, for example), we often suppose that there could be persons who are merely features of another thing. For instance, a hologram of a person is merely a feature of a computer program in the *Star Trek* story. Interestingly, as I will argue here, the idea from the Middle Ages that persons must be self-existent rules against this possibility. It would also rule out the possibility that we are merely somebody else's dream and will vanish when that person wakes up. There are many versions of the virtual-person scenario in contemporary culture but, if self-existence is a property of persons, then all of those scenarios describe something impossible.

For the following argument we will need a distinction of tokens from types. A *token* is a particular thing, while all things that are alike in relevant respects are of the same *type*. For example, there could be other people who are very similar to you—that is, of the same type—but you are likely more concerned with the survival of one token of the type, yourself. Another example is that there are many tokens of a particular type of word in this book. Take the word "the." The many individual occurrences of this word in this book are all tokens of a single type or members of a category of words.

Now suppose that persons are self-existent. In that case they cannot exist merely as a part or a property, a quality, or a feature of another thing. For instance, the token of redness on a red, rubber ball would not exist if the ball did not exist. Of course the type redness might exist independently of particular tokens of redness as either a relational property or a Platonic Form. Now what is a virtual human being but a dependent part of a program, a dream, or the like? Such a human being is similar to the token of redness, not similar to the ball. Without the program or the dream, there would be no such human being, just as the token of redness would vanish if the ball ceased to exist. A virtual human being cannot then be self-existent. A virtual human being cannot, for the same reason, be a person. Let us illustrate this with an example from the popular media. The doctor on *Star Trek*, a hologram, goes out of existence when the power is off or his program is not running. Various tokens of the doctor that are very similar exist in sequence. None of these tokens is self-existent. A virtual human being can be the type of a person, but it would not necessarily have a single token, as would a real human being. You are an individual in the sense that there is only one token of your type, and the type and token exist or do not exist together.

Argument 2: Objections to argument 1

It is not clear that anything is self-existent. The red rubber ball may just be a bundle of tokens of properties: redness, roundness, elasticity, and such. Even if the ball has a substance in which these properties inhere, that too is dependent for its existence on background conditions such as the environment that supports it. If the temperature, for instance, were too high, the ball, substantial or not, would cease to exist. That is not essentially different from a token of a program ceasing to appear when the power is turned off. Persons seem to be dependent for their existence on their environment as well, unless of course we are indestructible after all. Self-existence applies only to some indestructible continuing thing. In the Middle Ages, the soul filled this function, and it still does in some religious conceptions of a person. It is, however, not at all clear what souls are supposed to be or whether there are any. Even if there are such things, the first argument has given no reason why virtual persons could not have them. It appears that we have one of two possibilities: nothing is self-existent—in which case, the first argument presupposes an inadequate definition of a person, or souls are self-existent and virtual persons might have souls. In other words, the first argument starts from a mistaken assumption, or it is possible for computer-generated images of human beings to have or be souls. In either case, we should reject the first argument.

Part 3

Modern Philosophers' Views on Persons

CHAPTER 5

The Renaissance and the Early Moderns

Mechanism versus humanism

As it is in our own age, particularly in philosophy, so it was in the Middle Ages: the devotees of logic, precision, and clarity turn out to be the most difficult to read. Montaigne wrote: "I can't recognize most of my daily doings when they appear in Aristotle. They are decked out or hidden in another cloak for the benefit of the schoolmen."[1] Part of the problem was the corruption of Aristotle's texts that were used by the scholars of the Middle Ages. Even with better translations, closer to the original, most of us would still agree with Montaigne. Nevertheless, reading good translations is much to be preferred to reading bad or stilted ones.

Erasmus' humanist tradition

Erasmus, the greatest promoter of humanism in the Renaissance, set about providing editions of scripture in which the elegance of the language was preserved and the stilted, ritualized language of some scholars was avoided. The incipient democratization of things intellectual that was the result of Erasmus' efforts had a great effect on concepts of a person both by creating new avenues for discussion of

---

Notes to chapter 5 are on pp. 479-80.

the topic and by making acceptable the idea that those at the bottom of society's hierarchy were also worthy and capable. As learning spread downward, through this democratization, the idea that the value of persons was determined by their place in the social hierarchy became harder to maintain.

Erasmus also attacked the view of the person as distinguished essentially by intellect, the view inherited from the Greeks and from Aquinas. The attack on the overweening importance of intellect was part of Erasmus' attempt to democratize religion. Faith was something one could pursue with the heart, Erasmus thought. He did not think heaven would be populated by intellectuals only. He did not deride reason by any means, but he thought there was more to the person than Aquinas and some of his predecessors had noticed or, at least, emphasized. Humanism is, partly, a return to the richer view of Augustine in which such things as the capacity to love are important features of persons. This helped to establish the atmosphere in which the idea of the dignity of persons, no matter what their station in life, could emerge. The humanist tradition is essential to the contemporary moral force of the term "person."

Protestantism

At the same time there emerged a criticism of the old order much stronger than the criticisms from Erasmus. Arguing that both the corrupted mediaeval doctrines and the Protestant Reformation were driven by vast exaggerations, Erasmus tried to steer a middle course. "The whole world," he said, "is now shaken by the thunder and lightning born of the collision of such exaggerations."[2] On the one hand Erasmus opposed the clergy who magnified the importance of the papacy and, thereby, of their own role. Some were making a tidy profit selling salvation in the form of plenary indulgences and such. On the other hand, Erasmus found the cure for this corruption as bad as the disease; of the Protestants he said: "They liquidate the freedom of the will and teach that man is driven by the Spirit of Christ."[3] The dignity of persons was undermined both by those who said that heaven could be earned by fattening up the priests and by those who said that it could not be earned at all. One side reduced the spirit to commerce. The other negated the freedom that is essential to persons.

Taking aim particularly at Luther, Erasmus asks: "What's the good of the entire man, if God treats him like the potter his clay, or as he can deal with a pebble?"[4] This shows the importance, to humanists like Erasmus, of free will as a characteristic of a person. Luther, by contrast, while lashing out at Erasmus, leaves open the possibility of the worth of any person through God's grace. Unfortunately, this worth is entirely reflected from God; there is no real personal worth. By Luther's lights, the most meritorious of saints in fact, cannot be saved without God's beneficence. Nothing one does is ever good enough to merit salvation.

Not only was Luther unmoved by human freedom as a value, he also preached diatribes against intellect. Luther took the primacy of faith even further than his predecessors so as to exclude the usefulness of reason in supporting religious belief. Erasmus' emphasis on the positive features of people and their capacity for moral improvement was dashed by Luther's return to the mediaeval view that man is by nature corrupt.[5] The worth of the individual person is utterly denied. Intellect and achievement are derogated in favour of subjugation of oneself through faith. Whatever its achievements in rooting out the corruption of the church, the Protestant Reformation tended to promote a backward-looking idea of persons.

Montaigne

Erasmus was not, however, alone in the revival of the humanism of classical antiquity. We have already noted Pico Della Mirandola's *Oration on the Dignity of Man* with its praise of human freedom.[6] Erasmus' friend Thomas More wrote of the near perfectibility, through reason, of people and their government in his *Utopia.*[7] The humanist movement put forward freedom and reason as the essentials of a person. Though they did not neglect the emotions, it was usually reason on which the dignity of persons depended. This attitude is nicely summed up by Paracelsus: "He who knows nothing loves nothing. He who can do nothing understands nothing. He who understands nothing is worthless. But he who understands also loves, notices, sees."[8]

Another admirer of the classical period of Greece and Rome was Michel de Montaigne, sometimes called "the French Socrates." He was influenced by the Skeptics of the ancient period. Their method, quite opposed to that of Socrates by the way, was to hold tightly to no doctrine, submitting all to doubt so as to live to the full. A life hemmed in by preconceptions about the way things are is not likely to be a happy one. Montaigne wanted to break down the strict, ritualized worldview of the Middle Ages in favour of one more flexible. One should not, on Montaigne's view, adopt final answers to very subtle, variable questions. Dogmatism is not the way to truth. We might do well to heed this advice, noticing the final answers both sides have adopted concerning the nature of persons prior to engaging in the debate on abortion.

Montaigne, like Erasmus, tended to promote the idea of the dignity of persons. He asserted the humanist idea of our interconnection: "Every man carries within himself the whole condition of humanity."[9] He exalted our judgment as opposed to faith or intellect: to be a real person is to make conscious choices based on experience.[10] Montaigne, however, did not wish to overthrow the political system and customs that provided some stability within which one could pursue philosophical wisdom, at least if one was, like Montaigne, of the nobility.[11] This conservative attitude, as a result of doubt about absolute ends to which society should move, is very similar to that of the Sophists with whom Socrates contended. It comes too from an emphasis on personal rather than political development. It is, however, folly to think that the two can be separated. Montaigne's own development depended on his privileged position in society.

As to our concern about the nature of persons, Montaigne the skeptic would have warned us that constant change denies us access to this or any other nature: "And if by chance you fix your thought on trying to grasp its essence, it will be neither more nor less than if someone tried to grasp water: for the more he squeezes and presses what by its nature flows all over, the more he will lose what he was trying to hold and grasp."[12] Like the humanists before him, Montaigne was amazed by the variability of people. Nonetheless, Montaigne spent his life in personal development and advice to others on this difficult subject. To do this, one must know in some sense what a person is. The impressive variability of persons is, in fact, one of the things about us which makes us what we are and that, in turn, is dependent on our freedom.

Galileo and the new science

Generally opposed to the new focus on personal issues was the development of a new kind of objectivity in science, which was accompanied by a mechanistic materialism as the underlying philosophy and a successful use of mathematics in prediction and control. Discussing Galileo, who was one of the pre-eminent practitioners of the new science, Stumpf[13] draws a clear opposition between the attitude toward persons promoted by science and the humanist notion of the dignity of persons. Galileo thought of reality in terms of primary (objective) qualities such as motion, size, position, and density, which can be quantified and dealt with mathematically. Opposed to these are secondary (subjective) qualities such as colour, taste, emotion, and sound. We can talk about human beings in terms of primary qualities. Personal characteristics, Stumpf asserts, are usually represented by secondary qualities. According to Galileo's philosophy, these secondary qualities are either fictional or are to be reduced to the mathematically manipulable reality of primary qualities. Stumpf concludes: "In either case, the unique dignity, value, or special status of human beings in the nature of things is severely diminished."[14] Leonard Cohen has said, "We are so small between the stars, so large against the sky."[15]

What about Daphne?

Although Erasmus elevates people from the role of plaything of the deity, it does exclude people like Daphne from the essential source of dignity. Daphne would have agreed. That is why she chose death over a life of dementia. Without the ability to choose her own actions freely, Daphne really is reduced to the potter's clay from Erasmus' point of view. Since she has no free will—the main feature he holds out against the Protestants and the new science—she seems to be stripped of her dignity. Daphne herself saw matters this way when she anticipated being reduced by dementia to a mere mechanism. She demanded euthanasia as a protection from this fate.

What I like about Renaissance thinkers

The Renaissance, then, provided an atmosphere in which one could begin to think of persons as having dignity and moral worth by virtue of their own achievements, not just in the reflection of a deity. Individual freedom begins to assume more importance in conceptions of a person. At the same time, there were opposing views of the person presented by the severe Protestantism of the Reformation and the mechanistic, materialist philosophy underlying the new science. Protestantism made people out to be evil while mechanism reduced them to material things and, thereby, reduced their dignity and worth.

The oldest moderns

The success of empirical science in the prediction and control of events in the natural world gave philosophers pause. The mediaeval idea that pure intellect could find the truth was giving way to the modern recognition of the need to use the five senses in observation as well as the intellect to gain knowledge.

Hobbes: The emerging modern worldview

Thomas Hobbes, best known for his political philosophy, ushered in the modern era by accepting completely the scientific method and its underlying assumptions. He believed in the need to observe and gather facts prior to erecting a theory.[16]

Hobbes also accepted empiricism; that is, he believed that our knowledge comes from information we get through our five senses. Distinguishing himself from Descartes and his followers on the continent, the Briton Hobbes was a materialist. Recall that materialists believe everything is made of matter. Minds and spirits, if they exist at all, must be material. Hobbes's moral theory, moreover, was a precursor of today's social contract theories in ethics. David Gauthier in *Morals by Agreement*, for instance, considers himself to be developing Hobbes's idea of mutual constraint as the source of ethics.[17] Moral rules are justified by showing that, by constraining ourselves under such rules, we create our mutual benefit. While Hobbes held all these views in a form that was to be refined by later thinkers, he set the tone for much of later philosophy, especially in Britain.

Living as he did in chaotic times, 1588-1679, under threats of invasion, revolution, fire, and plague, Hobbes wished for security more than anything else. This political aim dovetailed with his materialistic philosophy. He believed that he could understand the way persons behave in terms of mathematical laws governing bodies in motion.[18] If a person is a physical system whose behaviour can be predicted and controlled just as the course of a billiard ball on a table can be controlled by a master player, then the key to security is to understand the physical principles of human behaviour well enough to fashion a political system that can banish chaos and uncertainty. The political system Hobbes describes turns out to be complete totalitarianism, in which value and dignity of the individual person is largely ignored. This is not terribly surprising, given the view that persons for Hobbes are merely elaborate mechanisms. Although Hobbes did not accomplish anything like the aim of finding the mechanical principles needed to predict and control persons, he bequeathed this aim and his view of the person to his philosophical heirs.

The success of mechanics in Hobbes's day misled him into his vastly oversimplified view of persons as mechanical systems. The success of computer science today has the same effect on his heirs, who also try to reduce mind and persons in general to matter. Some wish, for instance, to treat the brain as a computer and the rest of the person as programs. Hobbes's concept of a person as an elaborate mechanism has merely been updated with currently fashionable scientistic jargon. Hobbes wished to reduce mind and spirit to material bodies in motion. Current reductionist theories differ from Hobbes's mainly in the complexity of the thing to which they wish to reduce these features of a person. In their degree of overconfidence, these theorists are Hobbes's equals. On the other hand, Hobbes and later empiricists re-established the healthy attitude of Aristotle that takes our sense experience seriously. Attention to the here and now and lip service to common sense marks the work of Hobbes and his descendants. Wild speculation about persons untrammelled by the limits of experience is supposedly anathema among empiricists. One cannot help but smile, however, when asking how well founded, empirically, are their materialistic conceptions of persons. Such theories tend to go well beyond the evidence available from the senses and, in true empiricist fashion, they ignore equally strong evidence from other sources.

What about Daphne?

Metaphysically, Hobbes would see Daphne as merely a defective machine. Morally, Hobbes would treat Daphne as having no rights.

Gauthier points out that, following a Hobbesian morality based on mutual constraint for mutual benefit, we cannot rationally justify treating those such as Daphne as persons, as members of the moral community. There is, after all, no expected benefit to come from treating such human beings as persons and protecting their interests.[19] They cannot return the favour. Competitors restrain themselves according to rules that make all competitors better off than unlimited competition would make them. Daphne and others like her, however, are not in the competition.

Cartesian Egos

To many, Hobbes's view of the person seems to be not a propitious beginning to the life of that concept in the modern era. This era began, however, in cultural schizophrenia. A view opposite to Hobbes's and equally extreme was proposed at the same time by the renowned philosopher and mathematician René Descartes. Descartes and his school in philosophy are the arch-rivals of Hobbes and his. Hobbes's empiricism is countered with their rationalism. Rationalists not only deny the empiricist claim that sense experience is the source of all knowledge, they assert that reason alone is a much better source of knowledge than experience. Anything we get by experience must be filtered through our rational critical faculties before being accepted. The empiricist says that we should believe our eyes and ears. The rationalist tells us that we should not trust these unless reason supports the information they give us. The mind is glorified as Hobbes glorified the body. Descartes, however, does not wish to reduce the body to the mind. He is a dualist, one who believes that both mind and matter exist. Mind is just a lot more clearly known than matter.

The person, according to Descartes, is an amalgam of mind and body. This is a view which, today, is still often taken as common sense. Prior to Descartes, however, the distinction of mind and body was not at all clear. The ancient Greeks made no such distinction, although it is sometimes incorrectly attributed to Plato.

The distinction of mind from body seems undeniable to many of us. As is often the case, what was once a contentious theory has seeped down into the general consciousness to become obvious common sense. We no longer think with the ancients that thought and mind are merely subtle forms of matter like air. Most of us, outside of philosophy departments, suppose that mental events are quite different from physical or material events. If I say that I have a pain in my nose after witnessing my dog get stung on the nose by a bee, for instance, you might tell me it is all in my head. You might say the pain has a mental cause rather than the physical or material kind of cause which my dog's pain has. We are often very unclear about the exact nature of the distinction, but most of us staunchly affirm the Cartesian idea that mental and physical events are different. Descartes has had a profound effect on the way we think about what it is to be a person.

Perhaps the most famous saying concerning persons is Descartes' reply to the skeptics who think we should doubt every claim since there is nothing we can know for certain. The first thing Descartes thinks we can be sure of is the self. He asserts confidently: "I think; hence I am."[20] Descartes means that he cannot think and at the same time doubt that he exists. What would be doing the doubting if he did not exist? Here, Descartes seems to return to the Greek and early mediaeval emphasis on intellect as the essential feature of persons. Actually, thinking, in Descartes' terms, is much more than mere intellectual thought. When he defines a self as a thinking thing, he packs a lot into the word "thinking": "But what, then, am I? A thinking thing, it has been said. But what is a thinking thing? It is a thing that doubts, understands (conceives), affirms, denies, wills, refuses, that imagines also, and perceives."[21] The interior self which directs the body and does this thinking is often referred to as the Cartesian Ego. Descartes thinks it is independent of the body and would exist even should the body cease to exist.[22] While many think that nothing could be more certain than the existence of such a Cartesian Ego, others claim that there is no such thing. Since Descartes still has a corner on common sense in our era, the philosophers who claim there are no Cartesian Egos really have their work cut out for them. While dualism can still claim to be common sense, it may nonetheless be in danger of losing that status. Problems arise. Is this thinking thing, the Ego, a thing that must be thinking to exist? What happens when we are asleep? Perhaps we must say with Unger that Descartes thinks the Cartesian Ego is always conscious, but sleep is a kind of forgetting of what was consciously thought during the night.[23] This seems rather desperate. Why can the body not preserve our continuity instead of some mysterious Ego?

Descartes, in any case, does not leave Cartesian Egos unhoused. Like Plato's intellectual soul or self, Cartesian Egos have a body to direct. Unlike the Platonic soul which is made of a subtler form of the same stuff as the body, the Cartesian Ego is different in kind from the body. This gives rise to the interaction problem: how can a non-material self interact with a material body? If I want to walk to the store, I do it. But my wanting goes on in my mind, which does not exist in space, as my body does. How do the two of them get together? The mystery of how a mental event, like wanting, can cause a physical event like walking is just not solved by Descartes. In fact, I do not think it is solved at all. The common sense view of persons has, to this day, this completely paradoxical feature. We think of persons as minds with bodies, but we do not know how the mind makes the body do the simplest thing, nor do we know how physical events, passionate kisses for example, are associated with their complex mental concomitants, doubts for example.

Descartes was not too concerned with this problem. In a religious age such as his, it was still possible to argue—as his follower Geulincx did—that, when I exert my will to make my body do something, my mind has no direct effect on my body. Stumpf reports that according to Geulincx's theory, God intervenes to make my body do what I want it to do.[24] Some of you may wish to accept this solution. Many more will wonder why we have the problem. Perhaps common sense is not so sensible in this instance.

Descartes was much more concerned, with respect to persons, about the problem of how we know what we are. We think we have bodies of a certain sort, but the skeptics argued effectively that we could be mistaken. I might be dreaming that I have an ordinary human body but, when I wake up, it may turn out that I have three orange eyes and green feelers. Perhaps I have no body. Could it be that I am just a disembodied mind? If such oddities seem too strange to contemplate, perhaps I might wake up and find that I have a body like a dolphin's and that I was just dreaming that I was a human being. Descartes wanted to show that we are justified in dismissing such speculations. He thought he could prove that we are what we seem to be.

His proof is structured like this. Once I accept the indubitable claim that I exist, I can examine some of my thoughts as a thinking thing. I conceive of God. Descartes argues that I could not conceive of a being such as God without there being a God. Descartes thinks he has established that God must exist. God, however, would not deceive us all of the time. Consequently Descartes thinks he can know not only that he is a thinking thing but that this thinking thing, or Cartesian Ego, is housed in the body it seems to have. I will not wake up one day and realize that I have three orange eyes and green feelers all along.

Unfortunately, Descartes' certainty that we persons are minds in bodies is not really underwritten by his argument. Part of Descartes' method is to try to doubt everything and to accept only what we clearly and distinctly conceive to be true. He admits, moreover, that we could be systematically deceived. Even our basic reasoning processes which we rely on to do simple arithmetic might be faulty.[25] But if all this is so, the complicated reasoning Descartes gives for his belief in God must surely be doubted. We are left thinking that we are just thinking things until we move over to Hobbes's camp a little and accept some of the evidence of our senses without rational proof.

In any case, Descartes has given us good rational grounds for believing that we are thinking things in his wide sense of "thinking," and Hobbes is right to accept the evidence of his senses and to say that we have bodies which are prone to act when caused to do so. Much modern and contemporary philosophy has set itself the task of figuring out the nature of the thinking and bodily parts of the person and the means of their interaction, if indeed they are separate. Descartes left us also the closely related problem of understanding how our freedom of will operates. The picture of the person that emerges from Descartes is of a Cartesian Ego which supports a conscious mind operating a body, a free individual being responsible for all her own actions.

What about Daphne?

Daphne seems barely able to understand what is going on around her. Descartes might think that her Ego is trapped within a body which no longer responds to its commands. The Ego is what is essential to Daphne; hence, she has survived. The same person may, indeed, survive changes no matter how harsh, since the Ego is indivisible and hence indestructible.

The thinking thing that is the essential Daphne no longer thinks as a philosopher but as an infant does. When Daphne could express her thought, she gradually descended from high intellectual expression to infantile speech. It would be horrific torture if she had locked-in syndrome rather than dementia, but neurologists rule that out. Where is the indestructible Ego when she needs it? Descartes' view is rather like the religious view from which Descartes took his lead. Christians would say that the soul remains the same while the mind and body have deteriorated; hence the same person exists. The difficulty of course is that there is no way to tell whether the same Ego or soul persists in a person, since all outward show is irrelevant to that determination.

Spinoza: The unity of all persons in God

Not all rationalists took this Cartesian approach to persons. Spinoza believed that God was the whole universe and that a person is just a mode of God's being. He thought he could establish this by the use of reason and a higher means to knowledge called "intuition."[26] Although persons have both minds and bodies, both are just attributes of a single substance, namely, God. There is, then, no interaction problem. There is, however, no free will either. Speaking against Descartes and others, Spinoza reminds us that we are part of the natural order and, as such, subject to its laws: "Most writers on the emotions and on human conduct seem to be treating rather of matters outside nature than of natural phenomena following nature's general laws. They appear to conceive man to be situated in nature as a kingdom within a kingdom."[27] Spinoza, like Aristotle, sees the universe as unified. Every human action and every event whatsoever is determined, and there is no purpose or final cause, in Aristotle's sense, for individual persons, the human species, or the universe. God just is. A person can be thought of as merely a way in which God contemplates God, not as a separate free agent.[28] Spinoza, it seems, moves us away from individualism to the Oriental idea of absorption of the individual into the greater whole.

Since Descartes and not Spinoza holds sway in the popular conceptions of a person, few of us may find what Spinoza has to say immediately plausible. It is a view which opposes the individualism and belief in freedom that is a part of our main Western cultural doctrines. Spinoza's belief in the necessity of all our actions leads, as it did with the Stoics, to resignation and acquiescence.[29] The predominant Western concepts of a person are of beings who control, to some extent, their own actions and the events in the world around them, beings who ought to strive to get it right rather than simply accept whatever happens.

What about Daphne?

Spinoza gets by a very different route to Hobbes's estimation of Daphne's importance. She is to be valued as everyone else is. After all, through Spinoza's approach, Daphne is just one more way in which God contemplates God, like the rest of us. There is no harm in saying that Daphne has survived the immense changes wrought by dementia. An event of self-contemplation has changed in character. Since all is God, the importance of individuals in themselves is diminished as it was for Hobbes through their absorption into the state.

Locke's neutral ground

Locke may be the most important philosopher in history with respect to determining current Western concepts of a person within philosophy. So many philosophers are now either furthering his way of thinking of persons or objecting to that way of thinking.[30] One who currently wants to improve on Locke's account is Derek Parfit[31] at Oxford, whose views we will discuss in chapter 13. The opposition from Thomas Nagel,[32] for example, revives some elements of the Cartesian understanding of the subject of experiences.

While Locke is an empiricist elaborating the tradition ushered in by Hobbes, he attempts to find some neutral ground between Hobbes's materialism and Descartes' dualism. Locke is very much concerned about what changes a person can undergo while remaining the same person. His reason was the religious one we have discussed before, the resurrection of the dead.[33] One wants, of course, to have the person being rewarded or punished on Judgment Day to be the same one who did the deeds being judged. He asserts that neither the same material substance nor the same non-material substance preserves the sameness of the person. For example, neither having the same soul or Cartesian Ego on the one hand nor having the same body on the other hand will preserve the sameness of the person.[34] It is, rather, sameness of consciousness that makes sameness of persons.

Locke's reason for this view about identity of persons is his understanding of a person as a self: "Self is that conscious thinking thing (whatever substance made up of, whether spiritual or material, simple or compounded, it matters not) which is sensible or conscious of pleasure and pain, capable of happiness or misery, and so is concerned for *itself* as far as that consciousness extends."[35] Consciousness is crucial to Locke and apparently consciousness might be had by a Cartesian Ego or by a mere living body. Locke also says:

> to find wherein *personal identity* consists, we must consider what person stands for; which, I think, is a thinking intelligent being that has reason and reflection and can consider itself as itself, the same thinking thing in different times and places; which it does only by that consciousness which is inseparable from thinking and, as it seems to me, essential to it: it being impossible for anyone to perceive without perceiving that he does perceive.[36]

The person, self, or thinking thing is like an eye with a mirror which always sees itself as well as any object seen. This idea of the person as self-conscious consciousness pushes the problem of persons one step back. Now we must ask what consciousness is and why one can only have consciousness along with self-consciousness.

Now we have seen that persons had been explicitly a subject of philosophical conversation since the Stoics used the Greek term *prosopon* to mean "person" in the sense of "role." The term "consciousness," however, comes on the scene about the same time as Locke, if Wilkes is correct.[37] Locke's view apparently marks an important departure where concepts of a person are concerned. To understand Locke's concept of consciousness we must, unfortunately, also look into the mysterious concept of substance. We need to distinguish continuity of consciousness from continuity of a thinking substance, since Locke says persons are not thinking substances even though they are thinking things.[38]

For Locke, a substance whether it is material, mental, or something else, is the thing which has qualities but is not itself a quality. The things we can know through our five senses are qualities. For example that a thing is round, red, and made of wax can be known through the senses; therefore, roundness, redness, and being waxen are qualities. What has these qualities is a substance, the thing that lies beneath the qualities. That is almost all we know about substances—that they have qualities.[39] Perry, however, reads a little more than this into Locke: "The concept of substance is of the ultimate things in a causal sense: those things whose properties and relationships explain (or would explain, if known) the properties and relationships of the larger composite entities we deal with as human beings."[40] Substances may be material or immaterial. Persons are composed of bodies—which seem to be based on material substances—and minds—which may be based on immaterial substances. Locke is not committed to their immateriality, however; importantly, the substance which thinks, possibly an immaterial substance, is not identified with the person as it was for Descartes. Perry describes Locke's concept as: "The sense in which immaterial substances are said to think is analogous to the sense in which our hands can be said to grasp things."[41] Now, if being grasped is important, not which hand is doing the grasping, then one hand will do as well as another. Being conscious is what is important for persons, by Locke's lights, and it is unimportant which things, body, mind, or combination of these, support the consciousness. The person is the thinking thing in the sense of the continuing consciousness, no matter which substance is used to continue that consciousness.

Consciousness is, if anything, even more mysterious than substance as explained by Locke. Consciousness includes memory and knowledge of past events and current happenings as well as anticipation of the future. It is the source, according to Locke, not only of our identity but of our concern for ourselves.[42]

Consider, first, a common understanding of consciousness today: awareness of what is going on in oneself, particularly in one's mind. If I am unconscious, then my return to consciousness is a return to knowing what is happening to me now, or at least how I perceive what is happening, and knowing what I am thinking. It is as well a return to the knowledge of what I have done and am likely to do—in short, a knowledge of who I am. As Noonan[43] reads Locke, in addition to this weak kind of consciousness as a kind of knowing one's own current states, there is a stronger type of consciousness frequently presupposed by Locke, namely that of knowing together with someone. Noonan tells us: "To be conscious of one's acts is to share, *qua* witness, knowledge of their occurrence with oneself, *qua* agent. And having been witness in this way to one's own acts one can retain the knowledge of them thus gained. It is such shared knowledge had by a present self of a past self's actions which Locke thinks of as constituting personal identity."[44] Both the weak and the strong sense of "consciousness" as used by Locke are senses in which we are not always conscious even during our waking hours. A severely demented human being may never be conscious in these senses, and most of us are not so during our unreflective waking moments. Perhaps the correct notion of such consciousness as we have most of the day is a dispositional one. If I were to reflect, during my waking hours, I would know who I am and thus be conscious in Locke's strong sense.

"Consciousness" is, moreover, closely related to "conscience." The Oxford English Dictionary tells us that "consciousness," in the sense of internal knowledge or conviction, is especially of one's own innocence, guilt, or deficiencies. Locke is, of course, using the term with this connotation of self-accusation since he is motivated by concerns about the resurrection of the dead and Judgment Day. He is thinking of the person who is conscious of former actions as punishable for those actions. Our current use of "consciousness" often drops this connotation of blame, but we carry along as a primary concept of a person the one Locke fashioned using consciousness. That is why it is often said that a person must have the capacity for self-awareness. This rules out infants, the senile, and many other human beings from the category of persons.

Because Locke is fixated on the Judgment Day when he speaks of persons and their continuation through time and change, he introduces some features into his theory that have been widely criticized. The main implausibility is that the theory claims that we have only done what we are conscious of having done.[45] If I go through a period of amnesia during which I remember nothing of my past life, I am, in

Locke's view, not the same person. Some might agree with this, but Locke actually thinks that we cannot rightly be punished for anything that we do not remember doing. If I should commit some heinous crime when drunk and not recall it at all, then I have not done it and cannot rightly be punished, according to Locke. He admits, of course, that people will be punished for things they do not remember in our merely human justice system; he reassures us that: "in the Great Day, wherein the secrets of all hearts shall be laid open,...no one shall be made to answer for what he knows nothing of."[46]

God in His goodness, Locke tells us would not allow us to have memories of things we did not actually do and, hence, to receive undeserved punishment or reward.[47] Outside of the religious picture, however, we must concern ourselves with this continuity-of-consciousness criterion for persons because it is not at all evident that we very accurately remember the things we have done or have done the things we seem to remember. Is there something else in consciousness, as conceived by Locke, besides memory that may provide a more adequate picture of persons? According to Noonan, one of Locke's early critics, Reid, claims that by "consciousness" Locke must just mean "memory."[48] Later critics have by and large accepted Reid's account of Locke but, while memory is a crucial part of consciousness, consciousness is broader. I may be conscious of a feeling of guilt when I awake from a drunken rampage even if I cannot remember what I have done. Locke's insistence on our knowledge of past actions, however, bars him from access to this broader concept of consciousness and leaves him open to Reid's interpretation that consciousness in this context is memory. Locke's account is therefore open to objections which follow from that interpretation.

Even before we get into the traditional objections about the nature of the narrower concept of memory, the problem of telling what a person is and telling when one has the same person by appeal to consciousness is this: we are not entirely clear what consciousness is nor when we have the same consciousness. This is especially difficult since consciousness may be interrupted by sleep, for instance. Why can it not, then, be interrupted by bodily death? Would it not be strange to say that Socrates, Pilate, and Caesar Borgia were all the same person? As long as they each were conscious of the actions of the one before, then this is what we would say by Locke's approach. Locke could reply, it seems, that, while this is logically possible, God in His goodness would not let this happen.

Yet Locke cannot make this reply, given the rules he plays by. He criticizes, for instance, those who would reject his idea that the identity of a human being, as opposed to a person, is dependent on "one fitly organized body, continued under one organization of life."[49] Those who reject this criterion, Locke tells us, will not be able to say that there is one person through all life's developments unless they also admit that Seth, Israel, Socrates, Pilate, St. Austin, and Caesar Borgia could be one man.[50] He objects that this is a strange way of speaking. I submit that the same argument which disallows such odd possibilities for humans also inveighs against Locke's use of "person."

Even if one is willing to accept the strangeness of Locke's concept of a person and to say that it is nonetheless one useful concept of a person, there may be problems which undermine it entirely. What kind of a thing is consciousness? Not a substance, apparently. It seems then that consciousness is a property of humans; hence, being a person is a property of a substance or substances. Locke handles identity conditions in terms of special properties called "modes." More precisely, a mode is an aspect, that is, a fully instantiated property, a particular not a universal. But it is not at all clear how we identify modes; hence, it is not clear what the identity criteria are for persons. Locke's solution is, officially, through spatio-temporal continuity and, unofficially and illegitimately, through reference to the particulars that have the modes.[51] Neither the official nor the unofficial account could explain how it is that Socrates and Caesar Borgia could be the same person, given one consciousness. Perhaps Locke's problem of identifying modes—and, hence, persons—over time could be solved in terms of higher-order essential properties. We might assert that two modes are identical if they share all their essential higher-order properties in common, where "essential" would be defined so as to exclude space-time location and "higher order" would exclude the modes themselves. Pursuing such an account does not, however, look promising. If, on this account, two simultaneously existing human beings have exactly the same memories, are they not the same person? The fact that the theory cannot rule this out except by appeal to God's goodness is, according to the rules Locke plays by when objecting to his opponents, ground enough to reject the theory of persons Locke presents.[52] In some cases, I think, we can refuse to play by those rules which require us to stick to common usage of the term "person." We can find a use for Locke's concept of a person, sufficiently modified, to survive in the more secular contemporary debate.

What about Daphne?

We have to be careful to note what human beings Locke excludes from being persons. Of Daphne, Locke would say she is the same human being but not the same person as we knew prior to the dementia. Indeed, it seems that, on his account, she would not be a person at all now, assuming that she has no self-knowledge nor sufficient memory to see herself as existing through time. Certainly I would go so far with Locke as to say that Daphne does not bear responsibility for the things she has done while in a demented state. To deny, however, the status of a person to all who lose their memory and the ability to know themselves leaves us in a bit of a quandary about how to treat such human beings. We shall have to look to later developments of the concept of a person for enlightenment.

What I like about Locke

Locke's excusing the drunks is morally obtuse whatever we want to say about my being the same person drunk as sober. Either we should say I am the same person—and Locke's criterion of continuous consciousness is not the correct analysis of a person. Or we can agree with Locke but point out that I chose temporarily to lose myself in drink and that this choice makes me culpable for any evils which result from my "absence." Most of us think that drunk and sober I am the same person, but you can well imagine someone saying that I am a different person when drunk, meaning that my personality changes radically.

Putting together Locke's concepts of substance and consciousness, it appears that Locke thinks of a person as a complex thing formed out of more basic substances. As my body develops, the changes happen to an underlying substance which persists. My consciousness too, may be made up of a series of changes to a thinking substance whether material or immaterial. Thus the person or self is a continuing consciousness making use of substances to live and think. The man that I am came into being at conception and, by all report, has continued uninterrupted to this day. The person who I am, however, goes out of existence when I sleep. It flickered into being about the age of two, when the earliest events of my life of which I am conscious took place.

Locke is not too concerned about this patchy picture of a person that his theory gives. He is quite happy to have gaps in persons because of sleep or drunkenness. The religious person accepting Locke's theory could still find a way to provide for punishment of a person's drunken rage. On Judgment Day, perhaps, our memories will be improved. Hell or heaven, I suppose, might well be perfect memory. Which of these two memories gives us would depend on how we had lived, but Locke does not engage in such speculation. We should not try to force Locke into a more sensible moral view about punishment than he wished to hold. We should be careful, moreover, in the contemporary secular uses we make of the Lockean concept of a person. We must make do with our memories as they are in real life and we cannot appeal to divine goodness to get us out of difficulties with our concepts. Even those who agree on the existence of a personal deity disagree on what His, Her, or Its goodness comes to. The extensive use of Locke's concepts today does not always make sense, given the wider audience and the loss of the background assumptions concerning resurrection and final judgment.

Even though Locke's concept should not satisfy Locke, it has, historically, been extremely influential in the separation of the concepts of human being and person. Locke's is also one of the first theories of persons to rest the whole weight of morality on the concept of a person, to the applause of some and the chagrin of others. Probably we should settle on a view between the extremes, saying that there are rights of persons which include the rights of human beings, while the rights of human beings do not include the rights of persons.

Locke's influence extends, however, much further than the moral sphere. Even Locke's style of argument, using thought experiments and emphasizing common usage, set the tone for British and North American philosophical debate on this topic up to the present day. Locke must, therefore, be treated as a watershed. It will be difficult to retain whatever insights we may glean from prior philosophers simply because their contributions are not in the style of Locke and do not share his emphasis. We must be watchful lest these insights are locked out.

The importance of memory may not be as great as Locke supposed, but we must take it seriously. It is also a good idea to focus on such abilities as consciousness independently of their causes or the substance underlying them. We need not settle the debate between the materialists and the dualists to talk sensibly about people.

Responsibility, which was much on Locke's mind, seems to be a key concept in our understanding of persons and the distinction of persons as a group within that of human beings.

I also approve of Locke's proposed general approach, which rules out of court the appeal to God to get us out of trouble when puzzles arise regarding identity or the nature of persons. Spinoza's approach is, from my perspective, too otherworldly. Cartesian Egos are a bit too much like souls for me. Much of what Descartes has to say about people as thinking things may be reworked without the baggage of religious metaphysics. In particular, we should focus on the subject of the experiences, not just the experiences themselves. This strains against Locke's neutral position between materialism and dualism, but can be brought inside its fold. From Hobbes we should retain the general idea of the importance of the body. Putting all this together will be an interesting cobbler's job.

Content questions

1. How, in general, did the democratization of things intellectual, through Erasmus and the humanists, affect the concept of a person?
2. What were Erasmus' objections to Catholics and to Protestants regarding their views of persons?
3. Why did Montaigne think we would be unable to grasp the nature of persons in general?
4. What is Galileo's distinction between primary and secondary qualities?
5. Briefly describe Hobbes's general view of persons.

6. How do rationalists disagree with empiricists?
7. What does Descartes mean by his famous saying, "I think; hence I am"?
8. What is it that philosophers refer to as the "Cartesian Ego"?
9. Why can Descartes not use God's beneficence to get him out of skepticism?
10. How does Spinoza's view of persons move away from individualism?
11. What preserves sameness of persons through time according to Locke?
12. What is substance according to Locke?
13. Why is sameness of a thinking substance not sameness of a person?
14. Explain why Locke's view that we have only done what we are conscious of having done is controversial.
15. What does Locke think a person is?
16. Could various human beings through history be one person, in Locke's view? If so, why?
17. Why can Locke not appeal to God's goodness to avoid problems with identities of persons?

Arguments for analysis

Skeptics are those who disbelieve. What kind of skeptics they are depends on what they disbelieve. A religious skeptic might doubt the existence of souls, heaven, or God. Cartesian skeptics accept Descartes' arguments for doubting that we can know things other than that we exist and that we have certain things going on in our minds—that is, ideas in the broadest sense including feelings. Here I will present some of Descartes' arguments. It is debatable whether Descartes himself was a Cartesian skeptic. In any case, his method is to take into his system of belief only those beliefs of which he can be certain. From these certain beliefs he will proceed by logically certain steps until he builds up a system of belief free from error. The first step is to throw out any belief that can be doubted, so Descartes considers various classes of belief to see which are based on something uncertain. He ends up throwing out most beliefs in the first of his famous meditations. Here then are some arguments inspired by Descartes' first and second meditations.

Argument 1: Doubting what we believe

First, to get beliefs that are certain, we cannot trust our senses: seeing, hearing, touch, taste, and smell. These sometimes deceive us. Even if things seem very real to us, we might be dreaming. We can, therefore, doubt that any of our perceptions correspond to something real outside of our minds.

Second, in our search for certainty we cannot trust such analytical beliefs as those of mathematics. We make mathematical errors. It may seem that some simple beliefs like $2 + 2 = 4$ are certain even in dreams. We could, however, be systematically deceived. What if an evil demon had control of our minds and forced us to believe falsehoods among our analytical beliefs? This is at least possible, so we cannot accept such beliefs as certain.

While we do not typically think in terms of demons today, we might update this last point. It may be that all human beings have too little mental capacity to get to the truth through analytical, logical operations. We might all share the same defect in our brains as a genetic inheritance from our common ancestors.

Argument 2: There are beliefs left of which we can be certain

Even if our senses and our inadequate analytical abilities systematically deceive us, there is nonetheless something each of us cannot doubt. Each of us knows that "I exist," is true each time that we think or say it. That is the source of Descartes' famous saying; "I think, hence I am." Descartes thinks we know this directly, intuitively, beyond the power of argument to demonstrate. For those who would like a reason, however, we can say that if I doubt that I exist, there must be something doing the doubting—myself. Beyond this we can be certain of the things that are directly present to our minds (ideas). I know what I am thinking, feeling, apparently perceiving, doubting, and imagining right now. I do not know that any of these ideas correspond to reality in any way, but I do know they are in my mind right now. That tells me what I am, a thinking thing. If Descartes left it there, he would be a Cartesian skeptic. That is someone who is willing to believe only that he is an existing, thinking thing with some ideas, but who doubts the existence of everything else, people, things,

God, and what have you. Descartes, however, gives an argument to show that God exists. It is not a very strong argument. He says that we are beings who have not the power to imagine a perfect God, but we have an idea of God. He argues that only God could have given us such an idea. Once he has a belief in a perfectly powerful and benevolent God—or at least says he has such a belief—Descartes goes on to say that such a God would give us a chance. He would make our experience correspond at least somewhat to reality. He would make our analytical reasoning capable of finding the truth if we reason carefully and accept only what we know clearly and distinctly to be true.

Argument 3: Descartes does not defeat Cartesian skepticism

Descartes' argument using a benevolent God to get us out of Cartesian skepticism does not work. The Cartesian skeptic can reply that we should not suppose our reasoning ability is great enough to use Descartes' argument for the existence of God. We could be deceived at each step in the argument by an evil demon or by our own inherited incompetence. Since we cannot be certain that we are not so deceived, we must remain skeptical about beliefs except for the belief in our own existence and ideas. If you accept Descartes' arguments in his first meditation, you are left with no way to show that solipsism is false. That is the view that there is only one mind in the universe and you are it. The rest of us and all things that appear to you are figments of your imagination. This odd metaphysical thesis would solve some of our problems about persons, since there is only one. It seems, however, that Descartes has painted us into a corner.

CHAPTER 6

More Moderns

Berkeley: The outer limits of empiricism

If one takes seriously the idea that all of our knowledge is the result of sensations of sight, hearing, taste, touch, and smell, then one can, paradoxically but consistently, deny the existence of the human body or any material thing. A smell or a vision or a feel of something is a mental event. As long as one has the right mental events in the right order, then it will be as if there is an entire material world causing such mental events in material bodies. But matter is an unnecessary hypothesis. There might just be a natural world of minds and ideas, including sensations. Natural laws, like that of gravity, would really be shorthand predictions about which perceptions would follow which perceptions. For example, if I perceive as if I drop a small object near the surface of the earth, even though there are no such things as material objects, then I will perceive as if that apparent object falls. The whole of the material world would be a kind of virtual reality. This world of ideas could, then, have a regularity just like the one which our laws of physics describe. This, in fact, was the view adopted by the eighteenth-century philosopher Bishop Berkeley.[1]

Notes to chapter 6 are on pp. 480-81.

Persons as minds

Berkeley's idealism has a corollary relevant to our topic. His view was that the idea of a person as an embodied mind or soul is incorrect. Rather, he thought persons are just minds or souls. Minds perceive as if they had bodies.

This idealist view of Berkeley's sounds strange to a materialist Western audience but, in a country such as India where it is widely believed that the material world is an illusion, Berkeley's philosophy would be almost a commonplace. In some ways, it should not make any difference whether we think we are all matter or all mind, as long as we are made of only one kind of thing. In practice, however, idealists like Berkeley tend to be more interested in the spiritual side of persons, and materialists tend to discount spirit. Reducing spirit to a material phenomenon seems in practice to deprive it of some of its grandeur and moral force, although it need not be so in theory.

Materialists tend to be less able than Berkeley was to deny the importance of bodily suffering. While these are tendencies rather than generalizations that hold for all idealists and materialists, the metaphysical views about what people are do tend to have a profound effect on moral views about the treatment of persons. It is interesting, in any case, that the empiricism and materialism that are so influential in our current concepts of a person can be replaced without loss by empiricism plus idealism. In a society in which metaphysical materialism is accompanied by the crass, commercial variety of materialism, perhaps a switch to Berkeley's strange view that we are minds without bodies is not so crazy.

Leibniz against the drunks

On the continent, a theory in some ways similar to Locke's was developed by Leibniz and then revised in the light of Locke's contribution. Leibniz's work has been less influential than Locke's because the metaphysical system in which it is housed is much less tied to common sense than Locke's own metaphysics. Like Descartes, Leibniz was a rationalist, and, since Locke, rationalism has taken a beating at the hands of empiricism in British and North American philosophy. Leibniz was, in any case, a philosopher and mathematician of genius whose ideas on identity in general have had a considerable impact on later thought. Noonan points out, moreover, that Leibniz's work on our topic anticipated some arguments of great importance in contemporary philosophy.[2]

Leibniz's common sense

Leibniz originally put out a theory of persons in his *Discourse On Metaphysics* prior to reading Locke. The two main similarities of Leibniz's theory to Locke's theory are in its being influenced by religious belief in a way uncommon today and in the treatment of memory and knowledge of the past self as necessary for continuation of the person.[3] With God in the background, Leibniz's theory has to be adapted with care to the contemporary secular debate, but—in spite of Locke's reputation for a philosophy tied to common sense and Leibniz's reputation for weaving a metaphysical tapestry that only a philosopher could believe—Leibniz's views on persons run afoul of fewer of the dictates of common sense than do Locke's.

Because Locke thinks that only the same consciousness is needed to keep the same person, one could change bodies and still be the same person. This is not so for Leibniz. Not only is the same consciousness, or at least memory, needed but the same substance is also necessary to retain the person, and a substance cannot possibly be emptied of one person to later house another—as Locke would think possible, albeit unlikely. Thus Leibniz could freely maintain against Locke—what most of us would accept, that a person does not become another person when drunk just because, later, that person does not remember the period of drunkenness. Even more remarkable is Locke's claim that the sober person should not be punished for what the drunk—who is another person according to Locke—has done. Leibniz's way out of this, if he has one in his earlier work on persons, would be to appeal to divine intervention. God does not let a single person go out of existence.[4] There are no persons popping into and out of bodies. This preserves both our immortality and our moral responsibility. It does not work, of course, without the background religious doctrine. That is what contemporary theories will have to replace outside of theology. With his later work, Leibniz gives us some clues about how to do this.

In spite of the antiquated language and the strength of the religious background, parts of Leibniz's writings have a remarkably contemporary ring. This is particularly true in the *New Essays Concerning Understanding* which he wrote in response to Locke.[5] Here Leibniz responds with revisions to the theory aimed at preventing such odd consequences as the innocence of the sober person for the actions of the blind-drunk. What he says is in fact an appeal to an incipient theory of the unconscious.

Subconscious selves

Since Freud we take it as a commonplace that there is much to the person beneath the tip of the iceberg: consciousness. Ralph Walker claims that: "Leibniz was the first to introduce the idea of the *unconscious.*"[6] Instead of requiring actual memories of our past life, Leibniz switches to requiring only a psychological continuity of the person based partly on perceptions of the past of which we may be insensible.[7] Walker reports that Leibniz: "points out that one can often recall having perceived something—some detail of a familiar scene, perhaps—although one did not notice it at the time: clearly one must have perceived it without being aware of doing so."[8] Further in aid of this drive to take the non-conscious part of the person seriously, note that even an amnesiac does not lose all memory. Elements of the personality, abilities, and other features may remain. These are outside of what Locke would call "consciousness." These phenomena are some evidence that Leibniz is right to deny that one can be stripped of all perception of one's past existence. Everything that happens to us leaves some impression on us, although we might not be aware of it; as Noonan puts it; "It is this continuity and interconnection of perceptions which makes someone really the same individual."[9] Our unconscious "memory" of our lives suffices to make us the same persons we were during periods of our lives that we have forgotten.

Copies of persons

Leibniz also anticipates an important contemporary criticism of Locke's account given by Williams and known as the reduplication argument. Consciousness is the only thing that distinguishes one person from another, in Locke's view. Leibniz points out that, however unlikely it may be, there is no logical impossibility, according to

Locke, in there being a human being whose consciousness is indistinguishable from that of another concurrently existing human being. There is then nothing to prevent us from saying that two human beings are one person in such a case. Since it is absurd to think that two human beings are one person, a theory that says so must itself be absurd.

In the face of this objection, the Lockean is faced with biting the rather hard bullet of admitting that two human beings could be one person or adding something to the theory to prevent this consequence. Remarkably, until Williams came up with another version of Leibniz's objection in 1956, this untoward consequence of Locke's theory went unnoticed.[10] This rather belated attention to Leibniz's objection demonstrates the need to pay attention to the history of philosophy.

A Lockean might reply that this thought experiment about two people with the same consciousness—or each with a consciousness indiscernible from the others—is not to the point after all. It will not happen in the real world. This is a hard tack for the Lockean to take. Locke himself is fond of thought experiments as ways of testing the limits of our concepts. Lockeans could do this, however, if they are willing to come up with a whole new slate of arguments for Locke's position, arguments which do not make essential use of such thought experiments. It is much simpler to accept Leibniz's recommendations in some modified form. Few would accept his particular construal of continuing substance, but some acceptance of the body, or at least the brain, as crucial to the person is motivated by Leibniz's objections. The cure, however, is not simple, as we will see when we look at contemporary Lockeans, such as Derek Parfit, later on (see chapter 13).

Leibniz on identity

Before we bid adieu to Leibniz, for the time being, we should look at his contribution to the concept of identity, since the concept of a person is often understood, especially since Locke, in terms of personal identity. The reason for the close association between the topics of the nature of persons and personal identity is this: one knows the nature of a kind of thing if and only if one knows how to distinguish and identify particular things of that kind. I will know what persons are, for instance, if and only if I know, in principle, how to tell persons apart and how to tell when I encounter the same person twice. Many philosophers believe that there is something essential to persons, something without which a being would not be a person. For Locke, for instance, consciousness was this essence; so person A and person B would turn out to be one and the same by virtue of having the same consciousness. Leibniz thought this was necessary but not sufficient for identity of persons. He has, moreover, a general answer to the question of whether A and B, be they persons or whatever, are identical.

A is identical to B, Leibniz asserts, if and only if A and B have all their properties in common. This principle, called Leibniz's law (recall chapter 1), is not at all a simple principle, depending as it does on what we mean by "property." On most meanings of "property," however, half of the principle is uncontroversial: if A is identical to B, then A has a property if and only if B has that property. If Andrew is identical to Bob, for example, then Andrew is intelligent if and only if Bob is intelligent. But look at the other half: if A and B have all their properties in common, then A is identical to B. This principle is also called the identity of indiscernibles. Is it necessarily true? Is it possible for A to be totally indiscernible from B without their being identical? Philosophers have been arguing about that ever since Leibniz said it. It turns out that there are many different things that one could mean by this principle, some of which are necessarily true without much doubt. The interesting versions, however, are still being debated.[11]

With respect to Leibniz's objection to Locke, the problem boils down to roughly this. Suppose that A is a consciousness and B is a consciousness. Suppose further that there is no property which A has that B lacks, or vice versa. According to the identity of indiscernibles, A and B are the same consciousness. If, however, A has the property of being associated with the body of Alain and B has the property of being associated with the body of Bernard, then we can distinguish A from B, given that we can distinguish their bodies. But this is not the kind of distinction between one consciousness and another that Locke wants to use. Bodies are supposed to be non-essential to persons. We ought not refer to anything but some feature within the consciousness itself, whatever that means, to distinguish that consciousness. Consciousness itself, moreover, is all there is to persons. If, however, it is possible that Alain and Bernard could have indiscernible consciousnesses, then we have to admit that it is possible that they are one and the same person with two different bodies. This seems to Leibniz to be absurd.

Whether this objection really succeeds depends, however, on some very complex issues. Not only does one have to clarify the real meaning of "property" in this context, but one has to complicate the appropriate principles, such as the identity of indiscernibles, to take into account changes in an object across time which are not to be understood in the same way as differences between two objects at a given time. Such complexities will have to await discussion of the contemporary debate about persons.

The subconscious and responsibility

This subtle kind of continuity through the subconscious may be available to people even in severe dementia. Without the surface of conscious self-awareness, one may be the same person underneath in the poorly understood areas of the subconscious or non-conscious. These areas of the person's mind, as well as the conscious, may be destroyed by brain damage, of course, but it is at least not necessarily true that the loss of conscious self-awareness is the loss of what underlies it as well. It seems to me that common sense would agree with Leibniz in saying that people are, though greatly reduced in ability, still the same persons owing to other sorts of continuity, such as the continuity of the body and the non-conscious mind.

Now, while Leibniz seems to me more in line with contemporary common sense than is Locke, perhaps he carries his concept of person a bit too far in the other direction. Locke gives the sober man no responsibility for the drunk's actions and Leibniz gives him full responsibility. While, in my neck of the woods, we are becoming less tolerant of drunkenness, full responsibility still seems too much to most of my contemporaries. Often, today, we might consider drunkenness as a legal and a moral mitigation—an argument for lessening responsibility and punishment—but not an excuse. If one kills while drunk, one is guilty of getting drunk and creating the circumstances for the tragedy. This is not, perhaps, as great a guilt as one bears for killing while sober in full knowledge of what one is doing, although Mothers Against Drunk Drivers and Leibniz may not see it this way. The controversial idea is that drunkenness is a mitigating but not excusing factor where punishment is concerned. The culprit did not have the appropriate mental attitude to be said to have done the act completely intentionally. There is a problem that one may intend things while drunk that one would never intend while sober, but we only take sober intentions as the prerequisite for full culpability. It is as if we think that a person has temporarily, though willfully, suspended good character by deliberately becoming drunk. One can be punished for the deliberate suspension, but one cannot be punished fully for the acts while the suspension is in effect.

Consider now another kind of case, the case of a mental patient who has a real fugue state (that is, dissociation of the personality), supposing there are any such states. Such a person temporarily acquires a different personality and memories. The temporary personality and the normal personality do not influence one another. During the period away from the normal personality and memories, the patient has committed murder. Should we punish the person who, cured of the mental illness, remembers nothing of the murder? In a recent case a woman was exonerated in court of murdering her mother because she was temporarily in such a state as a result of taking prescription sleeping pills. She took them as prescribed. Leibniz would have counted her guilty. The testimony of others that she did such a thing is enough to maintain what Leibniz called her "moral identity," which entails personal identity.[12]

Whether in fact Leibniz is going too far in such cases depends, in part, on how much we think we are responsible for programming ourselves with our tendencies to act in certain ways when our minds are absent. If such chosen tendencies really are operative when our minds are absent, or our memories are not recording what we do, then perhaps our actions at such times flow freely from choices of which we were conscious. There are documented cases of automatic behaviour such as a doctor taking detailed notes in a thorough examination of a patient but remembering nothing afterwards.[13] If a criminal were to commit a crime in such an automatic state and remember nothing after the commission, then, even if we believed that the memory lapse were genuine, we might wish to place some blame if we thought the crime flowed from a character deliberately acquired. We might, in similar fashion, wish to praise the doctor for being so practised in good routines as to care adequately for the patient even though normal memory processes were suspended. On the other hand, were the doctor to make an error under these conditions, we might be less ready to blame the doctor. Our intuitions are overtaxed in such cases because our concept of a person is fuzzy. Leibniz, at least, knows what he would say about these situations. Part of his confidence in his concepts, however, is based on his views about what a benevolent God would permit to happen. Those who do not believe in such a God or in the same workings of His benevolence will want to tidy up the concept of a person to deal with fugue states and automatic behaviour.

Wilkes suggests that we simply ought to deny the extreme importance of consciousness, our inheritance from Locke. Fugue states and other dramatic aberrations in our lives are really no more a threat to our continuity than sleep, in her view:

> Longer-lasting fugues interrupt the unity and continuity of consciousness more dramatically and drastically; but, if they do not seem to disrupt our intuition that we have, unproblematically, one and the same person here, that must be because the unity or continuity of consciousness, or perhaps even consciousness itself, are not quite as important as one might at first think.[14]

The problem, of course, is to say what really is important for continuity—that is survival—of persons. Leibniz has given us a start.

Butler and Reid reacting

If we leave Leibniz and cross both the channel separating Europe from Britain and the gulf between the rationalists and the empiricists, we find that there were other and more famous objections to Locke's criterion of personal identity coming from within the ranks of British philosophers.

Fear of change

Butler and Reid make the peculiarly Cartesian claim that persons are indivisible, unchanging things. They are thinking of identity in terms of Leibniz's law or something like it. Any change of properties over time would constitute difference. Any temporal period in which a change of properties takes place will do. One second is enough. When we talk about the same tree, for example, at an earlier time and a later time, we really mean, according to Butler, two very similar trees.[15] A person, however, is unchanging and indivisible; so that person is the same at earlier and later times. Butler and Reid are concerned to found moral claims on the concept of person; so they return to something like the immortal, unchanging soul of the religious tradition and reject the developing, changing consciousness that Locke has used as the essence of the person.

The views of Butler and Reid about identity are confused. In trying to say that any change makes for a difference of the earlier from the later thing, they conflate identity across time with identity at a time. Even if we accept the idea that a thing must be unchanging to be self-identical over time, persons as conceived by Butler and Reid would not fill the bill. After all, persons have bodies, and those bodies change. We could then say that the earlier person has the property of having a young body which the later person lacks; so the two persons must be distinct. If Butler and Reid object that only properties of the persons themselves—and not properties which relate them to other things are relevant—then they are appealing to what have been called "purely qualitative properties" as distinct from "relational properties." In fact, however, properties which seem to be purely qualitative all turn out to be relational. Being red, for example, may mean appearing red to an observer within a certain frame of reference, or it may mean reflecting light at so many Angstrom units of wavelength. As I have argued elsewhere, there is no precise definition of "purely qualitative property" that gets around the problem.[16]

Reid's brave officer

Reid has, however, an objection which at least requires fans of Locke's memory criterion of identity to revise the criterion. Perry puts the criterion this way: "Person-stages belong to the same person, if and only if the later could contain an experience which is a memory of a reflective awareness of an experience contained in the earlier."[17] Roughly, if I remember something someone experienced from the inside as that person would have experienced it, then I am that person. Memory is taken to be veridical in this context. Merely seeming to remember guarantees nothing. To have a genuine memory, I must be the person who witnessed the event remembered.

Reid imagines a case in which this criterion leads to paradox.[18] He imagines a boy who is flogged and who later becomes an officer who performs a brave deed. The officer eventually becomes a general. The officer remembers the flogging; so he and the boy are one. The general remembers the brave deed; so he and the officer are one. The general, however, fails to remember the flogging; so he and the boy are two. This is, of course, absurd. If both the boy and the general are identical to the officer, then they must be identical to one another. Much of the contemporary work on personal identity is an attempt to improve upon Locke's criterion to make it immune to such objections.

Butler's charge of circularity

Butler has, moreover, another objection of note, namely that Locke's account is circular. A problem arises when we consider how we identify memories, or consciousness. Butler considers it self-evident that consciousness of personal identity presupposes, and therefore cannot constitute, personal identity.[19] One way to interpret what he is saying is this: to say that consciousness A is identical to consciousness B is to say that they are the consciousness of the same person. We can hardly, therefore, define without circularity "same person" in terms of "same consciousness," since "same consciousness" has already been defined in terms of "same person." Noonan says that Locke can respond to this charge of circularity since he distinguishes between persons and thinking substances. Roughly, Noonan would say that consciousness A is identical to consciousness B means that they are the consciousness of the same thinking substance. "Same consciousness" is, therefore, not defined in terms of "same person" after all.[20]

Both Butler and Reid, however, attack the distinction between thinking substance and person. In Locke's view the person is an evolving, changing sort of thing. The consciousness develops over time as it gains new perceptions and has new thoughts; so the person as a thinking thing changes. Underlying this change is the mysterious, unchanging thinking substance in which properties, such as the property of being conscious, inhere. This substance is what some philosophers have called a bare particular. All we know about the bare particular is that it is whatever has the properties. Butler says that, if a person is, as Locke says, a thinking intelligent being, then that person is a substance, and Reid says about the same.[21] This puts Locke in hot water. He wanted to get away from worrying about mysterious things like substances and to be neutral with respect to whether material or non-material substance underlies consciousness. Only consciousness itself was to be essential to persons.

Lockean responses

There are a number of ways for Lockeans to respond. Noonan suggests Locke might just bite the bullet and say that thinking things are not thinking substances. This apparently raises the odd question whether, as Chisholm puts it, If I want my dinner, does it follow that two of us want my dinner?[22] In other words, do the thinking thing and the thinking substance both want the dinner? According to Noonan, to remain consistent Locke must say that the thinking substance wants me, the thinking thing, to have my dinner and must think that strange thought by thinking, I want my dinner.[23] Once again, Locke seems to be a long way from common sense. He can buy logical consistency only by multiplying the entities that make up a person. Each of us begins to look like a crowd. Perry, however, has suggested that I think through the thinking substance as I grasp things with my hand.[24] I do not have to say that both my hand and I pick up my fork to eat my dinner. Similarly, I do not have to say that two of us want my dinner. My wanting is done with my thinking substance as my grasping is done with my hand.

This still looks distant from common sense, but not so distant. Common sense is, in any case, not always the most sensible view, but if we accept the mysterious underlying substance and the rest of Locke's concept of a person, then we do so only because we are driven to this mystery-laden doctrine. The empiricists, after all, wanted to demystify our concepts, which they saw being routed into fantasy by such rationalists as Descartes and Leibniz. As their views are pushed to the limit, we see the empiricist tradition garnering more mysteries. Hume's famous disappearing self is not the last but is the next mystery to be considered.

Hume and our disappearance

Hume is almost out of place among the moderns. He is too contemporary in his motivation for his theory and in his kind of theory of persons. As you have noticed, no doubt, God is still everywhere in the modern period, as He was in the mediaeval period. Locke and Leibniz, for instance, are motivated by religious concerns. Hume not only drops the concern to explain such doctrines as that of the Judgment Day, he plays by a tough new rule: when one's theory implies the possibility of some absurdity, one may not call upon God to rescue the theory. One cannot, for instance, say that God's goodness would prevent duplication of people or getting the memory of an action and, therefore, the responsibility for that action, associated with the wrong consciousness. What is new, then, about Hume is that he tries to give arguments that will appeal to intellect only, not even indirectly to faith. He was not a big hit with the clergy.

Where am I?

Hume, like Locke, is an empiricist. He observes that we have a concept of a person and spends his efforts trying to explain how we could come to have this fiction through ideas produced ultimately from sensory input. That's right; he does not think there are persons in Locke's sense. For Hume, there is just a powerful fiction that persons exist. He reduces the metaphysical problems about persons and personal identity which we have been investigating to psychological problems about how we could possibly be so deceived as to think that persons exist and endure through time. It is hard to beat Hume for sheer iconoclasm, but we contemporary philosophers have been trying our best. The modern period has a lot of kick left in it following Hume but ultimately his secular, ferocious style of thinking wins out. Philosophers now demand that our concepts defend themselves, and concepts are given no quarter. If a sanctified concept such as that of a person appears to be contradictory, it gets the boot.

At the outset of his discussion of personal identity, Hume sets up the concept he is about to attack: "There are some philosophers, who imagine we are every moment intimately conscious of what we call our SELF; that we feel its existence and its continuance in existence; and are certain, beyond the evidence of a demonstration, both of its perfect identity and simplicity."[25] Hume says that those of us who think we are aware of our selves are imagining things. There is no self or person continuing through time. Once people believed in the existence of unicorns—fabled horses with a single horn growing from the middle of the forehead; one could explain a belief in unicorns by pointing, perhaps, to the remains of beached narwhals, which might have been the source of the idea of the unicorn. Hume takes his task to be finding some cause of our belief in another fiction, that of the self.

No doubt some readers are about to say, Hold on a minute Hume! Although I do not expect to ever see a unicorn, I am intimately acquainted with a self, mine." "For my part," Hume responds, "when I enter most intimately into what I call *myself*, I always stumble on some particular perception or other.…I never can catch *myself* at any time without a perception, and never can observe any thing but the perception." From this Hume concludes that we are "nothing but a bundle or collection of different perceptions, which succeed each other with an inconceivable rapidity, and are in a perpetual flux and movement."[26] Persons or selves are reduced to vortices in the great stream of perceptions.

What Hume has jettisoned is what he would consider metaphysical and religious baggage that merely encumbers our thought. Plato's doctrine of an immortal soul, which is carried on through the Christian philosophers, is given the heave-ho. Not since Aristotle had there been such an influential secular philosopher as Hume and, while Aristotle just got rid of immortality, Hume wants to get completely rid of the soul or substance underlying consciousness. Look inside, Hume says, and what you see is what you get: "The mind is a kind of theatre, where several perceptions successively make their appearance; pass, re-pass, glide away, and mingle in an infinite variety of postures and situations. There is properly no *simplicity* in it at one time, nor *identity* in different."[27] Once he gets rid of the religious need for an immortal soul or substance which remains through change, Hume finds only a constantly changing river of consciousness. He takes Heraclitus' dictum literally—one cannot step into the same river twice.

Identity oversimplified

Like Butler and Reid, Hume takes the simplistic concept of identity—which led to the concept of substance in the first place—and objects to the identity through time of anything like Locke's concept of a person. More than this, however, he realizes that the concept of an immortal, simple substance of the sort Butler and Reid would substitute is not possible. Nothing can endure through time without changing some of its properties. As long as a change of properties guarantees a loss of identity, Hume avers that this entails that nothing can endure through time. Objects we think of as enduring are really just a series of very similar things. We ourselves are such series.[28] We take similarity to be identity, just as the ignorant once may have taken a narwhal's tusk to be the horn of a unicorn.

Hume has other things to say about his predecessors, things which are less than complimentary. Memory as a criterion of identity—which is in effect Locke's criterion—comes in for some criticism. Even those who favour Locke's criterion would have to admit that Hume is persuasive when he says: "memory does not so much *produce* as *discover* personal identity, by shewing us the relation of cause and effect among our different perceptions."[29] Since we do not remember our entire lives, memory just helps us to see how we are each a chain of causes and effects, a stream of causally related perceptions. With memory to show us parts of the stream, we extrapolate to fill in the rest and thereby come to our concept of ourselves. What Hume is pointing out here is that our concept of personal identity—he does not really accept it as identity—comprises much more than an intellect with a memory. Emotions, imagination, sensations, and other events in this stream of perceptions are seen as part of the self with the aid of memory as we fill in the blanks in our causal story: "'Twill be incumbent on those, who affirm that memory produces entirely our personal identity, to give a reason why we can thus extend our identity beyond our memory."[30] Since Hume's critique, followers of Locke have, by and large, extended the description of psychological phenomena which they appeal to in producing a concept of a person.

Ahead of his time

Another feature of Hume's account, which has a decidedly contemporary ring to it, is his claim that many questions regarding personal identity have no answer or must be settled by semantic fiat rather than philosophical investigation. When we ask whether, in principle, a person can survive such and such changes, we may stretch the concept of a person beyond its limits. Because we have not genuine identity, according to Hume, but degrees of similarity, there are bound to be cases where, because similarity varies by subtle degrees, we enter a grey area in the meaning of "same person." Disputes in such cases are, by Hume's lights, merely verbal. We simply have to make a legislative definition of "same person" to decide how much difference will be tolerated before we give up our fiction of personal identity.[31]

Since Hume's time, many philosophers have tried to defeat his skeptical arguments about persons, and many have tried to develop and refine them. This debate is still very vigorous and it is generally carried on using Hume's methods. Reducing apparent questions of metaphysics to verbal disputes, for example, is a very popular contemporary gambit anticipated by Hume.

Hume did a great deal, as well, to contribute to the current fashion of keeping philosophy and theology independent. But Hume was much ahead of the fashions, and later philosophers returned to the religious fold. They did so, however, as much more knowing sheep than their forerunners. The chains of church dogma, which had long been loosened, were now borne only voluntarily.

What about Daphne?

If, as Berkeley supposes, persons are just minds, their bodies mere illusions, then Daphne is more severely reduced than would appear. Her body is almost all that remains. Leibniz would tell us that, even though her conscious mind is all but gone, there may remain nonconscious features of Daphne's mind which preserve continuity. So strong are such features as preservatives that Daphne would even be considered morally responsible, on this view, for things she did as she was descending into dementia. Her disease, multiple sclerosis, causes personality changes as it attacks the brain. Daphne said and did hurtful things in her downward slide for which I and others did not hold her responsible. After all, her inhibitions were removed by the disease and inhibitions are things we cultivate in keeping up our own characters and personalities. Leibniz seems to go too far.

On the other hand, Leibniz's solutions seem preferable to Butler and Reid's mysterious underlying substance or to Locke's memory criterion of identity. The non-conscious part of ourselves is not to be neglected. Indeed, Hume's disappearing act is premised on there being nothing to us but what is on the surface of the mind. He would say that Daphne is a stream of ideas, sensations, and perceptions which has narrowed from a torrent to a trickle. He solves the problem by destroying the concept of a person, or attempting to do so. Daphne is in no worse state than any of us are, through Hume's approach.

As the religious doctrine of the soul loses its grip on our concept of a person, the danger arises that human beings with severe dementia and other kinds of mental incompetence will be treated as unworthy of concern. Taking Hume seriously, however, we can determine the extension of the concept of a person in a conventional fashion. Our conventions can be tailored to match our pre-existing moral concerns. If we want to include the demented in the moral community, then—given the power of the term "person" in our moral discourse—we should arrange our conventions so as to call demented human beings "persons" both before and after a tragic decline into dementia. This does not presuppose that sameness of persons is preserved through such a decline. Suppose your mother, through Alzheimer's disease, becomes severely mentally disabled. She is still, under such tragic circumstances, a person. Since she does not remember you or her earlier life and since most of her abilities have changed, we might adopt conventions to ensure that, although she is not the same person who raised you, she is the same human being. This preserves some continuity for moral and emotional purposes but avoids pretence.

Another way of looking at the situation through Hume's spectacles would show us that one who suffers a decline into dementia has not lost status, metaphysically speaking, as a result of her great loss. We should not concern ourselves with the question of whether she is the same person she once was, since none of us is. Her life took an unexpected course, much as a river whose bed is upturned by an earthquake. We, most of us, hope for a less dramatic course. In any case, the kind of survival we ask about with Locke hovering in the background does not take place for any of us, if Hume is right. There is no enduring self to survive. In Locke's terms, using the distinction between human beings and persons, there are no persons—just human beings who have, at any given time, a fiction about being persons who have survived from an earlier time. By Hume's standards, you cannot meet the same person twice, not even in the mirror.

What I like about these moderns

Leibniz's emphasis on things other than consciousness to preserve continuity of persons is a healthy emphasis. The body and the non-conscious mind must be kept in view. Memory should not be put above all else, given the problems to which Locke is heir. Hume points out the need for a much clearer understanding of what it is we are looking for when we ask about identity. He is also right to point out the conventional nature of the concept of a person, though I think we can take his point without his iconoclasm.

It is time to swim the channel again, if only to escape from such hard-nosed British philosophers as Hume. We will see what comfort we can find among the elegant continental philosophers.

Content questions

1. What is Berkeley's idealism?
2. How does Leibniz avoid an odd consequence of Locke's view of persons, that we are not morally responsible for doing things we have forgotten doing?
3. What is the contemporary objection to Locke by Williams that Leibniz gave long before?
4. What do Butler and Reid think preserves personal identity?
5. Why can we not identify people by their purely qualitative (non-relational) properties?
6. How does Reid object to Locke's memory criterion of personal identity?
7. Explain Butler's circularity objection to Locke's criterion.
8. What does Noonan suggest in reply to Butler, and how does Chisholm object? Give Perry's reply to Chisholm.

9. Why does Hume not think there is a self over and above the perceptions a person has?
10. How does Hume avoid the problem of identity of persons through time?

Arguments for analysis

You should find neither of the following arguments fully convincing. Can you extend the debate between idealists and dualists or materialists? Berkeley's *Three Dialogues between Hylas and Philonous* is one place to look for a series of arguments and counter-arguments on this topic.

Argument 1: Persons as minds

Recall the discussion of materialism, dualism, idealism and neutral monism in chapter 1. Berkeley takes the empiricist program to its logical conclusion in idealism. Persons are just minds with ideas. Here is an argument for the conclusion that matter is an unnecessary hypothesis. This argument presupposes the *experience principle*: as empiricists, we should not affirm the existence of that which we do not experience.

We do not directly experience matter. We experience, rather, the properties of things that we suppose inhere in matter. For example, we experience the redness, roundness, and elasticity of a red rubber ball. We do not experience matter or its cousin, substance. In fact, redness, roundness, and elasticity are ideas in our minds. We accept the hypothesis that there is a material ball causing these ideas. It is, however, not at all clear why we should think that matter, whatever that is, can have any causal effect on mind. Our minds and ideas, on the other hand, are things with which we are directly acquainted and we do not need mysteries to explain them. What we have knowledge of is a regular sequence of ideas. When I bounce the ball, I have a predictable series of ideas of redness, roundness, and motion. To say that there is an additional material ball in a material world independent of my mind does not help. I should say, rather, that the world is just the sequence of ideas that minds have. The regularity of the world that science studies is just the regularity of the sequences of ideas that exist. Objects, such as the ball, are just semi-permanent possibilities of perception. When I have ideas that I describe as looking in the closet for the ball, I have the ideas that make up the ball. I will have such ideas just as long as some mind has had the ideas we refer to by saying, I left the ball in the closet. To say the ball ceases to exist is just to say that no mind will have perceptions of it in future. We know persons, like the ball, as sequences of perceptions. To themselves persons are known both by perception and by other ideas, such as memories. The notion of a material body is no more helpful in understanding a person than it is in understanding the ball. Minds and ideas (in the broad sense including any experiences) are all that we need to have a universe such as the one we know by experience. Matter is an unnecessary hypothesis.

Argument 2: Objection by way of solipsism

Unless I want to accept the outrageous view that I am the only mind or person in the universe, I must reject the experience principle. We do not experience other minds. We have only our perceptions of others' words and bodies to assure us that others exist. We must infer the existence of things by their appearances. Just as we may infer the existence of other minds from experience, we may infer the existence of material things by experience. The persons-as-minds argument assumes that appearances can exist on their own without anything to appear. Supposing that the world is a sequence of uncaused appearances does not simplify our hypotheses; it mystifies them. It provides no way of explaining why those appearances persist for a while or why distinct minds experience similar appearances. The existence of material objects provides a cause for the appearances. Matter is a necessary hypothesis, for it provides the simplest way of explaining what we see.

Argument 3: The drunks argument against Locke

A common kind of counter-example to Locke involves showing that persons who deliberately abandon their own consciousness could avoid responsibility for what they do. Suppose, for example, that Terence intentionally drinks alcohol to excess. While drunk, Terence commits horrendously immoral acts. When Terence is sober, he does not remember what he has done. According to Locke's view, he should not be held morally responsible for what he has done while drunk, since that person is not really identical to the sober man. This licenses the worst crimes, so Locke's memory criterion of identity must be mistaken.

Argument 4: Reid's person-stages objection

Locke's memory criterion of personal identity is explained on page 143. Roughly who you are depends on what you remember doing. You are the person who did those things, who witnessed and remembered your own actions. Reid's objection to this is also on page 143, but I will explain it further here. Reid is giving a counter-example—an example that shows that something is wrong with Locke's criterion. His argument based on this counter-example is a *reductio* of Locke's criterion (that is, he tries to show it has absurd consequences). Suppose Locke's memory criterion is correct. Now consider a human being through three stages of life: being a boy, being an adult, and being a senior. Call the persons associated with the human being in these three stages x, y, and z. Suppose the person y remembers the actions of x. It follows, by Locke's criterion, that y is x. The person in stage z remembers the actions of y but does not remember the actions of x. It follows, by Locke's criterion, that z is y but z is not x. Now since z is y and y is x, it follows that z is x. Therefore, z is x and z is not x, but this is absurd. We must, therefore, reject the memory criterion that leads to this absurdity.

Argument 5: Butler's circularity objection

According to Locke, A and B are the same person if B shares A's memories. To tell whether they are really the same memories that are shared, we must be sure that they are the memories of the same persons. Thus sameness of persons is defined in terms of sameness of memories and sameness of memories is defined in terms of sameness of persons. To use Locke's memory criterion of identity we would have to go around in circles. Therefore, Locke's memory criterion of identity must be mistaken.

Argument 6: Hume's disappearing act

This argument also presupposes the *experience principle*: as empiricists, we should not affirm the existence of that which we do not experience. If we have a self that is constantly the same throughout our changes of mind and body, then we must be aware of the self. We would have a constant sensation of the self throughout our lives. When we introspect, however, we only notice changing ideas, feelings, perceptions, and the like. Therefore, there is no constant self in any of us. A consequence of this argument is that persons are just fictions if we think of persons as existing through time. We are each a sequence of similar things, not one constantly existing thing. A presupposition of this argument is that experiences can exist without someone to experience them. Instead of minds, persons, or selves, there are just sequences of experiences.

CHAPTER 7

Yet More Moderns

The late modern emphasis on morality

In the latter half of the modern era, widely differing views of what we are were proposed. A common thread, however, was the primacy of ethical concerns in the development of concepts of a person.

Rousseau

Rousseau makes a passionate attempt to give philosophy a human face. In the age of the Enlightenment the glorification of the intellect over the heart had furthered the concept of a person as an intellect with whatever else is needed to keep that intellect going. This was sometimes a tendency in the Middle Ages as well, as we have seen with Aquinas. Yet, in mediaeval times, the tendency was moderated by the emphasis on faith. As faith gave way to reason in the Enlightenment, admiration for the intellect knew no bounds. Rousseau dug in his heels.

Rousseau opposed equally the religious doctrine of original sin and the Enlightenment doctrine of the betterment of persons through intellect. He viewed people as naturally good. Education and civilization, however, destroyed this natural goodness. In his view, a native morality common to simple folk belied the theological doctrine of the

Notes to chapter 7 are on pp. 481-83.

evil inherent in people and was evidence against the efficacy of education. Education achieved its ill effect by suppressing the individual personality and making us all conform in manners and dress.[1] This makes it difficult to read people's hearts and minds; thus, deception and other vices are made easier.

Rousseau, then, is among those who promote the view of persons as individuals. His thought is important in the long tradition of the West moving away from the Oriental attraction to absorption of the individual into the universe or at least into some larger social group. At the same time, Rousseau is concerned to prevent the egoism that comes from overemphasizing the individual. Rather, he seeks to achieve the preservation of the native morality in us through the furthering of individual character.

What about Daphne?

Although Daphne's character outlived her intellect, she no longer had any way of furthering or expressing the character she once developed. Her options for individuality and morality are closed.

What I like about Rousseau

Rousseau champions the individual which, within certain limits, I approve. The idea that people are naturally good is also attractive, though sometimes it seems daft. When, however, I see the wicked world as peopled by a species most motivated by greed and fear, I remind myself that the opportunities for evil are far greater than those of which people take advantage. That slavery, for example, is widely shunned though not totally abolished, cannot be explained by base motives alone.

Kant

Although Kant admired and was strongly influenced by Rousseau, Kant wished to take morality out of the affective realm and back to that of the intellect. His view of persons as moral beings depends on their being quintessentially rational. Kant, however, like Rousseau, champions the individual. Kant advises us to:

> Act in such a way that you always treat humanity, whether in your own person or in the person of any

> other, never simply as a means, but always at the same time as an end. [He further clarifies:] Only rational agents or *persons* can be ends in themselves. As they alone can have an unconditioned and absolute value, it is wrong to use them simply as means to an end whose value is only relative.[2]

Here we have two of the themes we have noted in earlier developments of the concept of a person: the heavy emphasis on rationality as essential to persons and their being valued above all else. Kant is telling us that we may not use persons only to achieve goals; rather, all our goals must be subject to the betterment of people.

Kant sees as the enemy not merely the herding effects of education, which Rousseau decried, but utilitarianism. Utilitarianism takes the happiness of the greatest number of people to be the moral guide. Kant thinks that one may not trample on the rights of the individual in order to achieve this mass happiness. The terms in which I have put this may be somewhat anachronistic, but later philosophers who defended utilitarianism found in Kant their major opponent.

The emphasis on metaphysics (the theory of reality) and epistemology (the theory of knowledge) in the British empiricist tradition of Locke, Berkeley, and Hume finds its place in Kant's work as well, but always in balance with ethics (the theory of moral value). As the concept of a person is central to Kantian moral theory, Kant must reject the Humean skepticism about persons. The empiricists, who began with a return to common sense, ended with the Berkeleyan view that persons are mere disembodied minds or the Humean view that there are no persons.

Kant believes, contrary to Hume, that perceptions must occur in a perceiver. The mere fact that we have knowledge and experience in a unified way necessarily implies that there is a unified self having the experience, but this is no guarantee that there is a single subject of experience over time.[3] Something has to hold memory, imagination, sensation, and the various faculties of the mind together during a given period of consciousness. Persons, however, if they exist over a longer time than just a brief period of self-consciousness, cannot be proven to do so. Kant says:

> For since the only permanent appearance which we encounter in the soul is the representation "I" that accompanies and connects them all, we are unable to prove that this "I," a mere thought, may not be in the same state of flux as the other thoughts which, by means of it, are linked up with one another.[4]

We could—given the evidence of introspection—be nothing more than a series of persons each of us deceived into thinking that we are each one with the earlier ones. This is only a mild improvement on Hume's doctrine that we do not exist as continuing selves at all. Kant does, however, believe in our continuity, for moral rather than metaphysical reasons. Indeed, as we see below, he believes in our immortality.

Contrary to Berkeley, Kant believes that perceptions of objects are caused by objects outside the mind. Kant, however, distinguishes the things as we see them (phenomena) from the things as they are (noumena). On Korner's interpretation of Kant, persons too are apprehended by us in the phenomenal world, though they have noumenal existence which we cannot know.[5] We cannot even know our noumenal selves, though we can know that we exist. Without the person, there would be no experience, but the person as noumenon is beyond her own realm of knowledge. Hume was right to think he could not know himself but wrong to suppose there was nothing to know.

This qualified denial of what, from a Kantian point of view, are the excesses of the empiricists is crucial to Kant's moral theory as well. By limiting our knowledge to the phenomenal world, he is able to explain how there can be personal freedom. While my every action seems to be an event caused by other events in the phenomenal realm, for me to be morally responsible for my actions is for me to be free to have done otherwise. This antinomy of caused actions being free is, in Kant's view, explained by making freedom a feature of the mysterious, unknowable noumenal realm. We are empirically causally determined but transcendentally free. In other words, we are caused as phenomena, but we are free as noumena. Although we cannot understand our freedom as it lies in the noumenal realm, which is beyond our knowledge, we can nonetheless exercise our freedom.[6] To do so rightly, we must obey a moral law, the categorical imperative, which can be known by reason alone.

One of Kant's formulations of this law encapsulates Kant's famous doctrine noted above that persons must be treated as ends and not simply as means. That is, persons are not to be used only as tools to achieve goals; rather, valuing persons must be central to our goals. Because no person can be discounted as a mere means to achieving the goals of others, we are all required, according to Kant, to act only on rules that we could, without contradictory purposes, universalize. For us to universalize a rule is to accept it as a rule for all people who find themselves in a situation similar to the one in which we are acting. Kant believes that reason alone will tell us which rules can be universalized. Those that cannot be rationally universalized will lead us to contradictory desires when we accept such rules for all. We would want opposite kinds of things to happen, if we wanted such a rule to be universally followed. For example, if we try to justify breaking promises to create good outcomes, then we might, in effect, wish for promises to go out of style and wish to benefit from making false promises. The rule we are following—break a promise when it leads to good results—is a rule we cannot rationally universalize. Kant thinks that, when we contemplate universalizing a bad rule of action, we are trying to have our cake and eat it too.

This Kantian view of persons, reason, and morals is an extreme case of the emphasis of the intellectual component in persons. We are, for Kant, essentially rational beings. In this lies our value. We must recognize the same value in all other persons.[7]

Kant does not, of course, deny our affective features. He believes, however, that the emotions have absolutely no place in moral decision making. His is a stern view of duty understood by reason alone. Most people, he knows, will be guided by moral sentiments. In truth, however, the real reason that what they do is right is that it conforms to the moral law; the categorical imperative.[8]

Kant affirms, moreover, that nothing is good in itself except a good will.[9] It is not the consequences of our actions which make the actions right, but the intentions we have when we do them. The imperfection of this world is such, however, that the consequences of the exercise of a good will may not lead to happiness. Virtue is not often rewarded. Our reason tells us that virtue and happiness ought to coincide, an idea which leads us inevitably to postulate our immortality; otherwise there would not be enough time for us to achieve the moral perfection and consequent happiness for which we strive.[10] So, like Locke, Kant thinks that persons do not go out of existence. But, while Locke took that as a starting point and tried to explain how we could survive our bodily death with our responsibility intact, Kant takes responsibility and perfectibility of persons as given, to deduce our immortality. We are rational beings striving for moral perfection. We need the time to achieve the goal, but our immortality cannot be proven.[11]

While Kant's views on immortality have not, perhaps, penetrated popular morality, his view of persons as beings of intrinsic moral worth is quite often taken to be common sense now. To some extent it coincides with the long development of the idea of individual worth which is central to the Western theological and philosophical traditions. Kant focuses that idea through a systematic philosophy. He joins it, as well, with the Aristotelian view that rationality is crucial to what we are. The principle that all persons, as rational beings, have dignity and must be taken into account when our actions affect them is an idea that has permeated the contemporary world. This principle may be honoured more in the breach but is so generally accepted that we feel we must rationalize each breach. For example, when bigots mistreat a particular group of human beings, they may still feel constrained to deny that those in the group are "real persons" of the sort they perceive themselves to be. Kant's influence has seeped deeply into our culture.

On the other hand, the centrality of rationality in what we are and what we ought to do is often challenged. Kant's influence on contemporary views of persons is moderated by a Rousseauesque appreciation of the native moral sentiments. A psychopath, for instance, may be perfectly rational in the sense of logically pursuing egoistic goals. One might well say that the psychopath is, nonetheless, not a complete person for lacking the native moral sentiments of compassion and guilt. This is probably a more common contemporary response than the Kantian approach of trying to show that psychopaths are actually irrational since they universalize contradictory rules.

What about Daphne?

While Daphne appears to be absent from her body, which remains, Kantians could believe that her unknowable self exists yet in the noumenal realm. Her lack of ability to benefit others is, from a Kantian point of view, irrelevant to the treatment she should get. Her value as a person does not depend, as it does for Hobbes, on her place in the state or on her capacity to improve the general welfare. Perhaps a Kantian could argue also—as Kant does for our immortality—that Daphne's continuity is morally necessary, though unknowable and unprovable.

What I like about Kant

One rather general contribution Kant has made to the debate concerning persons is the demonstration that one can powerfully link three approaches to the person: metaphysical, epistemological, and ethical. These three pursue the questions of what we are, how we know ourselves and other persons, and what we ought to do. Where Kant has been unable to provide metaphysical proofs to his satisfaction concerning the permanence of persons, he relies on the necessity of our permanence for moral needs. Some would consider this a weakness. Many philosophical discussions today of the popular topic of personal identity narrow the approach to metaphysical questions alone. The motivation, however, to pursue the metaphysical questions and those of epistemology is often a moral one. This should be taken to heart, so that the three approaches through metaphysics, epistemology, and ethics can provide checks and balances for one another.

Hegel: God is still almost everywhere

There was a strong reaction to Kant from a school of philosophy known as German idealism or Absolute idealism. British and North American philosophers tend to look on this school with the same fondness that they display for German measles. Sallying forth into this territory will no doubt earn me the wrath of the dyed-in-the-wool subset of the Analytic philosophers of Britain and North America as well as the equal ire of their implacable enemies on the continent. That is a price I am prepared to pay for whatever insights about persons we might glean from either the Absolute idealists or my interpretation of them. Most philosophers on both sides of the great schism are at least willing to listen.

The main proponent of Absolute idealism was Hegel. Like Kant and unlike most Analytic philosophers, Hegel was a system builder. His main tool of construction was a method—dialectic, in which two contradictory propositions, the thesis and the antithesis, are resolved by a third, the synthesis. In Stumpf's assessment, applying dialectic to the concept of being, Hegel ultimately concludes that the universe is the product of an absolute mind.[12] Aristotle had earlier thought of the universe as a material organism with purposes realized in its parts, but Hegel is denying the existence of matter, as Berkeley had done. Hegel is also denying the separation of minds that Berkeley admitted. All things in the universe are part of one mind, the Absolute. The universe is a person. Individual persons are merely part of this larger person.

Stated baldly like that, the conclusion Hegel approaches with infinite pains is rather hard for the Western mind to accept. It seems more at home in some Eastern cultures, at least as perceived from the West, where the individual is routinely subjugated to the group and thought of as being reabsorbed into the One after death. This is not too far from the mark. Individualism is dealt a glancing blow by Hegel. He is, however, very much a Western thinker in many ways and has a role for the individual person within the larger person of the Absolute and in the political expression of that Absolute, the state. The Absolute, moreover, is a dynamic evolving process,[13] just as an individual person is.

For Hegel, everything that is known or understood is related to the Absolute idea or mind. This Absolute is all-encompassing; so we can make sense of individual things or persons only as parts of the Absolute. "The Absolute alone is true," says Hegel,[14] denying any use for a knowledge of some relative truth which obtains within a limited context. A piece of a puzzle cannot be understood on its own. As we seek understanding, we move dialectically, synthesizing opposites until we reach the Absolute, which makes the individual things and persons comprehensible. This process is illustrated when a person thinks of herself as opposed to things outside herself. There is subjective awareness of the thing outside and the objective existence of that thing independently of the person's mind. The subjectivity and the objectivity, thesis and antithesis, are synthesized in the Absolute. When an individual person is aware of a thing outside herself, this is the Absolute being self-conscious, rather like Spinoza's God. Individúal persons are, then, the way in which the largest person, the Absolute, knows itself. The subjective and the objective are unified in this Absolute.[15] The object is a thought of the Absolute. The person thinking about the object is the Absolute's self-reflection.

Seen from another point of view, objectively or from the outside, a person is, in Hegel's terms, a mechanism, a chemism, and a teleology.[16] Roughly, that means that we not only have mechanical and chemical aspects but also a system of purposes, both our own and those of the Absolute. Unlike mere machines or chemical reactions, human beings are not merely to be understood in the realm of nature which is governed by necessity. We are the self-awareness of the Absolute and, hence, free to choose. In the context of Hegel's philosophy this freedom is best understood in Shakespeare's apt phrase, "There is a divinity that shapes our ends rough-hew them how we will."[17] As the great, self-reflecting Absolute evolves through the ages, we are free to go, in various ways, with the flow of this evolution or to fight helplessly against it. We have room for a little swimming across the current, but there is no going against it successfully.

None of what has been said so far implies that the individual person is utterly subjugated to or absorbed into something beyond that individual. Even though all persons are one in that they are all expressions of the Absolute reflecting on itself, Hegel allows for many different sorts of self-reflection and, hence, room for individuality. The worth of the individual which Kant emphasized, however, takes second place to the worth of the group as the outcomes of Hegel's metaphysics for his moral and political philosophy unfold. Individual political freedom is minimized. Hegel's philosophy of history also leaves scant room for that metaphysical freedom which is opposed to determinism.

To begin with metaphysical freedom and individuality, these are absorbed into the freedom of the Absolute itself. By Hegel's approach, history is a record of the growth and development of this large person, the Absolute. What we see in history is the continual revelation of the spirit or mind which is the Absolute. The Absolute is evolving toward freedom, but the individual is merely expressing the spirit of her age, a stage in the character development of a much larger person. She is caught up in and swept along by that spirit will she, nil she.

> As it is not the brute, but only the man that thinks, he only—and only because he is a thinking being—has Freedom. *His* consciousness imports this, that the individual comprehends itself as a *person*, that is, recognizes itself in its single existence as possessing universality—as capable of abstraction from, and of surrendering all specialty; and, therefore, as inherently infinite.[18]

Here we see not only the familiar theme of rationality as essential to a person but also the unfamiliar idea that both the properties of having freedom and being a person require absorption of the individual, surrendering of specialty, being a part of the infinite, the Absolute.

As for political freedom in Hegel's view, the person who is most free is one who accepts completely the bonds of moral and political duty. This conclusion is also the end product of a line of dialectical reasoning. The thesis is that the individual person has a right to express individual freedom by, for instance, accumulating property. Opposed to this are the requirements of morality, the duties which restrict individual freedom. This antithesis is resolved with the thesis into a synthesis in which a higher freedom is found in the harmonizing of the individual will with the universal will. The individual no longer acts for herself but for all through the state. The state too is a person and is "the embodiment of rational freedom."[19] The only acts that one can rationally choose to do are those which are in accord with the public good. Therefore, if one is both free and rational in what one freely chooses, one accepts completely the bonds of social duty.

A theory like Hegel's can easily be perverted to the purposes of a selfish, totalitarian ruler. Hegel's understanding of it was, however, quite the opposite. Kaufmann tells us: "That history is the story of the development of human freedom, is the central idea of Hegel's philosophy of history."[20] Hegel thinks of the Absolute evolving through the history of humankind from the days of the single ruler, to the free society supported by slaves, to the society where all are free: "Universal History exhibits the *gradation* in the development of that principle whose substantial *purport* is the consciousness of Freedom."[21] In spite of Hegel's intentions, his excessive faith in the ability and willingness of people to act rationally leads him to put far too little caution in his remarks about the state. Theoretically, Hegel exalts the individual person as the Absolute being made self-aware. From a theological viewpoint, the Absolute is God. A version of the ancient idea of the divine in persons is thus preserved. One thinks as well of Spinoza's concept of a person. Hegel's views on morality, freedom, and the state are, nonetheless, effortlessly turned in their practical application to the suppression of the individual.[22] Although Hegel is a mystic of sorts and furthers the Oriental ideal of absorption of the individual person in a cosmic whole, he retains from Kant the requirement of rationality for persons.

What about Daphne?

On the one hand, Daphne may be a person in the sense that she could be one of the ways in which the Absolute contemplates itself. On the other hand, it seems that Daphne cannot think in a way that would allow her to comprehend herself as a person.

What I like about Hegel

Hegel provides a foil for the sort of philosopher I wish to emulate. The grand system, impervious to evidence, the opaque style, and mystic vision as opposed to precision are not my cup of tea.

Schopenhauer: God begins to disappear

Schopenhauer, whom Stumpf has with apt alliteration called "The Prophet of Pessimism,"[23] moves us further in the direction of contemporary concepts of persons by leaving behind in his account of what is essential to persons both the divine and the rational intellectual features. In his depiction of persons as totally driven by forces beyond their control one sees a foreshadowing of some of the dim views of persons which became popular in the post-Freudian world.

Schopenhauer takes as axiomatic the principle of sufficient reason "that nothing is without a reason."[24] "Reason" is here used in the sense of "cause." Once one accepts such a principle, pessimism is justified. Every human action along with every other event must happen of necessity. Free will is dead. We may be aware of our condition, but we can do nothing to alter it. At best one can view the spectacle of the misery of humankind with the compassion and resignation which come from generalizing love for an individual person to love for all persons.

In the course of delineating this cheery doctrine, Schopenhauer generates some interesting claims about persons. Self-awareness is often taken to be an essential feature of persons, but few give an account of what it is. How can the self be, simultaneously, the knowing subject and the object of knowledge? Schopenhauer explains that the self that wills is the object of knowledge for the self as knowing subject. He seems to be telling me that my intellect can step back and take cognizance of that part of me which is moved to action by my will. This use of the term "will" sounds peculiar to contemporary ears since we are used to thinking of will as itself under the guidance of reason. Schopenhauer, however, uses the term "will" as we might use "drives" to indicate deep-seated forces moving the person to act in ways that person cannot control. We can see the strings which move our puppet limbs, but we cannot be our own puppeteers. In self-awareness we come, sadly, to understand and see ourselves as puppets. The intellect is powerless against this "blind incessant impulse."[25] This is most clear in the will to live which normally overpowers reason.

This odd notion of the will as a cause that drives us to do the things we do quite independently of reason is fundamental in Schopenhauer's worldview. This kind of will drives all events in the world. He goes so far as to say the world is will. Clearly then, it would be an error to say that will is merely what later psychiatrists might call a subconscious drive. Will is broad enough to include types of energy and causation which occur in totally non-personal entities. Schopenhauer thus associates what drives persons with what drives any event in the universe. We are not different. We are absorbed into the general, heaving, life-seeking but otherwise purposeless realm of nature. For reasons in some respects different from Schopenhauer's, our contemporaries often view persons as merely more complex processes in the realm of natural processes. Although the scientific backdrop of this contemporary view is more detailed, there is the shared faith in the principle of sufficient reason which motivates both Schopenhauer and these contemporaries to reduce persons to causal processes.

What about Daphne?

Hegel and Schopenhauer both, in their different ways, see people as in the grip of large forces beyond their control. It is the Absolute, not the individual person here in the muck of the mundane, that is free. Given such views, it is difficult to differentiate Daphne from the rest of us. The Absolute is in an odd mood of self-contemplation in her case. She has the advantage over the rest of us of being unaware of her own condition, or so a pessimist like Schopenhauer might think.

What I like about Schopenhauer

The brief answer is not much. By focusing our attention on drives and then causes that affect our decision, Schopenhauer makes us face the problem of explaining what freedom of the will might be. The pessimistic view that persons are merely self-aware causal mechanisms is far easier to defend than alternatives that take free choice seriously.

Bentham and Mill

The movement of the concepts of the person from the religious to the secular realm was accelerated toward the end of the modern period. The positivism of August Comte and John Stuart Mill did something to move metaphysics more into the thought patterns of science and away from those of religion. Religions tend to expect faith on non-rational grounds. They treat the universe as either a person or something governed by an immensely powerful person or persons in whose terms all things have a purpose. What positivism substitutes for this universe with a purpose is a universe in which natural phenomena occur in regular ways governed by discoverable natural laws, but a universe which, in itself, has no purpose. The anthropomorphic and animistic views of the world are replaced with one in which the world is to be understood in terms of its regularity. This view puts persons in a special category, since they have purposes and values while the rest of the world does not. Such an understanding has made the immense power of science possible in the contemporary period and has contributed to its destructive tendencies. If nature is no longer our mother, she can be used like a whore—so one would judge by our present practice in which the planet, like an enslaved human, is being used up. By treating our surroundings impersonally, we have threatened their continuance and, of course, our own. Not only are persons not absorbed into a greater whole, they are encouraged to be so individualistic as to, egoistically, ravage the world for their personal benefit. Depending on what one thinks the results of less individualistic policies will be, one may find a partial antidote to this rabid individualism in the influence of the utilitarians, including Mill, who advanced positivism against the mother-nature view of the world.

In the interface between the modern and the contemporary periods, Jeremy Bentham and John Stuart Mill solidified and popularized utilitarianism, a view about morality which had been growing in strength since Hobbes's time. Hobbes, Hume, and even Locke were not utilitarians but foreshadowed what Bentham and Mill were to champion, the utilitarian view that what is good is happiness and that, hence, the right thing to do is what will create the greatest happiness of the greatest number of people. This is a far cry from the more traditional views about goodness and right action. In particular the idea that what is good is what God wills was replaced not only in the writings of these philosophers but in much of the realm of public affairs. Bentham and Mill were passionate, energetic, and effective social reformers.

The new ethics furthered by the utilitarians still competes with ethical views which do not make the rightness of an action depend only on the consequences of the action. Utilitarianism is, however, easier to defend than many other views in the contemporary context. Once one takes away a share in divinity as the source of the worth of persons and once one adopts a scientific, investigative attitude to persons, it is easier to support an ethics apparently based on observation. Looking at people's behaviour, we seem to see that they seek pleasure and avoid pain. Thus there is nothing mysterious about the utilitarian analysis of the good as pleasure. No appeal to the intrinsic worth of persons is required.

On the other hand, utilitarians tend to ignore persons as individuals in favour of the mass of persons. If one wants to maximize the aggregate of happiness, attention to the individual is not always necessary. In spite of the best efforts of Mill, this lessening of the importance of individual persons is a concomitant of the rise of utilitarianism and the secularization of the concept of persons which goes hand in hand with utilitarianism. If I have no individual rights, as act utilitarians claim, and I cannot say that my soul is special in the eyes of God, then there is nothing to prevent society using me as a means to the end of society's greater happiness, even if that results in my own lifelong abject misery. Utilitarians do a cost-benefit analysis. They find the unhappiness of one person justified by the happiness of the many. Mill thought that the happiness of the many could best be achieved by providing individuals with the liberty to make themselves happy, but that is a social/psychological claim which is open to empirical study. It may turn out to be false. If so, the utilitarian principles justify the absorption of the individual by the state.

One of the things I would like a concept of a person to provide is a theoretical underpinning for a society that is tolerant of individual difference without deifying it. Unfortunately, one can always find social/scientific support for greatly limiting freedom of the individual person, given that one's goal is to maximize happiness. Consider, for example, the uses to which Lawrence Kohlberg's theory of the stages of moral development might be put. According to this theory, very few people ever reach the stage of moral development in which they could properly apply their freedom as Mill would hope they would. They would not pursue their own happiness with respect for other people.[26] This seems to license denying individual liberty to most people and allowing it only to the highly developed few. This seems like a return to Plato's view of a just society in which the few ran the lives of the others. The absorption of individuals by the state is assured.

By another criterion for judging concepts of a person the utilitarians fare somewhat better. In cases of mental incompetence, I would like a concept which does not pin so much on rationality that it excludes a person from consideration because of a loss of rationality. The happiness of a mental incompetent is worth as much as the happiness of the most rational member of society to utilitarians such as Bentham and Mill. There are others who distinguish the kinds of pleasures one may have and thus would value simple pleasures less than those of which the incompetent is capable. Most utilitarians would accept pleasure of any kind as on a par with pleasure of any other kind.

This brings us to another feature of utilitarianism which may inhibit the effects of rabid individualism. The idea that the person is the crown of creation and may ravage the rest of the world for personal betterment is blocked by this fact: animals feel pain and pleasure. Since utilitarians view pleasure as good, the distinction between animals and people is minimized. The line to draw in moral matters is not between the rational and the non-rational but between sentient and non-sentient beings. Singer approvingly quotes Bentham on this score: "The day may come when the rest of the animal creation may acquire those rights which never could have been withholden from them but by the hand of tyranny.... The question is not, Can they reason? nor Can they talk? but, Can they suffer?"[27] The heirs of Hume minimize the importance of the person as a metaphysical unit, a chunk of reality, while the utilitarians undermine the importance of the person as a moral unit, one whose interests must be considered above those of other sentient beings. The influence of Hume's metaphysics and utilitarian ethics has the effect of widening our range of concern. As we shall see below, Parfit views this as an improvement. Certainly we have been woefully unconcerned about non-persons in this world, but treating fish and people as on a par is more than most of us wish to do to rectify this wrong. As a culture, we refuse to abandon the concept of a person, but we modify that concept to find a new role for persons in a world which may no longer be dismissed as mere material for our use.

What about Daphne?

The utilitarians tend to diminish the importance of the distinction of people from other sentient beings. Whether or not we wish to say Daphne is a person or is the same person will rely on our choice of categories within an empirical framework, but it will have little effect on the moral determination of the treatment Daphne should receive. Though her pleasures may be rather limited from an intellectual point of view, they weigh as heavily in the balance as those of the most refined minds.

What I like about Bentham and Mill

The positivist substitution of the natural world for the supernatural is a good trend in philosophy as is Bentham's and Mill's recognition of the importance of pleasure; that is, they are good ideas if one does not make a god of either science or pleasure. It seems to me important to consider the pleasures which are peculiar to people, not just because of their intensity relative to those of other animals but because of their difference in kind. People are animals who laugh.

Karl Marx and self-realization

We turn now to a system which paradoxically combines great respect for individual persons with the advice that dictatorship will be needed. Trigg claims[28] that romantic individualism seemed to be Marx's aim for those who would enjoy that utopia that Marx predicted would arise once the state had withered away. Could he be talking about *the* Karl Marx? In fact, Marx is known to many of us only through the caricature of his ideas which is seen in the media controlled by those he threatened most. It will take a bit of explaining to uncover the romantic individualist beneath the appearance of the inhumane totalitarian.

Marx might not have too much sympathy with the attempt to understand the concept of person except in so far as that is equivalent to the task of saying what human nature is. On the one hand, Marx seems to have believed that there was no invariant human nature and, on the other, that it was the very thing that makes us essentially human, or persons, which is alienated along with the products of our labour in a capitalist society. Consider first Marx's anti-essentialist doctrine that we vary as chameleons against the background of our society: "it is not the consciousness of men that determines their being, but, on the contrary, their social being determines their consciousness."[29]

Some contend that, according to Marx, not only invariant consciousness but an invariant human nature is non-existent. They attribute to him the doctrine that so-called human nature is merely a result of social forces.[30] There is, however, the notion in Marx that capitalist society alienates workers from the products of their labour and, thereby, "each man is estranged from the other, as each of them is from man's essential nature."[31] What distinguishes people from animals is that they produce the means of their own subsistence. The need to work and to be fulfilled in work is natural to us.[32] Here again we see the person being defined in terms of ability—not the mere ability to reason, but the ability to labour. Our need to identify ourselves with what we produce by our labour is essential to our being what we are. We are therefore depersonalized when the individual loses the means of production to the bourgeoisie, who distance us from the products of our labour. Marx is here describing needs and tendencies that, in some sense, are our nature.

Our nature does not, however, go so far as to include patterns of behaviour which many have put under the umbrella of human nature. That people are avaricious traders and fail to cooperate, for example, is something that could be changed, given a sufficiently thorough dictatorship of the proletariat which would enforce cooperation until it became habitual. In the resulting cooperative utopia, the state—that is, the dictatorship—withers away once enforcing cooperation is unnecessary. In the cooperative, classless society Marx envisioned, people would work creatively and be at one with both the products of their labour and the others with whom they created and shared these products. Cooperation would replace competition in human nature.

Marx thought this development would inevitably come. This conclusion came from his adaptation of Hegel's view of history. Hegel thought that the Absolute moved in its dialectic process through history to become ever more free. Marxist dialectic preserves this as the freedom of the individual in the utopia that must eventually come. In this anarchic, cooperative community we would be as free as Rousseau's noble savages, untrammelled by law. It is here that we see Marx's romantic individualism. Each person ought to be a free, creative being in harmony with other people and enjoying the full use of her abilities to satisfy the needs of all. Marx, however, thought of himself not as a romantic moralist like Rousseau but as a scientific historian and futurist making an accurate prediction of the way in which history must evolve.

This raises the question of determinism. If we are unable to resist the currents of history, are we not simply playing roles in a drama written before we were born? Do the concepts of a person which require personal freedom to choose assume what is necessarily false? Marx seems to allow personal freedom in resistance to or acquiescence in the inevitable. We can struggle to bring about or to prevent the coming of a classless society, but it will come in any case. The fine points of the metaphysical debates concerning what freedom is and how people can have it do not seem to concern Marx. His is a philosophy in which the details are not allowed to inhibit the call to action.

The dramatic failure of the Soviet Union to survive and to convert Eastern Europe or its own republics to truly communist states makes Marx's view of history and of people seem dubious. Admittedly his program required a worldwide revolution so that there would be nowhere for capitalism to breed. That revolution looks like an ever more distant prospect as people in the industrialized nations, where the workers were expected to rise against the bourgeoisie, take the money and run. Communist revolutions, as opposed to revolutions against communism, were, when they were still occurring, much more likely in agrarian countries of the Third World where people had nearly nothing to lose. The abolition of private property appeals mainly to those without any. Marxism is, however, flexible enough to allow for backsliding. The Marxist faith is that the revolution will come when history is good and ready. While recent events have given capitalists confidence, the long term looks bad for the capitalist system, which is devouring the ground on which it stands. The degradation of the environment may lead to cataclysms which, if they do not promote Marxism, will at least undo its main opponent.

In any case, unless one sees in it the romantic, beautiful ideals of fraternity and equality and the faith in people as naturally creative, free, and cooperative, the Marxist picture of persons will be unintelligible, and the Marxist fervour for revolution will be seen as pure malevolence. The effect of this betrayed faith has often been a horrific form of totalitarianism in which selfish party bosses enslave a country and degrade the environment even more than capitalist industry. This, of course, is not Marxism. It is what the failed attempts to establish Marxist states have led to, and perhaps this is predictable, given what people are really like. One cannot force cooperation.

In any case, to see Marxism through the caricatures in our newspapers is to underestimate its power as a movement with romantic, humanist ideals. In particular, one must see it as promising freedom and self-realization of the individual person. That is why people fight and die for it. Even within the most capitalist of societies, we accept the need for the self-realization of people, which Marx preached, and we have accepted many social reforms, which Marx envisaged, to this end. Marx would think we will eventually come around once we stop confusing real freedom with the free market. It is not clear to me from reading Marx what this real freedom comes to but, politically, it involves the power to create things in which we take pride and to share them with others in an environment where none are exploited, all contributions are valued, and all needs are honoured. Once one understands the ideal it becomes clear that the main sources of disagreement which most people in capitalist democratic countries have with Marx is over the questions of what people are like by nature and, hence, how to achieve the ideal.

What about Daphne?

If the capacity to labour and the need to do so are what is distinctive of persons, then few could have made better claim to the title of "person" than Daphne prior to her illness. She was never still but in sleep. Now it does seem as though the quiet woman who remains has lost what was essential to be Daphne.

What I like about Marx

While Marx's political theories seem ever more difficult to believe, it is hard to disagree with the ideal of a society in which people are each valued for their contribution, whatever it may be, each allowed self-realization and freedom, not merely under the protection of law, but through the voluntary cooperation of all. More pertinent to the topic of persons is the Marxist faith that there is no human nature which we cannot change. Rather than being like all animals driven by will, as Schopenhauer would have it, we can change ourselves fundamentally by changing the society around us. Whether we can effect such changes or not, the relativity of the nature of persons to their environment is an interesting idea.

Kierkegaard's attempt to depose reason: God reappears

In Mill and Marx one sees philosophers who are utterly opposed to the kind of philosophy done by Hegel, though not necessarily the structure of his theories. They might consider such systems as Hegel's to be castles in the air. They wanted philosophy which led to social reform. Yet in their attempt to achieve hard-headed philosophical views and to maintain what Russell would call "a robust sense of reality," each gives some attention to the humanist and romantic strains in our concepts of a person. Kierkegaard was a Danish philosopher of the time who gave far more attention to these strains in his own rejection of Hegel's Absolute idealism. He wanted to preserve, in the face of the scientific investigation of human beings and various kinds of materialism, something essential to persons. Like Schopenhauer, he found this in the will rather than in reason, but, dour as he might have been, Kierkegaard was far from the pessimist Schopenhauer was. Freedom is also central to the concept of a person left to us by Kierkegaard. The themes Kierkegaard pursued became the core of the mighty existentialist movement in Continental philosophy in our times.

Most importantly, against those such as Bentham who emphasize the good of the whole, Kierkegaard focuses mainly on the individual. Large systems, whether metaphysical or political, are to be understood in terms of the individual rather than the other way around. This is because, Kierkegaard postulated, it is the individual person's act of will, making a commitment, choosing between alternatives, that determines what is true. His subjectivist doctrine of truth is summed up in his claim that "the highest truth attainable for an Existing individual [is] an objective uncertainty held fast in the most passionate personal experience."[33] Ultimately, the individual person must choose what to believe. There is no objective certainty. There is no absolute.

Free choices are what make us what we are and choices present themselves to us everywhere. The criteria for choosing are themselves things we must choose on the basis of no higher criteria at all; that is, they are absurdly chosen. According to MacIntyre, Kierkegaard only sometimes restricts this sort of absurd starting point to the realm of morals or religious faith,[34] separating the kind of truth we can attain in this area from that of science. Whatever the limits of his subjectivist doctrine of truth, he does believe that people's actions cannot be explained by causes.[35] He assumes that freedom of the will is not compatible with causal determinism.

Like Marx, Kierkegaard is fundamentally concerned with self-realization, but he sees it as coming through the exercise of free choice in the development of personality. The Hegelian and Marxist idea that the unfolding of history determines the individual is anathema to Kierkegaard. There is, however, something like Hegelian dialectic in the development of the individual person who, if fully developed, evolves through three stages of personality led by guilt and anxiety. The initial stage of the aesthetic person is that of a sybarite in which the person aims at maximizing personal sensual pleasure. From this one may move to the ethical stage where one accepts the dictates of a reasoned morality, as Socrates did. This, however, is where Western philosophy has become stuck. Kierkegaard would have us go on to the religious stage in which one overcomes reason, making a leap of faith to believe what is rationally absurd. In this stage, one works out one's personal, subjective, and unique relationship to God. The ancient Greek ideal of rational ethics is deposed in favour of faith.

Unlike the faith of Augustine or Aquinas, however, Kierkegaard's is a faith in spite of what reason tells us, not one that can be bolstered by argument. Complete self-realization is hindered, on Kierkegaard's view, by the addiction to rationality. His is, however, not merely a non-rational philosophy. Reason must be given full sway during the ethical stage of development; it is not, however, the be-all and end-all in philosophical method. In this, Kierkegaard is out of step with the majority of philosophers throughout history. But his ideas on the limits of reason, often separated from religious views, have been taken up by contemporary philosophers, mainly those in the existentialist school. One notable philosopher outside that school, Thomas Nagel, currently takes the ability to sense the absurdity of one's life as a defining characteristic of persons.[36] Reason, the absolute, and objective truth have been on a less secure footing since Kierkegaard. In particular, the truth about what we are is challenged. The essentially rational nature of persons is disputed. The belief in our participation in some grand absolute is also undermined since the dour Dane wrote.

What about Daphne?

The concept of a person that emerges through Kierkegaard and through existentialist writing in general is of a highly developed human being, one who is supra-rational rather than sub-rational. The capacity for choice is fundamental. Thus those who seem incapable of choosing are left out of account. From this perspective, Daphne is incapable of doing what is crucial for persons.

What I like about Kierkegaard

I have no use for subjectivist conceptions of truth or reality. These would make philosophy no longer a debate or a conversation but a totally insular pursuit. Nonetheless, Kierkegaard is right to remind us that we choose absurdly to value reason. He just makes different choices to mine.

The turn of the century and the screw

Schopenhauer and Kierkegaard wanted to make reason play second fiddle to the will in their descriptions of what we are. Nietzsche was forcefully persuasive for a revision of standard views about what we ought to do and what we ought to become based on the will to power. He exclaims: "the strongest and highest Will to Life does not find expression in a miserable struggle for existence, but in a Will to War. A Will to Power, a Will to Overpower!"[37] A person, no less than a wolf, is driven to dominate. The person, however, seeks to dominate not only fellow creatures but the entire environment. If this is right, what a choking irony! We have succeeded in overpowering the environment. The struggling biomass on which we live is dying by our hand. Our will to life is killing that on which we depend to live.

Nietzsche and the death of God

Nietzsche saw the wild urge to overpower restrained in the Europe of his time only by the myth of the Judeo-Christian God. This myth was losing its efficacy as a restraint; so, with horrifying accuracy, he prophesied wars of previously unknown violence. People, according to Nietzsche, are different from wild beasts of prey only in the manner of the restraint of their will to power. This will or life force is the Dionysian element in a person and, ideally, Nietzsche sees it working in concert with the Apollonian side of the person, which provides order, restraint and form.[38] The will to power is merely destructive if it is not formed into an act of creation by the Apollonian element of the person.

This synthesis of the Dionysian and Apollonian sides of ourselves is Nietzsche's response to the antithetical concepts of a person which we have seen in the prior history of philosophy. The more Oriental view has the person as part of a mass while the Western influence moves the concept further toward that of the individual cut off from the mass. The worshippers of Dionysus became absorbed into the whole of nature in a trance. From this they derived great power and shed responsibility. Apollo, by contrast, was the symbol of the principle of individuation.[39] Nietzsche abhorred absorption as much as Kierkegaard, but he also abhorred the Christian doctrine in which Kierkegaard found solace. He derided it as "slave morality." He insisted that it turned love of the earth into hatred.[40] He accused it of elevating the mediocre values of the herd above the strength of the great.[41]

This is curious, in the large historical picture. Christianity was, in fact, part of the Western trend away from absorption of the person into the mass by valuing individual souls and demanding that they be identifiable for judgment. Nietzsche, however, thought that the virtues of humility, patience, and diligence which were promoted by Christianity were the virtues that the weak promoted to defeat the strong.[42] His hope was that our species might produce supermen who would rise above the common herd by exercising the will to power. Goethe was his model, not some precursor of Hitler. Such persons as now exist should be superseded by those who would not be afraid to drop the life-negating Christian virtues in favour of the virtue of cruelty—the will to power—which is the source of creativity, on Nietzsche's view. The ideal person would savagely exploit the weak, when necessary, to produce something of greatness.

The most successful executives seem to accept something like Nietzsche's superman doctrine, but they put corporate commercial achievement in place of the cultural achievements which Nietzsche admired. The heads of multinational corporations must accept a large share of the responsibility for the destruction of the environment which they have sought to overpower. It is hard to see how a will to power could generate much concern about future generations but, if Nietzsche is right about persons being fuelled by a mixture of Dionysian and Apollonian urges, the only hope for our survival as a species is in the harnessing of the will to power for the regeneration of our environment.

Nietzsche himself was in such agonizing need of physical regeneration that his writing was, perforce, aphoristic. Ironically, for medical reasons, he depended at the end of his life on the kind of virtuous help he had despised. Often, he literally could not bear to sit at a desk and write for long periods of time. He produced his ideas in short but immensely powerful bursts of prose, leaving us to fill in the details. What persons are and what they might become has been presented to us only in an adumbrated form. Nonetheless a provocative view as an antithesis to much of what philosophy has told us about ourselves was flung down as a gauntlet before later philosophers.

What about Daphne?

The Apollonian element is gone entirely from Daphne, but the Dionysian may have survived. This leaves Daphne far from the ideal described in the previous section. In fact, by Nietzsche's lights she seems to be half a person.

What I like about Nietzsche

Although it may be simplistic, the idea of achieving a balance between Apollonian and Dionysian elements is appealing. As a former hippie, I feel that reason and the Apollonian ideal of order have been overemphasized.

Peirce, James, and Dewey: Pragmatism and God's resurrection

Like Marx, Kierkegaard, and Nietzsche, three American philosophers, Peirce, James, and Dewey, wanted to bring philosophy back to earth. Their attitude to systems like that of Hegel was tersely summed up in one of William James's letters, "Damn the Absolute!"[43] They, especially James, wanted to ensure the connection of philosophy with the personal, immediate concerns of our daily lives. While the pragmatists are somewhat more at home with the British empiricists than with the continental rationalists, they thought that both groups were insufficiently respectful of the connections between thought and action.[44] Peirce coined the word "pragmatism" from the Greek *pragma,* meaning act or deed.[45] To understand what people are saying when they use terms like "person," the pragmatists would ask us to cash it out in terms of what those people using the term "person" would do under various conditions. Action is the underpinning of meaning.

To understand this theory of meaning a little, let us look first at a much simpler concept than that of a person, the concept of hardness. To say that *x* is harder than *y*, according to Peirce's theory of meaning, is to assert a series of conditionals. One of these conditionals is this: if a sharp point of *x* is drawn firmly across a smooth surface of *y*, then *x* will leave a scratch in *y*. What these conditional statements do is to relate the concept of hardness to things we can do to test for the applicability of the concept. Now to return to the more complex concept of a person, to explain to Peirce what I mean by saying that Kyle is a person, I would have to explain what effects this would have on my actions. I might, for example, say that in choosing between the mitigation of the physical suffering of my dog, which I dearly love, and the suffering of Kyle, whom I loathe, I would have to opt for the mitigating the suffering of Kyle. If I could only rescue one of them from a burning building, for instance, it would have to be Kyle. For Peirce, this sort of answer begins to explain my concept of a person. On the other hand, if I were to say that a person is a particular spatio-temporal expression of the ongoing dialectical development of spirit, Peirce would respond, Whoa! How does that affect what you would do? or words to that effect. If I told him that there were no practical effects of my use of "person," he would consider that usage empty of meaning. Eventually Peirce gave up this theory of meaning since it led him to subjectivism.[46] The theory of meaning and subjectivism were taken up and popularized by William James.

Peirce's method of looking for outcomes for action was carried on by William James, who wove into it the theme of the importance of the will. Like Schopenhauer, Kierkegaard, and Nietzsche, the pragmatists were willing to dethrone reason, but they did not make the will supreme. James tried to find a careful balance between the two. Unlike Schopenhauer and Nietzsche, who focus on the will to overpower others, James, like Kierkegaard, attends to the will to believe. When it comes to the truth of our beliefs, however, James, like all the pragmatists, takes the truth to be what works. Peirce thought of statements which worked in the sense of standing up to scientific testing. Dewey looked for the social usefulness of beliefs. James is the most relevant to our present purposes since he focused on what works personally. He speaks of passional grounds for belief which go well beyond what we might believe on the basis of scientific evidence. By passional beliefs he seems to mean beliefs based on emotion and will.

There are cases in which reason cannot decide an issue even in the way of saying which of two hypotheses would work best for us as a belief. James tells us that in such cases, it is reasonable to follow one's heart—rather than to adopt an agnostic attitude—if certain special conditions obtain. The conditions are that we have at least two clear, live, momentous hypotheses between which we are forced to decide.[47] A poignant instance is the decision between these: She loves me; She loves me not. These hypotheses are certainly clear, in pragmatist terms, since I know just what I would expect her to do if she loves me. They are live hypotheses in the sense that they have a strong connection with my life since I love her. They are momentous since, whichever I adopt, it will have a profound effect on what I do. They are forced since no answer is also an answer in this case. If I remain agnostic in the circumstances in which I find myself, that is as good as saying she does not love me and acting accordingly. This would be terrible if indeed she does love me. So how would William James advise me?

The option to believe she loves me or believe she does not is living, momentous, and forced, a genuine option in James's terms. In this very special kind of case of a genuine option and, only in such cases, James would tell me to exercise my will to believe.[48] Reason cannot help me. I should believe what I want to be true. I do this. If I believe that she loves me, this has profound consequences for action in the way I trust her, confide in her, and commit myself to her. If she responds in kind, my belief is confirmed. Yet I had to believe it first and have it confirmed later, unlike my scientific hypotheses. The truth, in such special cases, is only revealed if we first believe it. In some cases the truth is created by the will to believe it as it would be—if my belief and consequent actions helped her to come to love me after the fact of my believing that she loved me.

One might object that it is possible to proceed experimentally in such a case without adopting the firm belief that she loves me. This seems to me to be impossible if I really love her, but let us give the objection a run. First of all, one must be a very good actor to pursue such an experiment, as people are incredibly good at detecting inauthentic behaviour in others. James might also reply that in such a case the decision is not truly momentous for me. It would be momentous if, for instance, I had to take an enormous risk by trusting her—say the risk of my entire psychological, financial, social, or political well-being. One may still call it an experiment, but that is an odd name for betting one's life. Not mere curiosity or scientific interest but an enormously strong will to believe is required to make even the decision to act as if she loves me. And, in fact, if I really do love her, the devastating effects of dithering with experimentation in any way that might alienate her love make experimentation a fool's game.

Because James has this method of adopting beliefs on the ground of will, he personalizes pragmatism. Peirce and Dewey stick more to the experimental method. Dewey looks at people more as biological problem solvers trying to survive with intelligence as a primary means of adapting to the environment. One does not need, in this view, some Kantian notion of persons as ends nor essentialist doctrines about what we are to decide what to do. Each decision is taken on the merits of the particular case. The norms left to us by earlier philosophers and religious thinkers have to be taken as some among many that might be useful in solving a particular problem. In general, Dewey looked to the natural sciences for information which would be helpful in such problem solving. He thought we should pool our wisdom gained from experience to make moral and political decisions. The way to do this, from his perspective, was through democracy. Moral decisions look more like political ones in Dewey's version of pragmatism.[49] The emphasis on the individual comes out in James.

What about Daphne?

In general, a pragmatic approach to the problem of understanding the nature of persons and the criteria for their survival over time forces us to look at these concepts in terms of action. We need to know the difference it would make to what we do, should we adopt one or other of the many concepts of a person that parade by in the history of the topic. If, for example, it makes no difference to the treatment we accord to a demented person whether or not we say she is the same person she was before the dementia, then the question of her survival becomes uninteresting. Yet surely this would be a peculiar result. We should look then for the difference it would make. One example of a difference is in the gratitude we owe to some people but not commonly to non-persons. A person's good works in the past make us the more willing to make sacrifices on her behalf now. Were she a totally new person, such sacrifices would be completely supererogatory. One should feel no more motivation to make them than one should in the case of beneficence to a total stranger. It seems, then, that from the pragmatist point of view, the capacity to bring about debts of gratitude and their consequent actions is part of the concept of a person.

Another thing that at least James's version of pragmatism brings to the debate about persons is a response to the welter of confusion about facts pertinent to the discussion. In cases of dementia, we have no way of knowing what is happening in the mind of the affected person. Even if we could decide on some firm criteria of adequacy for survival, we might be always unable to decide, on the basis of the available evidence, whether the person we are dealing with satisfies these criteria. For example, if memory of certain crucial events in life prior to the onset of dementia is required for someone to be the same person, we might never know if she is the same person, since she cannot communicate. Under such conditions, James's passional grounds for belief come into play.

What I like about the pragmatists

The forthright insistence that we say what difference our theories make is refreshing. The idea that our beliefs about persons are relative to social or even personal decisions is interesting. The metaphysical and the moral are knit together in a new way by the links of our concepts to our actions through the theory of meaning.

It is interesting that, as pragmatism was ushering in the contemporary secular era, James was defending faith, including religious faith, under the conditions discussed above. In our own era faith of any sort is often considered suspect, so we hide it—even our own faith from ourselves. James wryly reports:

> I have long defended to my own students the lawfulness of voluntarily adopted faith; but as soon as they have got well imbued with the logical spirit, they have as a rule refused to admit my contention to be lawful philosophically, even though in point of fact they were personally all the time chock-full of some faith or other themselves.[50]

It is interesting to contemplate the decision to believe or not believe in God as a genuine option, living, momentous, and forced.

We now turn to a group of contemporary philosophers who, unlike most contemporary philosophers, tend to take a great deal on faith.

Content questions

1. What destroys the natural goodness of persons on Rousseau's view?
2. Why is it wrong to use people merely as a means to someone else's end?
3. What does Kant think about perceptions and perceivers in contrast to Hume?
4. Why is Kant's view only a slight improvement on Hume's where metaphysical personal identity is concerned?
5. How can there be personal freedom on Kant's view? Use the distinction of the noumenal from phenomenal reality in your response.
6. What is the only thing that is good in itself according to Kant?
7. Why must persons be immortal in Kant's view?
8. How does Hegel deny the distinction of perceiving a subject (a person) and the object that person perceives?
9. How does Hegel's concept of the Absolute leave room for individuality?
10. What is the principle of sufficient reason?
11. How can the self know itself according to Schopenhauer?
12. Summarize utilitarianism, and say how it undermines individualism.
13. In what sense does Marx deny that there is an essential human nature, and in what sense does he assert that there is one?
14. If people in capitalist democracies share many of Marx's ideals, what is the critical difference between Marx and such capitalists?
15. How is Kierkegaard different from most philosophers with respect to his attitudes to faith and reason?
16. What does Nietzsche think of the traditional virtues of humility, patience, and diligence?
17. How do pragmatists think we should understand the word "person"?

Arguments for analysis

Argument 1: Kant's objection to Hume

If there is an experience of something, then it always makes sense to ask who had that experience. The idea of experience, knowledge or perception without a person to have these is incoherent. In fact we do notice ourselves when we think of that which connects all of our experiences at a particular moment. Therefore there must be a unified self or person as the one who has the experience.

Argument 2: Kant's disappearing act II

Our introspective experience of ourselves as the connection between our othece on one occasion of introspection is identical to the self we experience on another occasion of introspection. If we rely on experience alone to prove the existence of ourselves through time, we would have to admit the possibility that we are a series of non-identical selves.

Argument 3: Kant's noumenal/phenomenal distinction

In response to the disappearing act II, Kant argues that we exist not only through time, but forever. He distinguishes between the world we know through experience, the phenomenal world, and the unknowable part of reality, the noumenal world that transcends the phenomenal. A sketch of the argument is as follows:

We are free and perfectible beings.

If we attend only to the phenomenal world, these things do not seem possible (because everything has a cause in the phenomenal world and there is limited time.)

There must, therefore, be a noumenal world beyond the phenomenal to make freedom and perfectibility possible.

In this argument, axiology influences metaphysics. It is also an example of a style of argument sometimes called "Dialectic." Caution, this word "dialectic" has various meanings. As used by Fichte, two opposites, the thesis and the antithesis, leads to a synthesis that unites the other two. Noumenal freedom is the synthesis that resolves the apparent contradiction between freedom and causation.

Argument 4: Hegel's dialectic concerning freedom

The individual person has a right to express her freedom.

The state has the right to restrict the individual expression of freedom.

Therefore, there is a higher freedom for the individual in harmonizing her will with the universal will (submitting to the state.)

Argument 5: Schopenhauer's argument against freedom

Every event has a cause.

Free will is only possible if our choices are not caused.

Therefore, there is no free will.

Argument 6: Bentham's arguments for utilitarianism

The good is that which all sentient beings seek, while evil is what all things avoid.

All sentient beings seek pleasure and avoid pain.

Therefore, pleasure is good and evil is pain.

The right action is the one that does the most good and the least evil. Since pleasure is good, while pain is evil, the right action is the one that maximizes pleasure and minimizes pain for all the sentient beings affected by that action.

Part 4

Contemporary Philosophers' Views on Persons

CHAPTER 8

Our Contemporaries (or Almost)

System builders are still around

It is popular today to think that our worship of science and technology has led us astray, that we have ignored Socrates' advice to know ourselves, that our attempt to conquer nature is leading to our own demise, and that we have left something important out in our way of gaining knowledge about the world. Early in this century, Bergson was arguing in concert with such thoughts that the scientific way of knowing is incomplete. Bergson develops a system of philosophy in which the distinction between analysis and intuition is fundamental. Analysis is our typical way of knowing an object. We compare it to other things. We look at its structure and its parts. We represent it in descriptions. In science we do this with mathematical precision. Knowing an object by analysis "implies that we move around the object," in contrast to knowing it by intuition, in which case "we enter into it."[1] Knowing a thing by intuition is knowing what it is like to be that thing, to have that thing's perspective in the universe, not to see it from the outside. It is very difficult to get a grip on the concept of intuition, especially as applied to inanimate objects, but, given the topic at hand, we will look only at the more comprehensible case of knowledge of other persons.

Notes to chapter 8 are on pp. 483-84.

Bergson: Seeing ourselves from inside

Bergson considers the way in which we know the hero in a novel through the detailed story about the character the author gives us. Bergson contrasts this analytical knowledge of the character with the empathetic knowledge by intuition. Speaking of the story, he says, "all this can never be equivalent to the simple and indivisible feeling which I should experience if I were able for an instant to identify myself with the person of the hero himself."[2] You have to stand in the hero's shoes to know the hero. You cannot just rely on comparison of the hero to others and such analytic ways of knowing the hero because these ways all look at the hero from the outside. The inside view, which we can get by intuition, reveals not what the hero has in common with others but what is unique to that person. This is the crux of the matter. Analysis gives us the common denominator, the ways in which a person can be compared to others. Intuition reveals the person's essence—which is the central core of that person and of that person alone—whereby a person can be distinguished from others.

The essence of a person or of anything whatever is inexpressible in symbols. It can only be directly experienced. Analysis, which relies on symbols, of necessity, leaves the essence out. We each of us know ourselves in the direct, intuitive way, so we know how inadequate mere analytic knowledge of a person can be. Bergson's system is aimed at getting us to take knowledge of ourselves as a model when we try to know other persons and, indeed, all other things.

When we use the method of analysis we are forced to describe persons and other things as if they exist at certain locations in space and time. This, however, is just a useful fiction, an intellectual supposition, which allows our analysis to proceed. It may be useful for prediction and control of events to proceed this way. Science and technology make use of that. We should not, however, confuse this description of ourselves with reality. In reality, as we know from seeing ourselves endure, things are always in the process of change and becoming, not a series of static states at points of space and time. Analysis, in effect, takes a series of snapshots of events and misses the flow and duration of things. Everything is always changing and moving. Bergson describes reality as "tendency, if we agree to mean by tendency an incipient change of direction."[3]

The whole of reality turns out to be, in Bergson's system, one large creative process he calls the Élan Vital, of which we are expressions, not parts.[4] Intellect, which can only grasp the symbolic output of analysis, cannot make sense of Élan Vital. Only by intuition can we see reality this way. By making us all expressions of a single indivisible process, Bergson has revived to some extent the Oriental absorption of the individual into the whole. In his view, however, persons each have a unique essence. Although we all express the Élan Vital, we all do so in our own ways. Seen from the inside, by intuition, each person is completely unique. Individuality is preserved after all.

Another familiar theme, that of personal freedom, is also taken up by Bergson. Intuitively we know we choose freely, but analysis falsely supports the idea that our actions are causally determined. In Goudge's assessment, Bergson appeals more to the strain of romantic individualism that we saw in the very different philosophy of Rousseau than he appeals to the empiricist tradition that he claims for his own.[5]

Whitehead: Persons as processes

The Romantic poets would have agreed with Bergson that science leaves something crucial out of its account of the universe. Expressing his agreement with this tendency in Romanticism, represented in the person of Wordsworth, Alfred North Whitehead says: "neither physical nature nor life can be understood unless we fuse them together as essential factors in the composition of really real things whose interconnections and individual characters constitute the universe."[6] Scientific method involves separating objects and processes from the whole, breaking them down and isolating them for study. This has led to rapid improvement of our ability to manipulate our environment through the prediction and control of events. While it was not so clear in Wordsworth's time that we were destroying the whole of our environment in our attempt to dominate nature, it was already evident that we were destroying ourselves in another way by becoming divorced from nature. Later Whitehead was to take up in the realm of systematic philosophy Wordsworth's theme of holism—the inclusion of the spiritual and the moral as well as the analytical knowledge of our world. Whitehead developed a philosophical system in which he emphasized process as opposed to isolated objects, and he sought to understand the interconnection of all things.

As with Bergson's system, perhaps one cannot understand Whitehead piecemeal, but for our present purposes what is of interest is that, like Bergson, rather than trying to force persons into the Procrustean bed of science, Whitehead takes our experience of ourselves as fundamental and understands other things in terms of that experience. Whitehead tells us that he is closely concerned with what Bergson calls "intuition."[7] What we experience is constant change. We are processes. Rather than a universe populated with static objects, Whitehead presents to us a universe which is like a person on a grander scale. This is a theme we have seen interwoven in other systems. Rather than objects Whitehead speaks of actual occasions which are, roughly, like our experiences, dynamic processes. Thus, instead of reducing persons to aggregates of static, analyzable physical objects of the sort that we postulate in order to pursue our scientific aims, Whitehead sees all of nature as an aggregate of actual occasions.[8]

Seeing persons, and indeed anything, as if what science says about them is literally true is, for Whitehead, to commit the fallacy of misplaced concreteness.[9] That is to say, we take the intellectual abstractions of science and treat them as if they were concrete things. The idea that there are bits of matter, for instance, at particular spatiotemporal locations is an example of this fallacy. These bits of matter are merely abstractions, not concrete parts of reality. Where persons are concerned, this fallacy leads to problems like the problem of the interaction of mind and body.

For Whitehead, there is no problem, since mind and body are merely abstractions, not real static entities which must somehow be shown to interact. They are just abstractions from the flow of experience, from the actual occasions which make up the whole of the universe. Whitehead speaks of "societies" of actual occasions which we can think of as, roughly, sets of processes. Mind and body are such societies. Just as the body politic is an abstraction, the body of a particular person is an abstraction, a way of looking at a particular set of processes.[10] Mind and body are interconnected, then, just as all things are, for they are composed of interpenetrating processes within the large process which is the universe. More prosaically, mind and body are just different ways we have of looking at our experience: "It is a matter of pure convention as to which of our experiential activities we term mental and which physical."[11] The experiences are real. Mind and body are things we make up to organize our thinking about the experiences. Persons, too, are societies of actual occasions, like eddies in the stream of the universe.

What about Daphne?

Bergson and Whitehead probably would find the puzzles about whether Daphne is a person and whether she is the same person she was prior to her illness result from a failure to see the limits of a conceptual scheme which works well only for scientific investigation. If we populate our universe not with individual entities but with actual occasions known by intuition, then it is merely a conventional matter how we solve our puzzles about Daphne. What is important is not what we call Daphne, but how we understand her changes and her current needs. Standing in her shoes is the task.

What I like about Bergson and Whitehead

The idea that we take our self-knowledge not as a goal but as a starting point interests me. It does seem that I have a certain intimate knowledge of myself that I can only in imagination have of other people or of other things. The notion of people and things as processes seems right from this perspective.

Contemporary Continental philosophy

The two main methods in contemporary philosophy are often labelled the Analytic and Continental schools. The Analytic school is the main contender in Britain and North America—although there are many philosophers on the continent who would consider themselves part of this school, as there are many Continental philosophers who do not reside in continental Europe. Some British and North American philosophers, like Whitehead, defy classification. As I was brought up in the Analytic school, I am about to give relatively short shrift to the contemporary Continental philosophers on the other side of a methodological chasm. As far as I can, however, I will try to draw out some of the influences of this important group of philosophers on our—the Analytic side's—current thinking concerning persons. At the very least, like the foregoing historical introduction, this can serve readers as a menu of ideas.

As to the methodological chasm between the schools, it is wide indeed. It is, moreover, only fair to warn those of you who have not yet encountered the chasm of which I speak that many in the Analytic school applaud these sentiments of David Berlinski: "Although great soupy volumes pour off the European presses with the inevitability of death, much of what results calls to mind only the perfect vacuum."[12] How you take this warning about soup—as an indictment of the Analytic school's attempts at clarity or of the Continental school's attempts at profundity—will depend on your own predilections. The soup results, according to Leslie Stevenson, from length, repetitiousness, and "a word-spinning delight in the abstract noun, the elusive metaphor, and the unresolved paradox."[13] Stevenson does, however, think that Sartre's *Being and Nothingness*, for example, contains important and deep analyses.[14] I think that Stevenson is right about the Continental philosophers having insights worth our attention, but it is not merely a difference in style which separates the two schools. Continental philosophers, at the very least, adopt a different methodology to investigate philosophical questions, and sometimes they are engaged in a wholly different project to that of Analytic philosophers.

Analytic philosophers seek, through objective, logical, rational inquiry, to understand our fundamental concepts. Some philosophers who were at least geographically continental—such as Husserl, Brentano, and Meinong, for example—would accept this as their project as well. Others, like Sartre and Heidegger, I suspect, adopt a much more literary approach, even a poetic one. The very word-play, metaphors, and repetition that annoy Stevenson and outrage Berlinski are their means to lead their readers to truths which philosophers of the Analytic school may take to be ineffable in their more precise language. The objectivity which Analytic philosophers seek is thought by the Continentals to be fool's gold. That is why, like mystics and poets, Continental philosophers allow themselves the statement of an unresolved paradox or two in their immense tomes. They seek to achieve with the weight of words what the weight of argument can never achieve. While the Analytic school accuses the Continental school of betraying reason, the Continental school retorts that profundity will not be found within the limits of rational analysis. Since it takes a fair chunk of one's life spent in study to read either school well, it is best to find out early on which kind of method attracts you most.

The roots, at least, of the Continental school are partly shared with those of the Analytic school. Both recognize the importance of the philosophers mentioned in the historical survey of previous chapters. Kierkegaard, however, is of seminal importance for the Continental philosophers since he introduces most of the themes of the existentialists. Along with existentialism, phenomenology—the creation of Edmund Husserl—is a key element in the thinking of many of the Continental school philosophers. I consequently begin my too brief exposition of the contributions of the Continental school to our topic with a look at Husserl's phenomenology.

Husserl: Phenomenology

Husserl, who began his career as a mathematician, has a painstaking and highly technical style of philosophizing which has not gained him many readers outside academic circles. This is in marked contrast to Jean-Paul Sartre, who has made his ideas accessible through his literary work as well as in stylistically more entertaining philosophical writings. Nonetheless, Husserl's influence is much felt among us even in lay circles, since it has been transmitted through Sartre and other widely read existentialists; this is not to say that existentialists generally agree with Husserl in detail. Husserl's influence spread well beyond philosophy, especially in psychology and theology, but in the human sciences generally. What we think of as persons now cannot but be affected by so pervasive an influence.

Although Husserl is moved, like the pragmatists and like the existentialists, by a reaction to the excessive claims of science to understand us, he is very unlike the pragmatists and existentialists in one key respect. They recommend renouncing the role of spectator and, instead, passionately engaging the world through decision and commitment. Husserl seeks, by contrast, to give a rigorous foundation to philosophy by utterly detaching himself from the world. His motive, as Stumpf sees it, is to save human reason from being misled by a naive scientific naturalism which erroneously seeks to reduce even the spiritual aspects of persons to physical nature.[15] From Husserl's point of view, if we are to understand ourselves, we must adopt a method quite different from that of the natural sciences, and we must give up many of the presuppositions of these sciences.

Science presupposes, for instance, observable objects existing independently of the persons observing them. Husserl wants to restrict attention to the evidence we actually have without such presuppositions; that evidence is our pre-scientific experience. The phenomena of experience—without any assumptions about their causal or other relations to things outside the experiencing Ego—are the data of the phenomenologist. Phenomenology is, according to its inventor, the science of phenomena. It will not replace the other sciences but will provide an adequate basis for their conduct. Husserl explains, in great detail, a method of looking at phenomena without the influence of all of our assumptions about where they come from and what they represent. This method of *epoche* or bracketing allows us to bracket out all distracting influences and observe the pure phenomena. Husserl tells us in the introduction to *Ideas* that it will take a lot of work to follow the method he outlines, that it is not everyone's cup of tea, but that we should not knock it until we have tried it.[16]

Husserl tells us that we will find, employing *epoche*, that consciousness is always directed to something and that there is always present the experiencing subject or Ego. We will attend to the full richness of our experience, not merely to the limited abstractions of science. We will see that this experience is quite independent of the existence of a world external to the experiencing Ego.[17] Our own consciousness and intentionality, the direction of consciousness to things of which we are conscious, are the fundamental facts to which we have access, not the supposed objective facts of science. These latter are really abstractions, extrapolations from our fundamental experience. Western man is in a crisis, according to Husserl, by virtue of taking science to be the sole source of truth.[18] This direction away from the human and personal to things outside ourselves cuts us off from the basis of knowledge, our own experience. We have to look inward again. This emphasis on the subjective elements of experience and their aspects ignored by natural science is part of what endears Husserl to the existentialist tradition. Nonetheless, there is a strain against that tradition which becomes evident when we see just how restricted is the realm explored by means of *epoche*.

Most of the things that philosophers have taken an interest in are excluded from our attention through *epoche*. This method is only for the study of particular pure experiences—which Husserl calls "immanental essences"—and is of no use for the study of things we do not meet in pure experience devoid of assumptions. The terms "man," "soul," and "person" are explicitly mentioned as referring to essences which are beyond the pale of phenomenology.[19] These are the kinds of things we can investigate only after we have established the firm foundation needed through the study of our basic experience.

Persons are, for Husserl, transcendental essences; that is, they are not met in our fundamental experience. Neither is the Ego, although it is always there having the experience. We have earlier seen Hume's denial that he can find an Ego in himself. What Husserl has to say in answer to Hume is expressed in a way congenial to both the poet and the mathematician:

> The Ego appears to be permanently, even necessarily, there, and this permanence is obviously not that of a stolid unshifting experience, of a "fixed idea." On the contrary, it belongs to every experience that comes and streams past, its "glance" goes "through" every actual *cogito* [act of thinking], and towards the object. This visual ray changes with every *cogito*, shooting forth afresh with each new one as it comes, and disappearing with it. But the Ego remains self-identical.[20]

There is still a debate in current philosophy about the existence of this Ego. The importance of intentionality, however, is almost universally accepted when the topic of persons arises. Husserl teaches that acts of consciousness are intentional, meaning that they are directed to something.

Persons, for some philosophers, simply are the sort of Ego of which Husserl spoke. Husserl himself, however, thought they were a more complicated kind of thing to be understood only after an ontology (a theory of objects) and an epistemology (a theory of knowledge) had been established phenomenologically as the underpinning of the philosophical and scientific work to be done. He had the effect of turning our attention from the exclusively empirical scientific outlook on persons to the things we can know only subjectively.

Heidegger: Being toward death

Jaspers, Marcel, and Heidegger write in such difficult styles that they seem intent on confirming the saying that the philosopher and the poet are neighbours on separate mountains. Kierkegaard, Jaspers, and Marcel retain a religious motivation for their philosophy, while Heidegger departs from this. Throughout these existentialist writings one finds an emphasis on the importance and uniqueness of the individual person and the theme taken up by Husserl of the distinction of philosophy from science. Personal self-realization is the main focus in Jaspers and Marcel. Heidegger set for himself the question of the nature of being and produced, in *Being and Time*,[21] one of the most revered works among existentialists.

Heidegger's question is rather more general than our present topic, but his way to an answer is through the elucidation of persons' awareness of themselves. As did others in his tradition, Heidegger inveighed against the objectification of persons who cannot be understood in the way that the objects of scientific study can be known. The attempt to define "person" by listing the essential properties that a thing must have to be a person is, for Heidegger, thoroughly wrongheaded. To avoid this error of treating persons as definable objects, Heidegger coins his own word to avoid the use of "person," "man," or "human being," which all carry with them the taint of previous philosophy's mistakes. Instead, Heidegger uses *Dasein* (literally: "being there"). I will stick to using "person" with apologies to Heideggerians. For Heidegger, to understand what being is, one must understand how a person has being. Like most philosophers on this side of the Analytic/Continental chasm, I do not have too much patience for being with a capital B. While I cannot be counted on to give a totally sympathetic account of Heidegger's project and achievements, I do wish to draw out some of the themes he attached to our contemporary concepts of a person.

Three things that Heidegger associates with a person (*Dasein*) are understanding, mood, and discourse.[22] It is tempting to read Heidegger as treating the capacity for these as essential to the existence of persons, but this would be contrary to his claim that no essence can be given. Under the general head of understanding, Heidegger speaks of the way in which particular things are meaningful to us in terms of purposes. We encounter things in the world as tools. What they are depends on our network of purposes. Thus the world is a characteristic of the person rather than the person being a thing in the world. Each of us has a world that depends on our purposes. Moreover, a mood, say, of despair or joy with which we encounter things will affect as well the way they exist for us. Before we can understand or feel about an object in some way, however, we must be able to talk about it. Thus the world for Heidegger depends on persons, on their understanding, mood, and discourse.

Heidegger teaches that we prepare ourselves to understand being when we recognize our own temporality, when we recognize that we are living toward our deaths in the dread of annihilation. The capacity of persons under the heading of mood seems to be most important as a capacity for dread and care. Without these to reveal to us the "nothingness" within us and our temporal finitude, we cannot know what we really are. Only if we recognize our limitations can we live authentically. To live so is to affirm what we really are and to live accordingly, not to deceive ourselves with thoughts of immortality or actions appropriate to some other kinds of being than what we are.[23] Understanding our own way of being in this world is a key, for Heidegger, to understanding being in general.

If indeed the world depends on persons, then there are many worlds. In each one what constitutes a person may be different from what does so in the other worlds. Questions about how we should view or treat others must all have completely subjective answers. The appeal of Heidegger's advice on authenticity and living in the recognition of our own finitude notwithstanding, there are no bounds on what may be justified by such a philosophy. Heidegger's own answer to the question of how to treat others included, as an important part, Naziism. Often this is excused as a naive mistake from which he retreated. Farias argues, however, that Naziism was fully integrated in Heidegger's thought and that he carried it with him to the grave[24]—a good place for it.

Be that as it may, it is not clear to me how a subjectivist theory of persons could oppose Naziism or any other doctrine on the grounds of proper treatment of persons. One of the points of discussing persons is to put up the barricades when Naziism and similar doctrines surface. During the Nazi era, destructive experimentation, involuntary euthanasia, torture, and genocide were carried out on people who had been pushed by loose Nazi theory beyond the pale within which persons were protected. The mentally incompetent were put to death because they were a burden to the state. People were put to death for being critical of Naziism. Individual people were not highly valued. More than the absorption of the individual into the state, however, brought about this Holocaust. The Nazis believed that they could do whatever they wished to the Jews, since they did not consider them to be full persons. Similarly, the Romans once thought they could treat slaves just as they wished, because slaves were not persons under the law. Settlers in the Americas thought—some contemporaries in my locale think—of Aboriginal peoples as less than persons. Clear thinking about persons is needed as a small but vital part of the rampart that we must erect against such horrific errors.

Sartre: What you do is what you are

Jean-Paul Sartre makes more accessible some of the existentialist doctrines through his literary works, though he also adds considerably to the corpus of inaccessible philosophical writing on existentialist themes. He, like Heidegger, develops an atheistic form of existentialism[25] and, like Heidegger, is influenced by Husserl's phenomenology. A major difference between them is in the focus of their interests. For Heidegger, understanding the person in the world is merely a means to the central question of what being is. Sartre, however, makes the individual person his main concern.

Action is foremost in Sartre's analysis of persons. It is what we do that is important. Think of the characters in his play *Huis Clos*: their hell is to look back on their actions and to be constantly reminded by one another that they failed to come up to their own personal standards. Through these reminders of their own inauthenticity they are denied the temporary solace of self-deception; they must contemplate what they did. To point out Sartre's emphasis on action is not to say that Sartre any more than Heidegger accepts the possibility of defining the concept of a person through consideration of capacities for action or any other characteristics. His motto is: "Existence precedes essence."[26]

To understand this, it is interesting to consider the idea of an unnatural act. There are none, as far as Sartre is concerned. There is no pre-existing nature or essence of a person which determines what the individual ought to do. We are completely free to choose, within the limits of physical possibility, what we do, and we are even free to choose the criteria in general according to which we make particular choices. Sartre is an atheist, so he denies that there is any God to foist on us an antecedent nature or essence that would make our action unnatural. First we come into existence, then, after we are able to choose, we make our individual characters or natures. If there were a God, then essence could precede existence, for we could be supplied with a pre-existing pattern of action or purpose to which we ought to conform.

It is tempting to say, paradoxically, that Sartre would say that it is of the essence of a person to be a free agent. The paradox is removed by noticing that "essence" in this claim does not refer to the kind of essence which is preceded by existence in Sartre's motto. The person first exists and then chooses her own pattern of action, values, or purposes—in that sense she chooses her essence. "Essence" in that sense is not a set of defining characteristics like being free, being conscious, or being able to act. Sartre is willing to assert the necessity of various characteristics of persons aside from their being free agents. In this other sense of "essence," in which essences are sets of necessary characteristics, Sartre could admit that there is an essence of persons prior to the existence of individual persons. There are, in other words, characteristics which all persons must have, according to Sartre, to be persons. What he wants to deny is that such characteristics determine what we as individuals do or ought to do. Our actions are free.

These necessary characteristics of persons distinguish people (beings for themselves) from objects (beings in themselves). A terribly important distinguishing characteristic—dare I say *essential* characteristic?—of people, for Sartre, is consciousness. As conscious beings, people—unlike their objects of consciousness—can distinguish themselves from their objects and choose for themselves the importance and purpose those objects will have. Problems arise, however, when conscious beings contemplate one another. Interpersonal relationships fascinate Sartre and reveal some of the essential or defining characteristics of the concept of a person in his philosophy. An existentialist would prefer to say that they reveal the general framework within which individual persons define themselves—that is, the human condition.

Consciousness, in Sartre's view, is—as with Brentano and Husserl—necessarily directed to something. Sartre also thinks that consciousness makes what is other than itself a mere object. Consequently, two conscious beings who are aware of each other will be trying to make of each other an object rather than a person. "[H]e analyses human life as a perpetual attempt to achieve the logically impossible," says Stevenson in great irritation; he goes on to say that this contradicts Sartre's claims about our freedom, since it seems we must try to make other people into mere objects whether we want to or not.[27] Perhaps Sartre could reply that we are not free to exert some superhuman form of consciousness which does not objectify others any more than we are free to fly by flapping our arms. If so, then he thinks he has discovered some of our mental limits. This is one of several tantalizing suggestions by Sartre about the concept of a person, but I find that closer examination of such works as *Being and Nothingness* does not help to clarify it. Sartre's writing often seems like an enormous impressionist canvas. It does not usually help to understand the work to look at it under a magnifying glass. We are left then with the suggestion that one limit on all persons is that they cannot see other persons as persons. One may have some dark moods if one comes to believe this. In any case, it is in the realm of intuitive psychology more than philosophy.

Most philosophical theories about persons either begin from or end in moral pronouncements about what persons ought to do. Sartre has denied that there is anything in the nature of persons that can determine what we ought to do. We each of us must choose our own moral values. Sartre does, however, follow earlier existentialists in condemning inauthenticity, bad faith, or self-deception. These occur, for instance, when a person wants to be a hero but acts in a cowardly way and then pretends that the action was beyond her control. Sartre despised such excuses as, I was overcome by subconscious forces, or I didn't know what I was doing. One who gives such excuses is being self-deceptive and acting in bad faith.

It seems, then, that while Sartre is willing to promulgate no particular moral view, he does offer a criterion for the acceptability of any moral view. One must adopt it in good faith. The particular standards of action are totally relative to the individual. Sartre cannot condemn Hitler as acting against absolute standards but only as acting against Sartre's personal standards—although in choosing standards for himself, Sartre chooses them for all. As long as Hitler did the same and lived by his chosen standards, Sartre would not despise him for being in bad faith. If, however, Mother Teresa undertook her charitable work in bad faith pretending, say, that she was forced to do it by God, then Sartre would find her life contemptible. This is another feature of Sartre's view to which Stevenson objects,[28] but I believe Sartre would just bite the bullet and accept these consequences. Mother Teresa would be more contemptible than Hitler if the former but not the latter were inauthentic.

Stevenson, like many of us who tear our hair out reading Sartre's philosophical writings, still believes that: "there is something important to learn from Sartre's deep analysis of how the very notion of consciousness involves that of freedom.…The vast verbiage of his philosophy issues ultimately in a directly practical and intimate challenge to us all, to become more truly self-aware and to exercise our power of changing ourselves."[29]

What about Daphne?

The themes that these Continental philosophers emphasize seem inapplicable to someone who cannot make choices or express them. Like Bergson and Whitehead, the Continentals would encourage us to drop the conceptual schemes in which our puzzles occur. They tend, nonetheless, to emphasize the relativity or even subjectivity of conceptual frameworks. There is no such thing as "the nature of persons" to which we may appeal to understand Daphne or our role with regard to her. It turns out to be our choice as to Daphne's status that we must examine. She may not be, in Sartre's terms, a being for herself, free, conscious, and able to act. In deciding how to think of Daphne as a being in herself we must choose authentically, not pretending that there is some essence which keeps her in continuation despite our own choices. In some ways, this seems as if we are saying that Daphne is not a person, since we others must choose for her.

What I like about the Continental school

Husserl makes sense when he speaks of the Ego as that which belongs to every experience without itself being experienced—like the eye which sees but does not see itself except through reflection. What sort of mirror, if any, would allow the Ego to experience itself? Here the analogy breaks down. The reiteration of the importance by Husserl and his school of the role of our subjective knowledge and experience is, in any case, salutary.

The Heiddegerian ideal of living authentically, in recognition of our own finitude, is useful. It leads into Sartre's denial of any human nature to which we must conform, a radical kind of freedom to choose what we are. Sartre's analysis may be deep, but it is muddy. The philosophical problem he leaves us is to see whether his challenge makes sense. Are we free in a way that allows us to change our characters and our moods? Can we overcome the influence of our cultures? I believe that Sartre has, in fact, insightfully described a kind of person, at least in broad brush strokes. I hope, however, that we who fit the description can, in special circumstances, overcome the tendency to objectify other persons and ourselves, for example, when we really love. Sartre might say that I misunderstand entirely the limits on consciousness. My initial reply is that I see the limits of freedom differently, but that leads to a story to be told after this brief survey of contemporary philosophy.

Derrida and Foucault omitted

More recent philosophy in Europe has departed even further from the school in which I find myself. There is a tendency to move entirely from the philosophical method to that of literary criticism and beyond. This is the natural outcome of complete subjectivism. Truth becomes a matter of taste. Rorty describes the new method as creatively ignoring one's opponents. Rather than offering arguments, one develops a new vocabulary and attempts to make one's opponents' vocabulary look bad.[30] Derrida may be adopting such a method. Foucault uses a multidisciplinary approach that goes well beyond the scope of what I produce in this work. I leave both Foucault and Derrida out of discussion here. Some may find that an unforgivable omission, but I can only refer my readers to these authors in the original. They, like poets, defy summary.

Content questions

1. What does Bergson mean by "intuition" as a form of knowledge of persons?
2. How does Bergson use intuition against the puzzle of whether persons have free choice?
3. How is Whitehead's system similar to Bergson's?
4. What is the fallacy of misplaced concreteness?
5. How does Whitehead solve the mind-body interaction problem?
6. What is the methodological difference between the Analytic school and the Continental school of philosophy?
7. In what way is Husserl's method of *epoche* very restricted?
8. How is the world a characteristic of persons for Heidegger? This reminds me of Protagoras.
9. Sartre's view of persons is sometimes characterized by the saying, To do is to be. Why?
10. In what sense of "essence" does existence precede essence for persons, according to Sartre?
11. Why are personal relationships doomed from Sartre's point of view?
12. While Sartre promotes no moral view, he does offer a criterion for the acceptance of any moral view. What is it?
13. Some philosophers, such as for example Bergson, Whitehead, Husserl, Heidegger and Sartre, take our subjective experience as something we must preserve in our explanation of the world. How does this avoid the puzzle of free choice? And why does it also make it impossible for us to be wrong about the world?

Arguments for analysis

Argument 1: The mind-body interaction problem

Here is a simple version of an argument that has been much discussed in the Philosophy of the mind through the ages.

The body is made of matter, but the mind is not. Whatever causes a material body to move must itself be made of matter. Therefore, the mind cannot cause the body to move.

Argument 2: Whitehead's solution to the mind-body interaction problem

Mind and body are simply conventions for the way we organize our experiences, and are not distinct individual things. Therefore, we do not have a problem about the interaction of two things.

Argument 3: To show that Sartre contradicts himself

Sartre claims there is no standard that we must follow in making moral choices; morality is purely subjective. Sartre also claims that it is despicable to be inauthentic, to act in bad faith. The previous statement is a moral claim that sets a standard for everyone to follow. Therefore, Sartre denies there are absolute moral standards, and Sartre elevates authenticity or good faith to an absolute moral standard.

Argument 4: A defence of Sartre against the charge of contradiction

Sartre denies that there is any standard that prevents us from choosing our own moral standards. He requires only that we choose these moral standards in good faith, authentically accepting them as our own free choice. Therefore, authenticity is not a moral standard but a standard for evaluating uses of moral standards.

Argument 5: A different defence of Sartre

Sartre tells us that in choosing a moral standard for ourselves, we choose for all, and he chooses authenticity for himself. Sartre chooses, therefore, authenticity for all. Choosing a standard for all, however, does not make that standard absolute but just expresses Sartre's wish that all would follow that standard. Therefore, authenticity remains Sartre's own subjectively chosen standard that others may freely choose or reject.

CHAPTER 9

Analytic Founding Fathers

Searching for precision and clarity

The group of philosophers within the Analytic school is very diverse as regards doctrine and even divided with respect to method. Stumpf prefers to call it a movement to warn of this diversity.[1] One can think of Analytic philosophy as, in part, a reaction to the previous trends in philosophy, many of which were thought to be extremely unclear in their language, ignorant of or opposed to science, mystical, religious, driven by emotion, and divorced from common sense. While they are very suspicious of the heavily metaphorical language of philosophers outside their group, Analytic philosophers do have a description which tips one off to their philosophical ideals: they like to call themselves hard-headed. It may be read from what they oppose that Analytic philosophers emphasize the role of language in determining thought and theory, and they demand clear and precise formulations of philosophical theory. Analytic philosophers often feel bound to take science and common sense seriously, explaining carefully any departures therefrom. On the other hand, they rarely think that common sense is sensible. Common sense is, however, a starting point, not something to be ignored. They often find their theoretical starting points in the science of their day rather than in

---

Notes to chapter 9 are on pp. 484-86.

religion or mysticism. Thoroughly argued iconoclasm is much admired in this school. Many within the Analytic fold are the intellectual heirs of David Hume. Usually they eschew grand metaphysical systems in favour of logical and linguistic analyses of concepts in a context much more narrowly circumscribed than a worldview. The task they set themselves is mainly clarification of the logic and language of science and the everyday conceptual framework.

At the outset of the twentieth-first century, the edges of the Continental and Analytic schools tend to blur into one another. In the early part of the last century, however, the distinction between schools was much more crisp. The Analytic philosophers universally conceived of themselves as revolutionaries casting out the old order of philosophers, whom they thought of as attempting to go beyond the scope of human knowledge in their metaphysical speculations. These early Analytic philosophers divided into two main streams. One included Bertrand Russell, the early Wittgenstein, and Rudolf Carnap, who thought of formal logic as providing a major key to philosophic understanding. Another stream flowed from Moore, the later Wittgenstein, and Austin, who thought that in ordinary language the collective wisdom of the culture was to be discovered and improved upon. Philosophers in both streams thought that most of the puzzles of past philosophers and their Continental contemporaries could be dissolved in the cleansing acid of logical or linguistic analysis. The single most influential source of this way of thinking is the philosopher I shall deal with first in this school, Bertrand Russell.

Russell: Aiming for scientific objectivity about persons

Some of you may have, on the basis of the foregoing remarks on Analytic philosophy, come to expect that Analytic philosophers would be opposed to everything you hold dear. That is why I begin with Bertrand Russell, a great humanitarian, political activist, and passionate social reformer. It is true that he wished to destroy the sort of philosophy that had led to systems of thought in terms of which some people had found their purpose in life, but he did so because he thought these folk were being led down the garden path:

> Philosophy cannot itself determine the ends of life, but it can free us from the tyranny of prejudice and from distortions due to a narrow view. Love, beauty, knowledge, and joy of life: these things retain their lustre however wide our purview. And if philosophy can help us to feel the value of these things, it will have played its part in man's collective work of bringing light into a world of darkness.[2]

Russell believed that prior philosophers had been led to an unfortunately narrow view of the universe and our place in it by the insufficiency of their tools. He believed that science and mathematics, including the new kind of formal logic, a system of which he and Whitehead had pioneered in *Principia Mathematica*, would open up a great many alternative conceptions where earlier thinkers had seen but one possibility.

There is an apocryphal story about Hegel speaking to a historian who told Hegel that Hegel's system did not agree with the facts of history. Hegel is reputed to have replied, "So much the worse for the facts." This story is used to undermine faith in systems which purport to tell us what life and the universe are all about—systems which admit only one possible way that we and our world might be. The story is designed to move us toward Russell's means of proceeding: when the facts and theory collide, abandon the theory. For this reason, we do not find one theory but a great series of them associated with Russell over his long and incredibly prolific career. Russell makes no apologies for being a moving target. He did not think, as many of his predecessors apparently did, that he had hit upon the absolute truth about us and our universe or that he merely had to explicate his findings in a grand system which could never be fundamentally altered. He adopted instead the attitude of the scientist who tries for some approximation to the truth in his hypotheses, puts them to the test, and abandons them when they cease to come up to scratch.

Russell did not focus on the concept of person in the detailed way that some of his contemporaries, such as Strawson and Ayer, did. The positions, however—which Russell fearlessly took, at a time when they were not at all popular—have had a great influence on the way those philosophers and philosophers since have approached concepts of a person. In particular Russell cast suspicion on the method of grand system building of the kind exemplified in Kant and Hegel. We have earlier noted that Kant exerted a great influence on thinking about persons. "Kant has the reputation of being the greatest of modern philosophers," says Russell, "but to my mind he was a mere misfortune."[3] Understand that Russell is speaking of one of the few philosophers who is revered on both sides of the Analytic/Continental chasm. One certainly sees the iconoclasm here, but this is not mere opinion: Russell's reasons are given for your assessment. In the passage just quoted, Russell is defending Hume's views on induction against those of Kant, but I will leave you to read those in the original if you wish. What I turn to now is another attack of Russell on Kant which affects the central position given to persons with respect to the nature of time and space. It is typical of Russell's wish to preserve a kind of objectivity of the universe outside of people's minds.

Kant argued that space, conceived as something existing objectively outside the observer, must be infinite and that space cannot be infinite. He concluded that, because our concept of space leads us to contradictory results, space was not objective after all but subjective. Space is in the eye of the beholder. In such a metaphysical view, the person is elevated to being, in effect, the creator of space. Russell informs us concerning space that "the non-Euclideans refuted the argument that it must be infinite, and Georg Cantor refuted the argument that it cannot be."[4] Russell here brings mathematics to bear on a former philosophical stronghold. This is characteristic of Russell and it is his way of bearing out the point made in the opening quotation. Earlier philosophy narrowed our view to one possibility only, in this instance that space is subjective, a feature of persons. Russell wants to use mathematics and science to undo the restrictive arguments of such systematizers as Kant to show that there are many possibilities for the way things are and consequently for the way people are. We have to keep our views about reality constantly open to revision in the face of new experience and new scientific and mathematical results. This makes philosophy quite a different discipline to what is being done under the name in the Continental School and what had been done in much of philosophy prior to the twentieth century.

What emerges in the background of the various views Russell adopts as he confronts new arguments and scientific results is a commitment to a generally Humean empiricism. One might expect then that persons would be analyzed away, and to some extent this expectation is realized. Russell certainly is attracted to a bundle theory of individuals on which individuals of any kind—cats, pumpkins, electrons, persons—are to be considered bundles of properties. By denying any Aristotelian substance in which the properties inhere, Russell in his later works seems to be leaving little room for a soul or a Cartesian Ego.[5] Nor is the later Russell sympathetic to the mind/matter distinction championed by Descartes. For a while, he calls himself a "neutral monist," that is, one who accepts only one kind of stuff out of which what we normally call mind and what we call matter is made. There is, however, a distinction in the way we know the two, for "mental events and their qualities can be known without inference, physical events are known only as regards their space-time structure."[6] To clarify Russell's metaphysical view that persons are special organizations of some of the basic things of which everything is made, we need to have a better conception of these basic things.

The philosophical question of what the basic things are is handled in a part of philosophy called Ontology. Russell's ontology changed considerably over his long career. In the famous, overconfidently titled volume, *The Problems of Philosophy*, he accepted a dualist ontology in which mind and matter were composed of different fundamental objects. Among the physical objects were sense data, "things that were immediately known in sensation," and among mental entities were sensations or experiences.[7] Examples of sense data are patches of colour in one's visual field and the sounds one hears. According to Pears, Russell seemed to think of persons as bodies with associated Egos which sensed the sense data emanating from objects and inductively inferred the existence of those objects.[8] Soon Russell moved to using sense data as the fundamental objects out of which objects external to the mind were constructed, an idea followed up by Carnap, Quine tells us.[9] Because he had problems with the nature of the Ego and of sense data, Russell eventually abandoned both ideas, trying to solve his difficulties by the move, in his middle period, to neutral monism. This was an attempt to construct both mental and physical objects out of components which were neither mental nor physical but neutral.[10]

Quine tells us that "Neutrality here has a bias, as it often has in politics; Russell's neutral particulars are on the side of sense data."[11] The status of sense data, mental or physical, was always somewhat unclear, though more physical than not in Russell's treatment. It seems then that Russell, and Analytic philosophy with him, took a step toward materialism. By 1927, Pears reports, he had taken another step in as much as he began to analyze sensations as physical occurrences in the nervous system of observers.[12] The view of persons that emerges gets further and further from that which had reigned since Descartes of a non-physical being with a physical body at its disposal.

After Russell abandoned the Ego, as Hume had done, and abandoned sense data which were sensed by the Ego, Russell needed a new word for his neutral particulars (that is, fundamental objects that were neither mental nor physical) and he called them sensa.[13] Pears calls them appearances which gives us some handle on what they are; we must not assume that they are appearances to a person but only things which, if a person were to be able to sense them, would cause something to appear to that person. They are the causes of sensation but not necessarily sensed. Using the word "appearances" for "sensa," Pears sums up neutral monism neatly:

> according to neutral monism appearances are grouped in one way to form physical objects and in another way to form minds. In order to get a physical object, you take all the appearances that radiate outwards from its position in physical space. In order to get a mind, you take all the appearances that start from surrounding objects and converge on its position in physical space. The difference is based on the distinction between input and output.[14]

This is very strange from the point of view of common sense. If I see a red rubber ball, I might think that the appearances of redness, roundness, flexibility, and others which it has are somehow given off by something underlying the appearances. Aristotle called the underlying thing "substance." Russell thinks of the ball, however, as just this radiating group of appearances. A person's mind, moreover, at least as far as perception is concerned, becomes a special group of appearances which are not radiating outward but which are interrelated with one another, causing what we think of as images and memories. Persons are then a combination of the body, which is a group of appearances radiating outward, and a mind, which is a group of appearances converging on the place where the person's body is. Belief, desire, and action are explained neurologically and behaviouristically by the latter-day Russell.[15]

Here we see the complete opposite to Continental philosophy, which thinks of science as hopelessly inadequate to understanding persons and which points philosophy inward to the knowledge of self gained by introspection. Russell does not ignore introspection, but he tries to balance what that shows him with the results of physics, psychology, and other sciences. He wields Ockham's razor—a minimalist principle common in philosophy, according to which entities are not to be multiplied beyond necessity—with zest. Ockham expresses the principle thesis: "What can be done with fewer [assumptions] is done in vain with more."[16] Russell tries to eliminate any concept he does not need to explain the facts he gets from introspection and from the examination of the world around him. Ideas such as substance or being are quickly lopped off as unnecessary appendages.

There is much that is problematic in these views. In particular, it is difficult to see how one can preserve the things Russell promised us in the opening quotation to this section. One is reminded of the sharp-toothed old saw, The grass never grows green again on ground touched by Analytic philosophy. How can bundles of appearances which are in no ontological way distinct from physical bundles find joy in life, love, knowledge, and values? The only thing which distinguishes persons from trees seems to be our being receivers of appearances rather than just senders. Actually, even trees might receive appearances in a limited way. We are just different kinds of bundles or different sorts of causal networks from trees. Trees might react to light through photosynthesis, while we might react to a similar appearance by producing images, memories, and behaviour—maybe getting out the suntan lotion. We are more complex, perhaps, but still causal, material systems like trees.

Of the lofty things mentioned in the opening quotation of this section—joy, love, knowledge, and values—knowledge is the one Russell spends the most time analyzing. The theories of knowledge which he adopts are empiricist theories which vary according to what is doing the knowing. When there are still Egos around in Russell's developing philosophy, they are acquainted with the external objects through sense data. We develop certain beliefs about the objects external to the mind and try to confirm them by seeing what other data we can get experimentally.

At the other extreme of a continuum of views, when Egos have been lopped off by Ockham's razor, knowledge is still understood in terms of confirmation of beliefs, but belief or assent to propositions is understood in terms of feelings the person has.[17] Love and joy are of course in this affective realm. Values as it turns out are, in Russell's view, also dependent on feelings, for he is an emotivist in ethics: "Since no way can be even imagined for deciding a difference as to values, the conclusion is forced upon us that the difference is one of tastes, not one as to any objective truth."[18] To call an action good or bad is not to make a claim to knowledge but to say how we feel about it.

Perhaps emotive feelings, like sensations, would be understood by Russell in terms of neurology in his later materialist period. In any case he thought of persons as causally determined physical subsystems of a physically determined universe: "I am persuaded that the behaviour of the human body is governed completely by the laws of physics, and could be worked out by a Laplacean calculator. I say this in spite of the talk of Eddington and others about atomic free will, which I regard as mere anti-Bolshevik propaganda."[19] It seems there is no room for personal freedom. Not only do we get subjectivism in ethics from Russell, but we are treated to determinism as well. By an enormously different route he brings us to the same conclusions about people as, for instance, Schopenhauer.

As for metaphysical views, what emerges in Russell's later writings is a view of persons that is anathema to many because of its materialist foundation. From Russell's standpoint, it supports many of those sorts of things which the anti-materialist values. Witness the opening quotation to this section. Those who feel this is a cheat will thunder away about the reduction of such precious things as love and values to neurological features of material things. One can see Russell with his characteristic twinkle and mischievous smile saying, "I am quite prepared to listen: what more do you think these things are?" Russell would summarily dismiss anything which is unclear or contradictory in response to this question.

In the twentieth century, on both sides of the philosophical chasm, persons have been changed into things which are hardly recognizable to earlier philosophers. Sartre's beings-for-themselves and Russell's irradiations and convergences of appearances are not the sorts of things we once thought ourselves to be. Absolutism has taken a beating as a consequence; both Sartre and Russell makes ethics subjective. While contemporary philosophers sometimes agree on ending or starting points in their investigations—both Husserl and Russell, for example, take our simplest experiences to be fundamentally important—the routes they take us between points are not different only in direction but also in the means of transport. Even within schools we see vast differences. This is evident as we move from Russell to his close associate, the formidable Wittgenstein.

What about Daphne?

Daphne is, from Russell's point of view, no different in kind to other persons. She is the centre of a vortex of appearances, as far as her mental life is concerned, and a radiation of appearances physically. Her neurological disease has, of course, limited her behaviour to a very small repertoire compared to what it was formerly. Like any of us, she is an ongoing series of causes and effects in a material universe. If we wish to use the word "person" to speak of Daphne in some moral sense, then for Russell we are expressing emotions but not stating facts. These emotions are themselves determined by neurological causes.

What I like about Russell

Russell shows us what we can get if we leave most of the poetry out of our philosophy of persons. Perhaps he has thrown the baby out with the bath water, but the water was extremely muddy. The trick is to get the baby back but not the mud. The attempt to work with an ontology of appearances is interesting. Egos and substances, such mysterious things, are not needed if we can make sense of appearances as independently existing entities without the need of anyone to whom they are appearances.

Wittgenstein: A different disappearance of persons

With regard to the relation of words to non-verbal facts, Russell tells us, there is a type of philosopher who maintains that there is knowledge not expressible in words but nonetheless uses words to tell us what this knowledge is: "These include the mystics, Bergson, and Wittgenstein; also certain aspects of Hegel and Bradley."[20] Wittgenstein speaks of using expressions as a ladder to climb to an understanding, from which height we can see the expressions as nonsense and throw the ladder away.[21] This ladder-heaving view Russell dismisses as contradictory.[22] Nonetheless, Russell avers that "Mr. Wittgenstein's *Tractatus Logico-Philosophicus*, whether or not it prove to give the ultimate truth on the matters with which it deals, certainly deserves, by its breadth and scope and profundity, to be considered an important event in the philosophical world."[23] Apparently, even for those who value his work highly, Wittgenstein is a terribly controversial figure in philosophy.

Like Russell, Wittgenstein dallied for a time with an ontology of facts; that is to say, he thought facts were the basic things of which the world was composed. Like Russell, Wittgenstein thought that the world was mirrored by a certain system of logic; logical atomism was what Russell called this theory. Language consists of propositions which can be broken down, ultimately, into atomic propositions. These correspond to simple facts about the world. All the complexity of the world can be expressed in terms of the atomic propositions combined according to logical operations. In such a view of the world, the self tends to get reduced to a group of facts concerning behaviour and neurology. We have seen this sort of materialist reduction in Russell's view of the mind. Russell is an heir to Hume. At first glance, Wittgenstein seems to be another heir to Hume. Wittgenstein puts the disappearance of the self this way:

> There is no such thing as the subject that thinks or entertains ideas.
>
> If I wrote a book called *The world as I found it*, I

> should have to include a report on my body, and should have to say which parts were subordinate to my will, and which were not, etc., this being a method of isolating the subject, or rather of showing that in an important sense there is no subject; for it alone could *not* be mentioned in that book.
>
> The subject does not belong to the world: rather, it is a limit of the world.[24]

As with the original Humean dissolution of the self, the immediate question arises, does this not reduce to absurdity the method which does the dissolving? It does seem to be the solvent, logical atomism, not the concept of the self which is endangered by such conclusions. If one insists on viewing the world through a form of empiricism that only a logician could love, then one will not find oneself. Nonetheless, the idea that the self is a limit of the world rather than a thing in the world may have important uses. It is reminiscent of Husserl's seeing but unseen Ego. Perhaps the appearance of disappearance is misleading. From an objective point of view, the self is not in the world but, subjectively, it is the perceiver of the world.

The person left after Wittgenstein's *Tractatus* has done its work is a combination of a body and any other things which can be described as facts in the world plus an encircling limit or self. One has to remember, however, that Wittgenstein is speaking of the world as *he* found it, not simply the world. The self then is the limit of a person's own version of the world, not necessarily of *the* world. For solipsists this comes to the same thing; for the rest of us, what Wittgenstein has really said is that a self is the limit of a person's world. To know oneself, one must know what, from one's own point of view, exists. The self is like a vanishing point, a point of perspective from which the world is drawn but not something in the picture.

Wittgenstein is often treated as two philosophers, the early and the later Wittgenstein roughly corresponding with the *Tractatus* and *The Philosophical Investigations*.[25] There are in fact some other developments in between these—"later" sometimes means from the Blue Book onward"[26]—but there is a remarkable unity through all his work on the topic of the self and the person. What we have is a philosopher who did not mind changing his views but who developed a skepticism about any objective self through all the changes. The later Wittgenstein abandoned the logical empiricism of the *Tractatus,* which limited attention to atomic propositions as the fundamentally important kind of language. He later thought of language on the model of a tool box with many different types of tools, while his earlier view had been restricted to one tool in the box. Wittgenstein did not, however, give up the idea that linguistic analysis is essential to philosophy, nor does the later Wittgenstein bring much cheer to those who found his earlier views of the person somewhat desiccated. In fact, by applying all the tools in the box, Wittgenstein still constructs a view in which there is no place for a self as the referent of "I."[27]

What seems constant through Wittgenstein's thinking on the subject of persons is that thinking of the self as a particular, as the referent of "I" is being misled by grammar. "I" takes the same subject position in a sentence as the sort of expressions which refer to a particular physical object, such as London Bridge. To think, however, that "I" in the sentence I am thinking, refers to something is to be mistaken about the use of "I." To illustrate the mistake, consider a foreign guest whose host informs her that, It is cold outside. The guest then asks, What is this thing that is cold outside, the cat? The host explains with patience and amusement that "it" does not refer to a particular thing outside, but indicates that the temperature is low. Wittgenstein claims that we are making the same mistake as the foreign guest in my example when we take "I" to refer to something.[28]

Wittgenstein also makes some brief remarks on personal identity in accord with his general concern to dissolve philosophical problems through careful attention to language.[29] We use personal names in the way we do only because of certain contingent facts about ourselves. Our bodies do not change so quickly that we cannot recognize people we see often on the basis of their appearance. Wittgenstein asks us to imagine that we all look alike but that there are different sets of characteristics associated with different bodies, for example, a low voice, jerky movements, and grumpy demeanour or a high voice, slow movements, and a mild manner. If the sets of characteristics stayed in sets but migrated from body to body, then we would be likely to use personal names not on the basis of sameness of bodies but to name sets of characteristics. Wittgenstein then discusses Jekyll/Hyde cases and an example aimed at the memory criterion of personal identity. He supposes a man has two separate streams of memory, one active on even days and one active on odd days of his life. These possibilities are used by Wittgenstein to try to persuade his readers that "the *ordinary* use of the word 'person' is what one might call a composite use suitable under the ordinary circumstances. If I assume, as I do, that these circumstances are changed, the application of the term 'person' or 'personality' has thereby changed."[30] We are free to choose, Wittgenstein thinks, how we are to use the terms in these odd circumstances. Thus, concerning the many similar examples that philosophers have used to try to clarify the concept of person, Wittgenstein would say that the examples show nothing more than that we are free to choose, in unusual circumstances, how we are to use "person." Once the background assumptions are changed from those with which we are familiar, the meaning of "person" is no longer fixed. One can only speculate on what the new usage might be.

This warning of Wittgenstein's about the chameleon quality of the meaning of "person" is seldom taken seriously. Even philosophers frequently treat "person" as meaningful and clear in extraordinary examples. Wittgenstein believes that "there is a great variety of criteria of personal '*identity*'" to be noticed even in ordinary cases.[31] Some contemporary philosophers such as Wilkes, do seem to appreciate Wittgenstein's point here. Wilkes, who recognizes the difficulty at least in so far as she avoids fictional examples, still treats the word "person" as meaningful in a constant way when dealing with such odd cases as multiple personality or fugue states, but perhaps she thinks her Aristotelian reconstruction of the meaning of "person" allows her to do this, stretching as it does to fit these cases as well as the ordinary ones.[32] Against Wilkes and others who try to establish one usage for "person" to fit a wide variety of circumstances, Wittgenstein seems to be claiming that there are many legitimate heirs to the ordinary usage of "person." It seems, however, that most philosophers disagree with Wittgenstein or forget his warning.

What about Daphne?

The later Wittgenstein would tell us that the answer to our questions about Daphne depend on linguistic usages. If none of the common usages is developed for the purposes of discussing such cases, then we may simply choose a way of using the terms "person" and "identity" in such a case. There is merely a decision about definition to be made, no profound question about who is whom or what is a person. Indeed if we wonder whether Daphne's self remains after her decline, we are merely misled by grammar. The self is not an objective entity but a limit on subjective perceptions of the world. Whatever limit Daphne has now is Daphne's self, but this is a very changeable thing, not at all like a Cartesian Ego.

What I like about Wittgenstein

Wittgenstein is clear about the limits of the strange examples which philosophers frequently use to understand such concepts as personal identity. They may reveal to us the ways in which we use language, but they do not reveal what is real or what is possible. His is an interesting idea, the self as a point of perspective outside the picture. If one stares at the picture, like Hume, one of course finds no self.

Logical positivism

When I was teaching in Europe in the mid-1970s, I noticed that the defenders of the Continental style of philosophizing often took it upon themselves to attack the Analytic school by attacking logical positivism. This was exceedingly strange given that, from the point of view of most Analytic philosophers, these Continental philosophers were flogging a dead horse. This sect of empiricism had already died the death of a thousand qualifications. It has, however, considerable historical importance and its influences remain.

Logical positivism was the output of a group of philosophers referred to as the Vienna circle, on which Wittgenstein was a major influence. To Wittgenstein they attributed their central doctrine, the verification principle; as Passmore expresses it, "the meaning of a proposition is identical with the method of verifying it—that is that a proposition means the set of experiences which are together equivalent to the proposition's being true."[33] In effect, the Vienna circle interpreted this in such a way as to accept scientific and mathematical statements as meaningful, while rejecting any claims which could not be verified by appeal to the five senses or to logic. Logical positivism contains, then, a theory of linguistic meaning according to which much philosophy consists of meaningless verbiage.

The logical positivists were particularly interested in destroying the German idealist tradition. Such proclamations as "The Absolute is beyond time," were thought to be absolute rubbish by the Vienna circle. More recent philosophy in the Continental school, while often opposed to idealism, tends to make claims in a way that the positivists loved to dismiss, for example, Sartre's claim that existence precedes essence. It is not hard to see why hatred for logical positivism has outlived logical positivism among the philosophers of the Continental school.

Much of our ordinary talk about persons would also qualify as meaningless by the verification principle. Unfortunately for the logical positivists, the verification principle also is meaningless when judged on its own. It is a self-destructive principle. To see this, consider the statement of the principle: *the meaning of a proposition is identical with the method of verifying it.* There is no method of verifying this statement. The two methods the positivists accepted were the empirical method of science and the analytic method of mathematics. The statement cannot be verified empirically, nor is it an analytic statement—that is, a statement known to be true or false by logic alone or one reducible to such a statement by the substitution of synonyms for synonyms. Disagreements about how logical positivism was to handle this problem and how it was to evolve eventually dissolved it as a sect into the wider movement of logical empiricism, in which such philosophers as Russell operated; these philosophers did not make such rigid demands on meaningful language. While this positivist view is well and truly dead, the legacy of logical positivism is evident in some contemporary Analytic philosophers' work. This influence is neatly summed up by Passmore:

> insofar as it is widely agreed that transcendental metaphysics, if not meaningless, is at least otiose, that philosophers ought to set an example of precision and clarity, that philosophy should make use of technical devices, deriving from logic, in order to solve problems relating to the philosophy of science, that philosophy is not about "the world" but about

> the language through which men speak about the world, we can detect in contemporary philosophy, at least, the persistence of the spirit which inspired the Vienna Circle.[34]

While Carnap and others in the Vienna circle might not like talk about being inspired by a spirit, what Passmore says here is meaningful and true. I speak from experience as one brought up in a philosophical tradition that fits Passmore's description. One could not speak to many of my teachers about, for example, Sartre's view that persons, of necessity, try to turn each other into objects. At least one could not express the idea without the kind of linguistic explication that Sartre would find otiose.

Logical positivism is sometimes so approximately construed as to include not only those who accepted the verification principle of meaning but quite different philosophers, such as Moore, Ryle, and Austin who are properly classified not as positivists but as ordinary language philosophers. Unlike their colleagues in the logical empiricist tradition, they laid much less emphasis on the help to be gained from formal logic and much more emphasis on the analysis of ordinary language. The most important member of this group, where the topic of persons is concerned, was Ryle.

Ryle: Exorcism of a persistent ghost

Ryle shared with Wittgenstein and Russell the Humean view that the self as a separate substance is a myth. Like the later Wittgenstein, Ryle thinks the difficulties we have understanding persons, the self, and the mind all fall away when one attends carefully to language and logic. His classic diatribe against the ghost in the machine, which one finds in *The Concept of Mind*,[35] extends the arguments of Russell and Wittgenstein and makes them more accessible.

One of the main battles concerning persons in contemporary philosophy is that between the heirs of Hume and the heirs of Descartes. Ryle lays the blame for our confusion about ourselves squarely on Descartes' doorstep, but he thinks that the arguments of many of those opposed to Descartes are also faulty because they commit an error to be discussed in a moment, an error Ryle dubs "a category mistake."[36] First let us look at the doctrine Ryle opposes.

The roughly Cartesian doctrine Ryle sets out to destroy is what he calls the official doctrine or the myth of the ghost in the machine. This is the doctrine that every person is a combination of a material body in a mechanical causal network and an immaterial mind insulated from that causal network: "A person therefore lives through two collateral histories, one consisting of what happens in and to his body, the other consisting of what happens in and to his mind. The first is public, the second private. The events in the first history are events in the physical world, those in the second are events in the mental world."[37] This doctrine, Ryle assures us, is absurd. He points to various problems, such as the difficulty of saying how mind and body interact and the tendency to solipsism if one adopts this doctrine. His diagnosis is that the dogma of the ghost in the machine treats the facts of mental life as if they belonged to one logical type or category when they actually belong to another.[38]

Ryle illustrates the meaning of "category mistake" only very roughly in a series of illustrations, for instance, this:

> A foreigner visiting Oxford or Cambridge for the first time is shown a number of colleges, libraries, playing fields, museums, scientific departments and administrative offices. He then asks "But where is the University?"...It then has to be explained to him that the University is not another collateral institution, some ulterior counterpart to the colleges, laboratories and offices....The University is just the way in which all that he has already seen is organized."[39]

According to Ryle, those who speak of the mind as if it were an entity collateral to the body are misunderstanding what type of thing a mind is. It is not that Ryle wishes to reduce mind to matter or matter to mind; he thinks both reductions are ridiculous, since matter and mind are not two contrasting things in the same category. He compares the attempted contrast to that between the sentences, She came home in a sedan chair and She came home in a flood of tears.[40] I take Ryle to mean that it would be silly to say that all mental events are really material just in the same way as it would be silly to say that someone could travel in a flood of tears as opposed to a sedan chair. Rather than engaging in the old debate among materialists, idealists, and dualists, Ryle tries to make their vocabulary look foolish, as Rorty might say,[41] and Ryle does a fairly good job of this.

This is not to say that Ryle wants to stop altogether the use of such terms as "I," "self," or "mind." We do, however, have to administer some astringent correctives to their usage. Ryle points out that: "'I' is not an extra name for an extra being; it indicates when I say or write it, the same individual who can also be addressed by the proper name 'Gilbert Ryle'".[42] Ryle is inveighing against supposing that "I" is the name for the self which is to be considered as an immaterial substance associated with the body. He also is unhappy with the idea that "an ordinary person is really some sort of committee or team of persons, all laced together inside one skin."[43] The Iliadic Greeks thought that way; we have seen, moreover, that Plato held that reason, spirit, and appetite were three selves within the person. Many people today still might talk, in Ryle's words, "as if the thinking and vetoing 'I' were one person, and the greedy or lazy 'I' were another."[44] In sentences such as, I caught myself beginning to dream, Ryle does not want to treat the two occurrences of the pronoun as referring to two persons or selves within the person.

To avoid this duplication of persons, Ryle analyzes "I" as an index word, which is today also called an indexical; he says such words "indicate to the hearer or reader the particular thing, episode, person, place, or moment referred to."[45] "Now," for example refers to the moment at which it is uttered. Ryle goes through a number of different uses of "I," "me," and "myself" to illustrate that they may mean "my body" or may just refer to the person uttering one of them. Ryle suggests that "I am warming myself at the fire" is equivalent to "I am warming my body at the fire," but that it is nonsense to say "My body is warming my body at the fire."[46] After going through some more peculiar usages, Ryle returns to the point that these pronouns are indexicals, so that in the statement, I caught myself beginning to dream, there is no reference to duplicate persons or selves within persons. To explicate Ryle, I would paraphrase this sentence just quoted as, "Gilbert Ryle at time t' noticed that Gilbert Ryle at time t was beginning to dream, and t' is later than t." Such analyses are intended to show that there is only one person to whom the pronouns refer. One may still, however, be dissatisfied. On introspection one seems to almost grasp an elusive referent of "I." Ryle attempts to take the mystery out of this as well.

Ryle speaks of the "systematic elusiveness of 'I'."[47] The general reason for this elusiveness of ourselves when we try to know ourselves is given in Ryle's principle: "any performance can be the concern of a higher order performance, but cannot be the concern of itself."[48] To understand this, consider Ryle's example of a book review.[49] A review of a book is a first-order review. A review of all prior reviews of a book is a second-order review, review of second-order reviews is third order, and so on. Now the principle tells us that a second-order review cannot be the subject of another second-order review. Consider now my reviewing my own performances with a view to knowing myself. One of the things I must leave out is my current reviewing, which is a performance that would have to be the subject of a higher-order performance later. When I look at myself, I always leave something out. This, Ryle thinks, is the source of the elusiveness of self. One cannot describe oneself fully: "Even if the person is for special speculative purposes, momentarily concentrating on the Problem of the Self, he has failed and knows that he has failed to catch more than the flying coat-tails of that which he was pursuing. His quarry was the hunter."[50]

Ryle also thinks this principle explains our feeling that we have free will and are unpredictable. Whenever we try to predict our own future actions we will leave something out, namely the current performance, the prediction we are now making. Looking at our past actions, we can see how they could have been predicted by someone in possession of all the facts, but our present self-knowledge is always missing one of the facts.[51]

It seems then that, although Ryle claims to dissipate the contrast between mind and matter, what he says is less abrasive in the ears of the materialist than in those of the idealist or the dualist. The materialist who typically accepts causal determinism will like what Ryle has to say about the prediction of human behaviour. It is also clear that Ryle accepts the existence of our bodies. What he says about minds, however, tends to rule out entirely dualism and idealism; for minds are largely known by observable behaviour.[52] While Ryle admits that there are things about ourselves which cannot be known by others—things to which we have privileged access—they are to Ryle, in the main, unimportant. The hallowed souls, selves, and minds within are reduced to a technical trick of inner speech.[53] He derides those who make something occult out of this: "They postulate an internal shadow-performance to be the real carrier of the intelligence ordinarily ascribed to the overt act."[54] Against this shadowy inner mind Ryle claims that describing mind or intelligence is describing conduct.[55] This is true of other capacities as well, according to Ryle: "I find out most of what I want to know about your capacities, interests, likes, dislikes, methods and convictions by observing how you conduct your overt doings, of which by far the most important are your sayings and writings. It is a subsidiary question how you conduct your imaginings, including your imagined monologues."[56]

Curiously, Ryle and Sartre agree entirely on the great importance of what we do as opposed to what we imagine we are. Ryle's method, however, is largely opposed to the poetic method of the Continental philosophers. The emphasis is on preserving as much as possible of common sense and usage while excising any absurdities and maximizing clarity. His critics might maintain that he has excised anything that was profoundly important in the concept of a person, while his admirers would say that he has banished occultists' mutterings in favour of plain truth. Certainly he has to be reckoned with when we come to give our own analyses of the concept of a person.

What about Daphne?

Ryle would tell us that it is silly to ask whether Daphne remains after the ravages of her illness. After all there she is. If we are asking about something other than what we see, then we are seeking a ghost in the machine, like the member of a non-industrialized culture who, on first seeing a locomotive, says It must have a very powerful spirit! If we want to know what Daphne is or who, we simply look at what she can do. To ask after the real Daphne within is to make a category mistake. There is nothing over and above that of which we take stock, no more than there is some entity, the university, over and above the buildings and the people in them.

What I like about Ryle

Ryle puts views about persons to be found in the ordinary-language school of thought into relatively sharp focus. He teaches us to be careful about the way we commit ourselves to the existence of things on the basis of the words we use. His picturesque metaphors and the hazy but evocative notion of a category mistake make us careful when we come to say what there is, over and above observable behaviour, in a person.

Taking stock after the iconoclasts

What remains of us after these founders of the Analytic school are through? We seem to be back where Hume left us, no place at all. Perhaps I should say, rather, we have been put in our place. There is no non-spatial Cartesian Ego left. What remains of us is a spatio-temporally locatable set of behaviours and a behaving body, which itself is a mere bundle of sensa, to use Russell's term, like any object. Thinking substances, essences, spirit, soul, mind, and self are banished along with the unicorn or, what amounts to a fate worse than banishment—reduced to neurophysiological events. The self is a grammatical illusion. Freedom is impossible. Moral claims are mere expressions of emotion. Some—Russell, for example—seem to be able to think and act as humanists in spite of believing in these iconoclastic pronouncements. This is not logically inconsistent if one describes what one is doing in the appropriate reductionist way. It is, however, difficult to motivate humanism under the stern aegis of reductionism.

In some ways such views simplify things. To ask whether, for example, someone who has permanently lost her mind has survived is to ask either whether a particular body has survived, or whether a certain repertoire of behaviours has survived. That explains our tendency to answer, Yes and no. Only the body has survived. This simplification of the issue of survival of persons is bought at the cost of trimming the rich fabric of our experience to fit the narrow frame of behaviourist or materialist reduction. Is it really plausible that a behavioural repertoire or a set of sensa can be made to explain what Bergson rhapsodically but unclearly referred to as our intuition of ourselves?

Knowing what it is like to stand in my shoes is to be acquainted with an extremely complex phenomenon, I assure you. To dismiss this as a limit of the world experienced, or to reduce it to atoms or sensa is not plausible without a much longer story being told than the cheerful British founders of the Analytic school have begun to tell. One should throw out bath water only after checking carefully for babies. On the other hand, this group of philosophers has shown us just how muddy the bath water was. Their demands for clarity can be met in a salutary way if we avoid oversimplification.

Content questions

1. Does Russell think that philosophy can help you find your purpose in life? What can philosophy do?
2. What are sense data?
3. What are sensa?
4. How does Russell distinguish minds from bodies?
5. What is Ockham's razor?
6. The early Wittgenstein thinks there is no objective self. How does the later Wittgenstein's view compare?
7. What is the verification principle and how did the Vienna circle interpret it?
8. Give an example of Ryle's idea of a category mistake.
9. What is an indexical?
10. How does Ryle explain the systematic elusiveness of "I"?
11. How does Ryle explain the appearance of free will?

Arguments for analysis

At some earlier stages in his philosophical development, Russell favoured a dualist view of the world, in which persons are mind-body pairs understanding the world around them through the sense data they get through the five senses. Here is a simplified argument for his view. The argument presupposes a commonly used principle of epistemology, inference to the best explanation (or, IBE). This is the principle that, if a hypothesis is the best explanation of the data then that hypothesis is true. It is a very controversial principle. Among those who accept it, there is a debate over what "best" should be taken to mean.

Argument 1: The inference to the best explanation argument for standard dualism

Our mental sense data occur as if we were observing a physical world, getting these data through the various neurological pathways that lead from sense receptors to our brains. There are, however, infinitely many different explanations for these sense data or appearances. We might, for instance, be brains in vats getting virtual reality rather than a picture of the real world. There is, however, no need to adopt such exotic hypotheses to explain our perceptions. By the inference to the best explanation, we should choose the simple explanation that our sense data are caused by objects external to our minds that are much as we see them.

Later Russell adopted a neutral monist view, through which persons and objects differed mainly by the distinction of input from output. The universe is composed of sensa (appearances). Persons and other observers of the universe are convergences of sensa. What we used to think of as material objects are irradiations of sensa. Objects send sensa out. Minds take sensa in. This view is reminiscent of Hume's radical empiricism.

Argument 2: Russell's argument against Descartes

When Descartes says, "I think; hence, I am," he illegitimately goes beyond the evidence. The evidence Descartes permits himself is that of sense data. All that one can conclude on the basis of observing the present operations of one's own mind is that one, at present, exists as a mind. "I," however, refers to a person existing through time, and our present sense data give us no certainty about any past or future of the mind that is presently considering its own sense data. More simply put, one cannot say, "I am" meaning "I exist as a person through time" on the basis of present thoughts. The past may be an illusion. The future may not contain the thinker of these present thoughts.

Argument 3: Some arguments of Wittgenstein against Descartes

The earlier Wittgenstein

If I make a complete catalogue of all the items of which I am aware, of the world as I know it, that catalogue does not include me. I am not an observed thing in the world but merely the limit of a set of observations. Instead of saying, "I think; hence, I am," we should say, "Thinking is taking place here and now." A group of thoughts just implies the existence of a group of thoughts, not a thinker.

The later Wittgenstein

If I say, "It is raining," I do not imply that there is some individual object to which "it" refers. If I say, "I think," I do not imply that there is some individual thing to which "I" refers. Descartes is misled by grammar into thinking that a pronoun in the subject position must refer to a particular in the world.

Argument 4: The positivists against Descartes

Descartes claims that he has shown the existence of a continuing and eternal Ego—rather like a soul—that thinks and knows of its own existence. The claim that such an Ego exists is, however, meaningless. To be meaningful, the claim would have to be an analytic statement (e.g., All bachelors are unmarried) or an empirical statement (e.g., There are two crows sitting on my roof). There is no reason to think "The Ego exists" is an analytic claim. The Ego, moreover, is featureless and, hence, unobservable. We cannot, therefore, prove its existence by empirical means. "The Ego exists" is neither an analytic statement nor an empirical statement. By the verification principle, therefore, "The Ego exists" is a meaningless statement.

Argument 5: Reply that the verification principle is self-defeating

The verification principle, as interpreted by the early positivists, claims that no sentence is meaningful unless it is either analytic or empirical. The verification principle itself, however, is neither analytic nor empirical. Therefore, the verification principle is, according to itself, meaningless.

Argument 6: Ryle against Descartes

If we think of the mind and body as two separate things, then we are unable to say how the two interact. Therefore, dualism is absurd.

If we think of the mind and body as two separate things, we only have direct access to the mind. In that case we can not be sure of the body or of other minds. We are led to solipsism, an absurd view. Therefore dualism is absurd.

If we speak as if the mind and body are two separate things, we are making a category mistake. There are not two kinds of things, the mental and the physical, within a single category. The contrast of the two makes no sense. It is like trying to contrast the two sentences, She came home in a bad mood and She came home in a taxi. If you say that a person is primarily mental rather than physical, that is like saying she came home in a bad mood rather than a taxi. The contrast is nonsensical.

One of the things common to all of the above arguments is their preoccupation with language, a hallmark of twentieth-century philosophy. Rather than accepting the old concepts of idealism, dualism, and materialism, contemporary philosophers have challenged the meaningfulness of the language in which these were expressed. Often this challenge backfires. Consider the argument above against the verification principle.

CHAPTER 10

More Contemporary Classics

Strawson: The concept of person as basic

Not all contemporary philosophers in the Analytic school are suspicious of traditional philosophy, in particular, metaphysics. A major contribution with respect to the metaphysical status of persons was made by P.F. Strawson in *Individuals: An Essay in Descriptive Metaphysics*. "Descriptive metaphysics," Strawson tells us, "is content to describe the actual structure of our thought about the world, revisionary metaphysics is concerned to produce a better structure."[1] More particularly, what Strawson wishes to describe comes from the great unsung commonplaces of thought: "For there is a massive central core of human thinking which has no history—or none recorded in histories of thought; there are categories and concepts which, in their most fundamental character, change not at all."[2] Strawson's work on the concept of a person is remarkable in the scope and generality of his undertaking and in his going beyond "the reliance upon a close examination of the actual use of words."[3] His main aim, as regards our topic, is to show that material bodies and persons are "the basic or fundamental particulars, that the concepts of other types of particular must be seen as secondary in relation to the concepts of these."[4]

Notes to chapter 10 are on pp. 486-87.

Self and other

Strawson's route into the forbidding territory of the philosophy of persons is via the traditional mountain passes, the problems of self-knowledge and solipsism: "Each of us distinguishes between himself and states of himself on the one hand, and what is not himself or a state of himself on the other. What are the conditions of our making this distinction, and how are they fulfilled? In what way do we make it, and why do we make it in the way we do?"[5] Think about how we distinguish two material particulars in the world such as the book we are reading and the telephone. Now think about how we distinguish ourselves from other things. It does not seem at all like distinguishing the book from the telephone. We do not hold up some particular—the self—in imagination and compare it to the telephone. So how do we do it?

Strawson sees a person's having an idea of herself or himself as a very strange phenomenon, which he describes in rather Humean terms: "it might begin to look impossible that he should have the idea of himself—or at any rate the right idea…if it is just an item *within* his experience of which he has this idea, how can it be the idea of that which *has* all of his experiences?"[6] To investigate our idea of self, Strawson turns to the language we use to talk about ourselves, to ascribe things to ourselves. We ascribe some of the same things we ascribe to physical particulars, for instance, height, colour, and position; yet we also ascribe things which we normally do not ascribe to physical particulars such as anger, diligence, or, more generally, consciousness. To understand this, Strawson decides to look into our reasons for ascribing consciousness to anything at all and our reasons for ascribing both physical and mental properties to people.

If, however, we look at people who are very young and outside of our culture, in non-industrial cultures, then Strawson's point about what we ascribe does not hold. A child may feel comfortable with an expression such as, The forest is angry. Poets and environmentalists in our culture may also use such expressions, though usually they are meant as tropes to underline our perfidy in sullying our own nest. Sometimes, however, the use is literal and draws on a system of values that is quite unlike the one Kant clarified by distinguishing persons from mere things. In the Kantian value system, things have value only in their service to persons. It is partly because we accept this Kantian doctrine that we are so willing to use up our natural surroundings rather than to preserve them for their own sakes. Strawson's acceptance of the Kantian doctrine may be backward looking. The point of distinguishing people from mere things was to prevent people being used improperly, but we will have to widen the scope of our protection. This may put a strain on the distinction of persons from mere things. It is to be hoped that we will refine the distinction so as to value some non-persons more highly rather than to value people less.

Having asked why conscious states are ascribed to anything at all and why to the same thing as physical characteristics, Strawson goes on to look at the way we have experiences. He argues that it is a contingent matter that our experiences are tied to our own bodies. The unique role, however, that our bodies have in our perceptual experience explains our attachment to them. This observation about our bodies does not, however, answer Strawson's questions.[7]

This unique role of the body might go further toward answering Strawson's questions if there were a necessary connection between the body and the experience of the person. The argument that there is no such connection consists mainly of a description of a fanciful case in which a person's visual experience is determined by the bodies of others. Like Kathleen Wilkes,[8] I am suspicious of such examples. In the unclear background assumptions which make them seem to work there may be hidden some contradiction. The philosophy, psychology, and biology of perception are insufficiently developed for us to comb this background for such flaws; so it is reasonable for us to remain, for the time being, agnostic with respect to the contingency of the connection of experience to the body.

What would persuade me that Strawson is wrong about this claim of contingency is sufficient experience of the sort described by the novelist Hesse in *Siddhartha*. Siddhartha, an East Indian mystic, is said to inhabit, while in a trance, the bodies of various animals and said to share their experiences. If I could see the world as if from the body of the bald eagle which I sometimes see from my window, and if I could later verify—say, by the use of aerial photographs—that my experience culled in this strange way was veridical, then I might accept the contingency of the role of my body in my experience. On the face of it, however, I lean, despite my agnosticism, to accepting a necessary connection of my body to my experience.

Owning experience: Cartesian and no-ownership views

Strawson continues his description of the structure of our thought with respect to persons by discussing the Cartesian and no-ownership views.[9] Both of these views he attacks as making the profound error of thinking that there are two senses of "I," one referring to the body and one referring to something else. The Cartesian view is one we have seen in the discussion of Descartes (see chapter 5). According to Descartes, the body is one substance, the mind or Cartesian Ego is another. When we speak of the person, we may refer to either or both. Mental predicates are properly ascribable only to the mind and physical predicates only to the body. While Strawson disagrees with this view, he thinks it is at least coherent. He does not accord the no-ownership view as much respect.

The no-ownership view is one Strawson thinks might be fathered on Wittgenstein and on Schlick, a central member of the Vienna circle which promoted logical positivism. The no-ownership view is the view that there are no owners of certain experiences which we ascribe to the Cartesian Ego. Strawson illustrates this view with his version of one of Wittgenstein's examples, which I simplify as follows: "I've got a bad tooth," means "This body has a bad tooth," but "I've got a toothache" does not mean "This Ego has a toothache." In fact, where "I" appears to denote the Ego, it denotes no such thing. "I've got a toothache" should be read as "A toothache is occurring now."[10]

The reason for adopting this strange no-ownership view, according to Strawson, is acceptance of what I shall call the transferability principle, which is that: "Only those things whose ownership is logically transferable can be owned at all."[11] Of course I could not transfer the ownership of my toothache to Ursula if it is my Ego which is having that experience. Ursula might have a toothache but not the experience I had—although it is logically possible that Ursula's body and not mine had this particular bad tooth. All talk of ownership of a toothache is dismissed since, by this transferability principle, I could not own that experience in the first place.

This no-ownership view is incoherent, according to Strawson. He accuses its proponents of assuming the ownership they are trying to deny when they state their no-ownership view. They must use "my" or some other possessive word to locate the experience. If they eliminate such possessives, they cannot, according to Strawson, talk about the contingent facts of possession of certain experiences by the body in the sense of being causally dependent on that body. (I will discuss the argument for this later in connection with Ayer's view.) If these facts are not contingent, then we do not have logical transferability of ownership as required. The no-ownership theorist has to make use of the idea of a person possessing an experience in order to deny that experiences are possessed by persons.[12]

Whether or not this no-ownership view is Wittgenstein's view, there is the Wittgensteinian ladder-heaving response to Strawson. The no-ownership theorist could say, Yes, I must use these possessives which reduce my propositions to nonsense, but these propositions are only used to bring you to a realization of the ineffable thing I want to say. Once you see that, you can discard these nonsensical propositions. Of course, if one has no special realizations on hearing these propositions, one can also reply with Wittgenstein's authority: "What we cannot speak about we must pass over in silence."[13]

The point of descriptive metaphysics which Strawson seeks to bring out by considering the no-ownership view is that the principle of transferability must be abandoned. A non-transferable kind of ownership is central to our thought about persons. In fact, without attributing them to persons, we have no way of identifying various particulars such as thoughts and pains. We need the basic particulars, persons, and this non-transferable ownership to be able to identify and re-identify these items in our scheme of thought about the world.

As to the questions on the Cartesian view with which Strawson began, one need not ask why both conscious and physical states are attributed to one thing, the person, since the person is really the Ego with two other things, body and mind, which it owns. This view, Strawson complains, does not answer why we should ascribe states of consciousness to anything. This must seem a rather odd complaint to a Cartesian, for whom the mind is the set of conscious states owned by the Ego. It is the same felt need for ownership of consciousness that drives both Descartes and Strawson. Strawson does not, however, like the sort of owner that Descartes came up with. The alternative no-ownership account, however, is anathema to Strawson.

In opposition to the no-ownership account, Strawson asserts the ascription principle: "it is a necessary condition of one's ascribing states of consciousness, experiences, to oneself, in the way one does, that one should also ascribe them, or be prepared to ascribe them, to others who are not oneself."[14] If I say to myself, No one could love her as I do, then, by this principle, I must be mistaken. It implies that, although no one could have *my* love for her, others could love her in a completely similar way. Others could have experiences like mine. Strawson insists on this ascription principle in opposition not only to the no-ownership theory but to the verification principle of the logical positivists.[15]

Person as a primitive concept

If we accept the positivist's verification principle, then the meaning of "I am in pain" must be very different from "He is in pain" for the methods of verification in the two cases are so different. Indeed, for the first sentence one might doubt the need for verification or the use of the sentence to ascribe a property to a person. Strawson responds that we use language to speak primarily to others; so both sentences would be used to let others know who is in pain.[16] This communication would be impossible if we were ascribing properties to Cartesian Egos which are inaccessible to us. Strawson suggests that—to preserve our ability to ascribe predicates—we must take the concept of a person as primitive. Cartesian Egos, if we wish to speak of them at all, will be defined in terms of persons, not the reverse, as Strawson notes: "The concept of a person is logically prior to that of an individual consciousness."[17]

This taking of the concept of a person to be primitive seems to solve, at one stroke, some thorny problems that have been sticking in the sides of philosophers since at least Descartes—problems such as how the mind interacts with the body and how we know of the existence of other minds. Strawson would also make people, not mysterious egos, owners of conscious states. On the face of it, the solution looks too easy. It seems to amount to saying that we do readily communicate concerning our experiences, so any view that implies there are difficulties with this is suspect. We should first adopt a concept which preserves the possibility of straightforward communication and only then concern ourselves with egos, other minds, and interaction. From the Cartesian point of view this seems to beg the question. Strawson tries to shore it up with a linguistic investigation of the kinds of predicates we use to speak about ourselves.

To clarify the taking of the concept of a person as a basic or primitive, Strawson roughly divides the predicates we ascribe to persons into two groups: M-predicates (M for "material," I suppose) and P-predicates (P for "person"), of which two kinds the P-predicates imply the possession of consciousness of that to which they are ascribed.[18] To say that the concept of a person is primitive means that there are not simpler concepts like that of a Cartesian Ego to which P-predicates apply and that of a body to which M-predicates apply which can be combined to make a person. Persons are those basic kinds of things to which both kinds of predicates can be ascribed.

The general argument for claiming that both P-predicates and M-predicates must be applicable to persons I would put as follows:

1. I correctly apply P-predicates and M-predicates to myself.
2. If I correctly apply P-predicates and M-predicates to myself, then I must be able to correctly apply P-predicates and M-predicates to others.
3. If I correctly apply P-predicates and M-predicates to myself and others, then these others and myself must be distinguishable members of a type of thing to which both P-predicates and M-predicates are correctly applicable.
4. Therefore, I and these others must be distinguishable members of a type of thing to which both P-predicates and M-predicates are applicable.

If I have not oversimplified, then we can see from this expression of Strawson's argument where it is most likely to meet challenges: (1) is true enough (for example, I say I am thinking, or I weigh seventy-three kilograms). (2) is a more general version of the ascription principle, which begs the question concerning other minds from the point of view of the skeptic. (3) just unpacks what is in (2). The part of (2) which is controversial is the part concerning P-predicates.

To be able to use P-predicates of persons, we must have a way to tell when they apply. Strawson tells us: "What I have said is that one ascribes P-predicates to others on the strength of observations of their behaviour and that the behaviour-criteria one goes on are not just signs of the presence of what is meant by the P-predicate, but are criteria of a logically adequate kind for the ascription of the P-predicate."[19] This conclusion would solve the problem of skepticism about other minds in what seems too easy a stroke.

Strawson claims, however, that we have to have this conclusion if we are to adopt the conceptual scheme in terms of which skepticism is stated. Thus, when we describe the structure of our thought, we see that skepticism is in a way contradictory: "So with many skeptical problems: their statement involves the pretended acceptance of a conceptual scheme and at the same time the silent repudiation of one of the conditions of its existence."[20] This is a bold move against skepticism with regard to other minds. It preserves common sense in the face of philosophical conundrums. But, it is not at all clear that the condition just stated for the ascription of P-predicates really is a condition of the existence of a conceptual scheme which skepticism must accept. The skeptic may balk at the ascription principle on which this condition depends or may cast doubt on the whole notion of logical adequacy presupposed here. Strawson has merely started to develop his position.

Strawson reminds us that P-predicates, as with words in general, acquire their meaning in a larger structure of interrelated uses. Those who speak behaviouristically or skeptically about the application of P-predicates are both failing to see the larger picture and supposing, wrongly, that these predicates can be meaningfully used in the narrower context without setting it within the larger one.[21] This is an argument for the ascription principle, but it would become convincing only if more were said about the language structure which requires us to have a primitive concept of person before we can have a concept of a Cartesian Ego. Mathematical systems are often arbitrary about which of several concepts one takes as primitive. Why should we be different in speaking of persons?

Perhaps the answer is, from a descriptive metaphysical point of view, partly that we just happen to have this conceptual structure in which the concept of person is primitive. We might have had others, but we do not now and it is far too complicated a structure for us simply to substitute another in a revisionist way. Of course the "we" I use here is "we of the European culture," and it may well be that descriptive metaphysics is culturally relative. I will pursue questions of the influence of culture on our concept of person in my final remarks, but let us stick to Strawson's own program for now.

As to the initial question of why to attribute consciousness to anything, Strawson seems to be saying that one cannot have concepts like that of consciousness without a primitive concept of a person. The other initial question concerning, in effect, why we apply both P-predicates and M-predicates to one kind of thing is also answered by the primitiveness of the concept of a person. We can do none other and still make sense within the larger linguistic structure in which Strawson suggests we use such predicates.

In Wittgensteinian terms, the language game in which words referring to persons—P-predicates—and M-predicates are used requires that the words for persons go in the subject place for both types of predicates. The question as to whether we play this game as a contingent matter of fact or of necessity is not fully dealt with by Strawson, but the answer in his intentionally fragmentary account seems to be that it is contingent, and contingent on what we do: "What I am suggesting is that it is easier to understand how we can see each other, and ourselves, as persons, if we think first of the fact that we act, and act on each other, and act in accordance with a common human nature."[22] It seems that any change of the linguistic structure to allow us to speak differently and see ourselves differently would depend on the way we act and interact.

Bodies: All for one, one for all, or none at all

One interesting example of this comes from Strawson's consideration of a theme that has often cropped up in our investigation of the history of the concepts of a person, namely, the absorption of the individual by the group, an absorption which is favoured more in Oriental than in Western philosophy. Speaking of speculation on the group mind, Strawson says: "The fact that we find it natural to individuate as persons the members of a certain class of moving natural objects does not mean that such a conceptual scheme is inevitable for any class of being not utterly unlike ourselves."[23] If, for example, human beings were arranged into groups which acted as perfectly disciplined military units, with one executive member controlling all their actions, we might think of them, as Strawson refers to them, as one "scattered body."[24] We would stop seeing individual human beings as persons. This example of Strawson's is fictional, but the Oriental ideal of absorption of the individual allows, in reality, the family sometimes to be treated as if it were a person. The state may also be so treated and not just in the Orient: witness Hobbes's *Leviathan*.[25]

The way we speak of persons now and of individuals having separate conscious minds would no longer make sense once we moved to a new linguistic structure in which groups of persons were the basic unit. It would be, within that structure, as strange to talk of the individual mind as it would be to talk of my liver, my kidneys, or my heart as individually conscious.[26] Even this latter scenario is not impossible. The Iliadic Greeks may well have thought this way.[27] If so, then Strawson might say that their language would have a different structure from our own, which makes their thought not about persons at all. He would say that they were speaking a language in which that concept had no part.

Another way of looking at it is that the various things within a human being that had executive agency were really what were persons for the Greeks. There were many persons within one human body. Strawson's scattered bodies could also be seen as the bodies of scattered persons. The person is the group. When we focus on action and decision making, as Strawson does, whatever is the agent is the person. It seems, then, that one thing we might glean from consideration of Strawson's example is the idea that a concept of a person is something we cannot do without. When we move to group persons or multiple persons within a human body, we merely change the physical realization of our concept of a person; we do not eliminate persons. Strawson, however, must strenuously deny that our actual conceptual scheme permits some of the alternative realizations. Without changing our conceptual scheme, by Strawson's lights, we could not treat Cartesian Egos as persons.

Having struggled might and main against Cartesian Egos, Strawson, in a curious concluding section, considers the idea of a disembodied person.[28] This is not, however, the idea of an Ego with no body. We can, he thinks, conceive of a disembodied person within our actual conceptual scheme only because we already have the concept of a person on which this concept of a disembodied person is dependent. Such a person would see and hear as if she had a body. Strawson's conception of a person, it appears, even retains the common idea of the possibility of survival of bodily death. I say "even" since what is remarkable about Strawson's view of persons is that it accords in many ways with Western common sense on the topic of persons. This is highly unusual for a philosophical analysis of persons. Of course no philosophical account can capture all of the richness of the common notion while remaining consistent. The main thing Strawson decides to give up is that element of our daily chatter about each other which we have inherited from Descartes. Philosophers, however, are bound to remain unconvinced by Strawson. One of the notables of this century who takes on the task of refuting Strawson is a part-time member of the Vienna circle, the great disenchanted (and, therefore, former) logical positivist A.J. Ayer.

Ayer: An unusual view of ordinary people

Ayer begins in a not too propitious way by telling us that he will be discussing persons "in the broad sense that every individual human being can be counted as a person. It is characteristic of persons in this sense that besides having various physical properties…they are also credited with various forms of consciousness."[29] Of course one of the questions in the current debate about survival of persons is whether to confer the status of person on those human beings either who never achieve consciousness during their lives or who lose it permanently without dying. There are questions as well about the forms of consciousness necessary to be a person. Someone whose consciousness is no more developed than a cat's may or may not be a person according to various conceptions of persons.

Ayer also takes consciousness, at least initially, in a rough and ready way: "All I can say is that I am speaking of it in the ordinary sense in which, to be thinking about a problem, or remembering some event, or seeing or hearing something, or deciding to do something, or feeling some emotion, such as jealousy or fear, entails being conscious."[30] Someone who is dreaming but sound asleep or, perhaps, even someone in a permanent coma can be conscious in this sense. Probably a cat can feel fear and see or hear things in a way sufficient to satisfy these examples of conscious behaviour. We may, however, wish to distinguish between being conscious in terms of our behaviour, being conscious in the sense of being aware of ourselves and what we are doing, and being conscious in the sense of having a continuing consciousness of the kind appropriate to persons.

Ayer, however, cannot be expected to solve the myriad problems swarming around our concepts of a person all in one essay, but it is worth noting his very liberal definition of the topic. Some of the problems that Ayer raises, like that of personal identity, require more precise notions of person and consciousness for their solution. The demand for precision, clarity, and attention to language which has become fashionable through the agency of Ayer and philosophers like him makes almost any attempt to deal with the topic of persons stillborn. No sooner does one speak than presuppositions to be clarified prevent one from continuing. Naturally, this leads to a certain amount of glossing over and passing off just to get on with the job. Ayer at least draws attention to the difficulties which appear in his own account by speaking of his approximate usage of "person" and "consciousness" while many others have simply assumed that the meaning of these terms is sufficiently clear.

Persons as bodies

Ayer attempts to show that Strawson is unsuccessful in his attempt to go between the horns of dualism and materialism. Ayer locates his own view by contrasting it with Strawson's: "I am...inclined to think that personal identity depends upon the identity of the body, and that a person's ownership of states of consciousness consists in their standing in a special causal relation to the body by which he is identified....This amounts in effect to adopting what Mr. Strawson calls 'the no-ownership doctrine of the self.'"[31] It is confusing that Ayer's view is not, on the face of it, the same no-ownership view that Strawson was talking about. Ayer speaks of conscious persons owning their states of consciousness. The no-ownership view, on the other hand, is one according to which there is no owner or subject of experiences; experiences just happen and, Strawson says: "it is a linguistic illusion that one ascribes one's states of consciousness at all, that there is any proper subject of these apparent ascriptions, that states of consciousness belong to, or are states of, anything."[32] Ayer's account looks more like a straightforward materialism rather than the exotic no-ownership view.

Strawson also says, however, that the no-ownership theorist is willing to admit "an admissible, though infelicitous" sense of ownership in which the body "owns" experiences or states of consciousness.[33] As we saw above, Strawson thinks this view is incoherent because the no-ownership theorist needs possessives such as "my" to single out experiences thus presupposing the ownership that is denied. For part of Strawson's argument, I left a promissory note on which I must now make good. Strawson makes use of the subordinate conclusion that the no-ownership theorist cannot do without these possessives and still maintain the transferability principle. For example, it would be illegitimate to say "my thought" and still require that everything one is thinking could be thought by someone else. It is Strawson's argument for this conclusion that Ayer wishes to undermine.

The no-ownership theorist, in accord with the transferability principle, requires that bodies have experiences as a contingent matter of fact, not of necessity. Strawson's argument puts the no-ownership theorist in the dilemma of asserting either something false or something necessary when trying to assert such a supposedly contingent matter of fact.[34] To see the dilemma—in somewhat less detail than Strawson presents it—consider a no-ownership theorist, Ludwig, who wants to dispel the illusion of the Ego through talk about the contingent fact that his body, B, has experiences. How can he talk about that fact without possessives like "my" or "Ludwig's"? He can no longer say, All my experiences are had by body B. When he eliminates possessives he says something false such as, All experiences are had by body B. Suppose Ludwig tries another tack by claiming that, All Ludwig's experiences just means All experiences had by body B. Then his statement of fact becomes All experiences had by body B are had by body B. This is a necessary proposition, not the contingent one Ludwig needs. It seems, then, that Ludwig will either say something false or something necessary when he tries to state the contingent fact about the relationship of his experiences to himself.

Against this dilemma Ayer defends the consistency of his own position: "The position is that a person can be identified by his body; this body can be identified by its physical properties and spatio-temporal location; as a contingent fact there are certain experiences which are causally connected with it; and these particular experiences can then be identified as the experiences of the person whose body it is. There is nothing inconsistent in this."[35] Ludwig can now say, with Ayer's help, that what he means by the original sentence—All my experiences are had by my body B—is merely that if B is in certain kinds of states, then certain experiences are caused to occur.[36] Suppose Strawson then says, Ah! but these are not just any experiences but Ludwig's experiences, and Ayer has left that out. Ludwig must then reply—from Ayer's perspective—that to say experiences are Ludwig's is only to say they occur in body B. The new translation of the original sentence then is, If body B is in certain kinds of states, then certain kinds of events called experiences are caused to occur in body B. Is this contingent?

Whether this last translation of the original claim is really contingent or not is impossible to tell, since it is so vague. It apparently depends on a rough materialist faith that we will be able to spell out scientifically the material causes within bodies of experiences and that we will be able to give a thorough description of experiences as events in material bodies. Depending on unspecified background conditions, on a general method of individuating events, and perhaps even on causal determinism being false, this new claim may be contingent. Ayer recognizes the vagueness of such claims and tries to address it, but at most succeeds in pushing the problem back to the problem of what counts as one event.[37] Ayer has, however, raised some doubts as to the dilemma posed by Strawson. Strawson, moreover, is threatened in his attempt to avoid the seemingly endless debates about the possibility of experiences being merely events in material bodies by speaking not of mind and matter but of persons. Ayer can say that, if Ludwig's last translation makes sense and is contingent, then the dilemma is finished as far as materialists are concerned. We are back in the old debate between dualists and materialists, which Strawson would like to short-circuit.

Quine: Convention rules

Quine is another major contemporary figure in the Analytic school who puts language front and centre in his consideration of philosophical problems. Quine's remarks on the topic of persons are, nonetheless, critical of the ordinary-language approach. The logical positivists—indeed, the whole empiricist tradition—is also subjected to a vigorous critique by Quine, who undermines the distinctions between the analytic and the synthetic and between science and metaphysics. He is also opposed to that empiricist linguistic reductionism which tries to translate all statements into statements about immediate experience.[38] None of this, however, makes Quine a friend to those who wish to promote grand metaphysical systems to explain persons and their role in the universe. Quine is a special kind of minimalist who values the desert landscape much above the lush jungle where his commitment to the existence of things is concerned.

Nominalism

For Ryle and philosophers like him, to say that John is a person is just to say something, in a very condensed way, about the many things John tends to do. Quine expresses some ire with this and with ordinary language analyses in general:

> There are those who uncritically accept the dispositional idiom as a clear matter of ordinary language. Say what a thing is disposed to do in what circumstances, and the disposition holds no further mystery for them. Solubility in water is the disposition to dissolve when in water, and there is no plainer English than that. Such is Ryle's position in *The Concept of Mind*, where he undertakes to clarify other more obscure and troublesome notions in dispositional terms and is content to leave them thus.[39]

Quine apparently thinks that dispositional talk is not explanatory. This is at least controversial. To say with Aristotle that a stone falls because it tends to seek the earth may explain nothing, but the law of gravity is also dispositional and is explanatory. In any case, Quine attacks both the logical empiricist, such as Ayer, and the ordinary language philosopher, such as Ryle. Since he attempts to sever both main strands of prior contemporary Analytic philosophy, it is hard at first to see what he leaves himself as a tether.

Quine is in the tradition of those like the mediaeval philosopher William of Ockham and Russell as we saw in chapter 9, who try to eliminate commitment to the existence of anything which is not necessary to explain what we experience.[40] For instance, we have a word "red" in our language so the word exists and there is no need to postulate a Platonic form of redness as well. This view is called nominalism, since the names of some things are accepted as existing rather than the things themselves. Quine's nominalism is in opposition to talk of ideas and concepts, yet he wishes to speak of the conjectures and abstractions of scientific theory. This seems impossible, yet Quine assures us: "There is a way: we can talk of language. We can talk of concrete men and their concrete noises. Ideas are as may be, but the words are out where we can see and hear them. And scientific theories, however speculative and however abstract, are in words."[41] Thus Quine shares Russell's dismissive attitude to the ineffable and to talking about it or around it. In fact, from such a severe philosophy as Quine's, one can expect a dismissive attitude to many things philosophers have spoken of over the ages. It is interesting to see what can be said about persons in this minimalist framework.

Survival

Quine raises, for example, the ancient puzzle of the endurance of the self through change, with a contemporary twist. Undergoing change as I do, how can I be said to continue to be myself? Considering that a complete replacement of my material substance takes place every few years, how can I be said to continue to be myself for more than such a short period at best?[42] Actually there are some brain cells that persist through the change of all other cells in our bodies but that is small comfort, even to a materialist.

On the other hand, as Quine points out, appealing to some immaterial unifying thing within us is the thin edge of a very large wedge: "It would be agreeable to be driven, by these or other considerations, to belief in a changeless and therefore immortal soul as the vehicle of my persisting self-identity. But we should be less eager to embrace a parallel solution of Heraclitus' parallel. problem regarding a river: 'You cannot bathe in the same river twice, for new waters are ever flowing in upon you.'"[43] There are indeed few left who would adopt the old animist worldview in which every persisting object, such as a river, has a soul. In a way, that is a pity. We might treat the environment with more respect if we saw its components in this way. We must, however, solve our conceptual problems within the bounds of the resources which we ourselves can accept. Quine's solution is instructive even for those of us who are less committed to minimalism with respect to existential commitments.

It would be unacceptable for most of us to solve Heraclitus' puzzle by giving the river a soul comparable to the one we tend to see in ourselves. Quine suggests that we solve the puzzle of our own continuation by the familiar means we adopt for the river puzzle. Quine sees the river, indeed any persisting object, as a series of momentary stages. One cannot bathe in the same river stage twice but one can bathe in the same river twice. Different stages will consist of different waters, but they are all stages of one river.[44] Similarly, Quine would see persons as a series of stages. One is not at the same person-stage one was ten years ago, but one is the same person.

Since he sees all individual objects as processes, Quine develops an ontology, a theory of objects in general, which makes it easy to speak of one object through great changes. I will adumbrate that ontology here and apply it to persons, but readers may retain the distinction of person-stages from persons without accepting the ontology.

Worming our way through space-time

Quine proposes a rather radical conception of what counts as a particular thing. To understand it, we need to get at least a loose grip on the concept of a four-dimensional space-time worm. Imagine, unappealing though it may be, a bookworm has gnawed its way through this book from cover to cover. As we turn the pages we see holes in various places. Since the worm bored through at various angles, the hole may be in the top, middle, or bottom of the page—different positions in space. Each page was bored through at a time. Each page represents a stage of the worm's progress. The pathway through the space-time continuum which every object takes is somewhat like the record of the worm's progress through the book. Quine therefore, calls objects space-time worms. They are four dimensional since they occupy three dimensions in space and one in time. At any given moment in its existence, an object exists as a stage of its whole progress through space and time. But suppose that there are some pages of the book with no holes and some pages with several holes, although this worm cannot bore backward any more than we can reverse time. Quine is willing to countenance objects which are many places at one time, scattered objects. Water is such an object. At any given time its parts are to be found in many locations. Objects also need not be continuous. They can skip a page or more in the great book of the universe.[45]

This view is radical because it allows us to take any assemblage of particles of matter at any time and call them a particular object. For the most part, of course, the objects we are interested in—rivers, people, and such—are not discontinuous in time or not noticeably so. A river might dry up for a while. Can a person have gaps as well? One hears of various cases of apparent death and revival. There are science fiction cases of prolonged hibernation or being dissolved and reconstituted, as in *Star Trek* teletransportation. Certainly Quine would have no objection to calling Captain Kirk a single object even when, during teletransportation, Kirk does not seem to be anywhere. What would Quine say about these various stages of Kirk before and after teletransportation being the same person? He thinks that such examples merely demonstrate deficiency of the word "person": "Any coherent general term has its own principle of individuation, its own criterion of identity among its denotata. Often the principle is vague, as the principle of individuation of persons is shown to be by the science-fiction examples; and a term is as vague as its principle of individuation."[46] In the world according to Quine, as medicine progresses we may be confronted with things which we are at a loss to classify. Our current means of individuating persons will not help us. New conventions have to be fashioned.

One final point on Quine's contribution to the current debate on persons is in order. Much of the contemporary literature has to do with the topic of personal identity which concerns the question, When is person *x* the same as person *y*? Quine reduces questions of identity, whether diachronic (across time) or synchronic (in the timeless present), to questions of kind membership. The real question we are asking is not about identity but about how best to construe the term "person."[47] Once we have made a decision about the nature of persons, we will be able to decide whether Kirk is the same person after being beamed somewhere or whether the Kirk who vanishes in the teletransporter has been killed and a new one very much like him created on his apparent reappearance elsewhere. This is reminiscent of the warnings of Wittgenstein on this topic.

Strawson, Ayer, and Quine laid the groundwork for much recent Analytic philosophy. Now we move into the discussion of the current debate, which always looks to this groundwork as something that it must include, replace, or adapt. Before that, however, let us look at what we can do with what we have taken just now from contemporary Analytic philosophy.

What about Daphne?

According to the metaphysical views adopted by Strawson, Daphne may or may not be a person or the same person we once knew, depending on what P-predicates we can truly ascribe to her. But what is it to be the same person over time as these predicates change? For Ayer, Daphne is the same person, since her body remains. For Quine, it is simply a matter of how we wish to talk. Our conventions for the use of "person" are, perhaps, not suited to such cases as Daphne's. We must decide how to extend those conventions if we wish to use the term.

While he leaves us up in the air, Strawson makes some interesting remarks about personal identity and re-identification.[48] By taking persons as primary, he believes he has avoided concerns about the unity of consciousness within these topics. Hume's problem, for instance, of finding an enduring self vanishes when the self, or consciousness, is conceptually derivative from the primitive concept of a person. What we re-identify are persons, and we need to make use of their bodies to do so. However, Strawson warns: "the criteria of personal identity are certainly multiple. In saying that a personal body gives us a necessary point of application for these criteria, I am not saying that the criteria for reidentifying persons are the same as the criteria for reidentifying material bodies."[49] We identify people by focusing on the body and applying M-predicates and P-predicates. That done, we can now identify and re-identify the consciousness of a person, even if it should migrate from one body to another. Strawson leaves it an open question how we should deal with extreme cases in the real world—such as that in which a person becomes demented—or with other science fiction puzzle cases, but he thinks that, if we take the concept of a person to be primitive, then we will have no trouble with identification and reidentification in the normal cases.[50]

In a case of dementia in which the set of P-predicates is greatly reduced while the set of M-predicates is reduced far less, it seems we are met with a person, from Strawson's perspective. But whether we are met with the same person is another matter. While that will depend on the relative weights we assign to various criteria for re-identification, it will not depend, according to Strawson, on the unity and continuity of a primitive item called the demented person's consciousness. Once we stop looking for this non-existent item, we will look at the whole person and see her consciousness as defined in terms of that person rather than the reverse. We will stop asking such questions as, Is the same person still in there since this fall into dementia? Instead we will ask, How should we weigh intellectual ability as a predicate required for continuity?

There remains the question, which Strawson leaves open, of how we are to assign such weights. Re-identifying persons becomes a matter of assigning weights to various criteria; that is, it is a matter of deciding what is important about persons. Quine would say that we can choose any convention we wish. Strawson lets himself be guided by respect for the structure of the conceptual scheme we actually employ.[51] The difficult task remains of describing that conceptual scheme with respect to the re-identification of persons.

It also seems unclear whether Daphne is a person at all, never mind the same one we knew, on Strawson's account, since some P-predicates seem to apply to her, but most do not. She may smile and we might say she is happy. It is difficult to suppose, however, given the extent of her brain damage, that she is thinking of things in the way that we do. Perhaps, if we decided how to assign weights to certain P-predicates, we could not only answer the question whether she is a person but also the question whether she is the same person we knew prior to the brain damage. Quine would say that choosing our conventions about what counts as a person will also settle issues concerning identity. It becomes clearer why Ayer would want to short-circuit this whole discussion and say we merely have to determine whether the body is the same body.

What I like about these contemporary philosophers

Strawson's attachment to our pre-existing conceptual scheme is refreshing, since so many contemporary philosophers encourage us to abandon it. Taking the concept of a person as primitive or basic may be a very useful device as long as the conceptual scheme is recognized as culturally relative. The primacy of actions of persons in our understanding of them is a good idea, especially with regard to actions of persons on persons.

We should retain from Ayer the idea of the importance of the body to our concept of a person, but we need not make it all-important. Ayer and Quine make us reflect on the conventions that Strawson tends to view as part of an ongoing conceptual scheme that weathers changes of time, nation, culture, and place. The challenge is to keep some of Strawson's insights in spite of the corrosive effect of Quine's and Ayer's arguments. This requires that these insights be supported by different sorts of arguments. In the search for such arguments in later chapters, we will hear the echo of Quine's warning about the inapplicability of some of our conventions to new cases.

Content questions

1. Why does Strawson call his metaphysics "descriptive" rather than "revisionary"?
2. What is Strawson's general method for investigating our idea of self?
3. Does Strawson believe that we must have the kinds of bodies we have in order to have our kinds of experience? Explain your agreement or disagreement.
4. What two views of persons does Strawson particularly oppose?
5. Why does Strawson think that the no-ownership view is incoherent?
6. What is the ascription principle? Explain whether you accept it.
7. Give a skeptic's objection to Strawson's argument on page 239.
8. Are persons necessarily individual human beings in Strawson's view? Explain.

9. Do persons necessarily have bodies at all in Strawson's view? Explain.
10. What is odd about Ayer's characterization of persons in terms of consciousness? Give a counter-example.
11. Why is it odd that Ayer says that he adopts the no-ownership view?
12. How does Strawson argue that the no-ownership theorist is incapable of describing the contingent relationship of himself to his experience?
13. How does Ayer reply?
14. What main strands of Analytic philosophy does Quine wish to sever?
15. Why does Quine object to the supposition that a person has some continuing thing like a soul that preserves personal identity?
16. What effect does Quine's view of persons as processes have on questions of personal identity?

Arguments for analysis

Argument 1: A defence of the transferability principle

When we say that we own something, we are implicitly drawing a contrast. Owning a car, then, contrasts with other kinds of possession such as renting. Without this contrast, the idea of ownership makes no sense. Even when we use it metaphorically—as in the phrase, You must own your own failures—we are contrasting taking responsibility with not taking it or assigning it to someone else. That is why the sentence, I own my brain, sounds silly. Brains are not transferable to other persons. If, in some science-fiction scenario, the brain is transferred, the person would probably be transferred with it. Since there is no contrast, the sentence makes no sense. These examples make plausible the principle that only those things whose ownership is logically transferable can be owned at all.

Argument 2: A counter-example to the transferability principle

Such an important principle for determining the nature of persons cannot rest on examples alone. Indeed, there are counter-examples to this principle. Suppose that it is part of the constitution of a country that all tidal lands are the possession of the nation in perpetuity with no possibility of transfer to any other legal entity. In that case, we would understand non-transferable ownership. The same can apply to our experiences, our brains, or anything else we own but cannot transfer. Examples, apparently, do not settle this matter, for they lend weight to both sides.

Argument 3: A defence of the ascription principle

Consider Strawson's ascription principle: if I ascribe states of consciousness to myself, then I should also ascribe them or be prepared to ascribe them to others. The reason for this is that my ascriptions become meaningless if this principle is not honoured. When I say, for instance, I am happy, I communicate something to others only if I could also say, She is happy, in a meaningful way. But if I say, I am greplfinst, and am not prepared to use this private sensation of mine to describe anybody else, then I communicate nothing. "Greplfinst" is meaningless until there are conditions under which I am prepared to say, She is greplfinst, or He is greplfinst. Knowing those conditions would tell you what I mean.

Argument 4: A counter-example to the ascription principle

Suppose I am a garage chemist, mixing up LSD and various other drugs. From time to time I experiment on myself with different combinations of illegal hallucinogens in order to test designer highs. Sometimes my experiments yield results that I cannot replicate. Indeed after I am no longer under the influence of the test drugs, I cannot always remember which combination of drugs brought on the experience and I do not know what my behaviour was like during the experience. There are, therefore, no criteria for judging whether others might be in a state of consciousness—call it "greplfinst"—that I was in during one such experiment. Nonetheless, while I clearly recall what it was like to be greplfinst, I cannot ascribe greplfinst to others because I do not know under what conditions others would be in that state. Nonetheless, I have a vivid idea of what it is to be greplfinst. In spite of what Strawson and Wittgenstein have argued, "greplfinst" is a meaningful term denoting a state of consciousness although I can only give an inadequate description of this state of consciousness to others.

In general, meaning is necessary for interpersonal communication, but interpersonal communication is not necessary for meaning. The sighted woman in the land of the blind cannot communicate to others that she is seeing a green tree. Nonetheless, she can tell herself this meaningfully.

Argument 5: An objection to Ayer

Suppose Opal wants to explain the sentence: All my experiences are had by body B, without using the possessive "my." Following Ayer's advice, we would translate this into: If body B is in certain kinds of states, then certain kinds of events called experiences are caused to occur in body B. But what states are meant? They are the states we call experiences. What this translation really says is not contingent, as Ayer claimed. What it says is this: If certain kinds of events called experiences are caused to occur in body B, then certain kinds of experiences are caused to occur in body B. That is necessary, uninformative, and wholly inadequate to explain what it means to say that Opal has experiences.

Argument 6: A reply on behalf of Ayer

Actually, Opal is not referring to experiences with the phrase, "certain kinds of states." For example, body B might be in the state of having light shining on the retina of the eyes of body B. This would cause a visual sensation, an experience, in body B. The kinds of states meant here are initial conditions that lead to experience.

CHAPTER 11

Wiggins and Williams

Wiggins' individuative naturalism

Wiggins, in the course of writing detailed essays on the concept of identity, has much to say about personal identity and the concept of a person.[1] He calls his view "individuative naturalism."[2] It is naturalist in that "person" is treated as a natural kind by reference to which we individuate its members. "Person" is a substance concept which applies or does not apply to a living being its whole life through. By contrast, "infant" is not a substance concept; it applies during part of a life.[3] For Wiggins persons are co-extensive with members of *homo sapiens*; so, spatio-temporally continuous living human bodies serve to identify persons,[4] but persons also have irreducibly psychological properties supervenient on their neurophysiology.[5]

Against relative identity

While Wiggins believes that we must individuate people under a natural kind, he does not accept the relative identity thesis (that is, the view that identity of things under one kind does not imply identity under other kinds). For example, in cases of dementia, it might be tempting to say that the demented individual is the same human

Notes to chapter 11 are on pp. 487-89.

being but not the same person as existed prior to the dementia, since many human attributes are still present after dementia sets in, while such properties as rationality and self-awareness are gone. Wiggins says, however, that identity cannot be relativized in this way and retain its formal properties of transitivity, reflexivity, and symmetry.[6] It is sufficient for our purposes to note that Wiggins holds that, if we identify some being as the same human being whom we once knew and that human being is also a person, then we have identified the same person as well. If indeed philosophers ought to speak of persons in Wiggins' way, this blocks many attempts to say, in a philosophically significant sense, that one is no longer the same person after losing one's mind. Denial of sameness of persons is often a preface to ethical considerations, so Wiggins' claim is of great importance in areas of philosophy other than metaphysics.

Aristotle's influence

In terms of the history of the concept of a person, Wiggins is lining himself up squarely with the Aristotelians against the supporters of Locke, who take continuity of consciousness to be the criterion of identity and who suppose that it is logically possible that we change bodies. Aristotelians think that the person or self is the form of the living body, hence inseparable from it. Aristotle's view about the inseparability of souls from bodies, which Wiggins thinks is nearly correct, is this: "So there is no call to ask whether the soul and the body are one, just as there is no call to ask this question with the wax and the impression in the wax, nor any call to ask this question for any substance and the matter of which this substance is composed."[7] Unfortunately for this view, Wiggins notes, a body is a substance, yet a dead body is not a person.[8] It seems, then, that the soul, or self, or person is separable from the body. The very brief form of Wiggins' answer is that the person is inseparable from the living body. The person is not, however, merely the living body since the person has irreducibly psychological properties.[9]

Since Wiggins is not willing to identify the person with the living body as materialists do, one may wonder why he is not willing to accept the dualism of Locke. He defends Locke against Butler's objection of circularity of the memory criterion for identifying persons and thinks that Locke is right to emphasize self-awareness, a profoundly important feature of persons.[10] Wiggins proceeds by revising Locke's account to overcome the problem of the imperfections of our memory.[11] In the end, however, Wiggins argues that a biological underpinning is needed for the consciousness of persons and that Lockeans overemphasize the intellect. The continuity of a ballerina needs explaining as much as that of a philosopher.[12]

Against functionalism

Part of Wiggins' argument for his doctrine that persons are substances—organisms more specifically—is the inadequacy of the denial of this doctrine. If we take persons to be defined by their functions, then the resulting concept is inadequate to bear the weight put on it from a moral point of view. Although Wiggins denies ethical naturalism, he asserts a neighbouring doctrine that the nature of persons is the basis of value in the sense of causally enabling objective agreement between persons.[13] Concerning this difficult doctrine Wiggins asserts: "If freedom and dignity and creativity are what we crave, we shall find more promise of these things in the Heraclitean prediction 'You would not find out the bounds of the soul, though you traversed every path: so deep is its logos' than in the idea that it is for men to determine the limits of their own nature, or mould and remake themselves to the point where they can count as their very own creation.[14] This can be understood partly through seeing that Wiggins holds that the functional account of persons allows what counts as a person to be a matter for interpretation while his own account makes it a matter for discovery. Person is not only a natural kind but a kind of such depth and complexity that Heraclitus' prediction is borne out.

Another dangerous path that Wiggins claims to avoid by means of his own theory is that taken by those who see persons as mere social constructs. Such is the concept used by the social manager who would engineer society to the manager's own political and moral specifications. This limits human potential and such constructs, once in place, are resistant to reform.[15] Those who try to be something more or something other than allowed under the manager's concept of a person are blocked by the social norms hallowed in terms of persons. If, on the other hand, we think, as Wiggins does, that what persons are is generally specifiable in biological terms but infinitely variable in the irreducibly psychological attributes which we may discover to be supervenient on that biological basis, then we do not limit human potential through the narrow vision of the social manager.

Natural kinds

A person then is a substance. If we have the same being, we have the same person; for, however one identifies a thing, it is the same thing. The spatio-temporal continuity of the living body will, therefore, be sufficient to individuate the person. The sense in which Wiggins accepts that the person transcends the body is that the person is realized in the living body. One can abstract the person from the body but not separate the two in practice. The criticism which quickly comes to mind in the light of current philosophical debate on persons is based on the possibility of brain transplants in which a person seems to leave her body, except for the brain, behind.

Wiggins is highly and rightly suspicious of science fiction examples. Of the brain transplant case, in which the character of the person goes to a new body with the brain, Wiggins says: "We are deceived by the high quality of the actors and mimics we see on the stage if with the help of greasepaint and props they have made us think this is as (relatively) simple as the transposition of music from one instrument to another."[16] Certainly it may well be in this and in other cases of radical change, including fission cases, we can appear to describe them without contradiction only because they are so badly underdescribed.

There may be another reason for thinking the various science fictions impossible. Wiggins uses a view based on Leibniz and Putnam which makes natural kinds determined by law-like principles discovered by attention to an arbitrary good specimen of the kind.[17] We take, for example, arbitrary good specimens of gold, which we have known for centuries, and discover the properties of gold as a natural kind. Now "person" may be a sortal term, such as "gold," based on law-like principles. It was once thought possible to make gold alchemically from base metals in certain ways which turned out to be impossible. Similarly, we think that persons can change in ways which threaten the use of spatio-temporal continuity of the living body as a criterion of identity. These may turn out to be impossible as well once we understand the law-like regularities underlying the concept of a person. This remains an open question.

We may possibly be able by some process not involving the philosopher's stone to synthesize gold. It would be real gold for all that. If, by some much more miraculous process,[18] we can synthesize people, then they would be real people, made of flesh and blood. They would not be just good-looking automata. If, by contrast, we accept mere automata because they function as people, then we open ourselves to the objectionable views mentioned earlier. What persons are becomes open to interpretation. We would still, therefore, by Wiggins' thinking, have to distinguish between real persons and artifacts which function like some persons if we want the concept of a person to bear the moral weight we put on it.

One response to this claim about moral weight is that given by Williams, whom we are about to discuss. Williams says that the concept of a person simply will not bear this weight, and we should reject this concept as a foundation for ethical thought.[19]

Williams' bodily criterion

Williams takes a dim view of the concept of person just outlined since he thinks that concept is not a true sortal or natural kind concept. That is why he does not trust it to bear the moral weight that Wiggins puts on it. Williams takes persons to be merely bodies, as we shall see.

Short of saying with Ayer that persons are merely bodies—sometimes this is restricted to bodies of the human kind—Williams argues, like Wiggins, that bodily identity is a necessary condition of personal identity.[20] That is, if person A is the same as person B, then A has the same body as B. Williams denies, however, that A's having the same body as B is enough to guarantee that A is the same person as B. Williams' thesis that bodily identity is a necessary but not a sufficient condition of personal identity, if true, would rule out the very popular view, for which Strawson argued, that one could survive apart from one's body.

Same body, same person

The essential point in Williams' argument to show that bodily identity is always necessary to personal identity is that any criterion of personal identity has to have a user.[21] The attempts by Locke and others to explain personal identity without the body rely, in Williams' opinion, on presupposing an impossible viewpoint from which to observe the non-bodily features of persons. This viewpoint is neither that from within the person (subjective) nor that from without (objective). The use of such criteria as self-consciousness and memory is illegitimate since these are not observable from the objective point of view.[22] From the subjective point of view, the question of identity cannot arise.[23] What we use to identify a person are actions and events, but we cannot associate these with a person without first identifying that person by means of a body. There are two points I wish to examine in this sort of argument: the viewpoint problem in general and the question of personal identity from a subjective viewpoint. We will see in chapter 14 that Thomas Nagel takes seriously the idea of a view from nowhere.

Even if one agrees with Williams concerning the viewpoint argument, the idea that a criterion of identity must have a user needs qualification. To require that a criterion of identity in fact be used by someone to make an identification is probably requiring more than Williams does here. Philosophers are not prone to restrict attention to what may be put to practical purposes. Let us suppose that he is saying, rather, that the criterion could possibly be used. Williams seems to be saying that I cannot use criteria like memory to identify others since I can have no access to their memories. What is required, then, is an argument to show that it is not possible to know another's memories. Such an argument is not given. Only an assertion about lack of access to the mental events of another bolsters this claim about memory.[24] Is mind-reading logically impossible? Even supposing that Williams is right about this impossibility, there remains the question whether a criterion of identity might not be correct even if it were inapplicable to the identification of others. That is to say, the criterion might contain a metaphysical truth but our knowledge of identities of persons might be limited by our not being able to apply the criterion.

Forget memory

Williams considers Locke's use of memory as "what makes a man be himself to himself."[25] Williams tries to show that this is absurd. His argument is puzzling, but it is his reply to objections that reveals what has gone wrong. He imagines this objection: "'You have argued,' it might be said, 'that no man can use memory as a criterion of his own identity. But this is just what shows that memory is the essence of personal identity; figuratively speaking, memory is so much what makes him a certain person that when provided with certain memories, he cannot doubt who he is.'"[26] To this objection, Williams replies, "A man who has lost his memory cannot say who anyone else is, either, nor whether any object is the same as one previously presented."[27] It appears that Williams is treating the memories used to identify a person as coming in an all-or-nothing package. That is, however, not the way memories are packaged. Apparently one can be in states in which large parts of memory are lost, like transient global amnesia or epileptic automatism,[28] not knowing who one is, but knowing much about other things and people. One can retain complex abilities and characteristics without remembering one's own history. Once memory of one's own history returns, one cannot doubt who one is.

My reply to Williams is a two-edged sword. If memory, during a state of epileptic automatism, for instance, is nearly intact except for memory of personal history, then memory of personal history does not seem essential to personal identity. This is hardly what the objection intended to support. I agree, however, neither with Williams nor an opponent diametrically opposed, a Lockean for instance. Memory of personal history is one of many marks of personal identity, including the body, personality, abilities, and other memories of the person. What I take from Williams, then, is the point that Locke and others have overemphasized the role of memory of personal history. On the other hand, Williams goes too far in his rejection of memory altogether. I address more of this toward the end of this work.

Personality is not enough

Personality also comes under withering fire from Williams' position. Williams resurrects the famous Beauchamp case of dissociation of the personality reported by Prince[29] to consider whether one may individuate personalities independently of the body. Beauchamp was reported to have various personalities in complicated relationships. Some of her personalities knew the doings of the others and some were supposedly in ignorance of others. Williams seems, at some points in the argument, to take it at face value that some of her personalities could not remember what others had done.[30] This is a matter in some doubt. The symptoms described by Prince are sometimes thought to have been produced by Beauchamp out of Victorian modesty and a desire to please Prince.[31] Whether the Beauchamp case is reliable evidence or not, let us assume for the sake of argument that Beauchamp's reported symptoms are possible. Note that the memories which make one oneself to oneself may be lost and regained if such symptoms are possible. While this occurs, other memories remain intact, in the Beauchamp story. Self-identification through memory seems to make perfectly good sense for Beauchamp in spite of Williams' claim that such self-identification is absurd. It seems then that the shaky evidence which Williams accepts, if it really is acceptable, provides a counter-example to his anti-Lockean claim. But let us see how Williams is using this Beauchamp case. His purpose is not to deal with the memory criterion, but to attack personality as a criterion of identity.

With respect to individuation of personalities, Williams claims that they are particulars only in the sense that character is a particular, that is, "a sense which is grounded in the particular body."[32] Here, of course, he is only speaking of the publicly observable personality and character. This is a point well taken. We could not begin to speak of Beauchamp's various personalities without first identifying her by means of her body. Her personality or personalities and her body are both part of what makes her Beauchamp; that is, they are parts of her identity, but we can know of that identity primarily through observation, which gives the body its central position in identification. This should not in itself impugn personality as essential to the identity of the person. It makes, rather, a point about how we may come to know that person.

Williams wishes, however, to claim more than this. Character and personality are not genuine particulars, he claims. They are parasitic on the body for their status as apparent particulars.[33] If this is so, then not only are they not the primary way in which we identify people, they are not metaphysically primary in the identities of people. The person is the body, and the personality is merely a set of properties of the body which may change without changing who the person is. Whether or not personalities are essential to persons, all Williams' argument shows is the epistemological point that the way we come to know them is through the body. This depends on our particular viewpoint from which we come to know persons. Williams' argument depends on saying that it is the only way we could gain such knowledge. This is the point of his saying that a criterion must have a user, and there must be some viewpoint from which we make the identification.

This brings us back to the viewpoint from which we apply a criterion of identity. Williams argues that it must be either subjective or objective, and then rules out the subjective viewpoint. We have just seen that it is not ruled out. It turns out then that publicity is not essential to identification. Beauchamp could identify herself when in possession of the appropriate memories. All those views of persons—such as Locke's and Descartes'—that result in criteria which are heavily dependent on subjective evidence, have not been laid to rest by Williams' argument thus far. Williams has, however, given us reason for caution in adopting Lockean or Cartesian positions by pointing out the epistemological importance of the body from the objective viewpoint. The subjective viewpoint, while not vanquished, is limited. It is logically possible that there may be incorrect self-identification of a kind, as reported in the case of Beauchamp. Should I wake up convinced that I am Bernard Williams, I could perhaps be persuaded of the falsity of that self-identification. One identifies oneself through one's body, personal history, abilities, and personality as others identify one. In cases of amnesia or dissociation of personality, the objective check of others may be needed to aid self-identification. If we could accept Williams' metaphysical position that persons are thinking bodies, we could simplify our conception of such difficult cases. According to Williams, Beauchamp would remain Beauchamp throughout her radical changes, while, in Locke's view, she must go into and out of existence frequently.

Persons as analyzable

Williams puts up three main contenders for the understanding of what persons are. Two of these we have discussed earlier. The three are Strawson's view that persons are unanalysable subjects, Descartes' position that persons are Egos in bodies, and the position Williams himself supports, that persons are thinking bodies. We have seen how Williams treats positions like those of Descartes and Locke, which have the Ego or the consciousness housed in a body and able to change residences.

Williams puts forth a variety of objections[34] to Strawson's position that the concept of a person must be taken as primitive, making persons unanalysable subjects in terms of which such things as person's minds and person's bodies must be defined. One of the simplest of Williams' objections is that treating persons as bearers of both M- and P-predicates is too inclusive, since animals may also bear both.[35] This is indicative of the general thrust behind Williams' objections. It shows that Williams does not take seriously the idea that the concept of a person is primitive, for his objection depends on taking that concept as defined in terms of M- and P-predicates. If there is to be any defining in this neighbourhood, it will have to be of the predicates in terms of persons, not the other way around. While I do not dispute that Strawson has insufficiently defined these predicate types, that does not, in itself, defeat the view that the concept of a person must be taken as primitive. One may object that Strawson has not satisfactorily shown us that so doing will lead to advantages in metaphysics. Williams may contend that taking persons as bodies which think, as material things to which psychological predicates are applicable, is a preferable basis for theory.

Against disembodied persons

One of the objections to his own position considered by Williams is that persons who once had bodies can survive in a disembodied state, that is, without bodies. Williams warns that this way Cartesianism lies. Apparently, while he takes Strawson's view of persons seriously, Williams thinks that a reduction to Cartesianism is a reduction to absurdity. Nonetheless, the possibility of disembodied persons is widely accepted, often for religious reasons, and our language reflects that. It is natural enough to speak of shaking off these mortal coils and departing from the body. Nor is this just figurative. Even the non-religious tend to take seriously the often reported out-of-body experiences had by people near death. Williams must argue that this common way of talking rests on a metaphysical error.

Williams first points out that supposedly disembodied persons would be indeterminate in many respects, just like fictional characters. There is no answer to How much does Sherlock Holmes weigh? nor to How much does Conan Doyle weigh? given that Doyle is now disembodied. Williams adopts a principle that, he claims, excludes such entities as disembodied persons from existence: "If we are given a specification of a thing of a certain sort, and are told that it exemplifies no determinates under determinables associated with things of that sort, we can standardly conclude that it is not the specification of any real thing of that sort."[36] The application of this principle in the present case simply begs the question. Why should we assume that disembodied persons should be determinate with respect to weight as embodied persons are? Is it that weight is essential to persons? Then one has assumed that persons are material or have an essential material component. Whether it is possible that persons can, like Cartesian Egos, have psychological without material features cannot be determined by the principle Williams adopts until we have decided what things of that sort, persons, have as determinables. Only if material properties must be included among these determinables will disembodied persons be ruled out. Since the reasonable alternative—that is, of saying that disembodied persons do not have such things as weight among their determinables—has not been dealt with, Williams' further arguments against the unreasonable alternative of saying that disembodied persons have a determinate weight of zero must be put aside as amusements.

Williams might retort that the onus is on those who imagine that there could be such things as disembodied persons to say what their class of determinables is. We know, roughly, for real people in what respects they are determinate. The answer that disembodied persons would be determinate only in those respects which do not require a body might elicit the response that there are none; all psychological properties are dependent on material bodies. This claim brings us to what Williams calls "the micro level"[37] of neurology and questions as to the causes of the psychological characteristics of people. The question then becomes one for empirical science.

Language rules

The philosophical questions that interest Williams arise not primarily from science but from consideration of the way we speak. For example, "Jones" and "Jones's body" are not interchangeable *salva veritate*; in other words, we can say true sentences using one of these two phrases which will become false sentences if we substitute the other. It seems, then, that these two refer to different things; hence, the person-as-body thesis seems wrong. In a way this is tricky for Williams since so many of his arguments rest heavily on our use of language, on what we may plausibly say. As he points out, however, there are phrases which are synonymous in some contexts and not in others; so we cannot rest much on the contrast between these two phrases in some contexts.[38] Williams is, moreover, revisionist in his metaphysics. He wants to change the way we standardly speak about persons.

Williams examines the difficulties of separating material from psychological properties of persons. This is the problem of Strawson's M-predicates and P-predicates revisited. Descartes takes extension to be the fundamental property of material things—their being in space and time. Williams thinks that defining material properties in terms of extension would exclude such properties as being observable by physicists as a property of material bodies.[39] That depends, however, on our analysis of observability. Williams looks at perception and memory as effects with causes in the body;[40] so he should see observability in the same terms. One can, it seems, accept extension as essential to material objects and say, consistently with Williams' other views, that observability is the potential of objects to cause our perceptions. This would not help Descartes, as it reduces psychological events, perceptions, to material events.

The difficulty here is to say something on either side of the issue without begging the question as to the truth of materialism, dualism, or idealism. Williams tries to be neutral prior to his apparently materialist conclusions but remarks that it is "far from clear that the idea of causal relations obtaining in an immaterial substance could be anything but utterly mysterious."[41] Idealists would say the same about causes in matter. Dualists, however, suffer from the interaction problem here, and it is mainly against Cartesian dualism that Williams seems to defend his person-as-body thesis. It seems, not too surprisingly, that Williams' rejection of Cartesian dualism leads him to materialism.

Williams glosses his objection to dualism in terms of class membership. If whales are mammals, then being the same whale is being the same mammal. Similarly, being the same person would imply having the same body, if the necessity-of-the-body thesis is correct. There is an infelicitous lack of parallel here. In any case, against this putative parallel, Williams considers a science fiction brain exchange case. Two people have their brains exchanged and their personalities go to the new bodies along with the brain. Williams seems to accept this as possible. Concerning this case, Williams refers to a problem—which Williams also attributes to Strawson—namely, that whoever accepts the brain exchange as possible must say how it is that the ascription of bodily properties to persons is not the ascription of anything to bodies.[42] One would have to be able to say following a brain trade, for example, that a person who used to be 183 cm tall with grey hair is now 152 cm tall and has not yet turned grey.

Putting aside the question as to the logical possibility of the brain-exchange example, it is odd that Williams requires of any user of the brain-exchange case that she overcome linguistic conventions when Williams was not willing to take them that seriously in his own response to the objection concerning interchangeability of "Jones" and "Jones's body." One could simply say, emulating Williams, that we ascribe properties sometimes to bodies and sometimes to persons; which it is depends on the context of the utterance.

Information is not enough

Williams also considers a science fiction case in which the information in one person's brain is recorded and transferred to another. Again, the logical possibility of this is not questioned. Since the contents of our minds seem to be heavily dependent on the actual structure of our brains, it seems that minds cannot be thought of as software to be recorded and transferred, leaving the old hardware behind. Let us grant, for the sake of argument, that the background assumptions could be spelled out so that such transfers are logically possible for beings like ourselves.

Williams is concerned that such transfers could be made in more than one case, creating a number of people who are exact copies of the original person. They cannot all be identical to the original. Williams calls this sort of copying reduplication. Reduplication seems to lead to puzzles if we depart from the bodily criterion of identity. Williams considers a way out for those who think in terms of character as a criterion of identity. Two tokens of persons cannot be identified with a third token. The problem of reduplication might be overcome, Williams speculates, if we think of persons as types, as classes of bodies.[43] This is, however, no advance. Williams considers what it would be like to fall in love with a person type and to want to be near any of several tokens of that type. "Much of what we call loving a person would begin to crack under this, and reflection on it may encourage us not to undervalue the deeply body-based situation we actually have."[44] As we will see in a later discussion, Parfit is not so concerned with tokens as with types. In his revisionist way, Parfit embraces the very conclusion that Williams finds repugnant. Williams, however, is also revisionist and admits that his own view may seem odd, entailing as it does that one who loves a person loves a body, but "the alternatives that so briskly flow out of suspending the present situation do not sound too spiritual either."[45] But must we really accept his view that the main remaining alternative to considering ourselves as bodies is to consider ourselves as types? I have tried to cast some doubt on his arguments leading to this conclusion.

Williams' arguments, however, make it difficult to keep to the Aristotelian position defended by Wiggins and even more difficult to occupy the large opposing fort where defenders of Cartesian Egos or Lockean consciousnesses reside. In particular, Williams has, through his consideration of reduplication, made it very important for any concept of a person to find an anchor lest it float into the region where persons become types of things and particular individuals may be just tokens of that type, more like particular copies of a frequently printed book rather than like precious crystals each of which is unique. Williams chooses the body as the anchor.

Person as a moral concept

Regarding the moral import of the concept of a person, Williams writes:

> The category of person, though a lot has been made of it in some moral philosophy, is a poor foundation for ethical thought, in particular because it looks like a sortal or classificatory notion while in fact it signals characteristics that almost all come in degrees—responsibility, self-consciousness, capacity for reflection, and so on. It thus makes it seem as if we were dealing with a certain class or type of creature, when in fact we are vaguely considering those human beings who pass some mark on a scale. To make matters worse, the pass mark for some purposes is unsuitable for others. If *person* implies something called "full moral responsibility," the lowest age for entry to the class that has traditionally been entertained is seven, but anyone who has lived with a six-year-old, or a two-year-old, has vivid reasons for thinking of them as persons.[46]

If, on the other hand, we accept the claim that the capacity for reflection and self-consciousness are the effects of causes "running through the body." As Williams puts it,[47] then, whether or not we accept fully that persons are bodies, ancient concerns about responsibility arise. The problem of causal determinism that there seems to be no room for people to have responsibility if all their thoughts, feelings, and actions are caused by material phenomena surely must be faced by any view that answers Yes to Are persons bodies plus their psychological effects? At this level at least, Williams' views on persons have a very direct impact on moral theory.

That is not to say that moving away from Wiggins' notion that the concept of a person is a sortal concept does not radically alter the ways in which that concept can be used in moral theory. If we must, moreover, disabuse ourselves of the opposing concepts of a person as a personality, Cartesian Ego, or Lockean consciousness, then these other ways of making the concept bear moral weight evaporate. Even if we can get over materialist determinist difficulties with motivating moral discourse at all, we will still have to forego Locke's forensic concept of a person and Wiggins' sortal or natural kind. We will not be able to talk of the rights of persons. If Williams is right, ethics has become a very different subject.

What about Daphne?

In terms of my constant example, one who becomes demented is certainly the same person, dementia notwithstanding, if Williams is right. It would be foolish to argue that Daphne's body is not the same body. What we see is, moreover, still a thinking body, though the level of thought is diminished nearly to the vanishing point. Depending on the height at which one puts the pass mark on certain scales, one might wish to say that a dementia patient is not a person, but this would be perhaps more revisionist than Williams would wish to be. In this identification of Daphne, Williams would, then, probably agree with Wiggins. But what follows from this identification regarding Daphne's right to treatment or our duties to keep her comfortable? Nothing at all for Williams. What we ought to do has to be determined, according to Williams, without appeal to, say, the dignity of persons. Saying Daphne is a person does not necessarily put her into the same moral class as you just because we say that you are a person. Person, for Williams, is not a sortal concept as Wiggins would have it.

Daphne's dementia, a radical change of psychological properties, does not, by Wiggins' approach, destroy her as a person. It would be foolish to say that she has a different body, although it has changed in some respects, including important neurophysiological respects. Since Wiggins argues against the use of relative identity to say that the sufferer of dementia is the same living body but not the same person, and since he denies that the person is separable from the body, he must count her as the same person through the radical changes.

A possible objection to this analysis using Wiggins' concept of a person can be worked out using the idea of our irreducibly psychological characteristics supervenient on our neurophysiology. Can Wiggins not say that, while the person cannot exist without the living body, the living body can exist without the person? Yes, he can. Probably he would do so in the case of a neo-mort. All of the psychological properties formerly associated with such a living body are gone. Daphne has certainly lost her intellect, but Wiggins thinks we place too much emphasis on intellect. Her remaining psychological properties, for instance perceptual and emotional ones, may well qualify her as a person on Wiggins' view; hence she is, from that view, the same person who once had a great intellect.

There is no doubt that Daphne no longer has the capacities she once had. By the functionalist account of persons which Wiggins criticizes, Daphne would be gone, though her body remains, as if a computer has been disabled and can no longer run the program we knew as a person. Wiggins rejected this account as unable to bear the moral weight we put on the concept of a person. In this case, one would be released from obligations to Daphne which were undertaken while she lived. By Wiggins' account of persons, such a release would be premature.

Daphne is, therefore, the same person she was prior to her misfortune, according to Wiggins' theory. This is morally significant since, for Wiggins, a person is a particular kind of creature, not merely a conscious body which can perform certain functions. Only a difference in kind is the moral basis for a difference in treatment. Daphne, according to Wiggins, must still be treated as a person.

What I like about Wiggins and Williams

Both Wiggins and Williams make the body important without actually identifying persons with bodies. Williams, however, comes closer to this position than Wiggins. Wiggins reminds us of the moral import of the concept of a person. Williams, through his iconoclasm against the spiritual or moral importance of persons as persons, drives us to clarify the way in which the concept of a person can be central to our moral thinking. Williams provides us, I believe, with a good example of the sort of revisionism which banishes concepts of a person to the museum of philosophical curiosities. Some such concepts, I will eventually argue, hold on to the door-posts and will not be forced into this unseemly retirement. For now, I will explicate more of this revisionist work in current philosophy of persons.

Content questions

1. What is Wiggins' individuative naturalism?
2. What is the basis of value on Wiggins' view?
3. What identity thesis would support a view, which Wiggins denies, that a human being could be the same animal as an earlier animal without being the same person?
4. Why is Wiggins' view like that of Kant, primarily an ethical position rather than primarily epistemological or metaphysical?
5. How are natural kinds determined?
6. Why does Wiggins object to the idea of a person as a social construct?
7. Why is Wiggins unimpressed with thought experiments that seem to show that persons are not tied to a single human body?
8. What does Williams think is necessary for identity of persons? Explain why it is or is not sufficient?
9. Why does Williams think the attempts of Locke and others to explain identity of persons without the body are unworkable?
10. What is wrong with Williams' response to objections to his arguments against Locke?
11. Why does Williams think that personality cannot be the criterion of personal identity?
12. What does Williams say is the viewpoint from which we must apply a criterion of identity?
13. What is the error in Williams' simplest objection to Strawson?
14. Why is it odd that Williams objects to ignoring ordinary linguistic conventions?
15. What does Williams think of the category of a person as a foundation for ethical thought?

Arguments for analysis

Argument 1: Wiggins' morality-first view

We must understand the concept of a person in such a way as to make it morally wrong to treat any human being without respect or dignity. If we treat a person in a functionalist way as a set of abilities that may be realized in various different physical forms, then the category of a person will not necessarily apply to all human beings. If the category of a person does not apply to all human beings, then it will not be morally wrong to treat some human beings without respect or dignity. Therefore the functionalist view of persons is wrong.

Argument 2: Objection from a functionalist point of view

This argument begs the question. We must first decide what persons are and only afterward decide what moral significance they have. The functionalist claim is purely metaphysical and cannot be criticized by appeal to felt moral needs.

Argument 3: Reply to the functionalist

On the contrary, we must look at the world systematically keeping our metaphysics, epistemology, and ethics synchronized. Insights in one area can and should influence choices in the others. The functionalist metaphysical claim is, whatever is intended, a claim with moral implications. Philosophy, like all disciplines, must start with intuitively acceptable principles. The idea that human beings are disposable when their abilities wane or before their abilities form is repugnant and far from intuitively acceptable.

Argument 4: Objection to the second premise of the morality-first argument

Premise 2 is false. We can adopt moral principles that value human beings whether or not they are persons. Even if respect for persons is more than respect for mere human beings who are not yet or no longer persons, respect for human beings may be very strong. Human dignity may be carefully guarded independently of dignity of persons.

Argument 5: The dead body objection to Wiggins

Wiggins claims that to be the same person, one must have the same body. The body, according to Wiggins, is a substance. Wiggins also accepts Aristotle's claim that there is no distinction between a substance and the matter of which it is composed. Now, when a body dies, the matter remains. The dead body, therefore, is the same body, the same substance, as the person had when that person was alive. The person, however, is gone. Therefore, the person cannot be identified with the body.

The idea behind this argument is that Miriam could not be the same as Miriam's body. If she were, then she would still be around when her dead body remains. We would not, however, think that her dead body is Miriam.

Argument 6: Wiggins' response to the dead body objection

A body is a necessary but not a sufficient condition for the existence of a person. The body must, moreover, be alive to support a person. A dead body does not have the psychological characteristics that are necessary for a person to exist. We can say that, if the same person is present, then the same living body is present and, if the same living body is present, then the same person is present.

Argument 7: The lost mind objection to Wiggins

Persons, according to Wiggins have irreducibly psychological properties. These psychological properties—supervenient on (or dependent on) the living body—are profoundly important. At the same time, Wiggins says that, if the same living body is present, the same person is present. There are cases, however, in which the body survives but psychological properties do not. If Raoul becomes permanently demented, then Raoul's body will remain but Raoul's mind will be destroyed. Important psychological properties like self-awareness will be gone. It is at least strange that Wiggins wants to call Raoul's body the same person when the psychological properties that Wiggins seems to value highly in persons are gone. Wiggins seems to be committed to the peculiar view that psychological properties such as self-awareness are profoundly important but not essential to persons.

Argument 8: A reply on behalf of Wiggins to the lost mind objection

The lost mind objection overemphasizes certain kinds of psychological characteristics—conscious intellect in particular. The retention of some psychological characteristics is essential to a person, but they might be subconscious or purely perceptual. Self-awareness, in spite of its importance, is not essential. Only when all psychological characteristics are gone is the person gone.

Argument 9: Williams' poor foundation argument

Being a person is a matter of degree, so "person" is not a sortal. A greater degree of being a person is needed for some moral purposes than others. Therefore the category of person is a poor foundation for ethical thought.

Argument 10: The missing premises objection to the poor foundation argument

On the face of it the conclusion does not follow from the premises. Williams must have in mind some additional premises such as the following:

- A category is a satisfactory foundation for ethical thought only if it is a sortal, or
- A category is a satisfactory foundation for ethical thought only if it does not admit of degree (ie, it is all or nothing), or
- If a category admits of degree, it is only useful as a foundation for ethical thought if, in all moral applications, the same degree is needed.

Unfortunately for this argument, none of these potential premises are true. The concept of fairness, for instance, provides a counter-example to each of these.

Argument 11: Reply to the missing premises objection

The point is not that every fundamental ethical concept must not come in degrees but only that the concept of a person is not useful if it does this. If moral rights are to be effective, for example, all persons must have them all of the time. To make a right to life, for instance, dependent on degrees of ability is to make it no longer a right but a privilege.

Argument 12: The missing premises objection rides again

Moral rights do, in fact, depend on degrees to which human beings are persons. Consider the right to autonomy. It is much more restricted for an eight-year-old than for an adult. This depends on their different degrees of ability to look after themselves. Neither rights nor persons need be all or nothing.

Argument 13: The neo-mort objection to Wiggins

There are living human bodies called neo-morts in hospital morgues waiting to be used for organ transplants. They are brain dead and kept otherwise alive with machines that keep them breathing. To the best of our knowledge they have no psychological characteristics whatever. Therefore, preserving the same living human body is not preserving the same person.

Argument 14: A reply on behalf of Wiggins to the neo-mort objection

Neo-morts are not living human bodies. Hospitals are allowed to use them for transplants because they are dead. Brain death is death. Some features of living bodies are simulated through respirators and such. This is not a counter-example.

Argument 15: Williams' viewpoint argument

Any criterion of personal identity has to have a user. Criteria, like the memory criterion, that can only be used subjectively have no purpose. A person knows who he or she is. Since we cannot determine objectively what memories another person has, there can be no user for the memory criterion and similar criteria. The only objective criterion is the body. It is the only criterion of identity that can have a user. Thus the only reasonable criterion of personal identity is the person's body.

Argument 16: A reply on behalf of Locke to Williams' viewpoint argument

Williams is thinking in epistemological terms about knowing persons' identities and misunderstands the purpose of metaphysical identity criteria. Locke, for instance, is not trying to give us a forensic criterion for identifying guilty persons. He is simply asking who is responsible for actions whether we can know for certain that a particular person is responsible or not. Responsibility depends on identity. Identity depends on memory. Even if only the guilty party knows for sure of her guilt, that does not change the truth about who is who nor the truth about who is guilty. Locke, of course, thinks God knows, but even without God's knowledge, the person and the guilt remain.

Argument 17: Williams' dog argument against Strawson

Treating persons as bearers of both M- and P-predicates leaves open the possibility that dogs are persons. Dogs can have P-predicates truly ascribed to them. One such predicate is "wants to go for a walk." Strawson's conception of a person is, therefore, too inclusive.

Argument 18: A reply on behalf of Strawson

Williams is assuming that "person" is defined as "bearer of M- and P-predicates." This is false. "Person" is a primitive term; that is, "person" cannot be defined. It can be used to help define M-predicates and P-predicates, but the reverse is not true. P-predicates are person-predicates. Every person will have some that are not applicable to non-persons. For instance, we might say Eva wants to change her standard desires so that she will want to go for a walk rather than wanting, as she typically does, to watch television. The complex predicate we attribute to Eva in this case is not attributable to non-persons.

CHAPTER 12

Nozick's Self-Makers

Crazy solutions

The concept of a person is slippery. Over the ages the problems which we encounter trying to explicate this concept are legion. Nozick admits that the solutions on which he speculates are crazy but thinks that, since all the sane solutions have been tried without success over the centuries, it may be that only the crazy solutions will work.[1] Some of the things he proposes do seem daft, but I will try to show how he is driven to them. What they reveal for those of us who hold out for sanity is important.

Crucial to Nozick's understanding of persons are two ideas, that of a closest continuer and that of reflexivity. Roughly, Nozick thinks of closest continuers as present people who most resemble those past people. Reflexivity has to do with a peculiar way some things, such as denotations of phrases like "this very phrase" have of looping back on themselves. The keystone in Nozick's arch of ideas between the concepts of a closest continuer and reflexivity is that of an action which creates the person who does it. As long as one can buy the notion that an act can take place independently of the person who seems to perform that action, one can feel at home with Nozick. Readers who want to turn the page crying, This way madness lies! may be reassured

Notes to chapter 12 are on pp. 489-90.

that the theory is able to account for some of our common sense views and to explain how they are sensible in spite of the powerful reasons to the contrary which are the heritage of philosophical thought about persons. While Nozick seems to put at least some of his speculations forth without full conviction, he does think they have some merit in providing us with fresh ways of wrestling with old problems.[2] He is right about that. In case readers lose patience as we follow Nozick through some difficult concepts and some strange examples, I issue this promise: before the end of this book, I will put some of Nozick's concepts to good use in talking about real people.

Nozick's closest continuer theory

The question about persons that Nozick faces first is a familiar one (unless you just opened this book to this page and began here). What makes a person at one time the same person at a later time? To construct examples I will use the names Tomas, Dick, and Heraldo, but these need not be different people. Consider any person Tomas on New Year's Eve and any person Dick on New Year's Day. What are the criteria, once Tomas has developed into Dick, for Dick to be the same person as Tomas? What criterion should we use to identify people over time? Nozick's answer is roughly that the identity of a person depends on who, among all the available alternatives, is the best candidate for being that person. As Nozick describes closest continuers, if Dick is the best candidate for being Tomas, Dick can be called the closest continuer of Tomas.[3] Now let us see what makes a candidate the best one or what makes a continuer the closest continuer.

Nozick describes the closest continuer of a person as not merely someone closely resembling the original but someone whose properties are like those of the original because the original's properties *caused* the continuer's properties. As an example of such a causal connection of properties, suppose Dick has strength of character because Tomas did since Dick is a later stage of a person who was previously called Tomas. This causal connection does not, according to Nozick, imply temporal continuity. People might have temporal gaps, as do the messages sent on telephone wires.[4] Thus all views, like that of Wiggins for example, that require spatio-temporal continuity for persons to continue are dismissed. "Continuer" really means "resembler" here.

The similarity metric: Weighted dimensions of closeness

So much for the concept of a continuer. To understand the other half of the phrase "closest continuer"—namely "closest"—is a difficult task indeed. Nozick speaks of a set of weighted dimensions and features in a similarity metric by means of which closeness is to be measured.[5] By "weighted dimensions" he seems to mean the properties of people, like having strength of character or having curly hair, plus the weight we give these properties in judgments about identity. Think of Nozick as developing a suggestion we saw from Strawson in chapter 10 concerning the weight we might give to the M- and P-predicates—the properties that tell us who is who.

Whether Dick is really Tomas will, of course, depend a lot more on their shared strength of character than on their sharing the same kind of hair. Character is, therefore, a dimension of much greater weight than hairstyle. What Nozick calls the "metric" is a complex of causal and qualitative dimensions of the person, to each of which we assign weights. This metric has to be taken into consideration in making judgments of closeness of continuation, but Nozick does not say in detail what is within the metric. He is offering a general schema to be filled in by whoever is making the judgment of identity. There are limits, however, on the ways we can select and weigh dimensions and thus fill in the schema. Nonetheless, there is not one correct answer to the question whether Tomas is Dick. According to the metric Dick selects, the answer might be Yes, while you or I might correctly deny this if Dick is too much changed from the Tomas we knew, according to our metric. Heraldo might be closer to Tomas as we see it. Closeness of persons, and hence identity as well, is relative to the metric used in judging it.

In spite of this relativity, not anyone can be identical to Tomas. There are four kinds of limits: closest continuer limits, that is, limits intrinsic to the concept of closest continuers; mono-relatedness, which has to do with predecessors as well as continuers and is not as bad as it sounds; metaphysical limits on classification; and, finally, social limits. Dick has a long way to go before he gets to be Tomas, but I will have to consider each of these limits before a picture of Nozick's theory begins to emerge.

Closest continuer limits

Nozick points out that, although we make different judgments of the identity of persons, we are still using the same general schema for making such judgments, and he thinks that his schema fits the judgments we do, in fact, make. Even though we can always pick a metric to suit a particular judgment about, for instance, whether Tomas is Dick, Nozick says that, "it does not follow that every group of judgments can be made to fit."[6] While individual judgments may vary, certain combinations of judgments are ruled out. We might, for instance, be able to adopt a metric under which Tomas is Dick, but then we could no longer deny that Sally is Andrea once we have chosen our metric. Picking a metric is deciding what we mean by "closeness of continuation" for persons, and that ties you to a whole set of identity judgments.[7] One cannot make such judgments lightly, I suppose, since they affect one's own case.

Mono-relatedness

Just as there are continuers of persons, as Dick might be of Tomas, there are predecessors of persons, as Tomas might be of Dick. Roughly, the person most closely resembling Dick who came before Dick is Dick's closest predecessor.[8] Now Nozick requires that for Tomas to be Dick, not only must Dick be Tomas's closest continuer, but Tomas must be Dick's closest predecessor. This he calls "mono-relatedness."[9] To see why Nozick does this, consider a case of merging two persons, Bob and Doug, into Al. Doug is more like Al than Bob is and exists along with Bob on New Year's Eve. Even though Al is Bob's closest continuer, Doug might be Al's closest predecessor. In that case, I think, Nozick would not think either Bob or Doug was identical to Al. Now you might remember the causal condition on closeness and ask how on earth Al on New Year's Day could arise causally from both Doug and Bob on New Year's Eve. Well it could not happen in the real world, so far as I know. Nozick, however, takes all examples to be relevant as long as they are of logically possible events. Now a fictional case in which Bob and Doug are in a terrible accident and clever surgeons cobble together Al from the pieces is, although disgusting, *apparently* logically possible. As an example it is under-described, so we cannot be sure that it is logically possible. Nozick's condition of mono-relatedness is intended, in any case, to rule out the identification of Al and Bob or of Al and Doug. If thinking of persons merging is too strange, consider a case of two rivers converging to flow into one another. Nozick would not count the resulting river as identical to either of the rivers upstream if neither is mono-related to that river resulting from their merger.

While we are on the topic of identity, note that Nozick does not think that mono-relatedness is sufficient to make Al identical to Bob, but it is necessary. In other words, if they are merely mono-related, it does not follow that they are identical—but if they are identical, then they are mono-related.

Metaphysical limits

The job of such classifying concepts as the concept of a person, according to Nozick, is to maximize the unity of a class of entities. This is to be done by maximizing the differences between classes and the similarities within classes in our classificatory scheme.[10] Persons, therefore, should be a lot like each other and as little as possible like non-persons. What we call a person, then, is not arbitrary, not merely conventional, nor is it arbitrary who we say is who. We need to follow a reasonable set of principles of classification. It follows that if I try to look upon my grandfather's departed pet cat as my closest predecessor, I can be making a mistake through adopting a classification scheme which fuzzes the border between persons and non-persons. I cannot, however, be wrong about who it is for whom I am seeking a predecessor. I am trying to figure out who I am in such a case, however badly I may be doing it.

One of the results of maximizing similarities among persons and maximizing their differences from other beings is the narrowing of the class of persons in some respects and widening of it in others. There are many human beings who, if included in the class of persons, would prevent maximization. One might include, for example, only those with the linguistic ability to say "I" meaningfully and those who will develop this capacity. (Nozick's reasons for this is revealed later.) This might exclude as persons some human beings with severely challenged mental capability but include Washoe, the chimpanzee who uses sign language. Nozick, an old hand at bullet-biting, should be willing to accept such a consequence, but he seems not to bite. At least he does not explicitly include non-humans in the class of persons. In any case, his general principles for classification limit what kinds of identity judgments he is willing to countenance.

Social limits

What happens if Dick tries, when deciding on his own metric, to include Heraldo's body or part of it as Dick's own? Assuming that Heraldo and Dick have distinct bodies, this will be frowned on in most societies, at least where slavery is unacceptable. Society limits our acts of self-creation. To this point Nozick says: "Rewards and punishments will lead to a boundary in a particular location along innate salient features or dimensions. Recalcitrant individuals who act on their deviant classifications wherein part of their own body includes someone else's arms, will be punished, institutionalized, or killed. Usually, the mutual compatibility of self-definitions occurs with less hardship."[11] The class of innate, salient features might include a great deal. Nozick does not help us with examples other than the inappropriate claiming of another's arms. The term "innate" leads me to suspect that he is thinking of features common to human beings rather than socially determined features. Not enough is said here, as Nozick skims over this point, but I develop it when I come to pontificate on the ways I think we should develop a concept of a person.

Self-creation and reflexivity

Nozick accepts that we ourselves are each, in part, responsible for determining who, by our own lights, preceded us and who continues us.[12] This gives particular tang to the question, Who do you think you are? We create ourselves—at least we share in our own creation—by deciding how we measure closeness of continuation. The self conceives of itself as a listing and weighting of the dimensions in the metric used to measure closeness. Nozick sums this up as: "Which continuer is closest to a person depends (partially) on that person's own notion of closeness."[13] Nozick does not attempt to say how much weight should be given to self-conception in the metric for closeness, but it must be considerable. He thinks that what distinguishes selves from other things and gives them special dignity is their self-synthesis, their determining of their own identity.[14]

The idea that we somehow create our own characters or personalities is not an uncommon one, but usually half-baked. Nozick, however, is a rather thorough and systematic baker. Although he takes on the whole person—not just the person's character—as a self-made item, he still makes the notion of self-creation somewhat plausible. One must, however, be able to imagine actions as events which may exist independently of the person whose action it later turns out to be.[15] The act of self-creation exists prior to the self which it creates. Consider a new example. In the year 2000 Dick chooses a metric for determining his closest predecessor and continuer. According to this metric, Tomas in the year 1990 was Dick's closest predecessor, and Heraldo in the year 2010 will be Dick's closest continuer. This newly unified person, Tomas-Dick-and-Heraldo, only comes into existence when Dick's action creates this person. Once this person exists, Dick's action is this person's action. Dick, of course, cannot choose any old Tomas and Heraldo. There are limits on the choice of metric, which were described above. But Dick can choose prior to the coming into being of the person Tomas-Dick-and-Heraldo.

Accepting actions which create people appears, initially, like giving up on people. Actions may be among the events which make up persons but which may be described without mentioning persons. This seems to lead to what I call "impersonalism," the view that people are not necessarily part of our description of reality. We could just describe the actions and leave people out of our account of what exists. If, however, as Nozick apparently sees it, one of a series of actions may be an act of self-creation, then, it seems to me, it is not possible to describe the action without mentioning the person created, the self which is synthesized. This is a good feature of Nozick's view, that people are real, not merely convenient fictions. By contrast, Hume, with whom we wrestled in chapter 6, made people disappear from his account of reality by his use of the device of actions existing independently from people. Parfit, who comes later in my account of contemporary philosophers, also favours impersonalism.

Reflexivity

Part of Nozick's explanation of self-creation involves an examination of the ability of people to say "I" in a special way. "I" is an indexical and, as we saw in the discussion of Ryle's exorcism of ghosts, words such as "I," "this," "here," or "now" index an item in our scheme of reality. For example, when I say, This tomato here on the window sill is green all over now, I pick out an object at a particular location in its journey through time and space. There is no contradiction in my pointing to the same tomato days later and saying, This tomato here on the window sill is red all over now. The indexicals keep straight which stage of the tomato's ongoing development I am indicating.

Reflexive self-reference

If, however, I use the word "I" to refer to myself, then "I" is an indexical of a very special kind. The difference between this use of "I" and the use of "this" is in the *reflexivity* of the use of "I." Nozick explains: "Some indexical terms have a reference that not only varies with the context of their utterance, but also depends essentially on the very utterance in which they appear; for example, 'this very phrase' refers to that phrase itself, and 'I…' refers to the producer of that token itself. Let us call such linguistic devices *reflexively self-referring*."[16] To put this a little less carefully (but perhaps more understandably) what "I" means, according to Nozick, is the thing that is referring to itself by using this particular instance of the special indexical word "I." "I" is special in that it points back at itself when we use it. The essence of the self is the capacity to meaningfully say "I."[17] Another way to understand reflexively self-referring terms is to say they are those which depend for their reference on the very utterance in which they appear. To know who or what "I" refers to on a given utterance of "I," we must know more than what is making the sound. A tape recorder may be making the sound, but it is the person who meaningfully said "I" into the microphone to whom this token (or instance) of the word "I" refers. Nozick has, thus, defined "self" in terms of the ability to use language in this special way.

It is not, then, the ability to speak or reason which distinguishes persons from beasts and machines which may possibly acquire these abilities to some degree, it is the ability to say "I" and mean it. If

Washoe the chimpanzee or multiple-parallel-processing computers can do this too, then they are selves with us, by Nozick's rules.

Nozick has clarified two things about his view of persons with this linguistic approach to the self. First, it is clear that "person" is not a species-specific concept as "human being" is. Second, the act of self-creation can be carried out through an act of reflexive self-reference. One need not speak the words aloud, I suppose, but when one says or thinks "I" and simultaneously has in mind some metric for closeness of continuation, then one creates oneself anew.

Think about a famous saying from Descartes, "I think; hence, I am." Could this be false? Applying Nozick's view, it could be. For example, in saying "I" a person may be trying to create something which goes beyond the limits that were specified above on making choices regarding the metric for measuring closeness. If Dick is saying "I" in such a way as to include Heraldo's arms in the reference of "I," then Dick's act of self-creation fails and Dick is not who he is saying he is when he utters, I am. Perhaps it would be preferable to say that Dick has not said anything rather than that he has said something false, since his use of "I" is non-referring. I prefer to say that Dick has made a fictional claim as if it were a statement about reality. Nozick puts it this way: "'I exist' might, strictly speaking, be false, in that the pre-conditions for the perfectly accurate use of the 'I' are not satisfied."[18]

Nozick also says that no thing in any possible world which always lacked the capacity for reflexive self-reference could be me or you.[19] This, however, is not clear without looking at an example. Always is ambiguous. We might say, for example, that Daphne in the stage or stages following her last decline into dementia always lacked the capacity for reflexive self-reference; hence, by Nozick's criteria, Daphne ceased to exist on becoming permanently demented. On the other hand, we might say that Daphne no longer has, but once did have, the capacity for reflexive self-reference. In that case, the demented Daphne would be a later stage of the same person as Daphne the philosopher. Nozick takes the former stance and would say that Daphne, once she has finally lost the capacity for reflexive self-reference, is no more.[20] Nozick of course makes the allowance for some periods of loss of the ability of self-reference without loss of self to provide for the brief interruption of the capacity for reflexive self-reference when, for instance, we are asleep. But he also makes an exception for those who have not yet developed the capacity of self-reference.[21] This creates an interesting asymmetry in his view. A fetus is a self as long as it will develop the capacity for self-reference, while a senile adult who has permanently lost the capacity is no longer a self. I wonder why he does not say the self is born with the capacity for reflexive self-reference just as it dies when that capacity dies. Perhaps the answer lies in the apparent fact that the fetus has the potential to develop the capacity while the senile adult does not.

Another interesting feature of Nozick's account is that there seems to be no theoretical limit on how often one could recreate oneself through reflexive self-reference nor any limit on changing one's mind about who one is. It might, however, be difficult to be sincere about frequent changes if one is mentally stable. Perhaps this could be worked into the social limits on one's metric discussed earlier. There are also the limits imposed by the metaphysical principles of classification. If people become too volatile, going into and out of existence all the time, it might be difficult to unify them in a class.

Reflexive caring

The theme of reflexivity, of things feeding back into themselves, is crucial to Nozick's understanding of a person, as we have already seen through his analysis of the meaning of "I." Nozick also imports this feature into his understanding of our concern for ourselves. Oddly enough, care for the self as the self, not as a bearer of some property or properties, is required by Nozick. The care is reflexive, looping back on itself the way the reference of the word "I" does. More precisely, it is care in virtue of a feature of the act of caring. Creation is an act of caring for the thing created; so self-synthesis is an act of caring for oneself.[22]

Four possible theories of identity of persons over time

Without saying which he favours, Nozick throws out four possible views about identity for us to kick around. To avoid any further technical terminology and to simplify these theories, I will use the metaphor of a cartographer mapping a previously unmapped river.

The cartographer must decide at various points in his journey down the river whether a body of water is the same river, a tributary, or an effluent. Nozick, because he takes seriously the logical possibility of odd things happening to people, must face similar decisions. He thinks, for instance, that a person can possibly split into two people as a river can split into two rivers.

The first theory: The closest continuer is identical

Nozick's first theory is that identity over time follows the path of closest continuity. A person would be a series of things each of which was the closest continuer of the one before. Death is the end of continuity. Our intrepid cartographer travelling downstream would compare bodies of water to what he had just travelled over. Like Nozick, he would use a metric, a set of scales of similarity, to make a judgment about which body of water was the closest continuer of the river. At a fork in the river, where it separates into two flows downstream, the cartographer would proclaim one flow an effluent and the other identical to the river. On this first theory, if the river forked so neatly that there were two equally close continuers of the river, neither of them would be the continuation of that river being mapped.

In Daphne's case, most of us would agree on continuity in spite of the massive changes until Daphne became demented. At this point, the different weights people give to the body, the personality, dispositions, abilities, and the mind would produce different answers concerning her survival. If we use Nozick's first theory of personal identity and do in fact give different weights within the metric of closeness, our infrequent disagreements about survival could be explained as differences in choice of a closeness metric. Whether one is the same person after a major change would seem to depend on who is making the judgment. Nozick, however, takes the closeness metric each person chooses for oneself as the important one for identifying that person. Within the limits mentioned, each of us is the best judge of who we are. This leads to puzzles in Daphne's case, since she changed her metric as she lost her intellectual abilities. At the end of her ability to consider such matters, it was by no means clear about where Daphne put great weight where closeness was concerned. Perhaps Nozick would be willing to say that Daphne, at the point of ceasing to be able to keep a metric in mind, becomes a person only to others. Her incapacity to evaluate herself makes her like a child. She becomes, in some sense, less of a person since she loses that self-determination which is the source of a person's dignity. From this point of view there is some truth in the adage that one must value oneself to be valued by others, though the adage is interpreted in rather a new way. Valuing oneself comes through self-creation, as an act of reflexive caring.

If we think of the river once again, we can see how Nozick's first theory allows for having many rivers made out of one stretch of water. We might call a river from its origin to the ocean one thousand kilometres distant the Blue River. But a shorter stretch within the Blue from kilometre ten to kilometre two hundred might be the Shiny River. Within the Shiny River we might have the Moon River which goes from kilometre one hundred to kilometre one hundred eighty of the Blue River. Various acts of self-creation in a person's life could have the effect of creating people within people in the same way.

It seems that, on Nozick's first theory, Who is who? becomes a question with more possible answers than seems plausible. The answers depend not only on whom one asks but also on *when* one asks. Daphne, before she lost the ability to do philosophy, put enormous weight on that ability. She would, perhaps, have had difficulty in conceiving of a continuer of herself who could not participate in that activity. Later, when participation was no longer possible for her, she saw herself as a continuation of the former Daphne, although it pained her greatly to be unable to do philosophy. She began to see other things as central to her being the person she was. In Nozick's terms, the later Daphne considered herself mono-related to the earlier Daphne, while the earlier Daphne would perhaps have denied this. Daphne the philosopher had a life which was part of the life of Daphne who came later, just as the Shiny River is part of the Blue River. The later Daphne created a new self including the earlier Daphne, while the earlier Daphne created a self which ended prior to the later Daphne. Since Nozick's view allows for many acts of self-synthesis associated with one body, Nozick is committed to the view that there may be many people associated with one body over a lifetime. Closeness of continuation may not be completely arbitrary, but it is certainly flexible.

The strangeness of Nozick's first proffered concept of personal identity, illustrated by the example of Daphne before and after she lost her most cherished ability, does not go away when we switch to any of the other proposals for identity that Nozick gives us. Nonetheless, Daphne thought of the woman whom she knew would result from her illness as someone other than herself, and there is some sense in this. The other theories, while strange, all capture something sensible as well.

The second theory: Switch from short-lived to runner-up

The first proposal was that identity follows the path of closest continuation. Nozick then modifies this to overcome what he calls the overlap problem. The problem, which I will explain through the river metaphor, is that two continuers might exist simultaneously, and we might have reasons to think of both of them as the closest. His solution is this: "Entity *X* follows the path of closest continuation, unless it is a short path."[23] To clarify both the problem and the solution, imagine that the Blue River forks, and the part that is most like the Blue before the fork ends after a short distance, say, one kilometre. This corresponds to a short-lived continuer (ie, person) on the short path of continuation. In this second theory of Nozick's, the less similar effluent that continues for a long way would continue to be the Blue River but it would only be the Blue after the shorter effluent ends. That is, one kilometre after the fork, its long effluent becomes the Blue river. From the fork for one kilometre along the longer effluent, there exists a very short river that is not the Blue. This is rather odd.

This short-path condition only comes into play when there are two or more candidates for being a continuer of an earlier stage of a person. It is quite ad hoc. If the closest continuer dies off, we switch conveniently to the next closest and much longer lived continuer. This has the same subjectivity as the plain variety of closest continuation, and it does nothing to overcome the difficulty that there may be many people associated with one body. Nozick would, perhaps, not consider these objections to be real problems for his view. He bites the bullets on which other philosophers only nibble. There is no doubt that Nozick accepts a best candidate theory of personal identity with all of its odd consequences.

The third theory: Ignore the short-lived in favour of the runner up

The Blue River, on this view, would not include its short effluent but simply go along the longer flow which is a less close continuer of the Blue before the fork. This third proposal for defining personal identity is that, instead of switching at the end of a short path of life—a short-lived closest continuer—one simply ignores the short path and becomes the second closest continuer at the fork in one's life. If we are not looking at this from some timeless viewpoint, we will have to wait to see how long a continuer lives before declaring it closest. Later stages of a person will determine whether earlier stages are part of the person or not. This is not quite as odd as switching to the second-closest continuer after a short-lived continuer as in theory two. Nonetheless, it is strange to think that I might not be the same person who began writing this book if I should die before I wake tomorrow and some reasonable facsimile comes along to finish this book—and my life. Perhaps that is ruled out by the social limits on continuation.

The fourth (and, mercifully, last) theory: The ur-person

Finally Nozick proposes what I will call an "ur-person," an original which every later stage must closely continue. Using the Blue River metaphor, the Blue might, at its delta, divide into many rivers. Part of this river and part of that could be cobbled together as the Blue. The stretches of water which most resembled the pre-delta Blue would be the Blue. Similarly, if the person divides in a kind of tree structure, then there may be segments of many different branches which would be assembled into one person because of their closeness to the ur-person. While I like the idea that there must be something central to all stages of me as I flow through life, I do not think that this quite captures that idea.

All of these theories of identity which Nozick puts forth have a drawback from within the closest continuer theory. That theory subjectivizes identity and these are attempts, albeit unsuccessful, to objectify identity. For example, a person-stage on a short path of life would consider herself to be the closest continuer of a predecessor which some other second-closest continuer would also take to be her predecessor. To say that one of them is right is to defy the principle of self-creation, the principle that who a person is depends heavily on that person's own metric for closeness of continuation. The weight given to a person's own metric, does not, therefore, remove the puzzle about who is who in every case. There could still be competing continuers, each of which had excellent grounds to think the other an impostor.

Some applications of closest continuer theory to puzzles

The science fiction puzzles dear to the hearts of philosophers talking about persons are solved by Nozick's theory in a way which he thinks preserves some important intuitions about persons. The main intuition he ignores is that someone who was very much like me but an impostor would not be me, even if he sincerely thought he was me and even if I were so insane as to agree with him. Nozick's theory also allows one to say that the impostor is me from the impostor's point of view but not me from mine if I am not deluded into agreeing with the impostor. This flexibility of Nozick's view does not help us much when we are trying to understand what persons are with a view to answering moral questions. If, on the other hand, we assert one of the four proposals for identity considered above as an objective answer to the question of personal identity, then we must delete the self-creation of individuals from the closest continuer theory. Yet this self-creation is the source of the dignity of persons.[24] If we can agree on some general conception of a person, then this objection does not arise. We each will allow others, within the limits of the general conception, to determine their own identities.[25] But how are we to agree on the general conception? Perhaps we are to choose among the four possible theories of identity mentioned earlier. Nozick must have made such a choice, for he offers the following solutions to the standard philosophical puzzles about personal identity.

Duplication

If I were duplicated, and both I and my double survived the process, then I would be me and my double would not be me, according to

Nozick's application of his theory.[26] I suppose this is because I am causally better connected with my earlier stages than my double is. If others, not me and my double, were making the judgment as to closeness of continuity, then this conclusion that the double is not me might follow, but given the vagaries of the act of self-synthesis and the importance of self-conception in that mysterious act, Nozick should not be so quick to judge. What if I develop a self-conception and my double develops a self-conception such that both of us agree that my double is the closest continuer of my earlier self? It looks as if I would no longer be me, my old self, that is. Even without this subjective element, it is not clear that Nozick is entitled to claim that the double is not me. Recall that the closest continuer of a person does not merely resemble that person but is someone whose properties are like those of the original because the original's properties caused the continuer's properties.[27] But that is true of both me and my double with respect to my old self prior to duplication. My old self is the cause of us both. Here Nozick might have to retreat to the concept of a normal cause, or the right kind of cause, but that is notoriously relative to the norms we choose. Perhaps Nozick would say that the norms are given by the social limits on continuation. If I and my double emerge from Williams' duplicating machine, our society would count the person who resulted from ordinary human reproduction as the real person.

Various thought experiments resulting in a closest continuer

Nozick considers the following cases to be cases in which the result is the closest continuer of the original: the brain is transplanted to a clone; the information in the body is transferred to a clone; there is a half-brain transplant with full psychological continuity, and the original dies; or half of the brain is destroyed. Even if we ignore the vast under-description of such cases, and accept them as logically possible, Nozick's conclusions about closest continuation ignore the potential interference of self-conception. He is at most entitled to conclude that these people could be the closest continuers of the earlier people who gave rise to them if they choose their closeness metrics in certain ways. The weight given to self-conception makes this claim trivially true. Because of this weight, anyone can be the closest continuer of anyone who went before.[28] Nozick might protest that the limits described earlier apply and would limit who is who. However, the social limits in such science fiction cases are simply not known. Our society has not had to face many such oddities yet. It is hard to see how the other limits could be used to make decisions in such science fiction cases either.

Nozick admits to having some trouble with certain kinds of duplication via transplantation of split brains. What really bothers him, however, is the overlap, or short-path, case.[29] I suggest, however, that closest continuation has been so weakened by the weighting of self-conception that no case is problematic, but this success is bought in a problematic way. We can be whoever we want to be. Again, to repair this Nozick would have to give far less importance to self-conception, which would undermine his view of the dignity of persons.[30] Having dignity depend on self-determination has something right about it, but perhaps the idea needs much modification before it is workable.

What a closest-continuer theorist cares about

Since closest continuation determines what we should care about, according to Nozick, it is crucial for Nozick to repair his theory to avoid the consequence that closest continuation is a purely subjective matter. Otherwise the theory produces the view that we should care about whatever we do care about as regards survival. For example, perfect fission of a person in which there are two equally good candidates for closest continuer is a case, according to Nozick, in which there is no closest continuer. The original no longer exists. Nonetheless, the original should not care. What is important is the survival of what would be a closest continuer, if it were unique.[31] Fission where is thy sting!

When reflexive caring was discussed above, the point was made that in the act of self-creation we care for ourselves as ourselves, not as a mere collection of characteristics which could be had by someone else. Nozick seems to forget this when he discusses fission. What seems evident to me is that we do and ought to care about survival of more than merely a closest continuer. It is not just important to me that someone very much like me will wake up tomorrow; I want to wake up myself. The puzzle of how to understand this is a Gordian knot, but Nozick tries to slice through it at a stroke and perhaps misses the import of it. A mere closest continuer is not enough for survival of the subject of experience which is at the core of the person. For instance, Franz might choose a metric which makes Franz the closest continuer of Franz's dead twin brother, Karl, and there is a causal connection between Franz and Karl; so the closest continuer theory does not clearly prevent Franz from being Karl's closest continuer except by social limits. Let us suppose those limits have changed. This is at least as possible as Nozick's examples. Now, clearly Franz and Karl do not share one subject of experience. What Karl wanted to survive was not just someone who could continue his genotype, personality, plans, and projects, but the very subject of his experiences. I think that it is perfectly reasonable for Karl to care about this continuing subjectivity and not just the continuing similarity which Franz can provide by taking over where Karl left off.

I can only be content with my replica as a closest continuer if I care not for myself as myself but as the bearer of certain properties which will be continued in the replica after I am destroyed. This is contrary to what Nozick says about such replication in a case of perfect fission.[32] I am not supposed to care that there are, if I split perfectly, two replicas and no me. I am supposed to care merely about somebody very much like me—the instantiation of properties which I now instantiate. Something has gone wrong with Nozick's view of caring. Perhaps no reasonable view can deal with a case of perfect fission, but then such fission may not be possible. The idea that we should care for ourselves as ourselves ought to win out for Nozick's supporters, if a choice is to be made between this and his solution of the fission puzzle, namely, saying that neither product of fission is the original person. One should also be suspicious of the facile solution to more mundane cases like that of the twin brother taking over. Similarity is not enough.

In fact, the datum that Nozick wishes to explain, that our care about our closest continuer is disproportionate to its degree of closeness of continuity, is explained only by denying the closest continuer theory. If, for example, I find that there exists a nearly perfect double of me who is causally unrelated to me, and hence not my continuer, I will care much more about my closest continuer. This double is not my closest continuer, since he is a person causally unrelated to me. My care for my closest continuer in this case is not because of its closeness via causation but because it is more likely to be me than my double. What I want to survive is me, not merely someone remarkably like me. Nozick tries to address this concern in his talk of reflexivity, but he ends, as I have been trying to show, by neglecting his own insights regarding reflexive caring.

Self as property

The view that the self is but a property of a body is one that Nozick flirts with. He puts it forth as a curiosity which may put old problems in a fresh light but which is insufficiently illuminating to adopt as a position.[33] If Nozick were to adopt this position fully, caring for oneself as an object—the self—and caring for the instantiation of a property would no longer be opposed. There would be no self as object to care for. In a case of perfect fission, the property of being myself would be doubly instantiated. When my replicas say "I" they will not be referring to me, nor to any individual. They will be asserting that they have a certain property which I used to instantiate. This points once again to the absurdity of fission, since the property of being myself must be uniquely instantiated, but Nozick actually takes the self-as-property view to provide a solution to the fission problem.[34] Unless the self-as-property is tied to a particular body as it is in Aristotle's enmattered form conception of persons, then problems are likely to arise. We will have Williams' oddities, as in his example, discussed in the previous chapter, of falling in love with a person type as opposed to a person token. Those who wish to follow Nozick's lead should read "dead end" on the person-as-property view or go back to Aristotle.

What about Daphne?

An earlier and a later stage of what appears to be one person need not agree on who is whom. Daphne, in fact, once held that her ability to do extremely abstract work in philosophy was a necessary condition of her continuation but, after losing that ability, she no longer thought so. In Nozick's terms the earlier Daphne would not count the later Daphne as a continuer, while the later Daphne would count the earlier Daphne as a predecessor. Now that Daphne apparently has no self-conception, she is still the closest continuer of the earlier Daphne according to those who give bodily continuity great weight in the metric for determining closeness. Since Daphne herself can now neither affirm nor deny this weighting of the body in the metric for closeness, she is deprived, in Nozick's view, of one of the essentials of dignity—self determination. This is one of those intuitively correct consequences flowing from Nozick's apparently wild view. Daphne herself held that she would be deprived of her dignity if allowed to live without her intellect; intellect is essential for making decisions about the metric, and hence is essential for self-creation or self-renewal. This is, of course, a matter of degree. Someone with Down's syndrome might have sufficient intellect for such purposes, but someone as severely limited as Daphne has no intellect.

What I like about Nozick

Nozick's craziness is a good thing. Although I wish to stick closer to common sense, Nozick's abandonment of sane solutions which have not worked drives us to dig in our heels. It forces those of us who think there is something right in the old views to ferret it out. It forces those of us who find something right in Nozick's relativism to say how it might be limited to prevent every Tomas and Dick from being any Heraldo. We need to add to the limits, particularly the social limits, which Nozick acknowledges.

The importance of similarity in our idea of continuity of people cannot be underestimated. Nozick takes it apart and puts it back together in a useful analysis. While closest continuation is not all there is to continuity, it is a major feature. A metric of dimensions is a good figure for understanding what Williams has called a series of sliding scales.

Being a person calls for pulling oneself up by one's boot straps. Nozick has given us one of the clearest discussions of the apparently insane topic of self-creation and has managed to inject some sanity into it. He has linked this usefully to the analysis of our use of "I", a vexed subject indeed. We will have to keep this contribution in mind as we come to consider what makes a person herself to herself.

I hope I have managed to convey some of the dizzying effect one may experience in a brisk climb up the steep slopes of Nozick's book *Philosophical Explanations.* What is harder, if at all possible, to convey is the view which one surveys after this steep ascent. It is worth a look, but I would like to stick closer to common sense about persons. That is feasible, Nozick's doubts notwithstanding.

Content questions

1. What is the first question about persons that Nozick faces?
2. What is Nozick's answer?
3. What, in addition to resemblance to person A, must person B have in order to be A's closest continuer?
4. How is resemblance to be judged?
5. Why is personal identity relative rather than absolute?
6. Why is personal identity nonetheless objective?
7. What is the limit on closest continuers of mono-relatedness?
8. How does our classification scheme provide metaphysical limits on closest continuers?
9. What is an example of social limits on closest continuers?
10. How does Nozick suggest we share in our own creation?
11. What linguistic and conceptual ability distinguishes persons from non-persons?
12. How could Descartes' expression "I think; hence, I am" be false according to Nozick's?
13. What is reflexive caring?
14. What four theories of personal identity does Nozick suggest?
15. On what does the dignity of persons depend, in Nozick's analysis?

Arguments for analysis

Argument 1: The crazy concept argument

Through the history of philosophy the concepts of a person that we have used have been incapable of solving the puzzles concerning persons that we face. All of the sane concepts have been tried. It is time to try a crazy concept of a person. This justifies looking at closest continuer theories of persons.

Argument 2: The true identity objection

Hume was right to distinguish between identity and similarity. Closest continuer theories of persons ignore this distinction and focus purely on similarity. They can, therefore, not give us metaphysical criteria for identity of persons.

Argument 3: The absolutist objection

Questions of personal identity are about who is who, not about who appears to be who to whom. Closest continuer theories make identity partly dependent on self-conception, hence partly subjective, and partly dependent on social acceptance, hence partly culturally relative. Such relativism provides a concept of a person that is inadequate for judgments of moral guilt or innocence of persons for their past actions.

Argument 4: The conventionalist reply

Questions of personal identity, like all questions with moral import, can only be settled by appeal to social conventions. There are no other standards that can be applied. Consequently it is reasonable to pursue a closest continuer theory of persons with the acceptable social limitations within our society.

Argument 5: The dignity objection

One of the advantages claimed for the closest continuer theories is that the dignity of persons is preserved by self-creation. Each person's own choice of similarity metrics is given considerable weight in the determination of who that person is. We are whom we think we are within the limits Nozick specifies. The four sample theories of personal identity that he gives us ignore this subjectivity. The responses to the short-path problem are made without consideration of who the continuers think they are according to their own chosen similarity metrics. This undoes the advantage that closest continuer theories were supposed to have in preserving the dignity of persons.

Argument 6: The built-in subjectivity reply

Actually the force of personal choice is already taken into account before the theories are applied. Take the second theory, for example.

Personal identity follows the path of closest continuation unless it is a short path. Before we can find out what is the path of closest continuation, we would have to look at the continuers' own similarity metrics. These would play an important role in determining who is the closest continuer. Only then would the second theory be applied to deal with the short-path problem.

Argument 7: The moral weight objection

Closest continuer theory does not give us an understanding of persons that can bear the moral weight that the concept of a person has traditionally borne. Consider, for example, Nozick's short-path problem combined with a question of moral guilt. Suppose that Tomas commits a terrible crime. Later in time when we try to catch up with Tomas, we find two continuers, Dick and Heraldo. Dick, the closest continuer, is on a short path of life about to die any day. Heraldo, the second-closest continuer, has a longer life ahead. Who should be punished for the terrible crime? By Nozick's first theory, Dick should be punished. By the second and third theories, Heraldo should be punished. By the fourth theory, there are possibly stages of Dick and of Heraldo which we might punish. We just have to catch each at the right time. On the face of it, this is arbitrary and unfair. Resemblance should not determine guilt.

CHAPTER 13

Parfit: The Oxford Buddhist

The creed of selflessness

Parfit, like Williams but unlike Strawson whom we discussed in chapters 10 and 11, is a revisionist in metaphysics. He is not content to describe the way we do think about persons but wishes to change it. Parfit is, in fact, an iconoclast where traditional concepts of a person are concerned. His motives for trying to discourage us from taking ourselves seriously include a moral one; he wants to make people realize that selfishness is irrational, even more so than one might think. Of his strange views about people he says, with typical understatement: "Most of us would accept some of the claims that I shall be denying. I shall thus be arguing that most of us have a false view about ourselves, and about our actual lives. If we come to see that this view is false, this may make a difference to our lives."[1] In fact, any converts to Parfit's view would have such a radically different self-conception that their lives would be changed beyond their imagining.

In popular Western representations of Buddhism, the self is something to be abandoned, excess baggage on the way to enlightenment. In effect, this is Parfit's view as well. Parfit tries to convince us that our selves are not what we should care about. Parfit's argument is general, opposed not only to Cartesian Egos but to anything like

---

Notes to chapter 13 are on pp. 490-91.

them—Christian souls, for instance—that would be an indestructible, unchanging part of a person.

Questions and theses

As I did with Nozick, I will try to convince you that Parfit's arguments challenge us in interesting ways though, as always, I will hold out for a stronger representation of Western common sense in our favoured concept of a person. Parfit says that he will answer these questions:

1. What is the nature of a person?
2. What is it that makes a person at two different times one and the same person?
3. What is necessarily involved in the continued existence of each person over time?[2]

After posing these questions, Parfit says "In answering (2) and (3) we shall also partly answer (1)."[3] Does that mean that he will answer his second and third questions? In charitable moods, I take him to be just pointing out the relation between the questions rather than issuing a negotiable promissory note, but I will argue that he certainly does not pay off any such note. The theory of personal identity in Parfit's main work on persons, *Reasons and Persons*, is circular.[4] He abandons the concept of the nature of persons rather than explicating it. Nonetheless, his views are provocative.

In terms of philosophers whose views were summarized earlier in this book, Parfit, by his own admission, is updating Locke in opposition to the followers of Descartes. I see him owing as much to Hume as to Locke. Recall that Hume looked for himself, found nothing, and concluded that selves are fiction. Descartes thought that our selves were indivisible and, hence, indestructible. I will call the view that there are such indivisible Cartesian Egos the indivisibility thesis. This indivisibility thesis of Descartes' is Parfit's main *bête noire*. In these pages I will often speak of Parfit's opponents as the Cartesians, meaning Descartes' followers, but anybody who believes we are indivisible is welcome to be offended by Parfit and, slightly less so, by me.

Parfit defends four main conclusions about people which I put forward here in brief along with some names by which I will refer to them:

1. the divisibility thesis: We are not indivisible Cartesian Egos; rather, we are complexes of psychological and or physical things which may be divided.
2. the indeterminacy thesis: We are indeterminate in the sense that the question, Am I about to die? does not always have a definite answer.
3. the reducibility thesis, or reductionism: It is theoretically possible to describe all of reality, including the unity of consciousness and the unity of a whole life, without mentioning people, since people can be reduced to the various things which make them up as complexes.
4. the fundamental value thesis: Personal identity is not what fundamentally matters, but psychological continuity and connectedness do matter fundamentally. Roughly, whether we survive should not concern us as much as whether our mind survives.

The last three conclusions are supposed to follow from his first conclusion, that we are complexes;[5] so I will first consider that view and its immediate consequences.

Divisibility: People as complexes

Since Parfit denies the existence of any continuing and indivisible self, soul, or Ego, he holds that people are, instead, made up of psychological and/or physical events. As an empiricist, Parfit thinks the matter of our divisibility should be judged in the court of experience. He notes that there is no experience which is generally acknowledged and is evidence for indivisible selves. If, for instance, people had memories of earlier lives which could be demonstrated to be genuine memories, then Parfit would be prepared to reconsider.[6]

One might think that the obvious rejoinder here is, I do experience myself! Parfit's response here is to point out that an indivisible self or Ego cannot be detectable in the way that changeable objects are. If an ordinary object is replaced by another object, we may notice the switch because of the difference in the features of the two objects. Egos, however, are things without features of that sort. Such features of people as being happy or being brown-haired, can change, while the Ego remains. Parfit wonders how we could tell if the Ego was switched with a different Ego since both could support the same psychological features and both could be associated with a single body. Parfit attacks all followers of Descartes by using the relay race argument. Parfit says that they "accept the possibility described by Locke and Kant. On their view, the Cartesian Ego that I am might suddenly cease to exist and be replaced by another Ego. This new Ego might inherit all of my psychological characteristics, as in a relay race." The Ego according to this version of the indivisibility thesis Parfit calls "the featureless Ego." He states that: "it is not clear that Cartesians can avoid this version of their view."[7]

On this version of the indivisibility thesis, it seems possible that one Ego could be replaced by another Ego and no one could notice. Neither the evidence of introspection nor publicly observable events would tell us of the change. Being something of an empiricist, Parfit thinks this makes the unintelligibility of the featureless Ego (perhaps of any sort of indivisibility thesis) probable, but he is content to rest his case on the facts."[8] The gauntlet has been flung down. The Cartesian must show how it is possible to detect a change of the Ego, soul, or whatever is the indivisible entity associated with the mind or body.

What is a Cartesian to do in the face of Parfit's attack? One could say that the Ego is not featureless. It does, after all, have features like indivisibility and determinacy. These, however, are not the sort of thing which we can detect empirically. I can see changes in my body. Introspectively, I can notice changes in my psychological makeup. How could I know if the current Ego has left some other body and mind and entered? This seems to make a change without a difference. On the other hand, if one gives the Ego features, like consciousness for example, then it becomes changeable and no longer the indivisible and indestructible thing which Cartesians want. These remarks apply equally well to Christian souls or any of the purportedly indivisible things which guarantee the identity of a person through change.

Cartesians can take some *small* hope in this, however: Parfit's two arguments strain against one another. The reincarnation argument complains that there is no evidence of egos and the relay race argument seems to rest on the idea that there could be no evidence of egos since they are featureless and thereby undetectable. Now suppose that through hypnotism people were able to get accurate memories of former lives. If I could, for example, remember where I had hidden treasure in a former life, and such experiences became common, then Parfit would, by his own lights, accept egos. In that case, it appears that they are detectable after all, although the detection is indirect. Egos, the Cartesian might say, could, at least in theory, become associated with new bodies, but they would carry memories and other psychological events with them. The Ego is not the mind, for the mind is changeable, but where the Ego goes, there goes the mind.

This sort of response would only serve to clarify but not to defeat Parfit's objections to the Ego. Parfit could say that there is no way to tell one Ego from another and hence no way to tell which Ego is dragging a particular mind around. Even if there were excellent evidence of reincarnation, there would only be inclining reasons to believe in egos or souls or some such indivisible component of persons with no guarantee that such indivisibles were not switched from time to time in an undetectable way. Such a response would show that undetectability is the truly objectionable feature of "featureless" egos according to empiricists such as Parfit. One need not be a very thoroughgoing empiricist to find the possibility of a relay race of egos rather disturbing. Parfit has at least put the defenders of indivisibility on the defensive.

Aside from these two arguments against the indivisibility thesis, Parfit argues that that thesis is too hard to believe since it conflicts with what we believe about our own continuation through time. This brings us to indeterminacy.

Indeterminacy: Dead, alive, or maybe

To parody Parfit's indeterminacy thesis, old people never die, they just fade away. As the pieces of the complex person are lost, the person gradually goes out of existence. Parfit argues mainly by presenting examples to convince us that we believe in our indeterminacy and, hence, in our divisibility. In other words, by trying to persuade us that there are situations in which the question, Am I about to die? has no definite answer, Parfit is trying to convince us as well that we are not Cartesian Egos. If we were, people would be alive or dead with no gradual fading away. Cartesian Egos have no parts, so they cannot go out of existence bit by bit. Parfit, moreover, varies his examples to deal with purely physical change as well as purely mental change within persons; so Parfit's arguments do not depend on a real distinction between psychological and physical events. In other words, he is, in his theory of persons, not presupposing any of the three views—materialism, dualism, and idealism—discussed in chapter 1.

Parfit uses prominently some science fiction examples, as philosophers are wont to do. This has the disadvantage of making philosophy look silly to intelligent lay readers. Even worse, it allows philosophers to speak of events as if they were logically possible without troubling to describe these events in detail. The minimal description may conceal logical inconsistency. Parfit tries to avoid this charge by claiming that he uses the examples only to reveal what we *believe* about ourselves as persons, not to argue for any conclusion about what we actually or possibly are. His argument against Cartesian Egos is that it is too hard to believe Descartes' view since it requires us to believe in our determinacy. We are supposed to see this by contemplating some science fiction.

The spectra example

His main fiction involves the spectra. The spectra ought not to be taken to show anything about what is possible. They may show that the indivisibility thesis is hard to believe. This is, in principle, *all* they could show, given Parfit's admission of the limits of the method of science fiction examples.[9] The psychological, physical, and combined spectra examples are cases of the gradual change of a human being.[10] Parfit might be (in lurid imagination if not possibility) changed from the kind of human being he is into one much like Greta Garbo, mentally, physically, or both. In a smooth and very gradual spectrum of change, there is no clear point at which one can say that Parfit is no more and some other person has come into existence. In other words, there is no place to draw the line, in the psychological or the physical spectrum of change, at which Parfit dies. This is taken as showing that we believe in indeterminacy; we believe, according to Parfit, that there is not always a definite answer to the question, Am I about to die? The belief in indeterminacy is inconsistent with the belief in our indivisibility. A Cartesian Ego cannot be gradually changed into something else since it cannot be changed at all. Change involves division into parts so that some parts may be hived off and different ones added.

The Cartesian could just bite the bullet here and say to Parfit that this Greta Garbo-like person *is* Parfit as long as the Ego remains. Parfit could reply that this only goes to show that the indivisibility thesis is too hard to believe. But Parfit's own alternative, embracing indeterminacy and losing oneself via Oriental absorption is, however, no joy either. Parfit tells me that, if I die and am survived by a replica which is psychologically continuous and connected with me, I should view that as about as good—or as bad—as ordinary survival. I am supposed to be happy that this impostor, a mere replica of me, will sleep with my lover and write my book. More of this story, which is Parfit's teletransportation example, later. The point here is that Parfit's main reason for rejecting the indivisibility thesis is that it is implausible. He then gives us a view which he admits is very hard to believe.[11] This does not seem like progress. Nonetheless we can learn from Parfit's explorations.

One thing we learn from such science fiction puzzles whether of the purely imaginary or the possible variety is that our common conceptions of persons are capable of dealing with persons as we commonly find them, not with special cases. Elements of our common conceptions can, however, provide us with more durable concepts of a person which will not break down as we approach new scientific facts. Medical technology is presenting us with puzzles about what we believe ourselves to be. These puzzles may not be as strange as Parfit's cases, but they do stretch our conceptions of ourselves. At this point I will merely issue another promise to deal with real people and to try to preserve much of what Parfit abandons. Parfit at least illustrates some traps we will have to avoid to continue thinking of ourselves as in some sense indivisible and determinate.

Reductionism: An impersonal universe

Another of the consequences of abandoning the Cartesian way of thinking of people is that the time-honoured glue that held a person together, the Ego or the soul, is gone. In particular, Parfit faces the problems of how one's consciousness remains a unified whole rather than a series of disparate events and how one's life is unified in spite of the vast differences between different stages of that life.

I will be so bold as to claim that common sense tells us that there is a unity of the consciousness of each healthy person. Memories, feelings, desires, and beliefs of which we are conscious may be united by the ownership of a person who has them. For example, the experiences I have had are united by their being *my* experiences. They can be widely separated in time and extremely different, but they are bundled together by being one person's experience. The unification of a person's whole life is done in similar fashion. What makes my life one unified life is my ownership of it. I am an entity existing apart from all that changes in my body and my mind during that life, *if* I am an indivisible thing like a Cartesian Ego. My persistence as a consciousness through change and the unity of my whole life are explicable for those who believe in the indivisibility of persons. The unity is preserved through the ownership by the Ego, soul, or whatever else in us continues indivisible and indestructible through change.

Thinking as he does that these two unities, consciousness and a whole life, are to be explained without the benefit of our indivisibility, Parfit thinks that the explanation must lie in the interrelations of the mental events and their relations to the brain. All this can be described, he supposes, without reference to the person. There is no owner of the experiences over and above the set of experiences and the body. Like Ayer, Parfit embraces what we saw Strawson deride, in chapter 10, as the no-ownership view. The world, according to Parfit, can be fully described without referring to persons.[12] Persons are ways of conceiving of some groupings of the furniture of the universe but not themselves pieces of that furniture. Similarly, we could refer to Granny's living-room furniture as some kind of unified whole. At auction, however, the same pieces would just be the red plush sofa (Oh where are its doilies now?), the ottoman, and the overstuffed chair. They could be described well enough without mentioning either Granny or her living room, bitter though the thought may be. "Person," as used by Parfit, seems to refer, conventionally, to a series of mental and physical events which we group together for convenience but need not have grouped together at all.

On the other hand, in the same breath as denying that we are entities existing separately from our bodies, actions, and mental events, Parfit asserts that "a person is an entity that is distinct from his brain or body, and his various experiences. A person is an entity that *has* a brain and body."[13] It seems that "distinct" does not mean "separate" here. While a person may be inseparable from one's experiences, it is wrong to say a person is *identical to* one's experiences. Parfit elaborates:

"A reductionist can admit that…a person is what has experiences or the subject of experiences. This is true because of the way in which we talk. What a reductionist denies is that the subject of experiences is a separately existing entity distinct from a brain and body, and a series of physical and mental events."[14] The crucial thing here is that people are a function of the way we talk. Conventions—not souls, Egos, or other separately existing entities—make people. Parfit's people are just handy shopping bags into which we put a series of events, but the events are distinct from the bags. We could have packaged these events differently.[15] Note, we could not package one series of events as two different people, but we could package it either as a person or in some impersonal way.

This reductionism which I have earlier referred to as impersonalism, the assertion that the universe is describable without reference to people, is the opposite of Strawson's view, in chapter 10, and to common sense. It is explicitly revisionist metaphysics, an attempt to change what we believe ourselves to be.[16] The opposition to common sense is not, however, total. Parfit is trying to get rid of such ghostly items as souls or egos while retaining the common sense idea of the person as distinct from the person's experiences. This is a good idea, which I will try to preserve and elaborate in a way different from Parfit's when I come to my own theory of persons. For now, I want to explore some other interesting claims of Parfit's concerning what we should care about.

Fundamental value: People do not count

The value we attach to ourselves should, by Parfit's lights, be attached rather to a series of psychological events. We care too much about the shopping bag and should concern ourselves about certain of the contents. To illustrate his departure from common sense, Parfit tells a science fiction story. Parfit uses the story of teletransportation to look into what we believe about ourselves and what we care about. It is also his vehicle for answering the sorts of questions which we have seen Nozick fretting over in the previous chapter with thought experiments concerning the overlap of people on duplication of a person. Recall the metaphor of a river which is split into two streams, the shorter of which is most similar to the original river. Nozick would consider the less similar but longer of the two streams the continuation of the river. So, hang onto your hat, here is a synopsis of Parfit's story[17] of a person dividing as a river might divide.

The teletransportation example

Imagine Georges is living in a future century when people routinely travel from one planet to another by teletransportation. Typically, people step into a scanner, on earth perhaps, press a button, and lose consciousness. After what seems like a moment, they awake in a replicator on, say, Mars. The scanner on earth destroys the body, including the brain, while recording the exact states of all the cells. This recorded information is transmitted to the replicator on Mars, which then produces from new matter a body exactly alike in every detail. This is teletransportation, which some consider to be a form of travel.

One day Georges steps into a brand new scanner on earth and pushes the button, but does not lose consciousness. Georges is then told that the new scanner does not destroy the body on earth but merely replicates it on Mars. Unfortunately, the new scanner is defective and has damaged Georges heart. Georges will die in a few days, but his replica on Mars is healthy.

In Nozick's terms from the previous chapter, the earthly Georges is the closest continuer of the person who stepped into the scanner on earth, but the next closest continuer is to be much longer lived. This is a case of Parfit's overlap in which personal identity follows not the path of closest continuation—since this is such a short path—but jumps to the replica on Mars. But Parfit does not accept Nozick's theory. The earthly Georges might have some difficulty thinking that the person on Mars is the real Georges. As Parfit points out, when Georges has his heart attack on earth thanks to the damage done by the scanner, his exact replica on Mars will feel no physical pain.[18] The replica, however similar to the person who stepped into the scanner, is not Georges.

Parfit's reasons for thinking the replica is not the same person as Georges are unclear, as we shall see in the coming discussion of personal identity. Now, however, I am interested not so much in his acceptance of the common sense opinion that the replica is a different person, but in his claims about how one ought to think about dying and being survived by a replica. He claims that this is about *as good as ordinary survival*.[19]

What is fundamentally valuable about you will survive. While Parfit's views on who is who seem ordinary enough as contrasted with Nozick's, his views on what is fundamentally valuable seem skewed. Surely, even if Georges is very unselfish, it should be little consolation to him that he is to be replaced by someone who will take over his life. If this replica is someone who will take over, for instance, his love life, it would be understandable if he felt a jealous rage against the impostor.

This is one of those instances in which we see the force of Parfit's general comments on his theory: "I believe that most of us have false beliefs about our own nature, and our identity over time, and that, when we see the truth, we ought to change some of our beliefs about what we have reason to do."[20] To persuade us that we should feel not rage but relief at the existence of the replica, Parfit argues that acceptance of divisibility and reducibility of people makes the question of who is who much less important.[21] Since there is no soul or Ego, saying that we are the same persons whom our mothers cradled in their arms at age one, is merely saying something about relations between experiences in a human life. Rather than fretting about the way in which one experience led to another, Parfit would have us concern ourselves with the quality of the experiences. Whose experiences they are is merely a question of the way in which experiences are connected but not as important as what kind of experiences they are.

I think that the idea behind this argument is that our relations to our future selves are no stronger than our relations to other people existing with us now in so far as the production of value is concerned. If we love somebody right now, that relationship is much more important than the relationship we have to our future self—perhaps some senile senior with whom we, now, have very little in common. Should we care more about that senior than others around us now? If we can use our resources to make others happy now, this would be, from my interpretation of Parfit, far more rational than hoarding them up to provide for that future senior. Indeed, if Parfit is right about people, the truth will set us free by breaking down the walls of our irrational selfishness.

Saints are unconcerned about themselves and concerned about others. That is not, however, what Parfit thinks is rational. To be concerned about others is to be concerned about people. A person, whether oneself or another, is not a proper object for moral concern.

Persons are, after all, merely conventional groupings of events. What is fundamentally valuable is the experience of persons. As a utilitarian in moral theory, Parfit is concerned with maximizing happiness; whose happinesses increases is not of great moment. Utilitarians are routinely criticized for insufficiently valuing individual people in their attempt to get the greatest happiness for the group. Parfit thinks that the utilitarian moral position becomes less implausible when we understand that people are not what counts.[22]

Personal identity: Who's who

To see better why he and other people are of little concern to Parfit, we must consider Parfit's views on personal identity—that is, on the question of what makes a person at two different times one and the same person. Since a person is a complex of things rather than a Cartesian Ego, personal identity must depend, for Parfit, on relationships among the things in the complex.

The circular criterion of identity

Parfit sums up his view on personal identity as follows: "Our existence just involves the existence of our brains and bodies, and the doing of our deeds, and the thinking of our thoughts, and the occurrence of certain other physical and mental events. Our identity over time just involves (a) Relation *R* – psychological connectedness and/or psychological continuity, with the right kind of cause, provided (b) that there is no different person who is *R*-related to us as we once were."[23] More simply put, each person is just a river of events. Some of these events are mental events joined together by an unclearly specified kind of link which Parfit is calling Relation *R*. Examples of the events in the river could include instances of thinking, remembering, dreaming, emoting, and so on. Parfit says that this river must have the right kind of cause, meaning it cannot be artificially produced, I suppose. So much for part (a), now let us see what happens in Parfit's part (b) in the foregoing quotation.

In part (b) of his identity criterion Parfit wants to rule out a fork in the river so that two different people in the present cannot turn out to be identical to one past person.[24] This seems reasonable enough, but part (b) makes Parfit's criterion of personal identity a circular criterion. We must use part (a) plus part (b) to tell when we have a different person. Part (b), however, relies on difference of persons. Parfit's criterion seems to depend on itself.

All in all, this is not too propitious a beginning. In much earlier work Parfit gave a version of the identity criterion which was not circular, since it did not include the word "different"; that version will not work unless we understand it to include implicitly the word "different."[25]

What Parfit may be trying unsuccessfully to do here with his rough criterion of identity is to define identity in terms of *R* without running into Williams' reduplication problem (see chapter 11). If people can be copied, then criterion (a) is not enough to guarantee personal identity. Parfit thinks duplication of *R*—roughly, duplication of consciousness of a person—is possible. (His reasons for believing in this possibility will emerge later.) He adds criterion (b) to rule out problems which might arise if people were copied or their conscious states were copied. Roughly, he does not want someone's consciousness splitting into two streams to make two people identical to the one whose consciousness split. Part (b) says that if the river splits, identity is lost.

Another feature of Parfit's identity criterion, part (a) plus part (b), which needs clarification is the Relation *R* itself. Parfit does not try to give any precise definition of its components, psychological continuity, and connectedness. He does say this: "*Psychological connectedness* is the holding of particular direct psychological connections.... *Psychological continuity* is the holding of overlapping chains of *strong* connectedness."[26] The psychological connections which Parfit uses as examples are memories, beliefs and desires, but he allows "any other psychological feature" to qualify.[27] This gives us only the weakest grasp on what *R* is. That is less of a problem if Parfit is not really concerned to give a precise definition of identity, but it is a bit odd in so far as Parfit holds that *R* itself is what we should care about instead of caring about our personal identity. As we saw in the last section, people are not what count; their experience is what Parfit holds to be fundamentally valuable. *R* is what holds experiences together in a sequence. Parfit, moreover, sometimes speaks not of experience but says that *R*, however it is caused, is what is fundamentally valuable. I can understand a utilitarian caring about the quality of experiences, but I am not sure why it should be so important that experiences be connected or why the relationship connecting them should be glorified. Indeed, if I am willing to give up on my continuation as a person in favour of the continuation of my mind in some other person, why should I not take a further step and say that any continuity is unimportant. I should only desire that experiences similar to my best experiences be had by me or others. Admittedly, for certain experiences, like writing the book Parfit was writing when he made these claims, continuity is needed.

Parfit's attempt to revise Locke is probably what drives him to use *R* as the all-important part of persons. Locke, whose views were discussed in chapter 5, told us that memory held a person together over time. Parfit wants to broaden this to include any psychological features which connect persons from moment to moment. He also wants to allow for loss of memories, beliefs, and desires by a person. As long as there are overlaps of my memories, I can be said to have continuous memory even though I do not remember what I did when I was ten years old. I do remember what I did when I was twenty and, when I was twenty, I remembered what I did when I was ten. This is enough for continuity of memory and continuity of the person, according to Parfit.

Parfit seems to be trying to avoid Reid's brave officer counterexample to Locke in which the officer has memories of his boyhood which he loses by the time he becomes a general (see chapter 6). The problem for a memory criterion of identity, for Reid, is that the boy and the general are both identical to the officer while the general is not identical to the boy. On Parfit's view, they are one person because overlapping connections are enough to do the job of maintaining a person's identity as long as there is only one stream of such connected events with no forks.

To fully reveal Parfit's picture of *R* it remains to be said what makes connectedness strong. To say I am *R*-related to some person yesterday is to say I have enough psychological connections with that person, for example, enough shared beliefs, desires, and memories. Parfit elaborates: "Since connectedness is a matter of degree, we cannot plausibly define precisely what counts as enough. But we can claim that there is enough connectedness if the number of connections, over any day, is *at least half* the number of direct connections that hold over every day, in the lives of nearly every actual person. When there are enough direct connections, there is what I call *strong connectedness*."[28] This is confusing and seems confused. The term "direct" is left vague. Worse, being a matter of degree is not related to imprecision as Parfit supposes. Support for a bill in the House of Commons is a matter of degree, but we can still precisely define enough support for a bill to pass. Parfit does, in spite of his disavowal, define "enough connectedness" by drawing a line at a certain degree of connectedness. I suppose he means to say that there is no non-arbitrary line to draw. To add to the lack of clarity, we are left unsure about what the connections are. Memories are the most obvious candidates. We are left unsure about what it is that Parfit thinks we should care about and what personal identity is, in his view. Both depend on *R*.

Let me try, a little more sympathetically, to see what Parfit probably thinks of as the same person. Perhaps Parfit should be saying, first, that if the body and the psychological states of a person, Tomas, are strongly connected to the body and the psychological states of a person, Dick, then Tomas is Dick. It does not work the other way around, though. That Tomas is Dick does not guarantee that Tomas is strongly connected to Dick. Second, he could mean that, if you are one in a series of people, each of whom is strongly connected to the preceding member of the series, then you are identical to all the people in the series, as long as the series does not split into two series. For example, if Tomas is strongly connected only to Dick, and Dick is strongly connected only to Heraldo, then Tomas, Dick, and Heraldo are all stages of one person—even if Heraldo is not strongly connected to Tomas. Thus I am the same person whom my mother held in her arms when I was two. I am not strongly connected to that person, but I am part of an appropriate stream of people—better, an appropriate river of psychological and bodily events—running from that gurgling two-year-old to me. As a reductionist, Parfit could just talk about the events in the river without mentioning people. The concept of a person is just a useful way of talking about a continuous, non-forking river of events of a certain kind.

Recall the questions Parfit seemed to promise to answer:

1. What is the nature of a person?
2. What is it that makes a person at two different times one and the same person?
3. What is necessarily involved in the continued existence of each person over time?

Parfit claims that an answer to the second and third questions will partly clarify the nature of persons, since "to be a person, a being must be self-conscious, aware of its identity and its continued existence over time."[29] The first question is answered by saying we are complexes. The second and third questions were answered roughly in terms of continuity of a river of experiences and bodily events. This tells us something about what kind of complexes we are, and what it would be to be aware of ourselves, not as egos but as a series of related events passing through time. To really get a grip on Parfit's answer to the second and third questions, we would have to have a definition of "direct connection," and we would have to have some understanding of a series of events which do not split and which do not depend on the identity of persons for its explication.

Cartesians and other believers in souls or Egos would, in any case, think Parfit has thrown out the baby with the bathwater. In a sense he would agree, for the baby was a fiction in his view. The answer to the second question shows that personal identity is a rather trivial matter. In fact, I think he is just trying to say enough about personal identity and the nature of persons to show us that in such concepts we will not find what really matters to us. I think of Parfit as saying that *R* is what matters in our futures and, if it turns out that one can only be *R*-related to one person, then identity matters, since it always accompanies *R*. Perry, who agrees with Parfit in large measure, puts the point by saying that the importance of identity is derivative.[30] We only should care about identity because *R* normally goes with it.

Although Parfit promises to give a criterion of personal identity, and does give a bad one, he also denies that he is offering a criterion of identity at all. He says he is a reductionist and that reductionists should not bother with offering such criteria, for personal identity is not what matters to them. In the particular context of this denial Parfit may mean that it is not important for reductionists to decide among materialism, dualism, and idealism as they interpret Relation *R*; thus they need not say what kind of thing—a body, a mind, or both—must survive for identity to be maintained.[31] In any case, Parfit appears to agree with Strawson's comment that personal identity is a problem of relatively minor significance.[32] Whatever Parfit intends, it seems to me that we need to know more fully what personal identity is before we dismiss its importance. We also need to know an awful lot more about *R* before we take it seriously as the fundamentally valuable thing about us. A little more about *R* can be gleaned from Parfit's real-world examples.

Parfit in the real world

Parfit, sensitive to the charge that too much rests on dubious thought experiments, seeks confirmation of his views in the findings of psychological research on commissurotomy patients and then extends this confirmation to more science fiction examples of brain bisection and brain transplanting. Parfit's argument is predicated on the idea that commissurotomy results, or may result, in a divided consciousness. "What is a fact must be possible," he asserts, "And it is a fact that people with disconnected hemispheres have two separate streams of consciousness—two series of thoughts and experiences, in having each of which they are unaware of having the other."[33]

Commissurotomy is an operation on the brain which does not split the brain in half as is done in science fiction examples of brain bisection. Links between the two hemispheres of the cortex (the upper brain) are cut, but the lower brain is not disturbed. This lower brain is completely indispensable to psychological functions. Philosophers should be more cautious than Parfit in making pronouncements about what actually happens to the consciousness of a person after commisurotomy. The empirical evidence, which is difficult to interpret, has led Trevarthen, a psychologist and psycho-biologist, to comment: "The tests of Zaidel and Sperry have shown that both hemispheres of commissurotomy patients have awareness of themselves as persons and a strong sense of the social and political values, or meaning, of pictures or objects."[34] It is a testimony, however, to the difficulties in the interpretation of this evidence that the same psychologist says, a few paragraphs later: "It does not appear necessary to imagine the 'self,' which has to maintain a unity, is destroyed when the forebrain commissures are cut, although some of its activities and memories are depleted after the operation."[35]

While it may seem very odd to speak of each hemisphere as being aware of itself as a person while there is but one self, one can remove the apparent paradox. Happily for Parfit, the means of removal is incompatible with the Cartesian view of persons. It seems that in such patients consciousness is not unified. That should not, however, be so surprising as it is not unified in people without commisurotomies either. The unity of consciousness, which the Cartesian explains by the mysterious Ego and Parfit explains by means of the mysterious Relation *R*, needs no explanation. It is a myth.

Before I go on to myth bashing, you may have noticed that I have attributed to Parfit views which are at odds with each other, namely, that the unity of consciousness is to be explained by the relations among experiences and that consciousness is not necessarily unified.[36] Perhaps he thinks that unity of consciousness is the norm—and that needs explaining, while exotic cases like commisurotomy examples show that there are exceptions to the norm. In fact, there are mundane cases of disunity of consciousness in totally normal people. Indeed, commisurotomy patients usually behave normally. I do not wish to defend the Cartesians against Parfit, but to point out that he brings out many dubious cases of unnecessary ammunition to fire at Descartes.

Parfit thinks that showing that the division of consciousness is logically possible shows that the Cartesians are wrong about our indivisibility: "This is one of the points at which it matters whether my imagined case is possible. If we could briefly divide our minds, this casts doubt on the view that psychological unity is explained by ownership."[37] Parfit imagines a commissurotomy patient who is capable of dividing his consciousness at will and working on two different problems in these two streams of consciousness. If this is possible, then Parfit believes he has some evidence against the view that we are each indivisible subjects of experience uniting our experience as ours. This view would entail, implausibly, that Parfit's commissurotomy patient is two people in one body, by a psychological criterion of personal identity. Parfit himself avoids this only by means of the circularity of his criterion, which was discussed earlier.

Wilkes's extended discussion of disunity of consciousness shows that the real-life cases are less dramatic and less clear-cut than Parfit supposes.[38] Wilkes points out that, for commissurotomy patients, "[t]he disunity holds against a background of 99 per cent unity. It is not far-reaching, does not consistently disrupt ordinary purposive action, tends to affect *only* the level of consciousness, and is avoided whenever possible."[39] Wilkes also is convincing on the point that exotic cases, such as that of commissurotomy patients, are not needed to illustrate disunity of consciousness.[40]

Imagine Grace driving a good friend to work on a route she takes routinely. Grace has an animated conversation with the friend with one part of her consciousness, while another part takes care of the driving. At the end of the drive she might remember only the conversation, although she exercised appropriate caution and reacted to various traffic events along the way. This would not make Grace a special case for philosophical explanation, nor should we think this of the commissurotomy patient. Even if the disunity is more dramatic in some cases of commissurotomy, not much philosophical hay can be made from this. A similar lack of hay is evident in the other real-world examples Parfit uses, but I shall content myself with his commissurotomy case as illustrative of the problems besetting such examples.

What hay can be made, Plato baled long ago. As we saw in chapter 3, people have a complex sort of consciousness, not an indivisible, unified whole. This is grist for Parfit's mill, but it does not ensure the logical possibility of all sorts of weird and wonderful science fiction.[41] Indeed, there is no need for it. Consciousness is clearly complex. This does not entirely defeat Cartesians, of course. The Cartesian can say that the consciousness is the changing part of the person while the immutable Ego owns this consciousness or even these consciousnesses if there are several in one person. In other words, the Ego is not the consciousness, but what has the consciousness, divided though the consciousness may be into various streams.

If Cartesians say this, however, then Egos seem not really conscious of themselves. Consciousness is of thoughts, feelings, and other things with detectable features. Egos cannot even detect themselves, since they do not have any properties which are detectable by consciousness. This would just bring us back to the argument discussed earlier in this chapter that there is nothing to prevent an undetectable relay race of Egos through a human being. Each Ego in turn would support the same stream of consciousness in the same body.

What about Daphne?

If Daphne is a person at all, according to Parfit, she is a different person from one hour to the next. Her short-term memory has long been dysfunctional. Her cognitive ability seems to be like that of an infant. Psychological continuity and connectedness, which Parfit thinks are crucial, are just what she has lost. Even if Parfit were willing to entertain concepts of a person through which Daphne survived the ravages of her illness, he would say that she lost what matters. Daphne was certainly of the same opinion prior to her descent into dementia. She did not wish to have her body live in that state.

Parfit's consideration of the spectra is particularly apt for Daphne. There are spectra of change, physical and psychological, beginning with Daphne the brilliant philosopher, a healthy vibrant woman, and ending with Daphne ten months later infantile in mind and nearly so in body. Parfit would say that this is a perfect example of a person's indeterminacy. It is not clear when Daphne, the philosopher, ceased to be. Different elements of the complex that was Daphne faded away at different rates. In any case, by Parfit's lights, what happened to Daphne in the first few months of this terrible period was the equivalent of ordinary death, although the exact point of death could not be determined.

What I like about Parfit

It is good that Parfit reminds us of our complexity. Parfit has at least undermined Cartesians and others who support the indivisibility, determinacy, and irreducibility of persons. We may wish to retain some version of these properties for ourselves, but probably not the ones Descartes had in mind. While I share some of Wilkes's concerns about Parfit's examples, they may, nonetheless, serve to prod us into re-examining our beliefs about ourselves. Parfit, in throwing out the baby with the bathwater, has shown us what sort of baby we are seeking, and it is not a Cartesian Ego.

Parfit has also given us some serious challenges concerning the clarification of our ways of valuing ourselves. I cannot, however, accept all of Parfit's views about what should matter most to us. Psychological continuity may be important to an intellectual, but much less so to an athlete. Parfit, like Aquinas, has elevated intellect to too high a pedestal. Views of the person based on the body have something to offer which Parfit neglects. Like Locke he is overvaluing psychological continuity, as philosophers such as Wiggins, Williams, and Wilkes would remind him. Nonetheless, there is some merit in considering later stages of ourselves less important to us now than other people at present might be. I should not, for instance, value my own comfort in retirement as highly as the present comfort of those I love. It is hard to argue with the need for some sort of war on selfishness. Nonetheless, as Parfit conducts it, the casualties are too high.

Parfit also encourages us in other ways to be here now. My later self might concern me less than my present self, especially if I think I will become very different from the person I am now. In anticipation of a diminution of my faculties, should I not spend my resources on the stage of my life when I am most capable of appreciating the results of such expenditures? Again Parfit pushes us to the limit, and we may not all wish to join him there. In any case, we are challenged to say why we should value later stages of ourselves as much as we appear to do.

Parfit has tried to convince us, in effect, that persons are not nearly as long-lived as the associated human beings. Since psychological continuity and connectedness are more fragile than their physical cousins, a human being may house a series of persons. There is something right about this, but it goes too far, as with most of Parfit's theses. Again we are challenged to come up with a concept of a person which allows personal identity to be a little more robust than in Parfit's view without making it implausible at the other extreme. It may be implausible to say that a zygote is the same person as the adult who later develops from it, but must we join Parfit in making people so volatile that they do not last from one stage of an adult to the next?

We should, perhaps, be somewhat revisionist, replacing the implausible views we have. We should not, however, replace them with outrageous views which only a philosopher could love. I accept Parfit's objection to the Cartesian view that it is hard to believe. Let us apply the same objection to Parfit and move on. What is plausible in Parfit's view will surface again in the roundup of ideas when I offer a new theory of persons.

Content questions

1. Is Parfit a revisionist (like Williams) or a descriptivist in metaphysics?
2. What questions about persons does he set himself?
3. Does he answer these? Explain your reply.
4. What are his four main theses with regard to persons?
5. What evidence would Parfit consider against the divisibility thesis?
6. What is the relation between the indeterminacy thesis and the divisibility thesis?
7. What may the examples of spectra of change show and what do they not show?
8. As a reductionist, to what does Parfit reduce persons?
9. Since "persons" do not have fundamental value in Parfit's view, what does?
10. Why is Parfit's criterion of personal identity circular?
11. Why does Parfit think that the example of two apparent streams of consciousness in one commissurotomy patient is important?

Arguments for analysis

Argument 1: The reincarnation argument

Following Parfit we can argue that persons are divisible by pointing out the lack of evidence for indivisible persons. If persons were indivisible, then they could be transferred from one body to another, or reincarnated. Reincarnated persons could remember their past lives and demonstrate that they did certain actions in the past. If we use the same standards that we use to have a living person prove she has done something, we find that supposedly reincarnated persons come up with no convincing proof. Until we have strong evidence for indivisibility—such as strong evidence of reincarnation—we should believe that persons are divisible.

Argument 2: An objection by distinguishing the Ego from the consciousness

For Cartesians, the Ego is not the consciousness but what has the consciousness of a person. The Ego could be transferred from one body to another without bringing the consciousness along. Strong evidence of the sort Parfit seeks should not convince us that the Ego has been reincarnated but only that the consciousness has continued from one body to another.

Argument 3: An objection to Parfit's empiricism

Parfit will not find empirical evidence for the Ego because it is not empirically known. It is known, as Descartes taught, by intuition. It is known each time any of us thinks or utters, I exist.

Argument 4: The relay race argument

Locke, Kant, and Parfit use this argument, in some form. Suppose the Ego is featureless. Then it could be interchanged with another Ego to support consciousness or Relation *R* or whatever without anybody noticing. There would be no feature of the new Ego to distinguish it from the old Ego. Indeed, the Ego currently supporting a person could be one in a series of egos that passes off the person as in a relay race. This makes the concept of an Ego appear rather silly. We should not accept the existence of indivisible egos underlying the person but stick with what we know, complexes of bodily and psychological features.

Argument 5: An objection to the relay race method

Our inability to rule out strange possibilities is no argument against a thing's existence. A completely similar body, for instance, could replace a human body and nobody would notice. Just because we cannot rule out this strange possibility, we should not suppose that the body does not exist.

Argument 6: An objection to the consistency of the relay race and reincarnation arguments

The reincarnation argument seems to say there could be evidence of indivisible egos and complains that there is none. The relay race argument seems to rest on the premise that there could never be any evidence of the presence or absence of egos. Parfit cannot have it both ways.

Argument 7: The spectra arguments

We can imagine people changing along a continual spectrum of gradual change physically. We can imagine the same mentally. Parfit, for instance, can, in our imaginations, gradually change into someone like the former movie actress Greta Garbo. There is no determinate point at which Parfit would cease to be Parfit and begin to be Garbo. This shows that we believe ourselves to be indeterminate. We should, therefore, also believe ourselves to be divisible. After all, an indivisible thing would be determinate.

Argument 8: The non-identity objection to the spectra argument

We can imagine many things that are not logically possible. As Parfit recognizes, this argument at most shows that we may have some beliefs. If one really imagines this case, one might be imagining an Ego changing all of its detectable properties. It would not be the person's essence, the Ego, that is indeterminate in this case, but the person's accidental properties that are indeterminate. Nobody doubts that sameness of consciousness and sameness of body are both difficult in this way. That is why we need the Ego to preserve the continuity of the person through bodily and psychological changes. Parfit gives us no reason to conclude that we should believe ourselves to be divisible. He merely forgets that the indeterminate consciousness is not identical to the determinate ego.

Argument 9: The teletransportation argument

We can imagine our bodies being destroyed and replicated elsewhere—as in teletransportation stories—with the same psychological characteristics. This would be about as good as ordinary survival in which one's body is continuous with one's past body. We should not, therefore, be concerned about personal identity but about the continuation of our psychological characteristics. It is Relation *R*, psychological continuity, and connectedness, that have value, not the person.

Argument 10: A counter-example to a premise of the teletransportation argument

A destruction and replication process through teletransportation is not about as good as ordinary survival. Suppose industrious Trish has an identical but lazy twin, Chris. Trish and Chris are out hiking and Trish is buried in a mudslide. Chris is mad with guilt at her failure to rescue Trish and becomes convinced that she is Trish. Chris takes over Trish's life and acts as though Chris has died. Now even if Chris is a great actor and perfectly replicates Trish, that would not be, for Trish, about as good as ordinary survival. Now an impostor is taking credit for Trish's achievements, taking the affection of Trish's family, and displacing the grief at Trish's passing. Even if Chris carries out Trish's projects and stands well in Trish's relationships, this would not be at all good for Trish. Trish would be gone but not missed.

Argument 11: The circularity objection to Parfit's criterion of identity

Part (b) of Parfit's criterion is that there is no different person who is R-related to us as we once were.[42] In the context of the whole criterion this says that nobody who is non-identical to a person is identical to that person merely by continuing that person psychologically. It presupposes that we already have a definition of personal identity before we define personal identity.

Argument 12: The commissurotomy argument

Once there were operations (commissurotomies) in which the entire commissure that joins the two hemispheres of the cerebral cortex of the human brain is cut through. This cut off communication between the two halves of the upper brain. There were some peculiar results, but these were rare. The Cartesians are wrong about our indivisibility. Persons with commissurotomies have a divided consciousness. If there were an indivisible Ego supporting consciousness, this would not occur. Therefore, there is no indivisible Ego.

Argument 13: The non-identity reply to the commissurotomy argument

The Ego is not the consciousness. The indivisible Ego supports the divisible consciousness and could, possibly, support more than one consciousness at a time. Parfit's example presents no problem for the indivisibility thesis.

Argument 14: The unity of consciousness myth reply

The unity of consciousness that Parfit wishes to explain by Relation *R* rather than an Ego is a myth. In ordinary people, never mind commissurotomy patients, there can be more than one stream of consciousness during a given time period. The two halves of our upper brain can think independently at times.

Argument 15: The river analogy reply

The consciousness may divide and rejoin itself much as a river does when it flows around an island. An island does not create two rivers, and a division of consciousness does not create two streams of consciousness. The divided consciousness remains one by its past and future connections.

CHAPTER 14

The Nagelian Perspective

Persons from inside, outside, and no side

Thomas Nagel thinks that Parfit and others, in trying to be objective, leave out something crucial about people, namely, their subjective viewpoint. We have been trained by many generations of philosophers and scientists to distinguish between mere appearance and reality. The way things appear, from a subjective point of view, is not necessarily the way things are, objectively. In *The View from Nowhere*, Nagel sets himself the task of combining the subjective perspective of a particular person inside the world with an objective view of that same world.[1]

The objective view is emphasized by most writers on the contemporary analytic philosophical scene to the exclusion of the subjective viewpoint. The pundits Nagel opposes would suppose that, even if one is subjectively aware of what is real, the same reality could be viewed objectively—indeed, the objective view would be superior. The underlying assumption is this: that there is in a subjective view of reality nothing different in kind from that which is observable objectively.[2] Against this claim, Nagel maintains the irreducibly subjective character of people's minds.[3] He thinks that objectivity is a valuable method of understanding the world but is overrated by those who

Notes to chapter 14 are on p. 491-92.

think it is complete in the absence of the subjective viewpoint.[4] People cannot be understood in a purely objective way.

The incompleteness of the objective perspective

Parfit, as we saw in the last chapter, believes in reductionism, the view that one could describe the universe completely from an objective point of view without mentioning people at all. The opposition, however, between Nagel and Parfit is not as clear-cut as this would suggest, since Nagel holds as well that the difference between subjectivity and objectivity is a matter of degree: "A standpoint that is objective by comparison with the personal view of one individual may be subjective by comparison with a theoretical standpoint still farther out.... We may think of reality as a set of concentric spheres, progressively revealed as we detach gradually from the contingencies of the self."[5] In spite of this fading of subjectivity into objectivity, people and their points of view are ineliminable elements of Nagel's world, while people are just series of objectively describable events in Parfit's view.

Objectivity as method

To get a preliminary grasp on Nagel's distinction of objective from subjective viewpoints, it is useful to reflect on some simple experiences of reality which people have. Suppose Patrick and Desmond are measuring the size of an object, say, a cube of metal. We expect them both to come up with the same measurements for the height, width, and length of the cube. If, however, one of them describes the cube as grey and the other calls it blue-grey, we are not surprised. Colour is unlike size.

An example which Nagel develops to explicate the objective/subjective distinction concerns such differences as the one we just noticed regarding size and colour.[6] The distinction of primary qualities of objects from secondary qualities has been used to explain the difference of colour from size. The primary or objective qualities of objects are supposed to be the properties they actually have independent of the perceiving subject, while secondary qualities are the powers of objects to evoke a certain experience in a subject of experiences such as you or me. Size is supposedly a primary quality while colour is a secondary quality. We can, however, take this time-honoured objective conception in which size is a property not relative to the observing subject and create new explanations in which size is no longer a primary quality. In Einstein's relativity theory, objects are not absolutely equal or unequal in size but only so with respect to a frame of reference. Einstein moves us out to a larger sphere of objectivity.[7]

From the new perspective which Einstein fashioned we can explain why, from the former perspective, we took size to be a primary quality. Size appears objective locally but, at extreme speeds and distances, depends on the observing subject. As we move from the way Galileo might have viewed size and colour to the way Einstein viewed them, we move from one of Nagel's concentric spheres of objectivity to another. We detach ourselves further from the contingencies of the self, for we now see things post-Einstein from a perspective which is not limited by the speed at which and distances over which our poor little bodies can travel.

If we now go back toward the centre of the concentric spheres and temporarily accept again the former primary/secondary distinction, we can see how, from Galileo's perspective, colour is not an objective or primary quality, although it seemed to be so in the smaller sphere of objectivity from which Galileo made his expansion. Colour seems like a primary quality of things until we notice that some people have different colour perceptions from the majority. These examples show us that, in thinking both colour and size are objective, we are in a smaller sphere than when we move to thinking colour is secondary in Galileo's sphere. This expands farther to Einstein's sphere in, which both size and colour are seen to be secondary.

Objectivity is, according to Nagel, merely a method of gradual detachment from the subjective point of view, and that is why the difference between the objective and the subjective is merely a matter of degree. Galileo is more objective than his predecessors and less objective than later scientists. One might wonder if it is possible to find some all-inclusive, absolute sphere of objectivity which would get us past any subjective elements in our thought.

Subjectivity is, however, incompletely reconcilable with objectivity, and objectivity is always limited, as Nagel sees it.[8] Our concepts become more objective by taking former objective conceptions together with an understanding of *ourselves* and putting the two together. The new conception explains how we had the former, given our subjective outlook.[9] The two perspectives are thus inextricably intertwined. Even the objective method has people's subjectivity at its core in Nagel's account of the matter.

False reductions of the subjective

Consider, now, in light of Nagel's opinion on the nature of subjectivity and objectivity, the reductionist thesis Parfit has presented. This is probably a case of what Nagel would call a false objectification or false reduction which merely reduces the explained rather than improving the explaining. The examples, however, which Nagel gives of such false reduction applied to people are not examples of Parfit's sort of reduction. Below I will show how Nagel attacks materialism, the view that everything—including each person—is made merely of matter, and a special case of materialism called "functionalism."[10] Functionalism—the idea that the computer is the right model for the mind[11]—is a view in which there is only a material brain and a program on which it runs, nothing mental beyond that. Parfit, on the other hand, only wishes to reduce people to mental and physical events without prejudice as to the nature of such events. Parfit can accept the falsity of materialism and functionalism while retaining his sort of reductionism.

Getting people out of the picture, however—even if one does not reject irreducibly mental states—must be wrong, given that people and their perspectives are ineleminable parts of the world. Such ineliminability is what I take Nagel to be pointing to with his claim that subjectivity is the core of all objectivity, the centre of all the concentric spheres of reality. Thus, although Parfit's view is not the direct object of Nagel's attack on reductionism, Nagel should consider it as false as any other sort of reductionism that leaves out the subjective viewpoint.

Objectivity is relative to the discipline

To add to the restriction of the objective viewpoint, Nagel thinks that objectivity varies from discipline to discipline.[12] This relativizes objectivity rather than having it serve as some universal, absolute standard by which to judge what we believe. Although Nagel does not make use of the relativity of the objective in this way, it could be argued that an objective description of the world which excluded people would have its objectivity only relative to the discipline in which the description is given, say, physics. This would not provide objective reasons for another discipline, say, psychology, to consider people eliminable. The reductionist thesis is probably understood by its defenders as being quite independent of disciplines; yet Nagel's relativizing of objectivity seems on the face of it quite plausible. At the very least, Parfit's reductionism is in need of clarification. In what discipline does Parfit envisage his unpeopled description of the universe?

Irreducibility

The irreducibility of the subjective to the objective comes up, so Nagel argues, in ethical values and truth.[13] Neither subjective nor objective values can supersede the other, yet they do not coexist without strife. As Nagel sees them, the same can be said of truths. The concept of a person is, in my opinion, at the centre of the vortex created by these opposing currents of objectivity and subjectivity. Nagel's insistence on opposing the scientism which requires us to neglect the subjective is, therefore, especially welcome.[14] Parfit is not alone among the influential writers[15] who have led many to believe that we can say what we need to say about ourselves while totally neglecting our subjective viewpoints in the world. It is this that leads them to suggest that personal survival is not what fundamentally matters. Nagel argues for the value of the subjective. I believe that this entails the importance of the very person who is the subject of the experiences. Replicas will not do.

Mind

Given Nagel's attitude to subjectivity and its importance, Nagel can be expected to attack vigorously the attempts of his contemporaries to understand people in terms of our objective understanding of machines. He does not disappoint this expectation:

> The reductionist program that dominates current work in the philosophy of mind is completely misguided, because it is based on the groundless assumption that a particular conception of objective reality is

> exhaustive of what there is. Eventually, I believe, current attempts to understand the mind by analogy with man-made computers that can perform superbly some of the same external tasks as conscious beings will be recognized as a gigantic waste of time. The true principles underlying the mind will be discovered, if at all, only by a more direct approach.[16]

To understand ourselves, we must look at ourselves, not at machines which can mimic some of our linguistic behaviour.

While Nagel does not yet know how to understand mind, he rejects materialism, idealism, dualism, and no-ownership theories as implausible or unintelligible and asserts a dual aspect theory. In other words he rejects the view that people are just physical bodies, the view that they are purely minds, the view that they are a combination of both, and the view that experiences can exist independently of the people who own those experiences. Instead of these he accepts the view that a person is one being made out of one kind of stuff with two sorts of features: a material aspect and a mental aspect. He forthrightly admits that talk about this dual aspect theory is largely hand waving.[17] Waving hands is, in any case, better than clenching them or wringing them in face of the inadequacies of the other kinds of theories.

Given the blanketing snowfall of Parfit's influence, I will single out just one part of Nagel's argument driving us in the direction of a dual aspect theory, the part which counters Parfit's reductionism. Reductionism is closely related to the no-ownership view accepted by Wittgenstein and Ayer and attacked by Strawson, as we saw in chapters 9 and 10. Of this no-ownership view Nagel says:

> I suppose I should also consider the "no-ownership" view according to which mental events are not properties or modifications of anything, but simply occur, neither in a soul nor in the body—though they are causally related to what happens in the body. But I don't really find this view intelligible. *Something* must be there in advance, with the potential of being affected with mental manifestations.[18]

The reductionist description of the world suffers from the same lack of intelligibility. If we try to describe, say, our own perceptions as events rather than as things which happen to us—all in aid of deleting people from the description—we fail to describe what really happens. From a subjective point of view, I have a perception. That is part of the world which gets left out when the physical concomitants of my having the perception are objectively described.

The question then arises, for Nagel, Who is the owner of mental events? Since they must be events in some soul or self, what constitutes that self? His answer is that the brain is that self.

The self as brain

According to Nagel, I can truly say, I am my brain.[19] The self just is the intact brain. Nagel admits this is an empirical hypothesis. What he supposes is that the brain is the seat of the person's experience, a conscious organ.[20] It follows that without survival of the intact brain, there is no survival of the person. Nagel rejects many thought experiments that seem to show otherwise. Such experiments confuse metaphysical with epistemological possibility.[21] What we *can be* should not be confused with what we *can conceive of ourselves as being*.

It might seem that Nagel is a materialist since he identifies the self with the brain. In fact, however, he believes that the brain has irreducibly immaterial properties.[22] He believes that physical parts of persons can have mental units.[23] He knows that this raises many difficulties for which he has no solution. His general tendency, however, is to preserve the richness of what is to be explained rather than to reduce it to something that can be handled given our limited conceptual framework and tools.

Pan-psychism

One problem that arises from Nagel's conception of the brain having irreducibly mental properties is that other things may have such properties too, even if they are not the sorts of things with which we would normally associate our mind.[24] The view that all things have minds or at least mental properties is pan-psychism. Nagel takes this to be a serious problem with his dual aspect theory. A conceptual revolution is needed to overcome such problems, in Nagel's view.[25] Leibniz, Schopenhauer, and Whitehead, among the dignitaries whom we have briefly interviewed in these pages, would reassure Nagel on this point. They accept forms of pan-psychism. The revolution anticipated by Nagel may lead us ultimately to see people as distinct from other things only in the degree to which they have mental properties. On this view, the mind is particularly well developed in people, less so in other animals, and very dim in vegetables. Certainly it is revolutionary to say that carrots, in even an extremely limited way, have mental as well as physical properties. One could, however, limit mental properties to those things with brains rather than buying the whole pan-psychism theory.

Contrast with Parfit

Although it may seem that Nagel has given us a view of ourselves that is diametrically opposed to Parfit's, they are not always on different streets. Before we explore their similarities, however, let us be clear about their differences.

Against Parfit: Not R but the brain

Recall Parfit's spectra examples—science fiction cases of gradual physical and mental change of one person into another person. Parfit's physical spectrum case was designed to show that the continuity of the brain is a matter of degree and that, in any case, not the brain but Relation *R*, which includes psychological continuity and connectedness of the person, is what really matters. Nagel asserts that the actual cause of such continuity is what matters, namely, the intact brain. Otherwise, he claims, personal identity would be illusory. Nagel has, however, no clear answer to the question, Why does the brain matter?[26] Perhaps for both Parfit and Nagel, the answers given to What matters? are close to bedrock assumptions on which the rest of the position is built.

One motive which Nagel does not mention for clinging to the brain, but which may be active behind the scenes in Nagel's presentation, is the irrelevant fact principle.[27] That principle, which underlies the argument of Williams in chapter 11, says that, if there is a question whether person Tomas is identical to person Dick, then that question can be answered by appeal only to what Tomas and Dick are like. Properties of other parties are irrelevant to the identity of Tomas to Dick. This seems like a reasonable principle, but best candidate theories of personal identity deny this principle. Such theories determine who Tomas is by looking for who, of various people, is the best candidate. If Dick would be best but for the existence of Heraldo, then not only Tomas and Dick are relevant to the question of whether Dick is identical to Tomas who existed earlier than Dick and Heraldo.

For example, we have seen Nozick's best candidate theory (in chapter 12) or the theory based on Relation *R* with which Parfit flirts but probably does not need to defend (in chapter 13). Best candidate theories tell us that, if there is some third person, Heraldo, who might along with Dick be a candidate for identity with Tomas, then we choose between Dick and Heraldo by checking to see which satisfies the identity criterion best. Parfit might think that, if Dick is more *R*-related to Tomas than Heraldo is, then Dick is identical to Tomas while Heraldo is not. If Dick and Heraldo are equally *R*-related to Tomas, then neither is identical to Tomas, going by the way Parfit speaks of his cases of personal fission. If Tomas divides, becoming Dick and Heraldo, then properties of Heraldo are relevant to the identity of Tomas to Dick contrary to the irrelevant fact principle. The sameness of the intact brain provides a criterion of personal identity that is immune to such science fiction fission cases. Even if the brain is divisible without the death of either half, the resulting halves are not to be identified with the original whole brain.[28] Nagel thus has a way of preserving our intuition that there is something under our consciousness that would preserve us even through radical changes in our mental life. Parfit seems to bite the bullet here, in effect denying this intuition about survival and denying the irrelevant fact principle.

With Parfit: Denial of the indivisibility thesis

Parfit and Nagel, in spite of their differences, do agree on some controversial theses. They both deny the indivisibility thesis of Descartes. This means that Nagel should accept indeterminacy of people. In fact, he does not think that there must be a definite answer to the question whether a particular experience is my experience. Nor does Nagel balk at believing that there could be two experiences both of which are mine but which occur in different subjects.[29] A single brain can continue in existence but, after some extreme experience, with a radically different mental life. This preserves the intuition that one can lose one's intellect and/or memories but still be the same person. In a case where large and important areas of the brain are altered, brain identity may be a problem for Nagel's view even if personal identity given the sameness of the brain is no longer a problem. The self as brain may not do all that the simple, indivisible self was supposed to accomplish, but it is better than the alternatives, if Nagel is right.[30]

Nagel, it appears, adopts a divisibility thesis which leads to *some* forms of indeterminacy of persons. But Nagel does not want to go to the extent that Parfit does in claiming that a person is a complex of things more like a nation than like a Cartesian Ego. Nagel admits that his reasons for resisting are question begging: "One of the conditions that the self should meet if possible is that it be something in which the flow of consciousness and the beliefs, desires, intentions, and character traits that I have all take place—something beneath the contents of consciousness, which might even survive a radical break in the continuity of consciousness. If there were no such thing then the idea of personal identity would be an illusion, but we are not in that situation."[31] Since Nagel insists on the intactness of the brain to fulfil this condition of the self, he would have to accept the odd consequence that one who survives the destruction of half of the cortex and who seems to be the same person by macroscopic observation is not the same person as the original victim of the brain damage.

Worse than this, the molecules that compose the brain change. Does this mean that the brain does not continue? If it does continue through this change, then the brain's structure—not the particular material of which it is composed—seems to be what is important. Nagel's view might, therefore, run afoul of Williams' reduplication argument. If we could produce a second brain identical to the first in structure, we would have two candidates for being a single person.

Since Nagel insists on actual causes of Parfit's Relation *R* (psychological continuity and connectedness), he might count only the first brain as determining the original person and the copy as having the wrong kind of cause to be the original person. A duplicate person might be, except for causal history and spatio-temporal location, indiscernible from the original: she would believe she was the original. Nonetheless, that causal history explains how she came to be and, hence, who she is. In this, Nagel agrees with Kripke,[32] yet another famous philosopher who barely gets mentioned in these pages. Nagel notes that Kripke comes close to a dual aspect theory operating through his claim that biological origin is the source of identity. Nagel disagrees with Kripke, however, as to the possibility of mental events without the brain. Nagel suspects that the conceivability of such detached mental events is dependent on our mental concepts grasping only one aspect of the mind.[33] When we think of our visual experience, for example, we may think of only one aspect of it and thereby delude ourselves into supposing that it can be consistently conceived of as existing independently of the brain.

In summary, then, Nagel rests identity of persons on identity of brains. He recognizes that identity of brains is problematic. He chose brains, in any case, because he thought that what mattered in survival was the actual cause of Relation *R*. When confronted with a case of two brains similar in structure or function, Nagel would look to see if one of them had the right kind of cause. If so, it would be the same brain we started with. It appears then that, for Nagel, what causes us to be as we are is crucial for our being who we are and, at the same time, is what matters about us. I should care about whether I survive, not just about whether my mind survives in someone or other. Personal identity and mattering are together again. This reunion, at least, is intuitively correct.

What is unintuitive is that the cause matters so much. Just how crucial is it that I am the result of a particular sperm and egg? Could not one of that sperm's squirmy brethren have contributed equally well to my birth? There seem to be a number of possible causes of my being which would not crucially have altered me as a person. Once we admit this, however, we stray from the causal theory which Nagel seems to be adopting from Kripke.

A good reason for Nagel to cling to a causal theory is his opposition to functionalism, the view of the person as biological computer. Once one gives up particular causes, such as a sperm and ovum, one is thrown back on the structure of the brain as the crucial thing about it for purposes of identity. Since every molecule of the brain will change every six years or so, there is no way to use a same-matter-same-brain criterion of identity. Structure is all that is left. Structures, however, can be duplicated, opening a Pandora's box of problems with which we have seen Williams, Nozick, and Parfit struggle. So Nagel is left with a brain caused in the appropriate way which has mental and physical aspects.

Problems

The difficulties Nagel faces are both linguistic and metaphysical. Because he has unusual ideas about what we are, he invents new terms to try to break out of unproductive ways of describing persons. I will try to some extent to tear apart the objections to Nagel's language from the objections to his theory of what we see.

The difficulty of defending a dual aspect theory

Nagel is defending very difficult ground here. Bravely, he tries to take a position between the dualist and the materialist in the full recognition that, like a pacifist protesting at the battlefront, he will be caught in the crossfire. The materialist will say that his talk of irreducibly mental properties of the brain is unfounded while the dualist will say that his identification of the self with the brain is unintelligible. Although Nagel admits to hand waving and question begging, he thinks the alternatives are even less able than his view to preserve both our subjective impressions of ourselves and our objective knowledge of our biological components.

Terminological problems

The terminology of Nagel's difficult position is somewhat puzzling. Nagel speaks interchangeably of personal identity and self-identity, seemingly making no distinction between selves and persons.[34] On the other hand, the self is defined as the same subjective consciousness.[35] While subjective consciousness is usually essential to our view of what we are, it is also usually a somewhat narrower concept than that of a person. Perhaps self-identity and personal identity always go together, but they must not be exactly the same thing.

Nagel also gives us his empirical hypothesis that the self is just the person's brain. Here the self is clearly distinct from the person: "What I am is whatever is in fact the seat of the person TN's experiences."[36] Here TN (Thomas Nagel) is a person who includes the brain which is the self. It looks as if the self is the subject of experiences if a seat is a subject; hence, the brain is the subject of experiences. We have already seen that the brain may survive a radical change in consciousness, so the subject of experiences is clearly not the consciousness.

Collecting all the bits, we seem to have the "person"; the "self" (which is also called the "subject" and is perhaps the "brain"); and the "consciousness" as, perhaps, three distinct entities. To this list we must add the strangest of them all, the "objective self." The picture we have prior to adding the objective self is of persons as normally conscious beings who may, however, lose their consciousness and remain the same so long as they retain the same brain.

The postulation of the objective self

In his quest to accommodate the objective and subjective perspectives to one another, Nagel postulates the existence of the objective self, a self each of us has but which has *no point of view*. This "true self" is abstracted from the person by treating that person's experiences as data for the construction of an objective picture.[37] This objective self functions independently of the person but is inseparable from the person.[38] By taking the view from nowhere this autonomous objective self helps in the reconciliation of the subjective and objective perspectives.[39] This will take some unravelling in terms of the meanings of what we say about ourselves.

From a semantic point of view this objective self idea allows us to distinguish three different meanings of the sentence uttered by Thomas Nagel, I am TN. It could be the content-free, TN is TN, or the practical communication, My name is TN. As a communication of the objective self, however, it says that the objective self is getting its sensory information about the world through the person TN. Nagel is replying to those who think we are misled by linguistic considerations into manufacturing a self from a misunderstanding of the use of "I."[40] That is, he is replying to the no-ownership view. The apparent strength of the reply depends, however, on one's intuitions about the existence of something in oneself fitting the description of the objective self.

Intuitively it is possible to stand back from ourselves and take an objective look at ourselves and the way others see us. Even in the midst of great anger, one can see one's anger as absurd from the outside. Nagel takes this kind of data seriously and drives the conception of persons from the contemporary unified picture back to a pluralistic conception. There are various decision makers within one person. This is somewhat reminiscent, in its pluralism, of the ancient Greek idea of a person as containing various autonomous decision makers—an idea used by Wilkes to hammer Parfit, as we saw in the last chapter.

Nagel's pluralism with respect to persons is certainly every bit as strange as its Iliadic cousin to contemporary understanding of the person. We could perhaps become accustomed to thinking of the self as the brain, but the objective self which takes the view from nowhere is an odd item indeed. Williams, in discussing identity criteria for persons, and insisting that they must be used by someone, has objected to the intelligibility of the view from nowhere long before Nagel makes use of it. Commenting on Hume's speculation on what we would see if we could see clearly into the breast of another, Williams says: "Others, in criticizing or expanding Hume's account, have written in terms that similarly require an externalized view of the contents of a man's mind, a view obtainable from no conceivable vantage-point. Theorizing which is in this sense abstract must be vacuous, because this privileged but positionless point of view can mean nothing to us."[41] It certainly seems to mean a lot to Nagel, but he warns against giving it a metaphysical interpretation, although it is real.[42] How can something be real and not countenanced as a real thing by our metaphysics?

This difficult doctrine is illuminated by another passage:

> The fact that I seem able in imagination to detach this perspectiveless or objective self from TN [ie, Thomas Nagel] does not show that it is a distinct thing, or that nothing else about TN belongs to me essentially. It does not show, as may at first appear, that the connection between me and TN is acciden-

> tal. It does show, however, that something essential about me has nothing to do with my perspective and position in the world.[43]

It turns out, then, that the objective self is real, but not really a distinct object from the person. It is a device for seeing an objective but non-physical part of a person. Is it intelligible, Williams notwithstanding? It is indeed difficult to moderate this debate concerning the possibility of a privileged but positionless point of view.

Williams is objecting to this viewpoint because no person could take it. Nagel might agree that no *person* could take it, but insists that *a part of a person* could. Stand back from your passions and notice, from no point of view, what you are experiencing. This essential part of you which does the standing back—rather, standing nowhere—is your way of being objective about your subjective experience.

One may answer these instructions in a Humean way, saying that there is nothing corresponding to the objective self which one sees when one introspects. Nagel might reply that it is the objective self which is doing the introspecting. We should not look for a distinct thing or a little person within doing this, but "a distinct part of the mind" viewing the mind's experience.[44] Here again is the pluralism which is contrary to many of our current ways of thinking and speaking. It is not contrary to all. You may find that you are of two minds about it.

While the objective self is still somewhat nebulous, it does tug at one's intuitions. There is an odd phenomenon of standing back from oneself even in moments of great heat. It is especially noticeable when one feels the absurdity of life.[45] The phenomenon may, however, be something more evident to those who have meditated on it than to others. My willingness to entertain, tentatively, Nagel's concept of an objective self as an essential part of a person is utterly dependent on my awareness in myself of this phenomenon of my standing back from myself even though there is nowhere to stand. It is quite possible that some do not experience this, whence their Humean replies to Nagel.

What about Daphne?

Daphne was the victim of massive scarring of her brain which altered nearly everything else about her. In spite of the changes to the brain, it is the same brain, by the causal criterion of sameness; so Daphne still exists as the same self. The self, however, is not identical to the person. Nagel does not tell us enough about the relationship, although he speaks as if self-identity and personal identity always go together. Daphne's former kind of consciousness is gone, although the seat of consciousness remains. Her current consciousness appears to be very limited. Her personality is reduced to mere remnants. Her capacity to interact with others is nearly absent. Would Nagel be willing to say, therefore, that a different person is now related to that continuing self, that brain? If so, then why is it the brain that matters? If not, then what is a person over and above the brain which that person has? Nagel's account, while insightful, is very incomplete.

What I like about Nagel's account

Nagel sees that there is something essential about the physical aspect of a person, although he does not take this insight far enough. Most importantly, he also articulates some of the uneasiness we reasonably have with reductionism. What reductionists leave out is our subjective viewpoint, and that is essential to persons. Nagel rightly resists the contemporary fashion of scientistic adulation of the apparently objective output by the empirical sciences. Nagel's analysis of the distinction between the subjective and the objective seems right. The proliferation of terms Nagel adopts to apply this analysis to persons is forced partly by the variety of questions about persons which is masked by a minimalist approach.

After too short a visit, we must bid a fond adieu to Nagel's territory in order to begin to draw together some of the ideas of the contemporary notables I have selected for comment.

Content questions

1. What do philosophers tend to leave out of our accounts of persons according to Nagel?
2. What is the difference, with regard to subjectivity, between Parfit's view of persons and Nagel's?
3. What view other than Parfit's does Nagel take to be a false reduction?
4. How does the discipline relativity of objective explanation impinge on Parfit's view?

5. What is Nagel's dual aspect theory of persons?
6. What is the essential self or person according to Nagel?
7. What is one very odd consequence of his view that Nagel must face?
8. What is the causal theory that Nagel uses to deal with problems of brain identity?
9. According to Nagel, from what point of view does Nagel's objective self observe Nagel's experience?
10. How would Williams object to the concept of an objective self?
11. How might Nagel respond?

Arguments for analysis

Argument 1: The irreducible subjectivity argument

Each person has an irreducibly subjective view of the world that is an essential part of that person. Each of us can tell that this is true in our own case. Therefore, any completely objective account of persons will leave something essential out.

Argument 2: The classy objection

Persons as a class may be objectively defined even if persons as individuals have an essential and irreducible subjective component. An objective account of an individual person may not be possible, but an objective account of the nature of persons generally could still be possible.

Argument 3: The objectivity of subjectivity compromise

Irreducible subjectivity is a real feature of persons, and that is what cannot be left out. The conclusion of the irreducible subjectivity argument must be revised to say that, although an objective account of persons in general is possible, any account of persons that does not refer to the subjective viewpoints of individual persons will be incomplete.

Argument 4: The ownerless objection

As Wittgenstein pointed out, there is no part of reality that is missed when we fail to describe the subjective viewpoint. It is like the point of perspective from which a picture is drawn. It is outside reality as the perspective point is outside the picture. Both are abstractions, works of the imagination, not something real.

Argument 5: The indirect evidence reply

It is an objective fact about persons generally that each person has an irreducibly subjective component, although, except in our own cases, we have only indirect evidence for this. We have, however, only indirect evidence for the existence of micro-particles that we cannot observe. That something cannot be directly and publicly observed does not make it unreal. Wittgenstein's persuasive metaphor notwithstanding, we should assert the reality of owners of experience and viewpoints through our direct observation of ourselves and our indirect observation of others.

Argument 6: The incoherence reply

It is incoherent to posit an experience without an experiencer, a thought without a thinker, or a subjective viewpoint uniting actual experiences without someone having that viewpoint. To deny owners of experience is to deny the existence of experiences themselves.

Argument 7: The degrees of objectivity argument

Objectivity, as Nagel says, is merely a method of gradual detachment from the contingencies of the self. This makes the difference between objective and subjective viewpoints merely a matter of degree. Therefore, a completely objective (reductionist) account of persons is not possible. There is subjectivity at the core of any objective account.

Argument 8: The Humean objection

There is no self to detach from gradually or otherwise. There is objective truth. What passes for subjective truth is falsehood.

Argument 9: The brainy reply

Admittedly, the concepts of a self or person, of self-perception, self-awareness, and personal identity have been vexed through their history. Hume is right to reject Cartesian Egos since these can make no difference to us. There is, however, a self or seat of consciousness, and it is the brain. This solution of Nagel's avoids the problems typically associated with other concepts of the self, but it retains the psychological aspects of the self or person. The subjective viewpoint that the brain has is one of the contingencies of the self from which objective fact is gradually detached.

Argument 10: The physical spectrum objection

The identity of the brain over time is problematic. The cells that make up the brain change over time, although some special neurons, the glial cells, remain. We do not want to say we are our glial cells. In any case, every six years or so, all of the molecules in the brain have changed. Since the brain is composed of different matter several times over the course of a human life, we would have to identify it by its structure. The brain, however, develops over time, changing its structure as, for instance, dendrites are formed and as cells die and are not replaced. We might, of course, identify the brain by its functions, but Nagel's brainy reply was intended to avoid functionalism.

Argument 11: The space-time worm reply

The brain is identifiable over time just in the same way that any continuing physical object or process is identifiable. By Hume's standards, we do not have the same tree from day to day growing in the park. In fact, we can identify trees and brains as rivers of matter through time or space-time worms.

Argument 12: The double trouble objection

The problem with processes is that they can divide into two. A river can fork. A stream of matter through time may give rise to two remarkably similar streams. Nozick's closest continuer theory is a response to this problem. Nagel's choice of the brain, however, is intended to avoid that sort of best candidate theory. He has no way to identify persons in the event of duplication of the brain.

Argument 13: The right cause reply

The brain is identified by its cause. It is not at all clear that we should worry about science fiction cases of duplication, but in any case the brain that is the duplicate would be caused by the duplicating machine while the brain that identifies the person whose brain was duplicated was caused by that person's conception.

Argument 14: The goofy gamete objection

This means that the person I am depends on the brain I have. That in turn depends on which two gametes got together. Had a different sperm contributing to conception caused me, I would not be the same person, no matter how similar I might be. Surely this is implausible. Any sperm bearing the same genetic information would have been adequate to the task of producing me.

Argument 15: The right kind of cause reply

Very well, we need not insist on a particular pair of gametes. Any cause of that type rather than that particular token would be adequate to support personal identity. A duplication machine would not, however, be a cause of that type.

Argument 16: The arbitrary kind objection

It is arbitrary what kind of cause gives rise to a brain and thence to a person. As biotechnology progresses, we may have various different ways of causing brains to exist. You exaggerate greatly the importance of the source of a particular process through this right-kind-of-cause reply. If our brains make us who we are, then it is the kind of brain one has, not what caused it, that is important.

Argument 17: The genuine original reply

Let us consider a case that shows that causal origins are important. If identical twins were disputing who was who, it would not matter that twin B had a brain that was a closer continuer of A's former brain than A himself now has. A would still be A and B would be B. Their brains are different causal processes.

Argument 18: The similar kinds objection

In the case of the twins, their origin gives them causes of the same kind, indeed the same token of a cause not merely the same type. You cannot rely on the right kind of cause as a distinguishing feature in all cases. The twins present a real case in which a stream of matter divides and causes headaches for those who overemphasize the importance of causal origins.

Argument 19: The linguistic reply

We know what we mean by "the same brain." Our use of the term "brain" is clear enough to distinguish cases like that of artificial duplication of brains from the twins case.

Argument 20: The conventionalism objection

That way conventionalism lies. What counts as a brain or as the same brain would be determined arbitrarily by our conventions for the use of the term "brain." Since we do not want to make personal identity purely a matter of convention, we must not identify persons with their brains.

Argument 21: The sanctified convention reply

The association of conventions with arbitrariness is mistaken. What we count as a brain or the same brain over time may be a matter of convention. This, however, does not show that it is arbitrary. In every viable society there are strong conventions such as that against killing people for fun or profit. These are necessary for the survival of societies, not arbitrary. Similarly, conventions affecting what we count as a person are far from arbitrary. They matter to us a great deal. They are chosen for good reason. We need to protect our interests as unique individuals. This may be more difficult for twins, but it is no arbitrary matter.

A fuller treatment of this conventionalist idea requires the social contract theory, to be introduced later.

Part 5

My Suggestions for Ways to See Ourselves

CHAPTER 15

Collecting Ideas

Five periods in the history of a concept

In the foregoing chronological record of the developments in concepts of a person, I have grouped theories of what we are into five eras. These are not individually united around any single doctrine but around sets of themes and concerns. As what we care about shifts, so does our self concept. Here, however, I will select some salient doctrines from each period that may help us to fashion a useful concept of a person for our use today.

Ideas from ancient Greece and Rome

The belief in a perfect world of Forms apart from the muck of the mundane in which we are mired is very pretty, but, as a device for changing behaviour, I put it with the belief in Santa Claus. There are times when it is good to temporarily suspend disbelief and act as if these things were so. There is, however, more in the Forms than in Santa. The Forms, with apologies to Plato, may be thought of not as real but as ideals to help us to organize our thought and action. It is useful to ask what the Form of a person might be. If we can construct a model and hold it before our minds, then we will be better able to

---

Notes to chapter 15 are on pp. 492-93.

say when a particular human being has enough resemblance to the ideal or model to be included in the class of persons.

Another kind of form, which is inspired by what was discussed in connection with Aristotle, is even more useful. Aristotle's forms are not otherworldly ephemera. The form of persons in general is a set of abilities. The foremost of these abilities is rationality, broadly construed to include much more than merely logical thinking. Logic can lead us from foolish starting points to foolish conclusions. Rationality includes the choice of good beginnings. Among the other important abilities which distinguish persons from other kinds of being are social and political abilities. Fundamental among these is the ability to communicate with others of our kind. There are also very basic abilities that are part of the form that are nonetheless not themselves distinctive of persons, such as the ability to move oneself. If we consider all of these various abilities as necessary to any person, counter-examples spring readily to mind. There are, obviously, people who cannot move themselves. There are irrational people as well. These counter-examples require that we say how one can be a person, albeit a deformed person, with only some of the abilities. Since nobody is perfectly formed, we are all in some sense "deformed." If we use this as a technical term rather than an insult, it can help to draw together ideas about what we are.

As will become clear, my perspective is heavily influenced by Aristotle. This is partly because I hitch my wagon to Western common sense, and Aristotle is one of the originators of what has come to be common sense. It would be anachronistic to say I will develop an Aristotelian concept of a person, but the inspiration for some of my theory blows from this doughty ancient.

As we try to make sense of the forms of people—both people as a class and people as individuals—we must keep in mind the lessons of the ancients which point to a complex, not a simple, indivisible self. Whether we call the parts of the self Reason, Spirit, and Appetite, or use contemporary psychiatric jargon, we must admit that a person is at times at war with herself or doing several things at once. This is inexplicable with the concept of a simple, indivisible self as a Cartesian Ego.

The Roman adaptation of the Greek ideas includes, importantly, the invention of the concept of a person (*persona*) as a concept distinct from that of a human being. Although there are those who wish to eradicate this ancient distinction—the anti-abortion activists for example—it is a distinction worth preserving. However we arrange our concepts, we must be able to tell when a person so loses the form of "person" as to be a mere human being or when a human being has not yet acquired that form.

Freedom starts to come into the picture in ancient times as well. The idea that slaves were not persons under late Roman law is a particularly nasty recognition of the importance of freedom in concepts of a person. As well as political freedom and its moral basis, there is linked to notions of the person the idea of metaphysical freedom. Persons, unlike automata, can be confronted with genuine choices. Most of us believe this, however difficult it may be to say what the freedom to choose is. We think we are responsible for our own actions. Of course, as we saw in chapter 3, the Stoics and Plotinus thought we were responsible while thinking that all of our actions are determined. I find this paradoxical. Give me freedom.

The political freedom that we may get as a consequence of being recognized as persons would not be worth much without the metaphysical freedom that is a condition that must be met for us to be persons. If we were like automata, we would not really be able to exercise political freedom. All of our actions would be forced, although the forces could be more subtle than those used by dictators.

Individuality as a part of what we are begins to grow in ancient times as well. The importance of the person as an individual over and against groups of persons, for example the state, is weaned in ancient times. It has become common sense in the West that the individual's interests, not merely the interests of the group, must be considered.

Mediaeval and Renaissance influences

Augustine keeps a version of Plato's value hierarchy alive—as Plotinus did before him—through his arrangement of the world via a system of values, with God at the top. For Plato the Form of the Good was at the top. For Augustine, people are valuable to the extent that they resemble God. This is a little easier to comprehend than resemblance to a form. God can be thought of as the ultimate person. In this system angels are better than us, but we are better than animals. Whether or not you think of God and angels as real or merely ideals, you probably think of people as more valuable than animals. This is a part of our common sense which is much under challenge nowadays. Nonetheless, with restrictions, there is something right about this. For example, it seems reasonable to allow animals to suffer in medical research so that people will have their suffering relieved. Much animal suffering, however, is inflicted for minor pleasures of people. This would not be justified simply by valuing people more highly than animals. Nevertheless, there is something appealing in the notion that people have a greater moral value than chimpanzees because of their greater resemblance to some ideal, some form, as the source of value. Is this appeal merely a hold-over from views like Augustine's that have seeped into what is now common sense? If there is a continuum rather than a sharp divide between humans and other species in the degree to which they match the ideal, then we must rethink our moral position concerning the treatment of non-human animals. I will give brief consideration to this in the final chapter.

Another contribution of Augustine's is the addition to the list of capacities of persons the capacity for mutual love. There is a strain, however, in Augustine's emphasis on love over such abilities as the capacity for rational thought. This might put some dogs above some people on a scale of resemblance to the ideal being, if that ideal is framed more in terms of love than rationality. While being a person is partly an affair of the heart, it is not only this. There are, of course, varieties of mutual love which require more intellect than a dog or even a chimp is likely to muster. In any case, we need to keep open a large place for the capacity for mutual love when we come to speculate on the form of a person.

Aquinas goes back to the intellect as a primary feature of us, and takes up the Aristotelian banner. There is, however, a new element. Following Aristotle's general way of thinking we would say that the potential person, the human infant, becomes a person in realizing some preset end or purpose. By Aquinas's way of thinking, the role of the person in making oneself is greater. Because we are responsible for forming our own characters, becoming a person requires pulling oneself up by the boot straps. There is something right about this paradoxical position on which we must try to get a handle. Perhaps Nozick's later views on self-creation will help.

A theme that takes root in the mediaeval period flowers in the Renaissance. We have seen, for example, Erasmus weaving into the humanist strand of thought on persons the idea that we achieve merit through our exercise of our freedom. Our dignity and moral worth come to depend on our own achievements. Of course a great achievement, in this context, may be merely in using well the poor hand that we are dealt by the accidents of birth. Through Augustine, Aquinas, and Erasmus, the importance of the individual and of what the individual does become further entrenched in our ideas of the worth of the individual as a person. For the religious, the value of a person resides officially in the approval of God. It is up to us, however, to choose to be either sinners or saints. This makes a person's worth depend ever more on that person. I wish to further this development with a gentle sort of individualism as a part of the concept of a person I put forward.

Help from the earlier moderns

Locke is the first to make the concept of a person a central issue. Ever after concepts of a person tend to be tied to moral concerns, especially Locke's worry about responsibility. Unlike Locke, I think people are responsible even for things they do not remember doing, but there is much in Locke that is useful. Like him, we should rule out appealing to religious solutions to philosophical problems. If our concept of a person, for example, is inadequate for telling who is who, it is not acceptable to say that God sorts that out. We should also follow Locke in trying to keep the debate among materialists, dualists, and idealists from clouding the issue. We want a concept of a person which will work with any of these metaphysical foundations.

Like both Descartes and Locke, we should attend to the subject of the experiences which a person has but, with Hobbes, we ought to remember the importance of the body. This does not rule out idealism. The idealist can reinterpret body talk as talk of ideas in minds. Whatever bodies are, they are crucial to people. Leibniz reminds us to remember also the non-conscious aspects of people, which hark back to Plato's spirit and appetite as parts of the self.

Hume's view that there are no people is an excellent prod. We must keep in mind his arguments against the self if we are to say anything sensible about it. His iconoclasm with respect to personal identity must also be faced squarely. There is, moreover, a theme in Hume that I will develop—conventionalism. The nature of persons is not something which can be discovered independently of a culture and its conventions.

Kant makes persons ends rather than means to achieving ends. The dignity of persons and respect for them as individuals with rights as opposed to mere parts of a larger society are things we should preserve. The strong linkage of metaphysical, epistemological, and ethical concerns about people is another valuable part of our Kantian heritage.

Contributions of the later moderns

Bentham and Mill, through making pleasure the foundation of morality, would undo Kant and allow people to be mere means. Although I think this is devoutly to be avoided, we should take from them the reminder that pleasure and pain are central to the concerns of people. We can admit that unnecessary suffering is evil. We can wish to protect animals from it. To value, as most of us do, people over animals, we must fashion a concept of persons which explains the difference. Otherwise we would be guilty of demanding a difference in treatment when there is no difference in kind. This is just what racists do.

Kierkegaard and the existentialists generally take the capacity to make free choices as central to what we are. This theme of freedom we have noticed in earlier philosophers. Marx, on the other hand, reinforces the idea of the relativity of people to their social and political environment. These need not be incompatible ideas, however. What we are, in general, may be socially determined, while the choices we make as individuals will create what we are as later individuals.

Contemporary pieces of the puzzle

The cultural relativity of the nature of persons is also furthered by pragmatist thinking. Any claims we make about people would have been assessed by James, Dewey, and Peirce by checking to see what difference it would make to accept such claims. It would be wise to ask ourselves what social and personal difference is made by accepting any concept we cobble together from these pieces of past philosophy.

Some Continental philosophers we have considered, Heiddeger and Sartre, reinforce the theme of the importance of personal choice and our subjective point of view. Such mottoes as We are what we do can be useful points of departure in our search for ourselves. Existence does precede essence in so far as one first exists as a human being, then gradually develops capacities which admit one to the class of persons and, by choice, fashions an individual essence. The difficulty will be in making this development by self creating understandable through a clarification of the two kinds of essence. Husserl, also in this continental tradition, influences me—somewhat in the way that Wittgenstein and Nagel do later—to see as crucial the unseen seeing part of myself but not to treat it as simply one of the items in the world which I see. It is a challenge to make something other than tongue twisters out of the things to be said about the viewpoint of the subject of experiences.

In the Analytic school of philosophy, Ayer revives the body-based view of people while Strawson picks up one of the Continental themes in emphasizing the primacy, for our understanding of people, of personal interaction. Strawson, however, unlike many philosophers in both schools, does not wish to shock us with the novelty of his views. Like him, I will take our pre-existing conceptual scheme as a guide. The difference is that I explicitly take this scheme to be culturally relative. To some extent, this is also a way of following Quine. He takes concepts of persons to be matters of convention. Like Quine, I think that once we can say what people are by specifying clearly the conventions regarding our use of the word "person," we can then understand what it is to be the same person over time.

In Wiggins and Williams we have seen further exponents of the body-based view of persons. Unlike Ayer they recognize the importance of the body without insisting that it just *is* the person. I will emulate them in this. We have seen Wiggins' warnings about the dangers of functionalism. While I will take them to heart, I will try to come up with a theory that takes the abilities of a person to, in part, define that person. Mine is not, however, a purely functionalist account. Williams is also concerned about the socially relative concepts of a person as an adequate basis for morality. He gives us instead a theory of person as a natural kind. I would like this to work, but it does not. We have to grasp the thistles of relativism.

Williams, on the other hand, thinks that the concept of a person is of little use in moral theory. I will side with Wiggins here, but I will try to overcome his conclusion that accounts which do not treat the concept of a person as a natural kind cannot provide for the moral weight that this concept must bear. I think that "person," like "infant," need not apply to a being from conception to death. I like Wiggins' revival of Aristotle and will use some of this groundwork, emphasizing the Aristotelian notion of the *psuche* discussed in chapter 3.

As we come to the very, very contemporary philosophers whom I have selected for comment, my debts grow larger. Nozick, for all that I reject closest continuers as not close enough, sets up some general structures which are a good support for my view. The weighted dimensions of Strawson or the series of sliding scales spoken of by Williams become Nozick's metric. This is a good device, though I have a somewhat different application. Nozick's views on self-creation and the use of "I" will also be incorporated.

Parfit, like Williams and Hume, often serves as the opposition to my view against which background I illuminate what I wish to say. Nonetheless, I accept the anti-Cartesian arguments which Parfit offers. Instead of Parfit's determined revision of our conceptual scheme, I support Strawson's descriptive metaphysics. The importance of psychological continuity and connectedness cannot be denied, but there are other kinds of continuity and connectedness to which we must give equal weight.

Although I found Nagel's account incomplete, his discussion of the distinction of subjective from objective is very valuable, extending and clarifying as it does some suggestive remarks from earlier philosophers like Wittgenstein and Husserl. Like Nagel, I think the bodily basis of persons is to be found mainly in the brain. Nagel's most valuable contribution, however, is the opposition to Parfit's reductionism and to pure functionalism by means of the subjective viewpoint of persons.

Some lessons of this history

The overview I have offered of the history of Western concepts of a person makes the construction of yet another such concept a little daunting. Metaphysically, it should tell us what persons are, in general, and what makes a person at one time the same person at another time. Epistemologically, it should help us make judgments about knowing who is a person and who is who. Ethically, it should help us make moral judgments about the treatment appropriate to persons. We have seen some philosophers despairing at finding any concept filling such a tall order. But the view that any concept of a person is inadequate to such tasks or to much of anything else is a mistake. This concept is central to Western European culture. This anthropological claim requires some support before we launch into the assembly of further desiderata for a concept of a person.

The centrality of a concept of a person

One might well argue that the concept of a person is merely a recent Western European invention, a cultural peculiarity rather than something central to our understanding of human beings. Marcel Mauss, while arguing for the importance of some concept of a person, gives a great deal of evidence opposed to associating persons with human beings in our one-to-one Western fashion. He details the ways in which other cultures see something like a series of persons through a single human life or a single person through various human lives. He tells us: "Those who have made of the human person a complete entity, independent of all others save God, are rare."[1] Are our memories just the ghosts of persons past? Or could it be that our bodily lives are just channels for persons who precede and survive those bodily lives?

Clifford Geertz, after investigating the Javanese, Balinese, and Moroccan ways of defining persons, concludes that: "The Western conception of the person as a bounded, unique, more or less integrated motivational and cognitive universe, a dynamic center of awareness, emotion, judgment, and action organized into a distinctive whole and set contrastively against other such wholes and against its social and natural background, is, however incorrigible it may seem to us, a rather peculiar idea within the context of the world's cultures."[2]

One might say, if Geertz is right, that our concept of a person is a defining characteristic of Western European (including British North American) culture (but not including native cultures in the Americas).

The anthropological data should at least give us pause. Perhaps current skeptics are right that the concept of a person should not be given the pride of place that it has had in Western philosophy since Locke's time. A look at cultural differences and at the sweep of the history of the concept does, at the very least, motivate our taking stock of the sort of concepts of a person which we are willing to take seriously and at the functions we expect them to perform.

For British and North American philosophers of the Analytic school, the main concepts of a person which are considered in the ballpark tend to be versions of Locke's concept of a person as a continuing consciousness. Wilkes notes, however, that the word "conscious" in the sense of "inwardly sensible or aware" only came into our language around 1620, and that neither the ancient Greeks nor the contemporary Chinese have such a word.[3] Even in contemporary Western European culture, we rarely limit the concept of a person, as it tends to be limited in philosophical discussion, to some sort of continuing consciousness or potentially conscious being where consciousness may be narrowly construed in terms of intellect.

Wiggins, whose individuative naturalism was discussed in chapter 11, points out that boxers and ballerinas as well as philosophers are persons.[4] Putting intellectual ability foremost in our discussions of survival has a parochial flavour. Philosophers dealing with the subject of persons tend to ignore most of the aspects of persons and to concentrate on those abilities that persons need to do philosophy. That is how Descartes got the idea that we are essentially thinking things. The emphasis on ratiocination and, in Locke, the emphasis on memory is, I think, due to this philosophocentricity. Recent philosophy has not changed the fashion much except to try to reduce these abilities dear to the minds of philosophers to abilities of the bodies of philosophers. I would like, instead, to keep an open mind about what kind of concept of a person will be useful.

There is of course the danger of keeping my mind *so* open that everything falls out. To prevent fallout, I will Moore[5] myself to Western common sense in my search for live hypotheses concerning the concept of a person, and I will try to be clear about what those who are not among the skeptics expect a concept of a person to do for us.

General features of a person to be preserved

Looking at the history of what philosophers have thought about persons, we see certain especially general features which their concepts of a person strive to maintain. These give us, in effect, a list of desiderata for any concept of a person being proposed. Any concept acceptable in Western eyes will have to allow for people to be complex individuals who are nonetheless irreducible and indivisible. They must be continuous and determinate. Persons have a certain mysterious cachet as well; they should be indefinable. All of these features need further explanation.

Complexity

People are many-splendoured things. In this I agree with Parfit. We have various parts, bodies, conscious and non-conscious faculties, for example. Views like that of Descartes, which try to make us simple atoms that are indivisible by virtue of having no parts, are on the right track for the wrong reason. We have some kind of indivisibility, and Parfit's reductionism is wrong. We are, nonetheless, complex.

Irreducibility

This is one of the features that Parfit tried to persuade us to abandon. Not just Descartes, but most of the philosophers we have discussed would wish to preserve this feature of persons in their concept of a person. Positively put, irreducibility requires that what we call persons must be more than merely the sum of their objectively describable parts. One cannot adequately describe a person by merely describing objects, events, or processes—none of which is a person. To abide with Strawson in the realm of descriptive rather than revisionist metaphysics, we should preserve irreducibility in our metaphysical views about people, recognizing that what we are describing is relative to Western culture. At the same time we must recognize what philosophers from Plato onward have emphasized, that we have an inner complexity. Irreducibility cannot be purchased at the cost of oversimplifying ourselves, pretending we are indivisible atoms of some sort like Cartesian Egos or souls.

From the moral standpoint, metaphysical irreducibility may be very significant. If, from a moral point of view, people deserve special treatment, then people must be special. What makes people special, what makes them ends rather than means in Kant's sense, may well be, in part, that people cannot be reduced to the things which are mere ends. Our dignity requires a contrast of ourselves with our social and natural background, else we are mere cogs in the social wheel or elaborate natural processes. Reduction is all very well if we wish to abandon entirely individual rights and to embrace instead the ideals of benefiting the social commonwealth or furthering ecosystems. Consequentialist ethical theories can benefit from the reducibility of persons, as we saw in looking at Parfit's views. Most non-consequentialist ethical theories, however, can tolerate no such abandonment. My presupposition is that our Western ethical mainstream is non-consequentialist, in the sense that it requires that we look at more than just the consequences of an action to determine whether the action is right. The ethical mainstream of our culture requires the dignity of persons to underlie such things as rights and virtues, which underlie non-consequentialist moral reasoning.

Epistemologically speaking, it would be easier if our concept of a person made a person a possible object of knowledge by acquaintance. Irreducibility seems to muddy the waters somewhat. A person's objective features do not in sum make the person, but they are the features with which we can be acquainted; so there is something mysterious about knowing a person. Consequently it is difficult to identify and re-identify another person with complete confidence. It would be easy if there were some unchanging mark of the person on which the irreducibility depended. If this mark could be objectively known then one could re-identify people with relative ease. Nothing, however, serves to identify people comparable to the way in which fingerprints serve to identify their bodies. Judging from my experience of myself, however, I expect bodies and people to be correlated one to one. Admittedly, generalizing from a single case is not ideal, but that is the limit of the empirical evidence we can have.

Self-knowledge, however, is another matter. Descartes was right to say that what we know about ourselves is not little. The subjective knowledge of a person by that person is of great importance and is closely tied to irreducibility. Socrates' ancient exhortation to Know thyself cannot be followed by merely investigating one's own characteristics as one would those of another. In fact, our knowledge of other people and things is based on our subjective self-knowledge. Bergson is right to take the self as the starting point in our search for knowledge of other things.

The viewline

Knowing one's own current subjective viewpoint and its history—that is, knowing one's viewline—is a large part of self-knowledge. My subjective *viewpoint* is the place from which I seem to be seeing the world at a given moment. My *viewline* is the locus of my viewpoint through space as it appears to me over time, that is, my series of viewpoints through my life. As I will argue, roughly following Nagel, this viewline is what makes us irreducible. Before coming to the difficult matter of discussing viewlines, however, I will mention some of the other features of people which will depend in part on subjectivity.

Individuality

Many of the same comments apply to this criterion as to irreducibility. That is because we are only individuals if we are not reducible to other smaller individuals which make us up as, for instance, a society is made up of us. If, to pursue an example of Strawson's (see chapter 10), there were groups of human beings who acted with one intellectual and emotional accord with such precision and unanimity that activities of members of the group could only be understood as part of an action of the group, then such a group of human beings would, nonetheless, not be an individual person. One person/one body seems to be one of our cultural mottoes perhaps because each of the members of the group would have a subjective viewline not shared by the others, however neatly they combined their wills in the objective realm. From an epistemological point of view, our classificatory criteria would be far too weak if we allowed such groups to be persons. We would not know who was who. In moral debate we tend to suspect the claim that the various human beings making up the group could not be held praiseworthy or blameworthy independently of the group. The buck of moral praise and blame stops with the individual. One cannot hide in the group. Individuality is dependent on irreducibility.

At the same time we must recognize the importance of society for our individuality. Some of the philosophers we have considered, particularly Plato and Aristotle, thought of people as importantly social. We need to understand ourselves not as metaphysically dependent on some larger group, but as fulfilled only in such a group. Even the hermit depends on society as a foil to make sense of her life. This does not mean that we should elevate the state, as we have seen Hegel doing, to that in accord with which the rational individual must act to be free.

The idea of our individuality recalls the property of persons which the mediaevals called self-existence. This is the idea that people are not essentially parts or properties of other things: we are individuals in our own right.

Continuity

One of the preoccupations of the metaphysicians looking at persons is that of diachronic identity—the question of what preserves the individual through change. Its epistemological cousin is the problem of re-identification. The metaphysician looks for the source of the continuity while the epistemologist seeks some mark whereby we may know it. Where continuity is concerned, I would turn Hume on his head and say that the one case where each of us does have direct knowledge of a continuing thing is our own case. The continuity of other things we understand by reference to our own continuity. I am influenced by Bergson in this (see chapter 8). Objective knowledge is a pale probabilistic reflection of subjective certainty. Unfortunately, even this subjective certainty is no unshakable certainty about others or even ourselves on the view I will propose.

Continuity is also necessary as a precondition of much moral thinking about persons. To say I am responsible for what I have done is to say, among other things, that I am continuous with the one who did the action. If one makes continuity too fragile, as does Locke with the memory criterion or Nozick with the self-creating closest continuer theory, then we let people off the hook too easily. It is also dangerous, from an Occidental perspective at least, to make continuity jump the bounds of a human life so that I become responsible, for instance, for what the holder of my title did prior to my birth. That is not the least bit counter-intuitive in some cultures, perhaps, but I am standing by Western common sense as much as possible in the delineation of a workable concept of a person.

The metaphysical problems which surround the attempt to describe what keeps people continuous are the problems of personal identity. A satisfactory answer to the question of what makes a person at one time the same person at another time may or may not help with the epistemological problem of continuity. How we know who is who will depend on the knowability of whatever it is that, metaphysically speaking, makes people themselves. Kant's doctrine of the noumenal self is an example of a metaphysical solution which makes the epistemological problem insoluble. I wish to avoid this as much as possible.

We know ourselves, subjectively, partly because we remember a viewline which our present viewpoint continues. We may, however, know ourselves well or badly. Unfortunately, some segments of one's viewline bear little relation to the objective locus of one's body through space. Suppose Tanya in Toronto gets stoned on acid and watches a movie taken as if through the eyes of Douglas in Vancouver. Her viewline may not correspond to the objective location of her body if the drug causes her to shut out completely her awareness of being in a theatre. Tanya may know herself in a way which is good for Douglas but bad for Tanya during the time of the watching of the film.

Nor does the viewline guarantee continuity. It may, after all, have gaps when we sleep. The subjective part of a person alone is not enough to guarantee continuity, but the continuity of the person can be guaranteed partly—as Wiggins and Williams would have it—by the continuity of the body. The subjective component is, however, necessary for indivisibility and irreducibility, as will be explained in the next chapter. A person, according to the concept I will explicate, must have a body, a viewline, and a set of abilities to continue through time.

Determinacy

The question Am I about to die? is metaphysical, a question about existence, about continuity of an individual. If it is always to be answerable, there must be some definite end point of every individual. That is another tall order for a concept of a person to fill, but it is too tall and not needed. The assumption that we cannot have irreducibility and continuity without complete determinacy is an unwarranted assumption. A person's life is not an off/on switch. Admitting some vagueness about the beginnings and ends of people's lives without thereby falling into reductionism is one of the tasks I set myself. I shall have to accept the epistemological consequence that it is sometimes impossible for anyone, even the person dying, to know whether that person continues in existence. I think, however, that this can be made more plausible than at first it seems. I saw it happen to Daphne. Morally speaking, there is in the vagueness of beginnings and ends of people much difficulty about matters such as abortion and promise keeping. We must, however, accept Aristotle's advice and not seek more precision than our subject matter allows.[6]

Indivisibility

Sometimes it seems reasonable to say one cannot speak of parts of persons except in the sense of body parts. We must be wary, however, of the mediaeval motivation for this. Indivisibility would provide us with indestructibility, something we might wish for but cannot necessarily be expected to have. I do not wish to argue for or presuppose any religious doctrines such as that of an immortal soul. The heritage I wish to preserve is secular, although the origin of much in that heritage is religious. Both the religious and secular traditions emphasize the importance of knowing oneself. Self-knowledge, however, requires a kind of indivisibility. But note, it need not be so mysterious as the indivisibility of the soul or of the Ego. I know who I am partly by knowing my viewline—the locus of my experience in space and time as it appeared to me, the history of my subjective viewpoint or perspective. To be a self-knowing subject, one must have a unique subjective viewpoint from which one sees the world, a viewpoint cannot be divided without becoming two. This indivisibility of viewpoint is morally important as well, in as much as I cannot know what I believe I have done unless I know my own viewline.

There is no infallibility here, since people can be fooled by tricks of memory to taking into their own viewline a sequence of perspectives which came from, for instance, a motion picture. One would have to be in some rather unusual state to suppose that one was living through what one was merely seeing depicted, but this can happen. More commonly we misremember the source of some of our remembered images. Usually, however, we are morally certain about what we have done and have not done because of the viewline from which we witnessed the events in which we took part. The viewline is not an objective part of these events. We should say, following Wittgenstein as explicated in chapter 9, that a viewline is not in the world but a limit of the way one sees the world. One cannot split such a limit. In that sense we, who contain such limits, are indivisible, but not indivisible in the way Descartes supposed.

Indefinability

Indefinability is the linguistic counterpart of irreducibility. If one of the fanciful machines discussed in earlier chapters—Parfit's teletransporter or Williams' duplicator—could read the information in a human and produce an exact copy, the result would be a replica rather than the person associated with the original body. Even before making sense of such difficult doctrines as the mediaeval doctrine of the intransmissible essence of the person,[7] we have a kind of indefinability. To support the metaphysical difference between a replica and the original coming out of a teletransporter, we note that they are different because they have different current viewlines now, although they seem to remember the same past viewline. As Parfit would express it, however, the replica has only a quasi-memory, not a genuine memory, of the events as seen from the shared viewline. From an epistemological perspective, the replica cannot have the self-knowledge that the original can have even if the replica seems to remember a segment of the original's viewline. The replica is deceived by the quasi-memory of this segment of the original's viewline. This has moral importance, since moral responsibility cannot be replicated. The replica might admit guilt for a crime of the original, but the replica is deceived and should not be punished. At least, this is consistent with Western common sense, but this understanding of moral responsibility is very clearly culturally relative.

Naturally one must put forward with caution the role of the subjective viewline in establishing ethical responsibility, else we end with something like Locke's implausible view that we are not responsible for what we do not remember. We must also avoid circularity and the sort of cultural relativism that amounts to little more than prejudice. Certainly, I will say more about viewlines as I develop a view through which I attempt to explain our indefinability.

Freedom

I agree with the ancient Romans, with Leibniz, and with contemporary existentialists that our freedom is essential to us as persons. If our actions are all determined by things over which we have no control, for instance, determined by such things as prior causes, then we are mere automata, not people. We would not be responsible for anything we did in that case. On the other hand, the attempts to make sense of the concept of freedom through the history of philosophy have foundered on conundrums. I believe the jury is still out on what freedom is and whether it is possible. Nonetheless, we have a rough idea of what concept it is we are seeking to clarify. It would, however, take a rather long book to say what can be said on this topic. Instead I will offer you, in the spirit of William James and Blaise Pascal,[8] a wager.

Bourgeois' bet

I speak only to those who agree that freedom of the will is essential to people. You are confronted with what James would call a genuine option: you can choose to believe that you are free or that you are not free. Reality may or may not correspond with your belief. You may really be free or you may really not be free. Consider now the four combinations of belief and reality. First, suppose you believe you are free, and you are free. In this case, you possess two benefits. You believe the truth, and you can live your life according to this true belief as a person. You win. Let us move to the second possibility: if you believe you are free but you are really not free, then you are an automaton programmed with misinformation. You lose. In the third case, you believe you are not free and you are right. Now you are a correctly programmed automaton. You lose. Finally, you might believe you are not free when you are, in reality, free. You would really lose badly in this case, for you would be a person who throws away the chance to use your freedom.

Since you do not know whether you are free or not, you have to adopt a belief under conditions of rational uncertainty. I suspect that after thorough philosophical investigation, no matter how hard you try, you will not be able to convince yourself fully by means of rational argument that you are free nor that you are not free. All you can do is place your bet. The only way to win, for those who think as I do that freedom is crucial, is to bet that you are free. James would not like this way of putting it, but he might say instead that, since you are confronted with a genuine option, you are justified in believing whatever you want to believe about your freedom. I believe I am free.

Enough has been said about the ideal functioning of a concept of a person. The time has come to put the pieces together and fashion a concept that will work.

Content questions

1. What different uses might we have for Plato's and Aristotle's forms?
2. Contrast the contributions of Augustine and Aquinas to the concept of a person.
3. What do Descartes and Locke have in common with respect to their views about persons?
4. How can we interpret Sartre's dictum, "Existence precedes essence" in terms of abilities?
5. Why should anthropological data make us careful about our philosophical concepts of a person?
6. What is a danger described as "philosophocentricity"?
7. What are complexity and irreducibility of persons?
8. What is a viewline?
9. What are individuality and continuity?
10. What are determinacy, indivisibility, and indefinability in relation to concepts of a person?
11. What is Bourgeois' bet supposed to show about freedom?

Arguments for analysis

Argument 1: The public evidence argument

Metaphysical, epistemological, and ethical concerns about persons are primarily those of the community of persons. By consequence, whatever general concept of persons we adopt, it must be a public not a private matter whether a given human being qualifies as a person. Plato's theory of Forms, however, would make it a private matter. The Platonic Form of person gives us no public standard but only a standard that requires a private, mystic apprehension. For this reason it is better to make use of an Aristotelian form of persons that depends for its application on publicly observable abilities.

Argument 2: The unevidenced abilities objection

The public evidence for a person's abilities may be lacking even when the abilities are still there. For example, people with locked-in syndrome appear to be in a permanently vegetative state but are really conscious persons with their abilities to communicate temporarily suspended. Their abilities remain even though they are not publicly observable. The danger is that we will treat some persons as if they are not persons just because we cannot verify that they have the abilities they do in fact have.

Argument 3: The useful concept reply

Even though we may not always know who qualifies as a person, the concept is generally useful while a Platonic conception would not be. With respect to the locked-in syndrome, however, the distinction of this syndrome from a permanently vegetative state is medically possible. We would assume in such cases that the person remains once we decided, by means of brain waves, that we were met with a case of locked-in syndrome. Even in this rare kind of case there is publicly observable evidence that will indirectly give evidence of abilities. In some even rarer cases, we may be fooled. That does not show the concept is wrong or not useful. Generally such a concept can be fruitfully applied even though our knowledge is, as always, imperfect.

Argument 4: The meritocracy objection

Analyzing the concept of a person in terms of abilities will lead to a diminution of persons of lesser ability. Those who, by the accidents of birth, have the most ability will be considered the most morally worthy; politically, this leads to a meritocracy. None of this would protect the interests of those who are disadvantaged by birth.

Argument 5: The wider view reply

This meritocracy objection comes from taking too narrow a view of the abilities that should be considered. In addition to the intellectual and physical abilities admired by Aristotle, there is the capacity for mutual love introduced by Augustine. There may, of course, be some human beings who do not have abilities to a degree that would qualify them as persons, but these would be exceedingly rare cases. They would, moreover, still be cases covered by human rights if not the rights of persons.

Argument 6: Leibniz against the drunks again

This analysis of persons will fall prey to Leibniz's objection to Locke. If a person becomes drunk and loses abilities—including the ability to remember—then that person is not really there in the drunken state. This could lead to using drunkenness as a moral excuse.

Argument 7: The culpable disability reply

Given that persons in general are understood in terms of abilities, the identity of particular persons will be affected by losses of abilities. This will have to be arranged so that only essential abilities are in question and that temporary losses do not wipe the person out. In any case, when we use inability as a moral excuse, it must be inability that we did not bring on ourselves. We are culpably disabled if we deliberately limit our abilities so as to have an excuse for immoral actions.

Argument 8: The existentialist objection

Sartre says, Existence precedes essence. This Aristotelian analysis, however, would make the essence of persons something pre-existing. This ignores our fundamental freedom to choose who we will become.

Argument 9: The adaptation reply

The Aristotelians can adapt this motto of Sartre's for their own purposes. We still choose whom we will become by choosing which of our inborne abilities to develop and in what ways we develop these. Nonetheless, everything that exists must already have an essence of a sort. Each person will share the general essence of persons. That precedes the individual developing a particular essence that depends on free choices.

Argument 10: The cultural relativity objection

Different cultures will value different abilities. The Aristotelian analysis will lead to the result that what constitutes a person will vary from culture to culture.

Argument 11: The best we can do reply

The best we can do in establishing a concept of a person is a culturally relative concept. This need not lead, however, to some of the most unfortunate consequences of relativism. There is, after all, an emerging global culture that can provide an overarching concept of a person.

CHAPTER 16

A Bourgeois Concept of a Person

Persons in a nutshell

Very roughly speaking, you are what you can do. You do not actually have to do it, just be able to. Abilities mark off not only individual persons but also the class of persons as a whole. Thus abruptly and unceremoniously summarized, my view is bound to spark many objections. So it should, as there is, of course, more to us than our abilities. Our subjective points of view through our lives are critical too. This summary statement of what we are gives only the scent of a theory that must be pursued through some rather dense thickets.

Essentialism

My view of persons is essentialist. Essentialists try to explain the nature of things by talking about the elements a thing must have to exist. Water, for example, is essentially H_2O. Being H_2O is essential to all samples of water. They may have other characteristics—being muddy, clear, solid, liquid, or vaporous—which are just accidental. It is fairly clear what the essence and accidents of water are. Persons are another kettle of fish.

Notes to chapter 16 are on p. 493.

To explain persons by describing the essence of a person we would have to list the elements essential to being a person. I will talk about the *general essence*, which includes those elements that all persons must have, and the *individual essence*, which is the essence of an individual person. My view, however, I dub "Byzantine essentialism" because it has—by comparison to the simple essentialism described above—a structure of Byzantine complexity. That is necessary because of the wild variation within the class of persons and within individual lives of persons.

Rather than say that there are features which all people must have, I am forced to say that there are features most of which persons must have most of the time in order to be "persons." Some of these are *subjective*, such as the conscious and non-conscious mind, the viewline—which is a series of viewpoints, and the experiences had from the viewline; others are *objective*, such as the body or the publicly testable abilities of the person. All this is without prejudice as to whether mind and body are one thing or two. Putting all the bits together, I get a kind of essentialism that is intended to preserve the general features of persons which any common sense, secular, and Western concept of a person ought to have, namely, the ones distilled in the last chapter.

Not only is my view Byzantine, it is relativist. Like Strawson I think of myself as doing descriptive, not revisionist, metaphysics. What I take myself to be describing, moreover, is not some absolute which is independent of time, place, or society. Most essentialists with regard to persons think they are describing *the* concept of a person, not merely *a* concept. This concept I describe is intended to work for us here and now, we who are heirs to the philosophers dealt with in this book. That is no small ambition, though more modest than the intention of most of those philosophers. I hope to produce an understanding of persons which is also cross-cultural in the sense that people from other cultures who may not yet have any of the Western concepts of a person will find this one attractive or at least not as repulsive as some of the others.

Subjective elements of persons

One thing which preserves the indivisibility and irreducibility of persons is the viewline. I have said that my subjective viewpoint is the place from which I seem to be seeing the world at a given moment.

My viewline is the locus of my viewpoint through space as it appears to me over time—that is, my series of viewpoints through my life. Think of one's viewline as a history of the places from which one *seemed* to be sensing the world. It is really line of viewing, hearing, touching, tasting, and smelling. Rather than being just one more item in our subjective experience, it is the series of apparent places from which we have had such experiences. It is an indivisible feature of persons.

Indivisibility and the viewline

Viewlines are indivisible in the sense that each viewpoint in a viewline is indivisible. If I seem to be seeing things from a certain perspective, that perspective cannot be split in two. It can change. It may even be shared with another person; that is, viewlines may intersect. One viewpoint, however, cannot divide without becoming two different viewpoints. This provides us with indivisibility. Not just persons, however, but any experiencing subject has such indivisibility; a cat does for instance. The viewline on its own is not enough to be the essence of persons.

Viewlines may appear to be divisible in some of the examples we have considered in previous chapters. Consider another fanciful example in which Tammy gets duplicated, resulting in two people, Dana and Harriet, both of whom seem to remember Tammy's viewline. This duplication may not really be possible, but it helps to ferret out what we believe about our viewlines. What apparently happens here is that Tammy's viewline has split into Dana's viewline and Harriet's viewline. Which of the viewlines resulting from the split—if either—is a continuation of Tammy's viewline? The one that corresponds to a continuous body continues Tammy's viewline. Tammy's body is the body which is part of the complex, the person Tammy. This body has a different history from that of the duplicate. The correspondence of viewline to body is somewhat complicated. Tammy's body is *usually* objectively in a location which is also Tammy's subjective viewpoint. The body also directly causes Tammy to have the viewline she does. This provides a close link of Tammy's viewline to Tammy's body, which helps us understand what is really happening in cases of apparent division of persons and their viewlines.

Let us say that, of the two people stepping out of Williams' duplicating machine, Dana has the original body of Tammy while Harriet has one which was produced as an exact replica. Tammy is Dana, but not Harriet. Tammy and Dana have one viewline. Harriet only seems to share the part of that viewline prior to the duplicating. Harriet, though, is a newborn with false memories of Tammy's viewline. Tammy, a.k.a. Dana, got her viewline through the use of Tammy's body. Harriet got only a short segment of real remembered viewline—through the use of Harriet's body; the viewline Harriet remembers as a result of duplication of Tammy's memories is not Harriet's. Bodies can be traced through time objectively, as what Quine calls space-time worms (see chapter 10). Harriet's body begins in the duplicating process. It is distinguishable from Tammy's; hence, Tammy is not divided nor is her viewline. Harriet is a mere replica, even if Harriet's self-knowledge is imperfect and includes the belief that Harriet is Tammy.

Suppose now that Harriet claims as much right to the remembered viewline as Tammy, since viewlines are subjective and Harriet has the same subjective impressions of her place in the world as Tammy. We could reply that memories of viewpoints are not viewpoints. Tammy seemed to see, say, Niagara Falls from the Canadian side in June of 1994. Harriet did not exist until August of 1994; so Harriet only remembers this viewpoint but did not have it. It is an objective fact that Harriet did not have that subjective viewpoint. Harriet has false memories of a viewline up to August of 1994, and a genuine viewline after that. It turns out that Tammy has not divided into Dana and Harriet.

We have to be careful here not to make of the viewline something like Locke's memory criterion. Recall that Locke circularly identified persons by means of their memories and identified memories by means of the persons who had them. Tammy is identical to Dana, according to Locke, because they share the same memories. They share the same memories, according to Locke, because they are the memories of the same person, namely Tammy a.k.a. Dana. We cannot chase our tails in this way if we approach the concept with the viewline. Tammy is identical to Dana because they share the same essence, including the same viewline. I do not, however, say that the viewline is the same because it is the viewline of the same person.

The viewline is a set of subjective experiences caused through a single body. The body must not have spatial or temporal gaps. The continuum of matter that is the body of Tammy and Dana has no gaps. If we move to Harriet's body from Tammy's at the time of duplication, we must cross a gap. Harriet's body begins at the time of duplication. Therefore, Harriet's real viewline begins then as well. That is why Harriet only seems to continue Tammy's viewline while Dana really does continue it.

This does not make Tammy identical with her viewline or body or the two combined. One continuous body could, at least theoretically, be inhabited by more than one person. A sufficient change of abilities could create a new person, a new complex of body, viewline, and abilities. Here I try to hold on to the Western common sense notion that a person cannot switch bodies but that the body may survive when the person fails to.

If all this makes common sense, Tammy is indivisible in the sense that she has an indivisible viewline. As soon as the viewpoint seems to split, as with Dana and Harriet at duplication, there are two viewpoints. Of course Tammy is a complex of many things, including a body, a viewline, and a set of abilities. These are not accidents of some indivisible Ego, as Descartes might have it, but they are all essential to Tammy. Tammy is, therefore, also indivisible in the sense that we cannot permanently separate the various essential parts of Tammy while Tammy exists. I pursue this when we come to look at Byzantine essentialism in detail.

It might still be thought—as Parfit apparently thinks—that, if a person's brain could be divided and the two halves transplanted into bodies so that each half-brain carried the viewline,[1] a person and a viewline would then have been divided. Our brains are not, however, so divisible.[2] The two halves of the cerebellum are different in function and do not carry the same memories. The lower brain is not divisible at all. If the reply is that this is merely a fact about us which does not exclude the logical possibility of such division, then the point has been missed. Creatures with brains so unlike ours would not be individuals as we are but pairs of individuals sharing most of a body, the brain excluded. If there were such pairs, we might be willing to revise some of our conventions about persons, but that is too speculative for all but science fiction fans. A workable concept of a person need not take such under-described cases, even if they are indeed logically possible, as a threat. They are not much more odd than the case of Siamese twins and do not provide a counter-example to anything I have put forward.

Irreducibility and the viewline

Consider our earlier discussion of Parfit's objections to our irreducibility. I reject Parfit's reductionism or impersonalism not because I believe I am a separately existing entity—a Cartesian Ego for instance—but because impersonalism leaves *me* out of the universe, and I am sure I am in it. I am not merely a useful fiction but a person knowing the world along a particular viewline. This is an adaptation of Nagel's response to Parfit which we also considered (see chapter 15). To preserve Nagel's point and some important characteristics of people we do not need a Cartesian Ego, a Christian soul, nor any other device which makes either being a person or being the same person akin to having a switch off or on. A person can, like a flame, gradually come into being, grow more intense, then gradually go out of being.

Admitting, as I do, that human beings are to a greater or lesser degree persons and that each person is to a greater or lesser degree herself is not admitting that people may be reduced to the objectively describable events or processes that make them up. This theory is not to be caught in the snares of Parfit's continua examples described in chapter 13. Parfit accepts the obvious—that people seem to change by degree—only by promoting the outrageous: the idea that there are no people. To keep both people and the gradual evolution and devolution of a person, I will use two kinds of elements in my concept of a person—the subjective kind—such as the viewline and the publicly inaccessible portions of the mind generally—and the objective kind—such as the body and publicly testable abilities.

Glover has a nice example to make the point about the irreducibility of the subjective to the objective. Imagine seeing on television a composite drawing of a dangerous criminal accompanied by a verbal description. You say derisively, What good is that? That could even be me. At this point the police knock on your door. You have been framed. You discover with a shock something about the picture and the description. What you have discovered can only be visible from your viewpoints or along your viewline. You could say with Glover, "however detailed or accurate it is, I do not get a shock until I realize the description is of me.[3] No objective description would give the same shock without the same realization. Parfit, it seems, would leave something out in his supposedly complete, objective description of the world if he indeed mentions no people in this description.

Mental abilities: A degree of objectivity

If I think, feel emotions, or have sensations, then I have a mind, however you may wish to analyze the concept of mind. I am willing to suppose that dogs have minds, but what makes people different from other beings is partly the degree to which they have minds. Some few human beings are limited to the mental capacity of dogs. They may have the potential to become persons, but they lack an essential characteristic of persons. That does not mean they should be treated like dogs. They have human rights, if not the rights of persons. I will consider a distinction of these kinds of rights in the next chapter.

Private and public abilities

From my view, we are essentially what we can do. Persons probably can think and perhaps feel emotions to a greater degree than non-persons. There are two great obstacles to specifying such degrees precisely. For one thing, the degree is culturally determined. "Person" is a concept relative to Western culture which is a rather hard thing to pin down, real though it may be. The concept of a person, in general, then relies on the amount of such things as intelligence and emotional sensitivity which are generally required in the West in order to join the persons' club. The second great obstacle is the inaccessibility of certain subjective features of persons. This affects not only what kind of thing a person is but who is who. Some of what we can do is private. Mozart could supposedly compose an aria in his head and write it down later. Only Mozart knows for sure if this is so.

Examples: Love, spirit, and aesthetic sense

Inspired by Augustine, I will try to say something about a subject which almost every philosopher ponders but few wish to address. Love is left to the poets. Some forms of love, however, seem to be peculiar to persons. Love can also illustrate the distinction of public from private abilities. Recall Ross's brave definition: "Mutual love seems to be a blend of virtuous disposition of two minds towards each other, with the knowledge which each has of the character and disposition of the other, and with the pleasure which arises from such disposition and knowledge."[4] Of all the kinds of love, mutual love between two people seems to me to be the sort which is peculiar to persons. The love of the parent for the child may be fiercer in a mother who is human than in a bear—yes, nothing matches the ferocity or love of persons—but the love seems to be of like kind. It can be all *one way*. An infant may be permanently comatose but not less loved. This is not to deny either that a mother bear may love her cubs in some other sense of "love" or that some human mothers are incapable of love. What partly distinguishes people, however, is the way they interact, a point I take from the earlier discussion of Strawson. It is, then, the capacity for *mutual* love which is peculiar to people.

Let us suppose that some human being, say Adolph, is incapable of taking part in a genuine mutual love. Does this incapacity rule Adolph out of the class of persons? The essence of a person which defines the class of persons is not simply a set of necessary conditions that are jointly sufficient for being a person. It would seem reasonable to say that Adolph is a person, albeit incomplete. Part of his potential is unfulfilled. He would not be remarkable, however, were he not a person. In using the capacity to love, like the other capacities mentioned here, we will have to fashion a concept of a person which is flexible enough to allow for persons of various kinds, even those who are in some remarkable way deformed. Being a person admits of degree.

The ability to participate in mutual love of the sort described by Ross requires a mind of a kind which bears probably do not have, judging by the behaviour toward each other of mother and father bears. Some would say that many a human being is ruled out of the class of persons if the capacity for mutual love is necessary. It is very hard to tell if this is so, given that we cannot peer into the hearts of human beings to detect the virtuous dispositions of which Ross speaks. We guess people's dispositions on the basis of behaviour. Even if we do not know for sure exactly how large the class of persons is, we can say roughly what kinds of being we think are in it.

Love illustrates another feature of persons which makes it difficult to be precise about the essences of persons in general or of individuals. Suppose Pierre discovers that he loves Marie. He might have come to love her all unaware. Pierre's non-conscious mind can do all sorts of things to which Pierre is not witness. Our subjective experience is not only inaccessible to others, it may be inaccessible to ourselves. This leaves us not so much knowledge as good guesses about who is a person and who is who. Even our self-knowledge admits of degrees.

Recall also the notion of spirit as the intentional togetherness of beings who are for themselves "I" and for others "You." (See the discussion of Smith's concept of spirit in chapter 2.) Often, primates may have spirit in this sense, but people develop the capacity to a degree of intensity and complexity that is staggering. The ways in which people unite with one another are almost infinitely variable. This distinguishes our behaviour from that of other higher primates whom we think of as acting from instinct. I am unable to say what this term really means, but at least our patterns of behaviour are much more complex and unpredictable than those of non-persons.

Another example of distinctive abilities of persons is the capacity to exercise aesthetic sense. Most non-persons seem not to decorate their environment nor themselves unless it is to some practical purpose. People, however, produce and consume art, especially visual and auditory art, in great quantity and variety. Certainly there are people with no aesthetic sense or at least people who fail to exercise and develop this capacity. It is *one* of those capacities in a group from which human beings must have at least one—to some degree—to be a person. Adolph might have aesthetic sense or spirit but lack the capacity for engaging in mutual love. This keeps him in the class of persons but not as a very sweet sort of person.

Anything which makes us think of people as special, as different from most animals, is a candidate for being in this grab bag of capacities from which a human being can draw to gain entrance to the persons club. Specifying the set of such capacities precisely is an ongoing and partly scientific labour. We used to think, mistakenly, that only people kill members of their own species. Do only people laugh with true humour? As we sort out the capacities peculiar to persons (not that all persons have them) we find that we may have them only to a greater degree than non-persons. This I will discuss below under the heading of "thresholds." Remember too that some human beings lack even the most rudimentary capacities of persons. People may choose, as well, to develop or not develop these capacities.

Self-creation and its limits: More objectivity

It may seem strange that self-knowledge can be imperfect. Since we choose what we are, it would seem that we know precisely who is who in our own cases. Difficulties with self-knowledge become apparent, however, when we look in more detail at this self-creation. Some of the philosophers discussed above have been helpful in delineating the peculiar tugging at boot straps which makes each of us who we are. This process is one in which there is a confluence of the subjective and objective elements of persons. We are what we can do, but we must give objectively acceptable weights to the various abilities in order to distinguish one individual from another and to distinguish people from non-persons. Something analogous to Nozick's metric of weighted dimensions, discussed in chapter 12, is what we need here.

When people talk of finding themselves, they are probably engaged in discovering their own abilities and dispositions and deciding the degrees of importance of these. They are making the non-conscious conscious. When Pierre discovers he loves Marie, in the way described by Ross, and puts that at the top of the list of important things he knows about Pierre, he is finding himself—finding out what he can do. His capacity for love may survive even a tragic break-up with Marie which is all too likely in a graceless age. Our capacities may be longer lived than the exercise of them; hence, we may outlive our most important deeds.

Epistemic and metaphysical social contracts

To say what we value most about ourselves is to choose what we are. The choice, however, is a choice within limits. These limits help to delineate the concept of a person. The limits can be thought of along the lines of social contracts. The social contract is a device usually used in ethics. For example, we might define what is fair by saying that it is what is according to the rules of an ideal social contract. This is the contract that equally powerful and intelligent self-interested human beings would choose to run a society, if they did not know what advantages or disadvantages they would have in that society. The choices we make about what to accept in our essences are choices which have to be in accord with an ideal metaphysical and an ideal epistemic contract, as well as the more usual ethical social contract. What norms are ideal is, however, a culturally relative matter.

The question as to how we know who is who, for instance, will depend on the ideal rules for re-identifying people. These will be, in turn, influenced by the ideal metaphysical rules for saying who really is who. Suppose Ralph, scion of a wealthy family, is lost for twenty years. Two people, Frank and Vince, show up claiming to be Ralph. Frank resembles the former Ralph most in character, general appearance, and in knowing the things Ralph knew, but Vince has the same fingerprints as Ralph. We in the West would choose Vince as the inheritor of the family fortune. This tells us something about the epistemic and metaphysical social contracts for both the general essence of persons and the essences of individuals according with Western common sense.

If we were choosing rules for re-identification would we not demand that sameness of body be essential for sameness of the person? Otherwise, an impostor could take someone's place. Against Parfit, and Nozick, most of us would say that having somebody remarkably like us take over our life is not the sort of continuity we wish. Individuality as summed up in the one person, one body motto is a part of our contract. This tells us, then, something about persons in general as well. They must have bodies and each must have only one. Must they be human bodies? At this time, yes. Extraterrestrials may land, causing us eventually to change our norms, but that is still science fiction. Chimpanzees or dolphins may in future seem to us to have abilities that gain them entry to the club. What is important here is that we admit that it is what we can do which makes us a person, not our species.

Wiggins' individuative naturalism is much opposed to this, as we saw in chapter 11. He thinks that persons are a natural kind of creature and that, if we are entrapped in contrary views, we will not be able to maintain the moral importance of the concept of a person. Just the reverse is true. Being a member of a particular natural kind has no special importance morally. This view could be called kind-ism, by analogy to racism. Racists take irrelevant naturally occurring characteristics to be morally significant. The morally relevant features of people are among their capacities, such as the capacity for mutual love discussed above. Not what kind of thing we are but what we can do, think, and feel determines how we ought to be treated and what our obligations are. Being of the human kind is just an accidental feature of persons even though it is, to the best of our current knowledge, a universal feature of persons.

It is crucial that one recognize the role of the subjective features of persons as well as such objective ones as sameness of body. Suppose that we have no fingerprints to go on. Does that mean that Frank, who has the winning hand with regard to other objectively determinable features, is Ralph? No, it merely means he would be mistaken for Ralph. Our metaphysical social contract does not specify that Ralph is whomever we would take to be Ralph. Rather, Ralph is the one we would take to be Ralph, using our standards for re-identification *if we could know which viewline was caused through which body*. From the inside, subjectively, Vince can know he is Ralph even if he cannot prove it objectively. Normally, you know who you are, even if the rest of us do not. That is because you remember your viewline. If you say that your viewline is that of Napoleon, you are put in an institution. We do not always know who we are, but usually we do. This shows that the viewline plus the body is essential to individual essences. The essence of persons in general would also include these. To be a person one must have a body which causes a viewline. If the body or the mind ceases to function utterly and permanently, then a person ends—although a human being may continue.

It also becomes clear in what sense our essences are intransmissible; that is, we see how individual persons cannot be defined in terms of their objective features. Whatever we include in our objective descriptions of Ralph, Frank, and Vince, it will not be enough to capture the viewline. One might suppose that this is merely an epistemological limit. We have no way of assigning coordinates to time and space and saying which of Quine's space-time worms would fully match Ralph's viewline. But the viewline may not fully match any worm in real time and space. Ralph's dreams or illusory experiences may affect it. He might have some experience of virtual reality. While the viewline is not at Nagel's innermost sphere of subjectivity, it is close. We cannot get there from here, outside Ralph's mind.

What this tells us about people in general is that they have an indefinability and, as we have seen, an indivisibility and irreducibility as well. What you see is not all that you get when it comes to people. To be in the class of persons, one must also be self-creating. This is part of the source of our dignity as persons: we choose what to value in ourselves. We are responsible for what we are. This distinguishes us from other intelligent beings we know about. Chimpanzees may have 98 percent of our chromosomes, some self-awareness, and the ability to learn limited languages, but unless they are self-creating—that is, choosing their own individual essences—they are not people. Until we change our minds about how much chimpanzees can do, we will not count them as persons. Nonetheless, they should get more consideration, because of their similarity to us in capacities, than they do get.

The results of the investigation so far are that persons are, although complexes of many elements, nonetheless indivisible, irreducible, and indefinable. To understand better how individuals create themselves, we should look more closely at the objective elements from which they have to choose.

The body and associated public abilities: Maximal objectivity

To accommodate the point discussed in connection with Wiggins—that ballerinas and boxers are persons as much as philosophers—we can look at the degree of weight attached to bodily features by the individuals possessing them. We need not go to the extent of adopting Wiggins' view that person is a natural kind. We have noticed that having a probably human body is essential to persons but, for each individual, the importance of the body may vary. The boxer may value his physical strength much more highly than his intellectual ability. He is most himself at peak performance. He defines himself in terms of what he can do physically. If he could, at the height of his powers, see his future body as a punch-drunk wreck sweeping the gym floor, then he might deny that the sweeper is the same person as the current champion. He has chosen, perhaps unwisely, to be very short lived as a person.

Private choices and public criteria

The boxer's choice does, after all, seem to be a complete departure from common sense. The one person, one body motto is being taken in only one direction. If there is one person, then there is one body. On the other hand, if there is one body, there is not necessarily just one person. I think, however, that we in the West sometimes take the motto only in the first way, even if we are not consistent about that. We often seem to talk as if having the same body were necessary but not sufficient for being the same person.

Consider the return of the long-lost Ralph once again. Vince is seen to be Ralph because the fingerprints match. Vince also chooses to own what Ralph had been able to do. Suppose, instead, that Vince says of Ralph, That was somebody else. He no longer has Ralph's abilities or even memories of Ralph's viewline and never reacquires these. In this extreme case, we might be willing to say that Vince is a different person, since Ralph's body no longer embodies the same form it once did. Some things essential to Ralph are missing. There can, in theory, be a series of persons associated with one body. It is just a very rare sort of thing if this happens. Most of us choose an essence so as to survive and do not undergo whatever extreme experiences turned Ralph into Vince, where Vince no longer has Ralph's individual essence. We are, however, reluctant to admit such cases as genuine. We would prefer to say that Vince is Ralph although he is deficient in self-knowledge through his loss of memory. The differences must be truly extraordinary before we say that a body no longer embodies the person it once did.

Our social contract is a little ill-defined in this area. Perhaps the rule once was that such self-defining choices as Vince's were unacceptable, although that may be changing. At least in cases of multiple personality, which have the imprimatur of psychiatrists, we tend to make moral allowances for more than one person per body. But this is not all. Self-creation could make possible persons within persons as well. The boxer as an old man and as a boy may include in himself everything that was or will be taken in along the viewline associated with the body that grows from that of the boy to the body of the old man. The boxer in his prime may repudiate this. The boxer in his prime is a person contained within the larger person determined by the choices of the boy and the old man. This, again, is not common sense. Perhaps we should say, rather, that the most inclusive person associated with a body really is the person, while the included "persons" within are just special stages of that overall person. The act of self-creation which really counts is the one which encompasses most of the viewline. In cases of extreme dissociation, we could admit that a person has been destroyed by mental illness although the human body is alive and is the body of some person or other.

This way of thinking explains why we should value our moral, emotional, and intellectual abilities more than our purely bodily abilities. The boxer should think of his courage as more important than his left hook. The ballerina should honour her dedication more than her stamina. It is such features which are primary in our saying that we are what we can do. In the case of the philosopher, pure intellectual ability may be chosen as foremost. This too is a trifle dangerous. A beneficent disposition is longer lived than brilliance. If we wish to maximize longevity, wise self-creation values long-lived features. While some may value intensity more than such staid features as longevity and continuity, they are not in accord with common sense.

The body, seen as a space-time worm in Quine's way, is continuous. This makes persons largely continuous. We may have periods of absence from our bodies. Morally, madness is accepted as such. Nonetheless, we each wake up in one body every day and remember a viewline. That the complex which is the person includes such a continuous body is sufficient for continuity of a person through most of the life of a human being, though the person comes into being after the human being and may well go out of existence before bodily death. Elements of the complex come together gradually and may disperse gradually.

A degree of determinacy is also preserved under the present concept of a person. The question, Am I about to die? has relatively clear answers in most cases. In the face of extreme change one can ask whether the abilities one values most will survive. Even if the body is going to live on, we can know that what is essential to us will not. Daphne knew this. The exact point of death may be unknowable. While I do not know how to make sense of life after death—meaning life of the person after death of the person's body—it is some consolation to preserve life during life. As persons, we live during most of our life with our body, usually. In cases like Daphne's, the body may live on for a rather long time while it no longer embodies the form or supports the essence of the person who used to inhabit that body.

Objective indivisibility

There is a kind of indivisibility of the person from an objective standpoint. It is fortunate, moreover, that objective indivisibility, like the subjective kind, need not be bought at the cost of accepting the featureless Ego. Must the impossibility of division imply having no properties? Why can it not be that the person is indivisible in the sense of having certain *essential* properties bundled together in an individual essence if and only if the person exists. If the essence is divided, the person is no more. One does not have the absolute indivisibility of the Democritean atom but the indivisibility of a democratic house which cannot stand divided against itself. Like a democracy, a person can survive considerable internal conflict but not unending civil war. The essence of the person must be intact for the person's survival.

Byzantine essentialism: Individual and general essences with thresholds

Part of the difficulty with the contemporary discussion of the essential characteristics of persons is the frequent assumption that these characteristics are all or nothing. But being a person is not like being a light which is turned on. It seems relatively easy to say what is essential for the light to be on, and if any of the conditions in the essence is lacking—say, there is no current through the filament—then the light is not on. People, however, have much more flexible essences than that. They can lose some of their essential characteristics to some degree or lose them temporarily while remaining persons.

We do not, for example, fall out of the class of persons just because we go to sleep. If having a viewline is essential to persons, it is essential in a flexible way. We must have a viewline *enough* of the time. We look to our social contract to say what is enough. If Bryan has only one lucid minute per day, he is no longer able to do the things which made him Bryan. He is not the person he was, but a living human body. We ought to treat that body with respect, but we could be quite paternalistic to the human being called "Bryan" without harming Bryan as a person. Often, however, the case is not even this clear-cut. We should do the best we can with the limited knowledge available to us to determine whether a given human being is a person. A reasonable social contract would put the onus of proof on those who wish to deny the status of a person to a human being.

Of course, even a light bulb is not really limited to being either off or on. It might be dim or flickering. We might be unsure whether or not to say it is on or off. All of us flicker. We go to sleep at night. All of us are dimmer at some times than at others. We can do less well the things which are essential at some times, or we can do fewer of them. Persons remain persons and remain particular persons to a degree of frequency and intensity. Stefanie must be careful if she constantly hears people saying of her, She's not quite herself today.

The essentialism I defend is not entirely at odds with Parfit's view of which I have been critical. In fact, I think Parfit is an essentialist of an odd sort. The particular realization of the Relation *R* (psychological continuity and connectedness) is what makes us who we are, in Parfit's view (see chapter 12). Since *R* is fragile and short lived—at least more so than are living human bodies—persons are ephemeral entities flitting in and out of bodies. It seems that what is needed to preserve common Western beliefs about persons is an essence that is more robust than *R* in the face of changes which we all live through as persons.

Complexity

Essentialism is a difficult doctrine since it is easy to put too much or too little into the essence. If there are a great many features which are required for being a person, or features which are short lived, then it is too easy to disqualify many human beings as persons. The claim from the pro-choice abortion camp, for instance, that persons are essentially self-aware would seem to rule us all out if we are asleep. Something has to be said about how such features can come and go in persons. If on the other hand we put in too few features or features which are too readily retained, the class of persons widens so as to become useless. This is what happens, for example, when those in the pro-life camp say that having human chromosomes is all that is essential to persons. This makes human cancer cells grown in a petri dish persons. The error on both sides of the abortion debate is oversimplification. We must keep the complexity of persons in mind and make the essence of persons support such flexibility.

We must take account, moreover, not only an essence of persons in general, but an essence of each individual person. Again, the difficulty is in specifying this individual essence in a plausible way. If we have too fleeting features in the essence of an individual person, then people will not last any longer than a new car. That is why the boxer is unwise to try to create himself as the champion. The fleeting essence is, as we saw in chapter 13, also what we get from Parfit. Putting in too many features will have the same effect. If, on the other hand, we put in too few or too easily retained features, Parfit can evolve into a Greta Garbo and still survive.

What goes wrong in this latter case may be that the essence of persons in general is mistaken for the individual essence. At each point in the spectrum of gradual change of Parfit into Garbo, we consult our concept of a person and say, Yes, there is still a person present. That is not, however, to say that the *same* person is present. The essentialism I seek has to allow for the belief that a human being can change so radically as to become a different person. I think that those who disagree with the possibility of such change most likely retain a belief in a soul or Cartesian Ego. Retaining just the viewline from this Cartesian view, let us try instead to make sense of people using an essentialism in which a viewline is an indivisible essential feature.

The seed of a believable essentialist view has been sown by Wilkes.[5] Wilkes, however, does not directly concern herself with the questions of individual essences. Perhaps she thinks the survival of persons through change is a matter settled if she answers her main question, What is a person? She answers, relying on Aristotle, that a person is an embodied form and a formed body.[6] Aristotle did not, however, have a separate word to distinguish persons from human beings.[7] Wilkes ignores this, although it may be as significant as something else which Wilkes emphasizes, Aristotle's having no word for consciousness.[8] In any case, I think Wilkes has Aristotle right; I wish to go beyond Wilkes's Aristotelian views on persons in general to a view of individual essences of persons that will fit with Wilkes's position as well as assimilate the insights but not the shortcomings of some of the other views I have discussed. Wilkes's position on the general essence of persons will also be revised to take into account the variability of persons as complexes.

Continuity

Let us recall Nozick's social limits on closest continuation and think of how these limits affect authentic continuity of a person on my view. Suppose that the limits of variability seem to have been passed. A woman comes forward claiming to be Sharon, but she is physically and in all other ways we can detect, extremely unlike Sharon. She is socially unacceptable as Sharon. Could she not still be Sharon? She could on my view. What is necessary to her identity is not what her community members accept but what they would accept if they could know her viewline.

It is, however, not merely some private and apparently non-physical aspects of Sharon which make her who she is. The separation of the physical from the non-physical aspects of persons which is the tendency of the Cartesian view is impossible in Wilkes's view, which I am adapting and extending here. One consequence of this, it seems to me, is that one who is destroyed and replicated is really destroyed. The replica is a mere replica. The original embodied form is gone, as Wilkes might say following Aristotle.

Taking the embodied form as essential to the person usually prevents long temporal gaps in persons. That provides for one of the features I like, namely continuity, albeit of a rough variety. The viewline alone does not provide continuity; but an objective part of the person, the stream of matter through time which is the person's body, is more stable. This is what motivates some of the body-based accounts of a person such as those of Wiggins and Williams (see chapter 11). We need not, however, merely by accepting Wilkes's account, take the body plus the form as a materialist conception of the person. Whether the form is immaterial or not is a question for another inquiry, and I do not wish to get bogged down in the debate here.

What Wilkes says about forms of persons in general is suggestive of a way for the essentialist to proceed in the search for an understanding of individual essences. One hopes for further gains in the direction of common sense. The form of a person is supposed to tell us what the nature of persons is. The individual essence of a particular person would, if we knew it, tell us what the nature of that particular person was and, hence, under what conditions that person would survive changes to the body. We should try to understand the individual essence, then, as the form of the individual along the lines of the form of a person generally. Before looking at survival on this kind of essentialist view, however, I must get more of the view out. Consider first the form of a person in general.

The form of a person is a special case of the form of an organism. The form of an organism is its *psuche.* Wilkes represents Aristotle's concept of the *psuche* as a pyramid of abilities.[9] Organisms which are not persons have some of the abilities in the pyramid of abilities associated with a person. The higher the animal, the more of the pyramid it takes in. What distinguishes persons as a class from other organisms is that our *psuchai* include, over and above the abilities of other higher organisms, the capacity for rational thought, both practical and theoretical. Crucially, this capacity for rationality includes the potential to be a social animal.[10] The ability to reciprocate with rational beings is essential to being a person.

How then do we know when there is life during life? That is, how do we know when the survival of a person goes with the survival of the corresponding human being? It is not enough to know what the class of persons is. We need to know something of diachronic identity (identity over time) as well. Suppose that we follow the essentialist's inclination and say that a thing remains the same over time just in case it retains its individual essence. What will an individual essence for a person contain over and above whatever in the *psuche* is essential to remaining in the class of persons? Well, we could throw in the fleeting characteristics, psychological continuity and connectedness, whatever they are.[11] But then one is certain to get a relay race of various persons through the body. With all that ephemeral stuff being essential, the person has to change as the stuff changes, often.

From Wilkes's view of persons, while one has certain capacities, one retains the status of person. I envisage an essentialism for individuals compatible with this essentialism for the class of persons. Roughly, one is what one can do. An individual essence might be fleshed out in terms of a particular set of capacities peculiar to an individual, over and above those essential for that individual to stay in the class of persons. Also in the essence is the viewline, the series of subjective viewpoints of that individual. To be who I am, I must have my past and present viewpoints. I need not remember all of them, the whole viewline. Nonetheless, having that viewline is part of what I am.

One advantage of thinking in terms of what the individual can do is that some abilities can survive considerable physical and psychological changes. One of Wilkes's many examples is of a doctor who suffered an attack of epileptic automatism while interviewing a patient. Although the doctor remembered nothing of the interview, he discovered from his notes that he managed to conduct a reasonably efficient medical examination.[12] The doctor was, apparently, a person throughout the attack. Was he the same person before, during, and after the attack?

Of course I do not want to say, with Lockean respect for memory, that the doctor lost one of his essential capacities—namely, an important part of his memory—and therefore went out of existence, to be replaced during the attack by a replica. That would not be a gain for common sense. To merely take a particular realization of the form which makes one a person and call that particular realization an essence would be too ham-handed. Some of the capacities in that essence might be *temporarily* lost.

These capacities may also admit of degree. Even the memory of the viewline is variable. It is significant that, as Wilkes describes the case, the doctor owned proudly the actions which he could not remember doing. We do not have to remember our experiences to have had them. The doctor did have the segment of his viewline during the attack but lost the usual benefit of it, since the portion of his viewline running through the examination is lost to his memory. Our viewlines, however, always become lost or strange as we sleep, perchance to dream. Since memory is one of these varying capacities, our retention of our past viewline in memory will also vary in degree.

Determinacy

Essentialism seems to preserve our determinacy as well, though only in a metaphysical sense. The question, Am I about to die? always has an answer, but it is not always one that can be known. One cannot always know whether certain thresholds have been reached. It might be impossible to check on the survival of a person when introspection is needed to view some part of the essence. For example, I might wonder whether I have sufficient emotional intensity to still be the person whose memories I share. My viewline may be the same, but that is only a necessary, not a sufficient condition for my survival. If I am sinking below the threshold, there is not a continuing person there to do the introspection needed. Yet nobody else could investigate by introspection the presence of some capacities in the essence to see if they are at levels above their thresholds. In this way, self-knowledge can be imperfect even for self-creating beings.

We are, in spite of these epistemological difficulties, metaphysically irreducible, determinate, and as continuous as we should be. The question, Am I about to die? always has a definite answer in terms of thresholds, although those near death may not be competent to give the answer. Those near death may be poor judges of their own thresholds, given their altered mental state. While most of our abilities are open to objective determination, it is interesting that our objective and subjective components get quite tangled up here. This epistemological problem, fortunately, does not prevent us from consolidating our metaphysical gains with respect to the concept of a person.

Return, too, to the question of life during life for such persons. Is there only one person associated with a living human body throughout its life? Not quite. It seems that a human being gradually develops capacities, gradually grows up to be a person. One can also go gradually in the other direction as one approaches senility. During the part of the life of the body in which one is above the threshold, however, one remains one person. In most cases, this is through most of a human life. I may reasonably refuse to take responsibility for something I did as a child because I had not fully become myself then. My children may not blame me for things I do in my dotage since I will have gone by then. There is, then, not life during life but life during most of life, usually. The Cartesian Ego and the Christian soul are attempts to provide continuity from conception to bodily death, but that is rather too much to ask.[13]

Individuality

One does, moreover, retain a variety of individuality within this essentialist view. A group of bodies cannot make one person, since their viewlines would be different. It may however be a bit too much to intone the one person, one body motto. There usually are not several persons having a single body at one time. One might think that the body is just a container for capacities and that it is easy to have differing sets of capacities associated with the same body in a Jekyll and Hyde fashion. If we add to a person's capacities, however, we are usually not adding another person but merely adding accidents to the essential capacities already there. Theoretically one could add enough capacities to kill off one person and bring another into being within a single human body, but the likelihood of this is diminished by the subjective viewline. Perhaps multiple-personality cases are genuine cases of multiple persons in one body, but I rather suspect that it is a case of one person with a great mental deformity. One person is having trouble keeping track of which self she created.

People with no illness at all, however, can undergo radical change with no threat to the one body motto. Suppose, for instance, I recall being a skid-row bum who reforms and becomes a social activist working to eradicate poverty. Probably I will accept the blame for my earlier condition, to some degree, and the praise for pulling myself out of it, to some degree. I will own the earlier limited capacities even though I seem to many to be a new person because of much higher present capacities. The kind of epistemic and social contracts we accept in the West allow for considerable variability in characteristics and abilities of persons over time. It is reasonable for Jekyll to accept Hyde's actions as his own. One who forgets a drunken spree should also own it, even though the viewline is forgotten in that segment.

One has reason to suppose that the viewline continued and that previous capacities, albeit diminished by the genie in the bottle, were sufficient to maintain one as the same individual during the spree.

Once again I have made use in my argument for Byzantine essentialism of the viewline. This is not strictly speaking an ability, although one could speak of that person's ability to know the world as if from a particular perspective in space and time. In any case, the crucial thing is that one cannot have more than one of these perspectives at a time and, hence, no more than one viewline. The thought experiments in which people divide like amoebae, if they show the essentialist anything about what we believe ourselves to be, show only that we may believe a person can be replaced by two remarkably similar people. A point of view cannot divide. A viewline can divide as a river splits, but after the divide there are two people.

We have subjective as well as objective individuality. Recall the theological use of *persona*, the Latin root of person, to mean something which is self-existent, that is, not a property or a part of another thing but a thing in its own right.[14] The individuality provided for persons, from my essentialist view, makes us self-existent. We are not just part of a larger whole; we are individuals. Larger wholes, such as societies, do not have one viewline.

Indefinability

The theological use of *persona* which we have seen stemming from developments in the Middle Ages includes intransmissiblity of the person's essence or indefinability.[15] There are also two senses in which persons are indefinable, on the view I am adumbrating here. First, a definition conveys objective information and cannot, therefore, capture the viewline. Second, while the objective information in an individual essence can be conveyed in theory, in practice it is too Byzantine in its complexity to be recorded. Each of us is the main record of what we are.

By now it is clear, I hope, that I accept to some extent Wiggins' claim, discussed in chapter 11, that: "If freedom and dignity and creativity are what we crave, we shall find more promise of these things in the Heraclitean prediction 'You would not find out the bounds of the soul, though you traversed every path: so deep is its *logos*' than in the idea that it is for men to determine the limits of their own nature, or mould and remake themselves to the point where they can count as their very own creation."[16] Viewed objectively, persons do have this deep nature which can only be partially known. This does not prevent us from making some choices subjectively—culturally limited ones—about what we are as individuals within the class of persons; thus far but no further I am willing to go with Nozick. From Nagel I take another crucial point in this discussion, that we have an irreducibly subjective component (see chapter 15).

The union of all these elements creates a new view of persons different from each of the theories which provided these elements, for each of these theories left out something crucial which another recognized. Putting all the foregoing views together, we come up with a fairly common sense picture of persons. Indeed, it was Western common sense which guided the selection of elements from the earlier theories. We retain important features of our Occidental heritage, but they are cleansed of contradiction. We are each in some reasonable senses of these terms which I have specified: *complex, individual, irreducible, determinate, continuous* (through much of our lives), *indivisible, and indefinable*.

There is, however, the wrinkle for the essentialist that a series of persons can possibly be associated with one body, as in Parfit's view. This is the relay race objection. This, however, is not likely from my essentialist view and certainly not required by Byzantine essentialism as it is by Parfit's essentialism. The capacities at the centre of what we are tend to be rather hardy. Very radical change may push us below the threshold of our own individuality, but usually we also lose the form of person as well as our own personal essence. Radical change not leading to death makes mere human beings of us more likely than not, as for example when brain damage leaves the mere shell of a person.

In such a case, we lose our freedom, and paternalism toward us becomes appropriate as it was before we grew up enough to pass the thresholds of our own individuality. We may still have considerable moral worth as human beings but not that special dignity which attaches to persons. If we are judged to be permanently below the threshold, we will be viewed differently from children who wear their potential to become fully developed persons as a special badge of worth. It is, however, medically possible to do such things as head transplants now. Who knows how this and other medical marvels will influence our metaphysical, epistemic, and social contracts in so far as they regard who is who. I consider it a strength of my theory that it allows in a limited way for but does not require the association of a series of persons with one body.

Another strength of this essentialist theory is that we avoid the distraction of worrying about the sameness of the body over time. Supposing that every molecule in the body is replaced every six years, we can still speak of the same stream of matter through the form. The form helps us pick out the beginning, end, and other boundaries of the space-time stream of matter. The form, remember, is a set of abilities. One becomes a person on acquiring the appropriate set and at the same time becomes differentiated from other people by the particular set of individuating capacities which make up the individual essence. Keeping the thresholds in mind, we can say, theoretically at least, when the person begins and ends which will be after the body begins and, in most cases, before it ends.

Freedom

Now, what about all that moral importance, social worth, dignity, and so forth that motivates the search for yet another concept of persons? While I think the individual essentialist view has a chance of preserving certain large chunks of common sense, I admit that it departs from our current legal notions of sameness of persons. That is inevitable, however, since our current legal notions are occasionally far from common sense. There are, however, some interesting connections of the view with the notions of Roman law, which I see as partly fathering our current common sense. What gave persons in ancient Rome their dignity, moral, political, and legal worth was their freedom, and freedom was understood in terms of capacities. Freedom was understood as the "natural power to do what you please unless you are prevented by force or law."[17] This is, however, the freedom we are granted under law if we are already persons. We must, in my view, have another kind of freedom to be persons. From the essentialist view I put forward here, an individual person is defined in terms of her powers to do certain special things plus the body and the viewline. A natural power to choose things is essential, but I am not thinking of the kind of freedom a dictator can take away. I am concerned that persons not be automata, that they have, metaphysically speaking, freedom of the will.

Thresholds

Both the individual essence and the general essence for persons will, it seems, have to allow for considerable flexibility. Our capacities may not only admit of degree individually, but the degree to which we have a complete set configured appropriately may also vary. This suggests various thresholds.

One threshold below which one could not fall while remaining a person or remaining the same person would be, very roughly, having a minimum number of capacities in the general or the individual essence. Focusing on the individual essence, for example, if one suffered the permanent loss of one's normal conative, locomotive, and affective abilities as well as memory—but retained intelligence, probably one could no longer be counted the same person. Here we depart from the current usage of "person" in law, but not in common sense. It is reasonable to say that the person who is devoid of former desires, physical abilities, and emotions, and who does not remember us, is not the person we knew even if she has sufficient rationality to stay in the class of persons.

The first threshold, then, is a threshold of quantity. There must be enough of the essential capacities in a being if that being is to be a person. Not all of the capacities, however, must always be present. Adolph is still a person, though a strange one, if his capacity for love is absent. The general essence of persons includes many features, but we do not have to have all of them all of the time. If Adolph now begins to lose his other conative abilities as well as memory and cognitive abilities, he at some point crosses the line from the class of persons into that of human former persons. The line is fuzzy since the essence is culturally determined, and cultures are fuzzy. There are other things which blur the line too. There is another kind of threshold, which I will come to later, applying to features individually. This makes quantity of capacities not the be-all and end-all of the general essence.

It is no doubt a gross oversimplification to speak in terms of a minimum *number* of capacities in the essence. Certain configurations of capacities would have to be present. The ways in which capacities might be added or removed could have incredible complexity. During a quorum call for capacities in the essence, there might well be particular capacities in a particular configuration which must be present for an individual to be a person or to remain the same person. I envisage here a general core of capacities which are necessary but not sufficient for being a person and a further core for survival of the particular person. These capacities would not form the whole essence but only a particularly important part of it. If they come and go, one flickers.

A person who is temporarily insane is temporarily not herself, or, less paradoxically, temporarily not housed in her body. Some part of her essence may be missing. A person may, for instance, be thought to have taken leave of the body on conative grounds. Suppose Irene undergoes a drug therapy, then does without compunction something evil that is totally out of character. While Irene lacks her essential shame, she is not responsible for the behaviour of her body. Courts have sometimes taken this position to excuse such horrendous crimes as matricide, at least when the killer was not conscious of having done the crime.

There might, in addition, be thresholds of each individual capacity. Once one permanently loses a certain degree of recall, for instance, one could not be counted as having the capacity for memory that was once part of one's essence. It would be quite difficult to tell where exactly the threshold for a particular ability or the threshold for the total essence would lie. This does not mean that there can be no such thresholds. The varying difficulty we have with Parfit's spectra might just reveal our varying degrees of confidence in our knowledge of our thresholds, our knowledge of who we are. It is too easy to say, however, that the metaphysical facts are totally independent of our epistemological difficulties. After all, as there is an element of self-creation in our choices of what experiences to own, indecision can be deadly. Given, however, that one has chosen oneself, one has a determinate threshold whether or not one is completely competent to judge its nearness of approach.

In some cases, as with persons who have Alzheimer's disease, a human being seems to fall below the threshold in various capacities, especially memory, and then to come back. It is as if the person is fading in and out. From this essentialist view, that is just what is happening. A person can be temporarily suspended, reinstated, and suspended again in the same body.

It might be objected, however, that this form of essentialism is just a dressed-up version of the old view of a person as programmed meat, functionalism. What is primarily different is this: functionalists leave out the subjective elements and the particular body is of no importance to them. The essences of persons, moreover, are enormously complex—Byzantine in their complexity. The comparison with computer programs is entirely unenlightening, since we have no examples of computers, outside of fiction, which can act as human beings do in a human society. Even if we did have such formidable, free robots, their programs might be quite different from our essences. If they had essences like ours, they would be persons, but how can we say whether such machines are possible? We cannot describe them in enough detail. We have enough trouble trying to convince ourselves that *we* are possible.

To clarify, I propose that we treat the general essence of persons as a set of abilities plus a viewline most of which one must have most of the time to remain a person. The abilities, their relative importance, and the thresholds of each one are determined by an ideal metaphysical social contract. The individual essence is a matter of an individual's choice, but is constrained by an ideal metaphysical social contract as well. An ideal metaphysical social contract is a set of claims about what is real that equally powerful, equally intelligent, self-interested human beings would assent to if they were utterly ignorant about the particulars of their own lives. This is a move in the direction of objectivity. It is not as strictly culturally relative as is, for instance, Nozick's way of saying who is who. The hypothetical human beings who write the contract do not know what culture they are from in the real world. Nonetheless, we who envisage such a contract cannot help but be influenced by our own culture. Still, we cannot simply take our own cultural rules as determining who is a person or who is who. We must argue that our judgments would be acceptable in terms of an ideal social contract. This broadens our perspective considerably. In fact our decisions about who joins the persons club and who we are as individuals must be justified according to ideal, ethical, and epistemic contracts as well. This further inhibits very subjective or culturally unique judgments. It fosters a higher degree of objectivity than pure cultural relativism and much more objectivity than subjectivist theories. At the same time, it appeals to no unbelievable absolute standards.

Admittedly, there are many problems with the view I am proposing for development. The use of social contracts, for instance, is tricky. I will illustrate their use in the next chapter. The pursuit of an essentialist doctrine using the idea of thresholds is somewhat Byzantine. People, however, are somewhat Byzantine. We can clean up the theory only if we ignore our own complexities. We are not much like nations. We are not much like computers. Nozick's closest continuers are not close enough. In fact, there is nothing I can name that is anything like a person, with the possible exception of the higher apes. It seems worthwhile, then, to put forward a program for investigating a rubbery, gappy, fuzzy, complex essence unlike the essences of non-persons. If this Byzantine theory should work, it would show that we do not have to go all the way with Parfit into the arms of Buddha merely to escape featureless egos.

Content questions

1. What is the difference between essential and accidental features of a thing?
2. What happens to the viewline if a person is duplicated?
3. What would Parfit's reductionism leave out of the description of a person?
4. List some distinctive abilities that separate persons from non-persons.
5. What is a social contract in philosophy?
6. Is being human an essential feature of persons?
7. How does the viewline make our individual essences intransmissible?
8. Why should chimpanzees not be considered persons in spite of their similarities to us?
9. Why should we value our moral, emotional, and intellectual abilities more than our bodily ones?

10. In what sense do we have objective indivisibility?
11. To what do we appeal to determine what is enough of any feature to keep the person in existence?
12. Why is it not sufficient to know whether a human being is still a person to know whether a given person has survived?
13. Why is social acceptance of a person as identical to a former person not enough to guarantee, from my view, that this is the same person?
14. Before even considering whether there is life after death, we need to ask whether there is life during life. What, in the view I present here, is necessary for preserving an individual through change?
15. Why is it that, while we have more or less determinate endings, we cannot always know when we are about to die?
16. How does the essentialist view preserve our individuality?
17. What are two senses in which persons are indefinable?
18. What is my response to the relay race objection?
19. How are such things as temporary insanity possible from this essentialist view?

Arguments for analysis

Argument 1: The moral weight objection to Byzantine essentialism

Williams said that a concept of a person depending on properties that come on sliding scales is insufficient to bear the moral weight we put on that concept. As evidence to this conclusion, consider those who are mentally or physically disabled. Making the concept of a person and personal identity depend on abilities would rule them out of moral consideration.

Argument 2: The common sense threshold reply

If we adopt thresholds that are too high, any of us could be ruled out of the class of persons. If we adopt thresholds that are too low, anencephalics are treated as persons with disastrous results for health care. Thresholds consistent with common sense would not rule out human beings from the class of persons in the dangerous ways you suppose. Even for those human beings who are, for instance, permanently vegetative, human rights would protect them where the rights of persons are not present. The threshold concept is not nearly so restrictive as you imagine, nor must it bear the moral weight alone. We have the moral concept of a human being to assist it.

Argument 3: The sold-out-to-Parfit objection

If you adopt threshold essentialism, you accept Parfit's indeterminacy thesis. Having already accepted the divisibility thesis, you will end up with a view prone to many of the objections you have brought against Parfit. Indeterminacy will follow from your view because there is no clear point at which a person goes out of existence. Parfit's spectra examples will work with your view.

Argument 4: The approximate threshold reply

This objection is a version of the heap paradox or sorites paradox. It is similar to the argument about one grain of sand not being a heap. Adding one grain to other grains will not change a quantity of sand into a heap. Therefore, no matter how many grains of sand we add, we will never have a heap of sand. For some purposes, we are willing to specify an exact number of grains that constitutes a heap and so avoid the problem.

Similarly, for some purposes we may want to specify a definite threshold or set of thresholds that will help us avoid indeterminacy of persons. In these sorts of cases we do not always know when the definite threshold has been reached. More often, however, we accept that thresholds are approximate. There may be a clear enough usage of "heap" to ensure that there is some range of cases of piles of sand that everyone calls "heaps" and some that nobody calls "heaps" and some penumbral range in the middle where people disagree. The same is true for both personal identity and being a person at all. The thresholds may be imprecise enough for disagreement even when all the facts are in.

Where we have precise thresholds, there is a definite answer to the question, Am I about to die? Where thresholds are approximate, there is still enough precision to answer the question for many moral purposes. Note that the question itself is not entirely precise. For both theoretical and practical purposes, we can usually get *enough* precision to answer the question. Hence, by Parfit's standards, we are usually determinate in spite of the continua on which the thresholds lie.

This is hand waving, but it is somewhat productive. I know that swallowing a fatal dose of poison would mean that I am about to die, even though I may not know exactly when death would occur. For moral purposes, the justification or lack of it for such a suicide would rarely depend on the precise point of time. Thus there is enough precision.

Argument 5: The split viewpoint counter-example

While you or I may only have one viewpoint at a time, it is not impossible for a single person to have more than one viewpoint at a time. Even the mundane example of looking through a telescope with one eye while looking outside the telescope with the other demonstrates this. Since the viewpoint is divisible, we are divisible.

Argument 6: The unified view reply

If I am on my deck looking at the trees in the park with one eye through the telescope, my subjective viewpoint is probably going to be unified. I will know where I am seeing the trees from, even though they appear closer in half of my visual field than in the other. I will still have just one subjective viewpoint, even though my visual field is distorted.

Now suppose you add other illusions involving all the senses, so that it is not clear to me from what point I seem to be sensing the world, my deck or the park. I would use my past viewline to determine my present viewpoint. If my past viewline placed me on my deck, I would continue to make my subjective viewpoint consistent with that and dismiss the conflicting sensations as illusory.

Suppose further that you could continue these illusions indefinitely, so that I always had a choice of two viewpoints to take as mine. This would probably cause me to be dysfunctional, to lose my normal capacities, and perhaps to go mad. I would cease to be the same person. I might, through madness, become two persons associated with one body. Unification of each subjective viewpoint and continuity of our viewline is needed to preserve a person's abilities and is, hence, needed to preserve a person.

Argument 7: The Nozick revisited objection

The scales with thresholds are just Nozick's similarity metric rehashed. All this view gives us is closest continuers. You have already said they are not close enough.

Argument 8: The beyond Nozick reply

This view owes much to Nozick and to others whose views have been presented here. It is importantly different from Nozick in demanding much more objective input into who is who. The emphasis on self-creation in Nozick led to a view in which only the broadest social restrictions limit what people choose themselves to be. The use of the social contract in this case puts much tighter constraints on self-creation. The objective limits on persons are considerably greater. In choosing constraints on the nature of persons and personal identity, the volunteers in the original position would want to restrict self-creation. Otherwise, people could reconstitute themselves to get out of keeping promises. This would undo the fundamental mutual constraints of the social contract.

The viewline is also used to prevent the fanciful cases in which the closest continuer is really only a replica not linked to the same stream of experience as the original. Attending to the viewline and abilities of a person focuses on the essentials, whereas Nozick's continuation can take non-essential resemblances to be deciding factors. In my view, the short path problem would always be decided in favour of the person who continues the viewpoint, not a replica. To use Parfit's example, teletransportation is replacement by a replica, not survival.

Argument 9: The complex viewpoint objection

A subjective viewpoint has many elements corresponding to the various senses that we use to experience the universe. Because it is divisible into these elements, it does not stop reductionism. We could, in principle, describe all of the universe without mentioning persons or their viewpoints. Instead we could talk about capacities, thresholds, and elements of viewpoints.

Argument 10: The no no-ownership reply

This is another version of the no-ownership view. It assumes that there can be an experience with nobody to experience it and a subjective viewpoint with no subject. That is incoherent, Hume and Wittgenstein notwithstanding. As for the divisibility of the subjective viewpoint, all the supposed elements are really what is seen from the indivisible viewpoint. We unify the input of the various senses by sensing them as if from some point. It may or may not correspond to the real location in space and time of our bodies. This is tied to the unified view reply. Suppose our senses do not agree; in that case, we treat some sensations as illusory. Suppose, for instance, that I am seeing the interior of the Chan Centre in Vancouver and hearing as if I am at a lecture in Massey Hall in Toronto. Probably, I count either the visual or the auditory sensation as an illusion or the result of some causally strange incident—such as picking up a radio broadcast through a dental filling. I create my viewpoint from the sensations available to me. If, as when I am asleep and dreaming chaotically, my sensations are too confused for such unification, then I have no clear viewpoint. The viewline has various gaps, but we unify the rest of it.

Argument 11: The discontinuity objection

If the viewpoint has gaps, then the person has gaps. The continuity for which you argue is a chimera.

Argument 12: The song goes on reply

Think of a token of a song played with various instruments and voices. Not all of them have to be sounding at once for the song token to continue. So it is with persons. The various parts of the essence of a person may have gaps, but they start up again in a unified whole. In a song, there may be a temporary pause of *all* the instruments and voices. The context of occurrence including the audience holds the song together through this pause. For persons, the body plays the role of the context of a musical composition; that reinforces the point that teletransportation would be death and replication rather than survival. In general, if there is too long a gap in any essential feature of a person, then the person does not survive. Similarly, if the melody of a song is essential to it and that melody pauses too long, that token of the song is over. What will be too long a pause is only roughly defined by the agreement the volunteers would make in the original position. We could make the concept of a person more precise only at the risk of making it inapplicable.

CHAPTER 17

Applications of My Concept of a Person

Fairness and a social contract

I will ask for your patience with some fanciful metaphors which allow me to simplify and condense the thinking behind social contract theories of morality. A particular notion of *fairness* developed by Rawls[1] I adapt and change here to suit my concept of a person, which Rawls does not share. Rather than using Rawls's ethical theory here, I am using some of the tools he developed to different purposes than his own. I will bring out some differences by considering some criticisms of Rawls's views and my own.

A metaphor for the original position

To begin, however, here is a smattering of social contract theory to illustrate briefly some applications of the concept of a person developed in the previous chapter. First there is an extended metaphor of an ideal social contract. This is a contract each person could agree to with assurance of getting a fair deal. The contract, as understood here, would govern all behaviour of persons to persons. Our moral rights are the rights we would have under the terms of such a contract. As mentioned above, this ethical section of the contract would

Notes to chapter 17 are on pp. 494-95.

be accompanied by epistemological and metaphysical sections. These tell us how to know, for example, what beings are persons and what it is to be a person.

Now consider an even more fanciful metaphor to specify roughly the method for determining what those rights would be under such an ideal contract. This metaphor makes limited sense; it is intended not as a possibility but only as a useful fiction to reveal what we might believe about fairness in terms of two concepts: the *original position* and the subordinate concept of a *veil of ignorance*.[2] I am not, like Rawls, trying to describe a perfectly just society.[3] Instead, I am suggesting uses of some altered versions of his concepts to help us in practical ethical debate. Of course the beliefs I reveal and the suggestions for ways to debate are my own. I hope they are shared by many, for I think they are largely in accord with Western common sense secular morality. Whether or not you agree with these beliefs about what is fair, you will, I hope, find the way of thinking about what is fair useful for revealing your own beliefs on the issues considered here.

To begin, let us consider the metaphor of *volunteers*. Suppose that a new anesthetic has been developed which makes people temporarily amnesiac. They retain their general cognitive, conative, and physical abilities, but they forget who they are, where they are, where they are from, and what their institutional memberships and personal relationships are. They are temporarily blind. They cannot feel their bodies except to the extent that they can speak coherently. These people, though rational, are behind a veil of ignorance about their own personal advantages and disadvantages in society. They do not know if they are crippled, average, or athletic in their bodily capacities. They do not know their position in society, what sort of personality they have, nor any other personal information—not even their gender, age, or preferences. They retain general knowledge about the human condition, but no particular religious or moral beliefs. This peculiar drug is put to an interesting political use. Persons in this hypothetical condition are in what is called the original position.

Under the auspices of the United Nations, a committee of volunteers takes this anesthetic drug in order to sit down and write a charter of rights of persons to apply throughout the world. They communicate with each other only indirectly through intermediaries.

As much as possible, the veil of ignorance is thickened. Even white lies are used. The anesthetized committee members are told that when they come back to normal they may be mentally impaired or much more brilliant than they seem to be now and, because of the strange situation in which they find themselves, they believe this white lie. In fact, the volunteers who have been chosen are equally intelligent, rational people who will remain so on coming out of the anesthetized state.

The purpose of this metaphor of the volunteers is to explain a concept of fairness. Fairness is what we have when people follow the rules that the volunteers would choose. The volunteers have no option but to choose fair rules. If they want to protect their own interests in the real world (after they come out of the anaesthetic) then they must choose rules in the original position (under the anaesthetic) that make sure that the volunteers will be treated well if the rules are followed in the real world, no matter what position the volunteers turn out to occupy in the real world. The rules the volunteers would choose are the rules that underlie our moral rights and duties according to a social contract theory of morality. To each moral right or duty corresponds a rule telling us what we ought to do. The ideal social contract (the charter of rights that the volunteers would create) is a set of such rules.

In the original position, the volunteers are not trying to follow any moral theory but only trying to protect themselves. Their ignorance of their own particulars in the real world forces them to unintentionally create the set of rules that would, if followed, provide fairness for all. In short, a general guide to morality is the set of rules that the self-interested volunteers would choose in the original position. We employ a useful fiction about self-interested, equally powerful, equally intelligent choosers of rules who are ignorant of their own advantages or disadvantages in the real world. We are characterizing fairness by means of this metaphor, so the volunteers import no moral principles to guide their decision making. They choose only on the basis of self interest. They are charged, however, with choosing rules that persons with ordinary human sympathies would follow. This is a heuristic for discovering workable moral rules. To know what we ought to do we must try to determine what rules the volunteers would choose and judge whether our actions are in accord with those rules.

First though, we need to be a little clearer about what it would be like to be a volunteer in the original position.

The volunteers are chosen from both genders and all sexual preferences as well as the widest possible variety of different cultures and nationalities. It would be best if each one of them speaks a different language (or at least a unique dialect) as long as a very broad cultural mix could still be achieved under this restriction. Even though they do not know their heritage, since they must think using a language, some of their thought will be culturally determined. For instance, a dialect of English in which there is one word, "mags," used to refer to both maggots and women could have a deep built-in misogyny that could influence a volunteer's choices. The breadth of backgrounds would possibly minimize such cultural effects on choice since the majority will rule on what code of behaviour is chosen.

Despite the attention to cultural diversity, I am not trying to achieve the impossible dream of a culture-free ethical system. The whole exercise reflects, after all, a Western idea of fairness. A contemporary Western idea of tolerance of differences also influences my choice of this version of the original position—that is, the imaginary position in which the volunteers find themselves while anaesthetized. I also must assume that the volunteers are in one clear way Westernized: they accept Western common sense standards of risk taking. Educated boldness is acceptable but not a foolhardy betting of the farm on a single roll of the dice. They also conduct themselves democratically in choosing rules. My choice of the original position for the volunteers is guided by Western common sense with an eye to the global dimensions of our moral choices.

These volunteers are also told that they must decide what the rights of persons are by forming the basic rules according to which societies and individuals will conduct themselves. They are instructed to think only of their own self-interest, not of any moral principle, and they obey this instruction. The volunteers on this committee are in a version of the original position. This departs, however, from Rawls's version in ways noted above. The volunteers on this strange committee are equally powerful, equally intelligent, self-interested people who will decide what rules should be in the ideal social contract, in ignorance of their own advantages and disadvantages.

An additional constraint on the volunteers has to do with one kind of compliance problem and with our partiality to those closely related to us. A minimal criterion for any ethical theory which proposes rules for action as social contract theories do, is that it should produce rules that people with ordinary human sympathies could follow. The volunteers in our metaphor are told they must foster compliance with rules by attending to sympathies, and they know enough about the human condition to state their general principles with appropriate exceptions. People could not, for example, comply with rules that tell them to ignore family and friends in favour of strangers. I do not, moreover, assume strict compliance with the rules as Rawls does in an ideally just society.[4] I am concerned with compliance in the real world. Of course the volunteers must think of their rules as generally being followed, so each volunteer could be told another white lie, that the rules they help craft will be strictly enforced as law in their particular society, whatever that may be. This induces a kind of presumption of compliance among the volunteers.

The point of the foregoing barely bearable metaphor is to explain how we could, in a rough and ready way, apply some concepts of social contract theory to resolve moral disputes. We could ask what rules we would agree to if we were like the volunteers. This would give us a practical understanding of fair rules applicable to the particular situation we are examining. These fair rules tell us what our moral rights and duties are as persons in that case. The self-interest condition is not there to produce egoism, nor would it. By acting in their own self-interest the volunteers would act in the best interests of any person simply because they are so ignorant about themselves, about their own advantages and disadvantages. For all any volunteer knows, she could be anyone. To help themselves they would be forced to choose rules that would be best for anyone governed by these rules, but they would do so with compliance in mind.

In light of the social contract as chosen by these volunteers in the original position, an important general principle of many moral theorists is illustrated. Moral rules must be universalizable: what it is right for a person to do is right for any similarly situated person to do. For instance, when a doctor behaves in a certain way toward a patient, the patient should be able to agree that, if the patient were the doctor, the patient would behave in the same way. The rule being followed by the doctor should be one that would have been chosen by the volunteers behind a veil of ignorance. Behind that veil there is ignorance about the relative positions of the people in the situation in which the rules are applied.

This does not mean that in the real world when we apply the rules the volunteers would choose that we ignore relationships among people or the unique aspects of each person's situation. Because the volunteers must foster compliance, they choose rules that people with ordinary human sympathies could follow.[5] Such rules could not require us to ignore the relationships we have. They will allow partiality to govern our actions to some degree in some situations. Perhaps a doctor would feel unable to treat a patient fairly because of his previous relationship with that patient. For such cases, the volunteers would provide ways for opting out. The doctor could ask that someone else care for this particular patient. General principles such as a rule of impartiality affecting the doctor in this case are not blindly applied to force people to act as superhuman ethical calculators. As I reply to the feminist critique of contractarian thought below, I will consider some aspects of balancing general principles from the volunteers with relationships in the real world to determine ethical decisions.

Objections to this use of social contract theory

Through a series of objections to the theory I propose, I will illustrate some of the practical applications of my view. Some of the interesting recent criticism of traditional moral theories has come from groups that feel ethics has been used against them as a tool of oppression. I hope to distinguish my view from the traditions that merit this criticism.

Ablism

It might be feared that the combination of the concept of a person that I have sketched together with social contract theory could yield ablist views. That is, the disabled would not be counted as full persons and the volunteers would disregard their interests. Even though the concept of a person explained in the last chapter is a concept heavily dependent on abilities, using a social contract theory would actually prevent the distribution of wealth or pleasure in a society purely on the basis of ability.

There are, historically, many instances of the sort of thing we would want our rules to prevent if we were volunteers in the original position. Nazis, for example, thought the disabled should be killed. Various schemes for developing meritocracies have been proposed by other groups. These schemes are opposed by the universalizability of moral rules which the social contract theory and most moral theories adopt. There might be different rules for those who are outside the class of persons than there are for those who are in that class, but within that class there is no ablism—that is, there is no favouritism for those already favoured by naturally occurring advantages in ability. Those behind a veil of ignorance, not knowing if their own abilities would be below average, would fear such ablism and prohibit it in the arrangement of offices and institutions. A person with common sense would protect herself by ensuring that public advantages are not distributed in ways which might deny her or her loved ones access to those advantages.

In fact, it would make sense for the volunteers to ensure that the playing field is levelled, as much as possible, so that natural disadvantages do not prevent a person from developing. That justifies having access policies requiring, for instance, wheelchair ramps. The most difficult problems, however, involve persons with fewer mental abilities than most. Almost everyone is mentally disabled to a degree by comparison with the brightest persons. In establishing thresholds for access to such things as holding public office, for example, the volunteers would have to take into account that ought implies can. In other words, if a person ought to do something, then that person can do that thing. Volunteers would not give people duties they could not perform. Nor would they give them rights they could not exercise. They might, however, accept a reverse onus rule that tells those who want to restrict access to some public advantage to prove that those who are kept out are indeed not competent to perform the duties that accompany that advantage.

One cannot, of course, legislate personal relationships, and the volunteers would not try. It would be silly to require us to ignore natural advantages that people have when we seek out friends. It is not immoral to seek out gifted people as companions as long as we do not deliberately and unnecessarily cause suffering to those with whom we choose not to be friends. Impartiality is required in our institutions, as kindness is in our personal lives. Where the public and private spheres merge, as in the hiring of a private secretary, it may require the wisdom of Solomon to know what to do. The volunteers can only give us general guidance.

It might still be argued that the volunteers know that their own mental abilities will be above some threshold that makes human beings persons. Given that I see metaphysics as determined from the original position as well, the volunteers would choose the thresholds themselves. The volunteers might reason that if, on coming out of the effects of the anaesthetic, they were non-persons, then they would not be the same persons who are now choosing rules. They would have no reason, purely from self-interest, to protect human beings who have mental abilities below the threshold for being a person. Their rules, however, must foster compliance. Our sympathies do not suddenly evaporate when someone ceases to be a person yet stays alive as a human being. Knowing this, the volunteers would have to protect to some degree human non-persons. I will consider this topic later as I try to distinguish human rights from the rights of persons.

Gambling

Now it may be objected that we cannot tell what volunteers would choose in the hypothetical original position. Perhaps they would be gamblers and choose favouritism in the blind hope of being among those favoured by the rules. But Western common sense is opposed to such blind gambling. The volunteers would not take silly chances with their lives. The standards of common sense which have guided this investigation throughout are not precise. Nonetheless most of us are, I suspect, fairly confident of our ability to decide what would be a reasonable bet in the circumstances I described to illustrate the original position. Of course I assume Western standards of reasonable risk-taking.

One, personally, might be inclined to take some bet which is not reasonable because one has a much higher than average—and hence, uncommon—tolerance for risk. Still, I ask you to judge my pronouncements about what people would do in the original position remembering that they are rational by the standards of Western common sense. It is common sense to minimize risks when venturing into the unknown. We may not wish to do so but, if you think of the volunteers as exercising this kind of caution, then we can see what sorts of rules they would recommend and, hence, what sort of moral theory is proposed here.

It might still be objected that even rational people have irrational moments. People are generally unpredictable. That is why the metaphor of the UN volunteers is used. It is hoped that the whole group would overrule any irrationality that may crop up in some of its members. Since the fanciful metaphor to illustrate the original position is contrived at best, I have no objection to making it more so and specifying that those in the original position are exceptionally psychologically stable and that the majority voting for rules will always be rational in protecting their interests. After all, this need not be a description of a possible situation or a likely situation but only of a situation which illustrates a kind of social contractarian view. Objections to my claims about what the volunteers in the original position would choose should be not of the form, I would not do that, or Real people might not choose that way, but That is not a bet a person would make in her own self-interest and in accord with Western common sense concerning risk-taking while trying to produce a rule that people with ordinary human sympathies could follow. While there are likely to be disagreements about what the volunteers in my illustration of the original position would do, there is, I believe, a large measure of agreement.

Sexism

One more general objection to social contract theories is that they try to come up with rules in isolation from personal relationships and that this is at best artificial. Why should we try to negotiate behind a veil of ignorance? This, it may be objected, will provide only ignorant moral views. Morality, some feminists argue, is undermined by the liberal individualist conception of persons and morality that gives us a false view of both persons and moral obligations, a view tailored to support male dominance.[6]

On the face of it, this is odd, since oppression of women or any other group is something social contract theories are ostensibly designed to condemn. The fundamental reason for negotiating rules as if in the original position is to promote fairness of those rules. A fair rule is defined here as one the volunteers would choose in the original position. Consider what is wrong with a judge in a court of law being partial to white middle-class men like himself and giving harsher sentences to women. The judge is being unfair. He could not justify the advantages given to his own group in the original position. The original position seems to provide us with a definition of fairness that can be applied to real cases with reasonable results. Feminists point out, however, that the appeal to rational impartiality in ethical theories has often been a tool for the oppression of women.[7]

A related major problem with social contract theories is that they get fairness via impartiality and tend to get impartiality to an unreasonable extreme. We might, if we are too simplistic, have a theory that requires a mother to let her children go hungry while she supports starving children in other countries. That is an insanely impartial treatment of the children. That is why the social contract theory used here requires that the rules be such that ordinary people with common human sympathies could follow those rules. This allows for special obligations of a mother to her children without ignoring the starving children abroad. The volunteers might, for instance, make it a moral duty of wealthy societies to send aid to the starving while allowing aid from individuals to be supererogatory. Within the original position, the volunteers would have to try to distinguish the kinds of cases where impartiality is required from those where partiality is merited. The courtroom, the legislature, and the stage of international affairs are different contexts from those in which families or friends make moral decisions affecting one another.

Some feminists, nonetheless, have tended to see this way of deciding moral questions as a wolf in sheep's clothing, or at best wrongheaded. The history of misogyny in the thought of such major philosophers as Aristotle and Kant and some social contract theorists is well documented.[8] Even Rawls, who says that gender is one of the advantages which is not known in the original position is suspected of sneaking patriarchy in by making heads of families the choosers of rules in the original position.[9] But I believe that the original position as I have described it avoids this problem. My version would not serve Rawls's purposes, but it may avoid the feminists' objections. I have a much less ambitious project than Rawls here. I wish to have a practical way for people to discuss moral questions including those that go beyond their parochial concerns.

Insidious individualism and impartiality

Even if I have managed to avoid the charge of misogyny, the moral theory and conception of person used here might be thought to be part of a tradition individualism for persons and impartiality in ethics that undermines morality.[10] There are two relevant themes in contemporary feminism that I shall, following Marilyn Friedman, refer to as the doctrines of "the social self" and "partiality."[11] First consider the social self. Many feminist and some non-feminist philosophers hold that:

> the self is inherently *social* to some degree or other. In its identity, character, interests, and preferences, it is constituted by, and in the course of, relationships to particular others, including the network of relationships that locate it as a member of certain communities or social groups.[12]

This brings us to partiality in ethics. Since we, as persons, are constituted by our relationships with other persons in the groups to which we belong, our moral obligations are seen, by some feminists, as explicable only in terms of our partiality to those with whom we are related. In the extreme case, the defenders of partiality see no place for impartiality in our ethical judgments.

Let us begin with examples of the opposed parties in the partiality debate. On the side of care ethics, adopted by many feminists, we have Nel Noddings, whose original form of care ethics made the relationship of reciprocal caring essential to moral obligation.[13] This strongly ties obligations to partiality. James Rachels draws out the contrast of care ethics with theories that accept general moral principles—akin to the social contract theory which I favour—by considering our obligations to starving children in distant lands. Rachels reports that because there is no possibility of a one-to-one encounter with these children in which they could acknowledge our care, we have no obligation to care for them according to Noddings.[14] Friedman notes, on the other hand, that feminists like Virginia Held, for instance, speak of developing concern for children abroad by learning to empathize with them using our relationships at home. Friedman still sees this as a limit of the social conception of the self, though "its inability to ground the widest sort of concern for others in unmediated constituents of the self."[15] Unlike some of the proponents of care ethics, I see this as a need for more than the social self and the ethics of partiality. Nonetheless, I think the feminist critique of ethics from Noddings, Held, and many others demands a response and a reworking of theories that leave out the importance of personal relationships in ethics.

On the other side, a sophisticated form of a social contract ethics abstracted from personal relations and depending on rational bargaining—represented via game theory—to justify cooperation is represented by David Gauthier.[16] Here the primary metaphor, the prisoners' dilemma, is of two prisoners unable to communicate with one another and placed in a quandary about whether or not to cooperate with the authorities. Now I will not attempt to do justice to Gauthier's views any more than to Noddings'. My purpose in putting forward these examples is to note an interesting similarity of the conclusions they draw, conclusions which I wish to avoid. Gauthier tells us: "John Locke wrote that 'an Hobbist…will not easily admit a great many plain duties of morality.' Although our understanding of human motivation and rationality is less restrictive than Hobbes's, yet the moral theory we have developed is clearly 'Hobbist' in its emphasis on mutual constraint." This emphasis, Gauthier goes on to say, does not give us conventional morality: "Animals, the unborn, the congenitally handicapped and defective, fall beyond the pale of a morality tied to mutuality."[17] Perhaps distant starving children would suffer the same expulsion from the moral community. Whether it is Noddings' mutual caring or contractarian mutual constraint, the mutuality will rule out some to whom we conventionally have obligations.

Following Jane English,[18] I have tried to allow for moral obligations without reciprocity and for rules which have some chance of gaining compliance by emphasizing sympathies. The volunteers in the original position are told that they must choose rules with which real people can comply. Therefore they must take ordinary human sympathies into account. That is why the volunteers would not hesitate to make charity begin at home and why they would not let it end there. Knowing that they would be very strongly bound to their own children, the volunteers would not want to have to sacrifice their children's interests to distant children, should they be among the fortunate who can feed their children well. Knowing that they might themselves parent starving children elsewhere, the volunteers would not wish to deny all obligations to these children by others distant from them. They would have to come to some view that allowed priority to be given to one's own without leaving the needy out of consideration, no matter how distant. Of course, the devil is in the details, but we can at least argue about how much to give to whom if we can agree on our duties to give in very general terms, at least nation to nation.

Three feminist objections

Three objections to social contract theories tend to be bundled together in the feminist critique:

1. The social contract idea of the original position takes away the context of relationships needed by the social self to make ethical decisions. I refer to this objection as decontextualization.
2. The use of general principles or rights applied impartially is artificial since each case of moral decision making is unique. I refer to this objection as artificial impartiality.
3. Metaphysical concepts of a person other than the social self promote a view of ethics as a contest by making persons atomistic individuals cooperating only out of necessity and adopting minimal constraints on their liberty. I refer to this objection as artificial isolation.

According to this kind of objection, understanding, love, sympathy, and care are pushed out of ethics in favour of the rules restricting competition in the interests of the majority of competitors. This combination of objections is sometimes aimed at views about persons and morality lumped under the heading,"liberal individualism." It contains elements of liberal views in the nineteenth century which have become conservative views of today. I will try to show that I avoid the excesses of such extreme individualism and avoid these objections. To respond to the feminist critique, I wish to distinguish the use of social contract ideas that I make from that which is oppressive and to try to find a workable view between the extreme positions on either side of the debate over ethical partiality. To do this, I will first consider the objections to ethical views and then work on the metaphysical aspects of individuality.

My response to decontextualization is that context comes into play when we are trying to decide the details. The general principles are established in the social contract. What we do in different cases may be very different things, although all are subsumable under one principle. In case it appears that I am trying to have it both ways, notice that we must accept varied applications of principles in all sorts of areas, not just in ethics. For example, it is a good principle of fire fighting that when we want to put out a fire we should deprive it of oxygen. To put out the campfire we might throw on sand or water but, if we have burning fat in the kitchen, we should use baking soda. The different contexts require very different actions in the application of one and the same principle. Similarly, a duty of beneficence requires us to do varied things for different beneficiaries of our actions depending on such things as the closeness of the relation of ourselves to those who benefit. The hunger of our own children is not the same sort of fire to put out as the hunger of distant children who are not related to us.

I hope it is clear from this discussion how artificial impartiality and artificial isolation are also avoided. Of course it is not required that we treat our children and other children impartially without regard to the closeness of the relationship. That would not be in accord with the requirement on the volunteers that they make rules that people with ordinary human sympathies can follow. The use of the social contract ideas that I propose can, moreover, deal with cases in which impartiality is required, the case of the judge mentioned above, for instance. Nor is there any need to treat real individuals as artificially isolated and combative just because we use the original position to look beyond our parochial concerns. The rich textures of our relationships are fully relevant to our moral decision making since they affect our sympathies. That is not to say that we leave competition out of consideration. The original position uses competing interests to generate fair rules but not in a way that ignores the importance of human relationships.

The problems for social contract theory mentioned here are only partially addressed. There is certainly much room for debate around such concepts as that of ordinary human sympathies. While there is not enough space here to include much more than the beginnings of the debate, at least I have indicated the general direction of my replies to certain interesting objections. I turn now to further applications of my views of persons and morality.

Allocation of scarce medical resources

The rules chosen in the original position (in my metaphor the rules the UN volunteers would choose) would include rules for allocating scarce medical resources to people rather than to human beings who are not people and are not likely to become people. But the committee would not accept a rule that says that those who have advantages shall get more advantages within the class of persons. Fearing, for instance, having a body which limits abilities, a volunteer on this committee would ask for democracy within the class of persons. Fairness of allocation of resources among persons would not treat the accidental advantages of birth as merits. From the original position volunteers would not accept a rule which tells us to save the most able-bodied and brightest people first, since volunteers would have no good reason to think they are among those people. Recall the white lie that the volunteers believe—that they could have impaired mental or physical abilities when they return to their normal state.

The rules for allocation within the class of persons would be closer to a first-come-first-served rule, but that rule would have to be qualified. Clearly a person with a fatal disease and weeks to live should not block a person with a chance for a long life from receiving treatment. Volunteers would consider their best interests over a lifetime, for they do not know their own ages. Unfortunately, actual decisions are rarely so clear cut. There are many things that we might weigh in the balance, such as gratitude for past actions, and abilities and propensities to perform future actions for which we would be grateful. Providing rules which do not conflict with ordinary human sympathy requires attention to our relationships and partiality.

Suppose, for instance, in a medical centre in the far north where resources and time are limited, we are faced with saving an old shiftless prospector from the south well known as a drain on the community or saving a well-loved elder who has served the community well. This elder's guidance is crucial for the community's well being. Are we really to flip a coin? Would we choose, in the original position, a rule which would deny the elder the care because she lost the coin toss? From the original position we might try to choose rules that would favour the elder since we would wish, in self-interest, to promote the society which results from such allocations. We would also think of where our sympathies would lie and compliance with rules. We might be willing to take our chances of winding up as the prospector in such a situation. Nonetheless we would frame our rules so that there is a heavy onus of justification resting on the shoulders of those who would depart from the first-come-first-served rule. The right to life-saving medical treatment of the individual would have to be weighed against the rights of others. In the case of the elder and the prospector, we honour more rights and offend fewer sympathies by saving the elder because of the dependence of others on the elder and gratitude to the elder. Seen from the original position, it is a better bet that we would be helped—rather than hurt by this weighing of rights.

Beyond consequentialism

But some will smell a whiff of sulphur here. If we really were to put such rules into practice, would we not be sliding into the pit of moral consequentialism where the end justifies the means? I think not, and I think the volunteers would not like consequentialism. The volunteers would want some individual rights to protect themselves against the ends of community benefits that can always be used by utilitarians to justify the means of harming individuals. In the original position it is in the interests of the volunteers to strike a balance between rights of the individual and the community. Volunteers would want to keep some advantages they might have in the real world, but not allow anyone to have enormous excess at the expense of most others. The social contract theory, however, tries to get some of the advantages of consequentialism without becoming totally governed by consequences.

In the original position, the volunteers would surely be reluctant to choose the simple consequentialist rule that whatever is in the interests of the majority is what is to be done. The volunteers know that, when they come out of the anesthesia and return to normal life, they may sometimes find themselves in a happy minority at an advantage over most others and they would not, therefore, choose a rule which always wipes out that advantage. On the other hand, they might well find themselves, on occasion, in a majority which suffers because a few have most of the advantages. One might make a trade. One could limit the depth to which one might be allowed to fall into a disadvantageous situation by limiting at the other end the height of the advantages one could enjoy. Rather than getting rid of all differentiation of people's positions, one might accept rules which would provide a safety net at the bottom and a ceiling at the top. No person could be treated as if she did not count and no person's merits could be trump. It is common sense to hedge one's bets.

The related point about sympathies is that no person could be treated as if she did not count no matter how slight her relationship to ourselves, and no person's relatedness to ourselves is trump. A mother who avoids putting her daughter in quarantine might risk illness and death for many others to whom her daughter might pass an infection. She cannot justify this because she does not wish to cause emotional trauma to her daughter. Her partiality to her daughter is understandable but provides a limited justification. In the original position, the volunteers would need to limit the degree to which our sympathy with those close to us could allow us to put them first. Special obligations are not always trump.

The way that consequentialism is also limited in rules chosen from the original position may be illustrated if we vary the story of the prospector and the elder. Suppose the prospector has arrived earlier than the elder and treatment of the prospector is well under way.

Treatment would not be abandoned in this case to save the elder, even though this would have a better outcome for the community as a whole. The anaesthetized volunteers would want advantages, once gained, not to be totally volatile.

Beyond meritocracy and egalitarianism

From the original position, both totally egalitarian societies and meritocracies would look bad because of their tendencies to reverse allocations already made and thereby to undo advantages which have been gained without force or fraud. Because it is in the interest of the volunteers to promote a stable society, they would oppose rules that take away advantages which were gained without force or fraud as opposed to luck or pluck. Common sense would tell the volunteers that their rules should allow them to hang on to what they have. On the other hand, they would want to arrange things so that nobody can monopolize advantages. Someone with so much luck or pluck that he corrals many advantages while others are needy should not be allowed to hold on to things that go to waste. Here we are applying a view of John Locke's, his spoilage condition that says we may take "as much as any one can make use of to any advantage of life before it spoils."[19] Another relevant proviso from Locke on keeping what you have is that enough of the advantage of the same quality is left for those who come later.

Where services in health care are concerned, scarcity of resources makes the application of Locke's ideas tricky. If I use services or medicines that the society provides, there may very well not be enough and as good health care for those who come later, even if I am careful not to hoard such resources.

Not just new and exotic treatments but standard health care becomes more scarce as populations increase and economies founder. Not only concerning life-saving medical care but, regarding health care in general, questions are being raised about the allocation of this care on a first-come-first-served basis. Ethics committees in hospitals, for instance, may be asked to suggest policy regarding the reserving of some treatments for those who are not so infirm or advanced in age as to make the outcome extremely dubious. A physician remarked to me, in the context of discussing this issue, that 50 percent of health care dollars in British Columbia are spent on people in the last six months of their lives. Long-term care facilities may house many patients who are well below any reasonable threshold for being persons and, hence, below the threshold for being the persons their families knew before advanced age or illness robbed those persons of their capacities.

Of course rules that gave summary loss of treatment to human beings as soon as they had fallen below enough thresholds to cease being persons would not be rules with which people with ordinary human sympathies would comply. We need some time to come to terms with the loss of a person that occurs before bodily death. Nonetheless, seeing themselves threatened by allowing far too much time for such accommodation, the volunteers would limit the degree to which treatment could continue when resources are short. It is strongly in their interest to do so.

Problems arise also at the other end of human life. In neo-natal care units we spend millions saving newborns even after a mere twenty-week pregnancy. These newborns will probably have ongoing health problems all of their lives. Locke's spoilage condition might be applied to some of these newborns who may become persons. If their lives are likely to be prolonged but not to their advantage, the resources should be given to others in need. Even those who never have the potential to become persons may use enormous quantities of resources. As our health care systems stagger under the weight of supporting such patients as if they were persons, we need to separate clearly the treatment which is the moral right of all human beings from the treatment which is the moral right only of persons. The rights of human beings are not a matter of genetics, but had by virtue of the close relationship between the class of persons and the class of human beings. As far as we know, given that Byzantine essentialism is correct, all persons are human beings, although not all human beings are persons.

We already make many decisions in accord with that concept of a person which I explained in the previous chapter. The medical profession in my locale has apparently stopped doing many life-saving operations on patients who appear to be clearly below some threshold. For example, one hears that few to no bypass operations are being done on those who clearly no longer have capacities for thought, memory, or emotion. If resources are dedicated instead to those whose abilities are obviously above the thresholds, few would take the reallocation amiss, given that there are not enough resources to give all who need the operation to stay alive. First-come-first-served is a rule which is constantly being qualified. We ought to devote resources first to people and only then to those human beings who are no longer—and likely never again to be—or not yet—and unlikely to become—people. Resources are not so tight that we are unwilling to err on the side of generosity in letting human beings be treated as people. Having human chromosomes is no longer a guarantee of treatment, if it ever was.

On the other hand, those who are not persons may have certain rights as well under the terms agreed to by the volunteers. For those outside the group of persons, it would be reasonable to differentiate treatment on the basis of their similarity to persons and on the degree to which they have a chance of becoming persons. Their similarity engages our sympathies. Consideration of sympathies is necessary for making the rules of the sort that people can follow. As far as the volunteers know, the potential to be a person is all that some of the volunteers may have once the rule-making exercise is completed. The volunteers believe the white lie that they will possibly be preserved for life in a later generation.

As seen from the original position then, egalitarian considerations have a qualified use within groups of people. This is a block to attempts to differentiate treatment on the basis of the degree to which a patient is a person. For those outside the circle, however, decisions about allocation might well look to the degree of similarity to persons or to the degree of potential for becoming persons. I seem to remember an outcry in the press when a well-known chimpanzee, who had demonstrated certain cognitive and conative capacities like ours, was to be used for vivisection. Well we might ask about the other chimpanzees who are used in this way without any notice being taken. Animals who are more like people than are some human beings should be accorded special respect because of their capacities. The volunteers in the original position would, in self-interest, demand respect for such abilities so that their own would be respected. They would not wish to undermine the sympathies of persons for persons by allowing people to act harshly toward those who resemble persons. It is reasonable for the volunteers to bet that they would have need of such sympathies once they are not in the original position but in the real world where their rules may apply.

Informed consent and access to information

From the original position volunteers would choose rights to information prior to giving consent to operations or to their use as experimental subjects. Indeed, volunteers would want information about themselves generally. These rights apply to all research on persons and to government record keeping. They are urgent questions as well in medical practice. By the nature of medical practice, the patient cannot have as much information as the practitioner. One very difficult policy to state is that regarding the degree to which consent must be informed. This will depend partly on the degree to which the patient is a person. Roughly speaking, the more one is a person the more one has the capacity to assimilate such information and make a judgment on one's own behalf. From the original position volunteers would choose to give the patient's own view of the patient's competence a very heavy weight in these matters. In short, volunteers would oppose paternalism because it is a reasonable bet that volunteers would turn out to be the best judges and protectors of their own self-interest when they got back to their ordinary lives.

Paternalism

In the past, doctors were brought up in a rather paternalistic medical culture in which they passed little diagnostic information to patients. Even now, legal difficulties to one side, probably the moral question most physicians would ask themselves is, Would this information do my patient more harm than good? The culture is changing, however, to admit that the autonomy of patients who are persons must be respected even when some harm will be done by such respect.

To see the knife-edge on which doctors must balance principles, consider an example. Diagnostic test results are generally considered information to which competent adults—as autonomous persons—have a right. If a gynecologist has a young patient who presents as a woman but is diagnosed as having testicular feminization and, consequently, a male chromosome profile, full information will not usually be disclosed to the patient. If the patient were told that she had the profile of a man, the patient might suffer from difficulties with gender identification. In some cases, full disclosure of this diagnosis has led to extreme psychological trauma and even suicide. Clearly health care professionals may come under conflicting requirements in cases of autonomy and access to information. From the original position, we would want our autonomy respected but not if it would injure us to no good purpose. To justify not respecting autonomy we would have to make a very good case that immanent harm (not wished by the person who would suffer that harm) would be avoided.

This illustrates the mammoth task of the volunteers in the original position. With each of the rules they would put forward in the original position, they would have many paragraphs of general exceptions and examples as guidance for the decision makers in real world societies trying to abide by these rules. It is, nonetheless, not an impossible task. It is more difficult than, but comparable to, the task each of us might face in writing a living will to specify what should be done in a future veiled from us by our ignorance of the future state of our health.

Moral limits on research and experimentation

Once again, the primary issue here is informed consent. Informing research participants fully may destroy a research study and inhibit the discovery of important data. Failing to inform them may constitute a breach of their rights as persons. Mainly universities and research hospitals face this dilemma, but the debates about informed consent are relevant to ordinary medical practice in many areas. For example, informing a patient about the details of a procedure may lessen the opportunities for success if the patient is sufficiently fearful. In this case as well, health care professionals are expected to make a judgment about which takes precedence, the autonomy of persons or doing what is best, medically speaking, for patients. The same rule discussed above requiring respect for autonomy except where justified by avoiding immanent harm to the patient seems to apply in this case.

Persons and informed consent

We may, however, forgo considerable benefits from research if we insist on informed consent. Consequentialists might think the concept of a person too weak to stand in the way of the general increase in human happiness that might come from less hobbled research. From the original position, however, we would want to be sure that we were not going to be used, without reasonably informed consent, as laboratory rats. While fully informed consent is impossible without giving the subjects an education like that of the experimenters, it is usually easy enough to see what the experimenter would be interested in knowing if the experimenter were in the participant's shoes. From the original position, one does not know which shoes one will wear. The rule is, therefore, that the experimenter should tell the subject what the experimenter would want to know if their roles were reversed and if common sense guided risk taking. This ensures treating the participant as a person rather than an experimental animal. It would mean foregoing some experiments which would be impossible with such reasonably informed consent.

Here too we must distinguish between merely human beings and persons. We tend to protect all human beings from harm in experimentation, but informed consent is only possible for persons. The protection for all, moreover, is justified in the original position by concerns about persons being mistaken for mere human beings and deep sympathy for human beings generally. In some cases, it is clear that we are dealing with a human but not a person. We allow experimentation, for example, on neo-morts in hospitals with the consent of the next of kin. Because the neo-morts' brains are not functioning, they are not persons. On the other hand, those whose brains function sufficiently to maintain them as living human beings without life-support systems but who probably have no significant cognitive function would not be thought to be proper subjects for experimentation. For instance, some permanently vegetative human beings in long-term care facilities would be in this category. Perhaps if we were as certain as we are with the neo-morts that these human beings would never again be persons, we would not have quite the same qualms, but their similarity to us is greater; so they would not likely be treated like neo-morts. The general rule chosen from the original position might well be this: when in doubt, protect a human being as a person should be protected. Since the volunteers are betting on rules with their own self-interest in mind, however, they would have to weigh carefully their chances, on the one hand, of being a person who is mistaken for a human being in a vegetative state and, on the other hand, being a person who suffers because of the lack of knowledge which might have been gained through more liberal experimentation. The volunteers might, however, let the general rule stand in any case just to support sympathy for human beings on which so many of their interests and the compliance with—and, hence, the usefulness of—their rules would depend.

Non-human subjects of research

Non-human experimental animals might also be accorded more respect according to the rules of the social contract than they are currently accorded. In their own self-interest the volunteers would want to have the advantages which come to people from the use of animals in experimentation, but the volunteers would also want to inhibit needless suffering in any sentient being, not just those which resemble us. To allow suffering is to undermine one's own security by undermining the sympathy on which security rests. Those in the original position would not favour the ideal of the dispassionate scientist. It is an ideal of scientists, not a view likely to appeal to those who are trying to minimize their risks in accord with common sense. I think the volunteers would want to promote a robust sympathy for sentient beings more than they would want to promote uninhibited scientific experimentation on sentient beings.

The case for preventing suffering in non-human animals becomes all that much stronger where the resemblance is greater. Previously I have noted that chimpanzees have 98 percent of our chromosomal makeup and may be able to use to some extent such languages as American Sign Language for the Deaf. If we justify vivisection on such animals to benefit ourselves through research, we are in grave danger of undermining the sympathies that prevent doing the same to some human beings. Since the volunteers would have to choose rules that people with ordinary human sympathies could follow, they will take resemblance to human beings as highly relevant when they set rules to prevent suffering and death.

Euthanasia

Euthanasia is taking over from abortion as the topic of biomedical ethics most in the public eye and before the courts. Consequently it provides excellent examples of pressures on ethical decision making which may go on in medical settings. Attention to even the abbreviated discussion here could, perhaps, urge the debate within those settings in new directions.

It is useful to distinguish at least six kinds of euthanasia: *voluntary*, in which the person requests death, *non-voluntary*, in which the recipient is incapable of making requests, *involuntary*, in which the person requests life-saving aid that is denied,[20] and each of these three may be *active* or *passive*. This last distinction is hazy. Is doctor-assisted suicide active or passive? In accepting a patient's refusal of life support is a doctor causing a death or merely allowing a patient to cause her own? Disagreements here are not merely about the moral value of actions of persons but about what constitutes an action and what constitutes a person. Actions are, roughly, the behaviour of human beings caused by the intentions of the corresponding persons, and corresponding persons are as described in the last chapter. On this view, not giving a patient antibiotics when the patient has pneumonia is as much an action as giving the patient a lethal injection. The question in either case remains, Is euthanasia morally justified in this instance? Given this rough characterization of action volunteers can consider what to say about the six kinds of euthanasia.

Acting in their own self-interest but behind a veil of ignorance about their lots in life to come, the volunteers would choose contractual terms that would make life worth living, as much as possible, no matter what lot is drawn. On the other hand, they would also, perhaps, permit the termination of the life of a person were it to be a totally unbearable life. A human body which was not a person could, under very special circumstances, permissibly be killed too. If brain damage, for example, in that body were so severe that no person were really present in it, killing that body would not be killing a person. Different rules would protect human beings who were not persons, though the volunteers would want to severely restrict harm to human beings as well. The self-interest of the anaesthetized committee, the volunteers in the original position, would lead them to provide for their continuation if they are once in the real world having lives worth living. If their lives in the real world became a burden to them, they would want to be able to have themselves killed without suffering at their considered and reasonable request.

Voluntary euthanasia

From the original position, then, one would want the power to end one's life in the real world if it were truly unbearable. People make mistakes about their future degree of suffering and about its probable duration. Sometimes they are glad to have lived after all, sometimes not. Voluntary euthanasia, therefore, should be allowed only under strict controls to prevent a person from accepting euthanasia because of pressure, misinformation, or temporary despondency.

One should also be able to make the choice of death while still a person and have it carried out later when one is no longer able to commit suicide. This would usually be called active euthanasia. When only the human being remains but the person has, prior to falling below some threshold, requested euthanasia, it should still be carried out. I suppose it could be called both "active" and "voluntary" in such a case, though some dispute the use of voluntary acceptance of death when much time has elapsed since acceptance was expressed. In the original position, however, volunteers would choose to be in charge of their own bodies in the real world even when they can no longer control their bodies, if only to prevent the mere behaviour of those bodies from being mistaken for their actions. The dignity of persons depends on persons' wishes about their own bodies being given great weight in any decision about how to treat those bodies. The volunteers would, in any case, be making a reasonable bet if they put forward rules which protect persons' power over their own bodies.

It seems we should not rest too much on the distinction between "passive" and "active." These terms have no precise meaning. Active euthanasia is, roughly, the mercy killing of a person assisted by some other person, while passive euthanasia is mercifully letting a person or human being die, or benign neglect. Neglect, however, is not always as benign as more vigorous steps to bring about a patient's death. In the original position we would choose a rule by which we could get help to end our own suffering in a hopeless case. Avoidance of needless, pointless pain is the way of common sense. Some may choose to suffer to the end, but it should be a choice. If there is a point to suffering to the end, it should be a point of the person who is suffering. As usual, I assume that it would be a reasonable bet, a rule of common sense, if we were volunteers in the original position, to keep our options in the real world as open as possible and keep as much control as possible over ourselves. If we had to make rules to govern us in an unknown future, it would make sense to maximize the personal choices we would be permitted in that future.

Non-voluntary euthanasia

In cases of non-voluntary euthanasia the will of the person or the remaining human being to be killed is not knowable with any certainty. One can consult those who knew the person when communication was possible and make the best guess. Protecting ourselves in the original position, we would want to distinguish two main kinds of cases. In the first, the patient cannot request euthanasia, because the patient is no longer a person. A patient in a permanent coma, for example, is a living human being but not a person. In cases like this, non-voluntary euthanasia is permissible. In cases, however, where there is some reasonable expectation of revival of a person in the body, non-voluntary euthanasia would not be permissible. The volunteers would choose to err on the side of keeping human beings alive pointlessly as long as the cost of this policy is not prohibitive. It would be in their interest to protect themselves in case of a future loss of abilities which might prove temporary, though temporary against all odds. On the other side they would have to weigh the costs to themselves of keeping others alive pointlessly. Probably the best the volunteers can do here is give guidelines for judgments to be made on a case-by-case basis. A chance of recovery should normally be a reason for keeping a person alive. This is consistent with saying that extreme circumstances make for harsher choices. For example, triage has been used where resources are very scarce.

In the second kind of case, much rarer, a person exists but cannot communicate. One could even be conscious but so severely injured that one cannot give instructions even by a sign. In the original position it would be rational to put stringent restrictions on non-voluntary euthanasia to ensure that it was only used on persons in cases where the patient could be shown, with moral if not epistemological certainty, to be incapable of regaining the capacity to communicate her decision. In the original position we might, out of self-interest, wish to have a decision made for us on the basis of what a reasonable person would do if so terribly injured. Medical experts could determine the likelihood of survival and the future condition of the person so far as could be known. If the prospects were only for agony, for instance, then non-voluntary euthanasia would be justifiable. Once again, I think common sense tells us to pick a rule which promotes our survival only if our lives are worth living. If possible, one's own judgments about what life is worth living should be used to decide one's own case.

According to some principle which I have failed to master, stopping life-support systems is often considered morally permissible in cases of non-voluntary euthanasia, while giving a lethal injection is not. The first is considered passive, the second active. The only morally relevant difference I can see is that the lethal injection is liable to be quicker, more effective, and less likely to cause pain to what may be, in some way, a sentient being. The similarity of this sentient being to a person should at least move us to minimize pain. People in the original position would take sympathy into account and rule in favour of euthanasia in such cases. Common sense urges us to end pointless suffering, but we must be at great pains to ensure that there is no reasonable expectation of the suffering human being becoming a person again who is able to decide for herself whether to live or die and able to communicate the decision.

The law is not in accord with morality on this; so further moral questions arise about the legal risks, if any, which health care professionals are morally obligated to take to do what is right for their patients. In the original position one would not know whether one would wind up in the position of the patient or the doctor. The rule might be framed that a doctor who could relieve extreme suffering through euthanasia with minimal personal legal risk ought to do so. Risk, however, becomes a morally adequate excuse for not acting in such cases at fairly low levels of risk, since those in the original position would exercise common caution. In self-defence, they would excuse readily in such cases a doctor's unwillingness to cause a death or to provide the means for others to do so. It would still be morally incumbent on all to seek a change in the law if the moral rules put forward by the volunteers were, indeed, at odds with the law.

Involuntary euthanasia

A person who chooses to live should be allowed to do so. Here, however, the distinction of active from passive begins to have some purchase. The ninety year old who is suffering terribly but afraid to die should generally be relieved as much as possible of pain and kept alive, but not at the cost of a misallocation of medical resources according to our earlier discussion. Such a patient could be allowed to die if the motive of mercy is combined with that of saving another person who can benefit much more from resources. In the original position, though, I suspect that considerations of autonomy would win out, denying the permissibility of any *pure* case of involuntary euthanasia. Even a patient who is suffering the tortures of the damned who chooses to live should not be shown to death's door actively or passively *if* the resources are available without misallocation to honour the patient's wish to live. Nonetheless, I would expect the volunteers to weigh more heavily the importance of having their lives saved when they might have much life left to live than the importance of having their lives saved when they are sure to die soon. This too seems to be common sense. Common sense prevails in moments of calm reflection, though one may lose sight of it when one, or one's dearest, is on the deathbed. The volunteers might agree to rules in the original position which they know they might not wish to follow under some circumstances in the real world. We make rules which force our future selves to be sensible.

What about Daphne?

Daphne, who requested euthanasia frequently during the three months prior to her final descent into dementia, is now in the condition she feared and wished to avoid via euthanasia. Daphne now is certainly not the person who existed before dementia overtook her. It is very doubtful that Daphne remains in the class of persons. She was reduced to being first like a babbling infant and then like a silent one with no potential to develop as an infant would. Now that her chance for a remission is certainly gone, her request for euthanasia should be honoured, on the face of it. The volunteers would want, were they to be in the real world, their wishes concerning their bodies to be followed. Even after their minds had gone they would want previously expressed wishes to be followed. At the very least, we ought not aggressively to try to keep Daphne alive.

In life, things are rarely as simple as they are in the abstract. In this case we discover conflicts of rights. First there are the rights of the physicians to refuse euthanasia. They would suffer severe legal sanctions if they practised it. This excuses them from following Daphne's wishes. Even the less controversial claim that we ought not to preserve Daphne in life is difficult to defend. Daphne's parents cannot quite believe that she has lost her former capacities except for what she has obviously lost—her abilities of locomotion and speech. They cannot believe what the neurologists say. As they see her, she may be simply trapped in a body which is out of her control. They strive heroically to maintain her in life and have spoken of pursuing alternative treatments to what standard medicine offers. The massive scarring of Daphne's cerebral cortex makes it certain that their view of the facts is incorrect. Daphne gradually lost the capacity to think and to speak like an adult. The intellect cannot survive the death of the brain tissue which supported it, nor can any treatment bring it back. Daphne's parents are willing, however, to hang on and hope for a miracle. Her parents spend most of their time and efforts on this. Saving Daphne has become their life.

The conflict of rights is primarily between the right of Daphne to determine what should happen to her body and the right of her parents to keep her alive and pursue various treatments. Not all cases of conflict of rights are this difficult. The parents' rights to protect their daughter with help from the public health care system would be extinguished, for instance, if Daphne were completely brain-dead, but she is not.

Reflecting on the original position, we get some help with resolution of conflicts of rights, but many points remain moot. If we are willing to allocate medical resources to keep human beings in Daphne's condition alive, then it is hard to see how we could deny her parents reasonable access to some resources. If the rules we make in the original position take into account that we can only follow rules which accord with our sympathy for persons, then we would arrange for honouring a parent's right to enlist society's help to battle for the survival of a son or daughter even when the prognosis is opposed to any return of the abilities of persons. When there is no probability of recovery, such a right can be extinguished by competing rights of other patients to medical resources. This is vague at best, and there would have to be limits on the type and quantity of resources used to keep a human being alive for the sake of parents.

In cases like Daphne's and in less clear cases in our society where medical resources are not yet taxed to the bitter limit, we fall back on the principle that when we are in even the slightest doubt we should treat a human being like a person. Indeed, even when our doubts are insignificant we tend to do so, at least when other persons' rights or sympathies for other persons or human beings promote such treatment.

We are not, however, taking the global view that those in the original position would be partly inclined to take. The world as a whole is reaching that bitter limit. If all resources were distributed without regard to nationality, we could not support human non-persons in life at the expense of people elsewhere in the world. Daphne herself was greatly opposed to the systematic wastefulness of the West and had great compassion for all who suffer. She would have, I believe, agreed that euthanasia in cases like hers would be morally right even if it were considered non-voluntary and active.

The volunteers, however, are to make rules which people who feel ordinary human sympathy could follow. We know, moreover, that our sympathies vary with proximity of persons to us both in geography and in personal relations. This undermines the global view. The volunteers would realize that rules which required distribution of medical or other resources without regard to the proximity of people to those doing the distributing would be rules that people could not or would not follow. Rather than distributing resources without regard to nationality or kinship, the rules chosen by the volunteers would require that people throughout the world be helped to attain some minimum standard. A global safety net would be the object of the rules. In case the volunteers found themselves on the outside of the resource-controlling countries looking in, they would want such a safety net. They would realize, however, that sympathy operates in such a way as to prevent any egalitarian distribution. To require such a distribution would make the rules ignored. This is a case where half a loaf is better than none. Putting this together with another bit of common sense, that charity begins at home, we modify the distribution of resources which the volunteers might otherwise like to make. Rules applicable by those with ordinary human sympathy do not include a rule requiring parents to let their own child die to preserve others with a better chance of a life worth living.

Discussing allocation of resources on a hospital ethics committee, a doctor remarked to me that our society has to relearn when it is right to let people die. Part of the problem is that our sympathy for the parents in Daphne's case makes us want to do things which are not necessarily in Daphne's interest nor in the interest of society. In the original position we would be willing to allow for what would otherwise be unreasonable treatment of a patient to alleviate the distress of others, but only to the extent that it put no one at risk. From a global point of view, our medical practices put others at risk, and they are beginning to do so even here at home. The volunteers would be ignorant, of course, of their economic circumstances. It would make only limited sense for them to assure those like Daphne her current treatment at the expense of those who are clearly persons in need of life-saving aid but who cannot afford it. We are not at that point yet, at least not locally. Sympathy still wins over harsh necessity within the wealthy countries.

The volunteers would put persons first, but in Daphne's case it is difficult at best to see how to do so. Daphne's own wish for euthanasia should be taken seriously. Her parents' right to protect her is very strong. Her parents are, moreover, currently persons while Daphne is no longer. This does not extinguish Daphne's right, but it affects her interests and capacity to suffer in ways which the volunteers would have to consider when deciding how conflicts of rights are to be decided. The right of persons elsewhere to medical resources, however, abets to some extent Daphne's right to die. We could, nonetheless, cut many luxuries before cutting medical care to such human beings as Daphne if we wished to provide better care elsewhere in the world.

The question seems, therefore, to come down to the competing rights of Daphne to euthanasia and of her parents to protect her. If it is a harm to Daphne to keep her alive and as comfortable as possible, then it is a harm that no person experiences. The harm to her parents, on the other hand, to be deprived utterly of their hope would be almost unbearable. The volunteers would protect the interests of persons much more than those of merely human beings. Daphne cannot now suffer as her parents can. Even though Daphne was a person when she requested euthanasia, it seems that to put persons first and follow rules consistent with sympathy is to support the parents in Daphne's case as long as Daphne is kept comfortable and the use of resources is not extreme. Her parents, on the other hand, cannot require the rest of society to provide aggressive, invasive treatment, nor are they morally licensed to inflict unnecessary suffering on Daphne through such treatment. Our duty to Daphne is to keep her as free from pain as possible. Our duty to her parents is to give them the resources, short of aggressive treatment, to keep Daphne alive. This seems to be the way to put persons first without ignoring the rights of past persons or of present human beings.

Abortion and infanticide

Here the central concept is often seen as the concept of a person. Pro-life groups argue that abortion is always morally wrong since it is the killing of an innocent person. Pro-choice groups deny that the fetus is a person. This opens up much larger questions which affect most medical care: What is a person? What are the rights of persons over and above those of human beings? and Does the potential to become a person confer any rights? A program for answering the first question has been suggested in the last chapter. The answer to the second and third questions are hinted at in this chapter by looking at the rules volunteers might choose in the original position. Each of these rules defines a right and, for persons, a duty. Since those choosing rules in the original position would want to protect their future selves in the real world, there would be a general prohibition against us killing innocent people who are not attacking us. This rule gives each person a corresponding right to life and a correlative duty not to kill other innocent people who are not attacking her.

Potential

A right to life is a poor thing, however, if a right to life-saving aid does not accompany it. A rule would be accepted which requires us to come to the aid of other people whose lives are threatened as long as we can do so without great harm to ourselves or others. How great a harm must be to provide an excuse for not aiding is a vexed question. I will reserve it for brief treatment by examples in the sections on foreign aid and future generations below. Here I will merely say that, while we may not be required to be good Samaritans, the opposite extreme is not likely to be acceptable to the volunteers either.

The right to life and the right to life-saving aid, however, are not obviously rights of a fetus. A fetus has not yet developed the capacities which take it across the threshold from being human to being a person. Persons in the original position would want rules to save persons, but not necessarily rules to save all human beings. Since they do not know whether they will be persons or only potentially persons when the anaesthetic wears off, the volunteers would be careful not to dismiss the interests of those who are not yet persons. A common presumption is, moreover, that a human being is actually or potentially a person; so any denial of rights to human beings would have to be carefully weighed.

Abortion should be treated differently from non-voluntary euthanasia for those whose minds are permanently gone because someone who has passed for the last time below the threshold for being a person has no potential to be one in the future. There is no person to protect. Someone who still is a person can choose to live or die and usually can express the choice, so euthanasia in such cases would only be permissible when voluntary.

The similarity of merely human beings to persons is also relevant in regard to the volunteer's choice of rules affecting the fetus. The fact that a fetus at an early stage of human development has fingers and the fact that it has gills are both relevant. The one arouses our sympathy while the other distances it. Compatibility with sympathy is a feature to be taken into account by any set of rules which is actually to be followed.[21]

When I am sleeping I have only as potentialities certain capacities which make me a person and other additional capacities which make me the particular person I am. Nonetheless, I expect my rights as a person and as *this* person to be respected. I may not be killed, and promises made to me may not be broken, just because I am not currently able to do the essential things on demand. Of course capacities are always potentialities in the sense that they are the potential to do certain things when they are required. We may, however, not be able to do things on demand when we are in various states from sleep to transient global amnesia. In these cases, though, there is good reason to believe that the abilities will be revitalized. The potential of the fetus is somewhat different.

Believing that people begin at human conception, some wish to treat fetuses as people. Fetuses, however, do not yet embody the essence needed to make a person. The question is begged, Why treat something which is clearly not yet a person as if it were? Even if we accept, just for the sake of argument, that fetuses should be treated as if they were persons, we can see that abortion would still not be completely ruled out. In the original position, a volunteer would not know if she would eventually be a woman needing an abortion for physical or psychiatric reasons. The volunteer would want to protect such a woman's interests since they might be the volunteer's own. A person who is being attacked, even by an innocent, may rightly produce even a deadly defence in some cases. The right to self-defence can overrule the right to life.[22] But this still avoids the main question, since few pregnancies are this threatening.

The difficult question is, What moral limits, if any, are there on the right of women to choose to end a *healthy* pregnancy? These limits, once we know them, can be modified to the degree that the health of the fetus or the mother are threatened prior to our facing the decision about abortion. To say that there is no moral reason to protect a fetus from abortion is to ignore the matters of similarity to persons and the potential to become a person. Since those in the original position would take sympathy into account, they would recognize that abortion late in the term would have to be justified by much more pressing interests of persons than abortion earlier in the term. And since they would want a rule which protects themselves when they are temporarily unable to function as persons, they would allow the potential to become a person to weigh in the balance when the decision to preserve or take human life is contemplated.

This potentiality too would increase as the pregnancy continued. As the fetus gains a greater probability of survival, it has more potential to become a person. Thus the common idea that abortion becomes morally less permissible the closer to birth that a fetus gets is buttressed by the conceptions of a person and of the social contract used here. On the other hand, the mother, as the most affected person, would be accorded strong rights to autonomy and bodily integrity by those in the original position. Within the limits of sympathy, the mother's rights would generally be more powerful than those of the fetus, as the rights of persons usually are over those of the merely human. The volunteers would be more concerned to protect their interests as persons because they would be more capable of suffering and pleasure as persons than human beings. It is common sense to worry more about what may happen to you when you can know about it and care about it than about what may happen when you would not know what hit you.

The foregoing raises the spectre of infanticide. There are few taboos stronger in our culture than that against killing innocent children. Yet newborn infants are not persons if membership in the class of persons depends on abilities. Their potential to become persons, however, is increased by birth since the probability of their surviving to become persons is greater than the probability of survival prior to birth. Our sympathy is also greatly increased once the infant is living in the world like ourselves rather than within the mother. Infanticide commonly goes beyond the limits of our sympathy.

It is useful to look at a culture in which infanticide has been deemed permissible, the Inuit culture. At times when there were insufficient resources to keep a family from starving, infants—as new mouths to feed—were put to death. In harsh conditions, a choice had to be made between the survival of a family and the survival of a newborn infant. To suppose that a human infant had an absolute right to live in such circumstances would be to condemn the family to slow suicide. When food is plentiful, the Inuit demonstrate abundant devotion to their young of the kind that one would expect of sympathetic people. The rules put forward by the volunteers would have to be applied in such a way as to give variable results with varying conditions. They would put persons first and protect human beings who are not persons as much as possible, while preserving persons.

Future interests

The right to life of persons generally outweighs the future interest[23] in a personal life of human beings who are not yet persons. To illustrate the concept of a future interest, consider a purchase of a valuable piece of art. The purchaser has, let us suppose, paid half the cost down and is paying the remainder of the price in instalments. On full payment, it is agreed, the purchaser will become the owner. Until then the purchaser cannot take the art. Nonetheless, the purchaser has an ever-strengthening future interest which, from a moral point of view, prevents the current owner from doing whatever she pleases. The current owner could not, for example, exhibit the work under risky conditions. Similarly, the closer a human being comes to being a person, the stronger entitlement that human being has, under the rubric of future interest, to such things as life-saving medical treatment. In Western societies, where resources are currently plentiful, the future interest of an infant is very strong indeed.

If we took a global view, then this future interest is weakened in competition with the rights of the needy persons already in existence throughout the world. Of course the sympathy for those close to us, particularly our own offspring, makes a usable set of rules take the global view only in so far as is necessary to provide some global safety net. No rule which required people to deprive their own newborns to save strangers in the Third World would be compatible with ordinary human sympathy. Restricting the number of children per couple in the wealthy countries would, however, be reasonable, assuming that a child born among the wealthy will use eight or more times the resources of a child born in the Third World.

Even looking only within our own society, there are cases where the future interest would be weak, indeed cases in which infanticide as a form of non-voluntary euthanasia would be permissible. Consider cases of birth defects too severe to allow a chance of development of the human infant into a person. If the prognosis were for two weeks of agony before an inevitable death, it would be better to kill a newborn infant than to merely allow it to die through the supposedly benign neglect of passive euthanasia. The very sympathy which prevents killing in most cases requires it in rare cases. Some cases will be very difficult to decide since we will have varying degrees of certainty about the chances a particular infant has to develop into a person. In our decisions, we should keep in mind the rights of the mother and other closely affected persons. These rights may outweigh the future interests of the infant. Fortunately, the cases in which these rights and future interests conflict are *relatively* rare. They are, however, heart-rending where they do occur, and we need strong principles such as those I have been suggesting to deal with them. We should put people first, just as the volunteers would require.

It may be thought that the deck is stacked if we ask the volunteers to write rules concerning abortion or infanticide. Even behind the veil of ignorance they would not believe they might be fetuses or infants. They are, however, unaware of their capacities. It might turn out that they are only potentially persons once the drug wears off, so far as they know. They would have to offer some protection to potential persons. Our sympathies toward potential persons to whom we are closely related amplify this point. Still, it makes more sense to be concerned about protecting one's life after one has developed to the point of being aware that one is a person. A failure of this protection could cause the volunteers greater suffering than a failure to protect merely potential persons. It is common sense to worry more about losing our life when we could agonize over it than about losing it when we would not be capable of valuing life.

Genetics and human reproduction

Questions frequently raised here concern the moral implications of selective abortion, genetic engineering, surrogate motherhood, and the rights and duties of biological parents. As we confront these issues, there are reasons to treat differently from persons human beings who are not yet persons. A look at some cases may illustrate the employment of the concept of a person introduced in the last chapter.

Selective abortion

Treatments for infertility, for example, may give rise to multiple pregnancies. This requires the abortion of some of the fetuses in such a case to maximize the chances of the others being brought to term. The rights of the parents as people are put foremost here. The future interests of the aborted fetuses as human beings are not dismissed, but they are outweighed by the rights of the parents plus the future interests of the fetuses which do live. The volunteers would be unlikely to change this given sufficient global resources to allow fertility clinics.

On the other hand, another case of selective abortion illustrates the ways in which cultures may collide because of disagreement about or lack of a concept of a person. Ultrasound clinics have opened that offer parents the knowledge of the gender of their fetuses. It is alleged that in some cases those who are anxious to have a male child abort female fetuses. Here the future interest of the female fetus in becoming a person outweighs the wishes of the parents, as we see things in the West. Unlike infertility, the lack of male offspring is not, in Western culture, often considered a significant harm to the parents. Human fetuses may not have a right to life, but they have a strong enough future interest in life to outweigh mere preferences as opposed to rights of persons. Putting persons first does not mean that any interest of a person will outweigh any interest of a non-person.

Population control

It is doubtful that the volunteers would uphold what we may suppose to be a right to have as many children as we wish. The whole discussion of fertility here has been, after all, within the context of affluent Western culture. If we were to take the global view, limits on the resources we use, including those we use by having children, might well be considered the right of those who are cut off from resources. Fertility clinics would perhaps be contrary to the rules the volunteers would write. Childless couples could be helped to adopt orphans from the Third World. Similarly, those with a strong desire for male offspring would be the objects of intensive education aimed at making the world's people care for the children who are already here rather than having many children to assure that one is a male. The desire to reproduce one's own genotype, however strong a drive it may be, can be sublimated in an affluent society, and there are many orphaned children elsewhere in the world needing our care. This moderates the effects of sympathy for the childless. To protect themselves, the volunteers would wish to restrict the creation of new people in cases where people in existence were unable to live good lives because of inadequate resources. Against this, the volunteers would have to weigh the degree to which having their own children would be essential to the development of their own capacities and thus to the enrichment of their lives as persons.

In any case, any restrictions on such personal matters as reproduction would have to be imposed in a way compatible with a counterbalancing interest of the volunteers. They would want to be as free as possible to make choices for themselves. For example, in case they turn out to be on the outside looking in, the volunteers would want to make sure that efforts to control population in the Third World were not coercive but aimed at bettering the economic circumstances of the people there, giving people the incentives and the education needed for them to want smaller families as we do in the wealthier nations. Giving women control of the use of their bodies for reproduction would probably also be favoured by the volunteers whose gender has been concealed from them.

Genetic engineering

Now that it seems imminent that geneticists will be able to stitch in genes for tallness, athletic ability, and other characteristics which parents may wish to have in their offspring, the question arises whether we should limit intervention in the development of the fetus. Are genetic alterations significantly different, from a moral point of view, to other advantages parents give to their fetuses and to their children? Certainly if there is a danger that the alterations will realize part of Mary Wollstonecraft Shelley's nightmare in the novel *Frankenstein,* then the future interest of the fetus and other potential victims would outweigh the parents' wishes. Stringent precautions must be taken to ensure fetal health and human development whether or not genetic alterations are induced. The self-interest of those in the original position would require this; they would not want to live in a world full of failed experiments.

Within reason, the rights of the parents to enhance the lives of their offspring are again foremost, and genetic alteration might be permissible by the volunteers' rules, if it is known with reasonable degree of probability to be beneficial to the fetus while unlikely to harm anyone else. After all, the volunteers would take into account their possible future role and desires as parents. It is difficult, however, to predict future harms coming from such radical changes. What if the people in the affluent countries could be made biologically superior to those elsewhere? Genetic engineering could widen the gap already existing between rich and poor both globally and within nations. The volunteers would try to make rules that would not exacerbate existing inequities. Use of genetic alteration would have to be strictly controlled to make sure that it was beneficial to most persons, not just a lucky few.

Surrogate motherhood

The questions here concern primarily the rights of the so-called surrogate mother. She, as a person, has a right to bodily integrity under the terms acceptable in the original position. She cannot be treated as a baby factory, nor can the fetus which is dependent on her body be thought of as the property of another. Those in the original position would be more concerned about protecting their interests in case they wound up in the mother's shoes than they would should they turn out to be one of those wishing to have someone else bear a child. The reason is that the mother is generally more vulnerable to harm, and the volunteers have no idea whether they are likely to be in the situation of the mother.

The resulting child in such a case might be in some ways better served by being placed in the care of the couple who hired the woman to bear that fetus. Usually the couple is wealthy and the mother acts out of financial necessity. Nonetheless, the future interests of the fetus cannot outweigh the right of the mother to determine what happens in her body. After the birth, the mother should also, if competent, be allowed to parent the child if she chooses. In the original position, those choosing the rules would frame them in such a way as to give themselves rights acquired by extending themselves physically as the mother has done. Rules which ignore the strong bond between mother and child, and the sympathy which people have for the mother, in this instance would be defeated by the conditions on the volunteers' choices. The disappointed couple might still have some rights to recompense for support given to the mother during the pregnancy. Perhaps they could even be given the option of co-parent-ing the child. Again, in the position of the volunteers, it makes sense to hedge one's bets to protect one's future interests, but they would protect the most vulnerable first. Common sense requires this of those who might turn out to be among the most vulnerable.

Foreign aid

Recall now the committee choosing the rules, a committee struck by the United Nations to hammer out a revised charter of the rights of people throughout the world. The participants, behind a veil of ignorance as they are, would not know what countries they come from. They would come up with rather different rules for distributing the world's wealth than do the wealthy and powerful nations of the world. These rules would, if the committee members each assiduously pursued her own self-interest, reflect approximately a 20 percent chance of landing in an economically good situation and an 80 percent chance of landing in a bad one. The volunteers who are instructed to act on self-interest would not want such a punitive redistribution of wealth as to destroy their luck if they were in wealthy nations. They would, however, insist that much more be done to give the poor a reasonable return for their labour and resources, most of the benefits of which flow rapidly into the wealthy nations. To develop to the fullest of one's abilities, to be as much a person as one can be, to have fulfilling relationships with other persons, one needs ample resources. Personal development is, for most human beings, dependent on economic development. Much of what is now considered charity coming from the wealthy to the poor would be duty under rules framed by the volunteers.

Heading into the unknown, the volunteers would want a chance for the best but not for the worst. It would make sense for them to limit the worst-case scenario for their futures even at the cost of limiting the best outcome. It would be wise for them to ensure that the duty of all was to provide a minimum standard of living for everyone in the world. This might involve population control, but probably the rate of increase of the population goes down as economic well being goes up.[24] Providing themselves with a safety net would be common sense caution for the volunteers even if it meant that they could only have the potential to be millionaires instead of billionaires, should they make a lucky landing in the real world. Certainly a right to life-saving aid would be a minimal part of the safety net. The wealthy would be required to overcome famine in other parts of the world.

This raises the question to what degree the wealthy could be obligated to suffer to aid the poor. The volunteers, remember, make their decisions based on self-interest. Since they have a chance of being wealthy, they do not wish to allow rules which require extreme sacrifice to aid others who are starving abroad. In any case, our sympathies are directed mainly at those with whom we are in close contact; so no rule requiring saintliness in aid of foreigners would be acceptable to the volunteers who try to fashion rules that people with ordinary human sympathies could follow. The volunteers might accept a rule which says that, far beyond the basic necessities, the wealthy could keep enough wealth—hence, enough power—to ensure reasonable security. They could keep the wealth needed to respond confidently to natural disasters and the attacks of other people. Even by such a generous standard, we have a surfeit in the industrialized nations which should be used to fashion a global safety net to prevent any person from falling out of reach of a minimum supply of food, shelter, and medical care.

Future people

The metaphor of the committee of anesthetized volunteers has been stretched to its limits. We can, however, extrapolate beyond them the notion of fairness which emerges from the preceding examples. Imagine, although it takes quite a feat of imagination, that the volunteers do not know when they will live. Ignorant as they are about some facts, they might believe a white lie to the effect that some of them would be preserved for life in the future. Would they share our current rules for preserving resources for future generations? For instance, we seem to act by the maxim: preserve only what is nearly extinguished. In self-interest, they would not want any generation to sacrifice its economic and personal development entirely for the people yet to come. Nonetheless, they would look askance at our current profligacy in using up whatever comes to hand. Sustainable development of resources would be, in the hope that one can make practical sense of it, a requirement laid down in the original position.

Current people would be required to keep options open for future generations as well. If we can use wind, geo-thermal, wave action, and solar power sources to supplement or replace the use of non-renewable resources and nuclear power, we ought to do so. In other words the volunteers would choose rules which bias decisions about resources so as to avoid doing anything irreversible. This reversibility rule and several other rules offered by Goodin[25] as an improvement on simple consequentialist reasoning characterize the application of common sense in the original position to management of resources for the future. The volunteers would be potentially at risk if they allowed current generations to leave radioactive waste as a legacy to future generations in the hope that they will find some way to deal with it. In effect, nuclear plants are forever. The decision to use other power sources is reversible. Some of Goodin's other suggestions are that decisions be biased to do the following: make the worst possible outcomes of our decisions as good as we can ensure, give special protection to the vulnerable, create sustainable benefits, and avoid causing harm as distinct from merely foregoing benefits. These are the sorts of policies which would be reasonable from the point of view of the volunteers who want to protect themselves wherever and whenever they land in society.

The interests of future generations cannot be ignored. At the same time future persons cannot be treated in the same way as existing persons. We do not know whether people will exist at all in the future. It would not make sense to sacrifice every luxury now to extend the best possible resource allocation to the future. We can still put currently existing persons first without ignoring future generations. We should not mortgage the future to provide current luxuries and preferences, but we should not sacrifice current persons' needs to those of persons in an uncertain future.

Respect for persons

From the original position, the desire of women to be treated as persons is completely reasonable. Ignorant as they are of their gender, the choosers of rules in the original position would wish to maximize their own chances of personal development. This is primarily a matter of exercising and improving upon one's capacities, given the way persons are understood in the previous chapter. The committee would strike down barriers to occupying any position in society which are based not on ability but on gender. Volunteers are charged with self-protection. They just do not know who they are or what gender they have.

Feminism

Objections may come from those who think that this plays into the hands of the liberal individualist tradition and ignores the ideas of the social person and partiality described earlier in this chapter. This is not so. Mothering may well be a person's most important defining ability. Realizing this, the volunteers would not set rules so as to devalue the abilities more commonly associated with women. The ability to hold together relationships and the partiality on which that depends would influence the volunteers. They would be wary of setting rules that would devalue such abilities and make them always secondary to the public life in which impartiality is necessary. Great judges and great mothers might be similarly honoured and compensated for their service in the sort of society that would protect all of the common interests of the volunteers.

Another kind of objection comes from those who think that fairness starting now would not be adequate given the systemic unfairness of the past. Some feminists, for instance, have asked for reverse discrimination in order to bring the genders into a balance of power. The idea is that to break some of the invisible barriers—glass ceilings and the like—we need to give women the advantage men have had for so long. A person on the committee would be concerned about turning out to be of a gender which is at a disadvantage and so might allow the judicious use of some tools such as reverse discrimination as a last resort. These tools would have to be carefully guarded to ensure that a balance was created between the genders rather than a new form of imbalance, since only by ensuring balance would those behind a veil of ignorance, which conceals their genders even from themselves, be likely to protect themselves.

Racism

The issues here are similar. Racists fail to treat some people as persons. They do this by not recognizing capacities and by preventing the exercise of capacities in some visibly different group of people.

Behind the veil of ignorance one does not know one's own skin colour. Rules and tools, such as reverse discrimination, would all be directed by the volunteers at giving every human being a reasonable chance to develop as a person. The volunteers would support the ideal of equal opportunity since they would have no idea what skin colour or what opportunities they might have.

It is worth noting as an aside that equal opportunity can only make sense for those who have the autonomy of persons. That is why it is a mistake to try to capitalize on the gains made against racial intolerance to institute the same policies where intolerance of the mentally challenged is at issue. Certainly the mentally challenged should be better treated, but it is folly to treat some as if they had capacities other people normally have. Under the banner of equal opportunity, some students in my locale have been placed in classes with regular students and, as a result, are ill served by being in a classroom which is hopelessly beyond their level of competence both intellectually and socially. Others have benefited greatly by such educational mainstreaming, but individual cases must be judged in terms of capacities for doing the work and forming the relationships necessary to thrive. Mental ability cannot be treated as an irrelevant characteristic such as skin colour when such decisions are made. What is fair in preventing racial discrimination does not necessarily work in every case where a group is singled out for different treatment.

Slavery and prostitution

What is wrong with people being bought and sold like commodities is simply that it is grotesquely unfair, as can be seen by contemplating the rules volunteers would make from the original position. Self-interest would surely motivate the volunteers to rule against any sale of persons. The capacities which give people their dignity are largely ignored in such transactions. Even if a slave is valued for an ability to write poetry or do mathematics, a great wrong is done in reducing her achievements to commodities. One is most oneself when one is exercising one's capacities to the fullest, and it is precisely then that it is most horrible to be treated as the property of another. People in the original position would want to be able to take their places in the class of autonomous beings.

Slavery has not been wiped out in our world. People are still bought and sold as if they were machines made to perform labour. Much more common than the purchased labourer, however, is the prostitute; most obviously when a prostitute is under the control of a pimp and forced to work to enrich that pimp, a prostitute is a slave. When there is no pimp, the question still arises whether the alternatives are so bleak that prostitution is a form of self-enslavement to a series of masters. Examples are not so far to seek: an obvious one is that, for children in the slums of Third World countries who must sell themselves to live, prostitution with no pimp is still slavery.

It is a moral commonplace that it is not only wrong to enslave others but morally wrong to offer oneself as a slave. From the position taken here, the sin is in both cases the same: one denies the existence of a special class, the class of persons. One reduces persons, in such acts, to the level of a trained bear, a being which cannot choose what it will be. This right to choose for oneself would be fundamental to the volunteers as they tried to ensure their future well being. A rule against slavery would be part of the safety net they would weave to ensure that no person could fall too far, no matter how unwise her personal decisions. Of course such a rule only makes sense within a network of rules ensuring that no one falls so low economically as to be reduced to slavery for survival. As in the other issues discussed here, the volunteers would exercise common sense caution if they fashioned safety nets to prevent themselves from falling too far. These nets would be worth the price which might be ceilings to prevent them from rising too high.

Civil liberties

Those in the original position would want to retain as much individual freedom as possible while protecting the global community by controlling such personal matters as reproduction. Most of us would prefer to be the judges of what is in our own interest as opposed to having the state decide for us. Freedoms of speech, association, religion, and movement are fundamental to putting people in charge of their own further development as persons. Where restrictions are necessary for the general good, as with population control, the volunteers would make rules that bias policies in favour of eliciting voluntary change. Education and economic betterment are, from the volunteers' point of view, far better means to controlling population than law. If more coercive measures such as economic disincentives are used to bring about the good of the global community, these should be applied in the same way to all, without favouritism. Many special interest groups have taken of late to calling their privileges "rights." If we look at these from the original position, we can, perhaps, better distinguish the two. At least the traditional civil liberties and other means essential to the maintenance and development of the capacities of persons should be protected as rights. It makes common sense for the volunteers to promote these.

Moral relativism

A favourite question of students in introductory ethics classes is Who's to say? A favourite answer of mine is, You are. There seems to be a common view that what is morally right depends somehow on persons, times, or places. At its most extreme, relativism becomes subjectivism, the view that what is morally right depends on each individual person's values. Usually the relativists one encounters are closet absolutists believing as they do that there are some absolute values which everyone must accept. For example, they often say, You shouldn't try to push your values on me! Everyone's got his own. This, if it means anything, is contradictory. The relativist is saying that it is absolutely morally wrong to interfere with others' moral decisions since morality is relative to individual values, not absolute. But this is to say that something—interference—is absolutely wrong although nothing is absolutely wrong. Another way of exposing the problem is to reply to the relativist who demands to be let alone, But *I* value interference.

Objective rights

Usually the absolutist tries to pin the relativist in a contradiction,[26] then goes on to promulgate some rule or rules of conduct which are said to be independent of when or where or by whom an act is done. Utilitarians ask us to look only at the consequences of the conduct. Maximize happiness and minimize suffering is the one rule of the hedonistic, act utilitarian.[27] The concept of a person becomes relatively unimportant, since any sentient being can be happy or suffer. Hence the distinction between the wider class of human beings and the narrower included class of persons which I have been trying to make is not morally significant on this view. Other moral theorists—non-consequentialists—emphasize the importance of something in addition to the consequences. Often the additional things are moral rights.

For every right there is a rule. The rules chosen in the original position, for example, correspond to a set of rights of persons and duties of persons. Suppose, for instance, the volunteers accept the rule that people ought to give life-saving aid to those people—or at least those in their immediate vicinity—who are in danger of dying as long as the saviours can do so without serious injury to their bodies or their life prospects. The rule would have to be further qualified and hedged to avoid counter-examples, but some heavily qualified rule of that sort would be in the self-interest of the volunteers. Now if Sam sees Erik drowning, Sam has a duty to save Erik, and Erik has a right to be saved, under the social contract rule; that is, Sam has such a duty if Sam, for instance, need merely throw in a life preserver. The question then arises whether such rights and duties are absolute, or relative to persons, times, and places.

I wish to say that there are some senses in which rights are relative, but that they are objective. Using Nagel's view on objectivity which was briefly explicated above, I will say that rights are to a high degree objective. That is to say that rights are mainly independent of the values of individual persons. Rights are, though, fundamentally rights of persons and, as I have argued, a person is a concept relative to cultures. Indeed there may well be cultures without any morally important concept of a person.

To illustrate, imagine that I am in a moral dispute with someone from a society which wants to revive an ancient custom that requires that women be burned alive on their husband's funeral pyres. My opponent accuses me of cultural imperialism when I try to persuade people of his locale to prohibit the practice. In his culture, he tells me, it is nonsense to attach great importance to individual human beings. There is no clear concept of a person in his society. The family is the morally central unit. Any individual within the family may be sacrificed for the family's well being just as we might remove tonsils from a human body as a preventative measure. The idea of persons and their rights as individuals makes no more sense to him than the rights of tonsils would to us. I would reply that I see it as my duty to change his culture. I would rather be politically incorrect than derelict in such a duty. I should work to change any culture, my own included, which treats people in a way so obviously inconsistent with the rules which would be chosen from the original position. While the nature of such rules may be moot in some cases, there can be no doubt in this one. The volunteers would rule against such practices as this sacrifice of women since it is clearly in their interest to protect themselves from such practices. Those who argue for such practices usually know they are not going to suffer from them. This illustrates the role of the veil of ignorance that hides from the volunteers their own genders.

How is my position different from that sort of missionary who goes into a culture with the idea of making it like her own and who has no tolerance or respect for the customs of the people in cultures foreign to her own? In the original position, the volunteers would not know what culture they came from. They would not want others riding roughshod over their customs in the real world. Tolerance and respect would be written into the rules in their self-interest. Nonetheless, they would want protection from their own culture where it would deprive them of life, limb or liberty for the sake of others' interests. They would not want any practice, like the funeral practice just described, that could undermine their interests entirely. The volunteers would rule out any form of ritual human sacrifice. They would insist on core personal protections to be observed in every culture (through a set of inter-cultural rules) while accepting the role of each culture in determining its own rules where persons are not threatened. Cultures could determine, for instance, whether polygamy or monogamy would be the norm, but according to the rules the volunteers would choose, no culture could institute torture of persons. My view, therefore, does not entail standard cultural imperialism. It does insist on protection of an individual's fundamental rights independent of the culture the individual occupies. The fundamental rights are those specified by the rules the volunteers would choose to protect themselves, no matter what culture they might turn out to occupy in the real world as opposed to the original position.

My decision to resist the horrific funeral practice has the appearance of being independent of my culture. My opponent, however, responds that the original position which I imagine makes no sense to him. What is a committee of persons? Make it a committee of families, perhaps, and the rules would alter to preserve less fanatically the individual. My opponent and I are clearly embedded each in his own culture as far as our moral thinking goes. Even if we put a high value on tolerance of the customs of others, there are limits to my tolerance if I take people and their rights seriously. There is no *absolute* standard to which we in the West can appeal as we argue with the Indigenous peoples of the Americas or the peoples of the Third World about dignity and respect for persons. This is not to say that anything goes, or that when in Rome we should do as the Romans do. There are various kinds of *objectivity* available to us even if no *absolute* standard is available.

First we can be objective in the sense of following non-contradictory sets of moral principles. My opponent cannot say that each culture determines its own morality; so my culture is morally wrong to interfere with his. This puts an absolute value on non-interference which would make him an inconsistent relativist. I could simply and truthfully say that my culture values interference where the fundamental rights of persons are at stake. Secondly, we can have the objectivity that comes from the veil of ignorance. As this element of the social contract is understood, the rules are those which would be in the interest of any persons in any culture whether or not they think of themselves as persons. There is then, a vast difference, to my opponent's objection to having the concept of persons introduced to his culture and his objection to having a foreign religion foisted on his people. Although we are a proselytizing culture, not all that we preach is religious in source nor need it be in the narrow self-interest of our own culture. Indeed, if we acted according to our own rules across cultures, we would treat other peoples of the world much better than we do. It is objectively right that we reform our own conduct and interfere with the conduct of others when it is not in accord with the rules that would be chosen from the original position. The unfortunate spouse on the funeral pyre might well agree.

The moral rectitude of this interference is, nonetheless, relative to Western cultural concepts such as that of a person. If I pretend that our morality is absolute, I contradict myself as a moral relativist. Yet I comfort myself with the objectivity of the moral claims which are based on the social contract. Concerning cultural interference I can say that I do not wish to change other cultures except in so far as they undermine persons. It is unfortunate that I must choose between my respect for cultures and my respect for persons, but persons must win. Mine is a Western morality. This is figuratively represented in the metaphor by the volunteers' use of Western standards of rationality and common sense as they choose rules in their self-interest.

The moral view summarized here is one which is intended to have a broad appeal since it takes seriously the rights of all persons at all times everywhere. It is a nod in the direction of the unattainable absolute standard of morality. While it fails to achieve such a standard, since person is a relative concept, my view does not devolve in the other direction to subjectivism. While I do not think that there are accessible to us any absolute standards, akin to Plato's Forms, I do try to view reality, knowledge, and value as part of a systematic whole. Our principles of metaphysics, epistemology, and ethics, seen as principles the volunteers would choose, are objective though culturally relative. We have a place to stand, a place from which to consider what we are, what we can know, and what we should do.

Human rights as opposed to rights of persons

It might be thought, however, that we could escape this cultural relativity by appeal to *human* rights instead of the rights of *persons*. Could we not use a social contract for the purpose of deciding what rights human beings shall have with the result that persons would have only human rights along with human non-persons? If the committee members could be ignorant of their status as persons, then they might decide questions differently concerning such matters as abortion, for example. But if the idea is to suppose that the volunteers are not necessarily persons, this is to suppose a contradiction. If any social contract is to be made, the makers have to have the abilities of persons pertinent to the making of a contract; hence, they must be persons, not mere human beings. It is, after all, impossible to be ignorant of one's capacities exercised in making a contract while one is making the contract which concerns honouring those very capacities. Even the general knowledge of people and the human condition, which those in the original position must have, would assure them that they are not mere human beings who lack the capacities of persons. Acting in their self-interest they would give themselves special rights over and above any they would give to human non-persons.

Potential

Most of the rights which would be granted to human non-persons by the volunteers in the original position would be granted because these humans will be persons or have been persons. Some will be granted because of our sympathy for those who resemble persons. To say, however, that human beings deserve different treatment from that accorded to other animals simply because they have human chromosomes,[28] for instance, seems rather arbitrary. Chimpanzees share much of our chromosomal makeup; they, however, seem to be unable to become persons who are self-creating. They apparently cannot choose what they want to desire, but act on desires they have by nature. If, however, they can be shown to have the capacities for free will and self-creation and other capacities above the threshold for persons, then their non-human character would be morally irrelevant. They would have the rights of persons. If they only come close to being persons but are below the threshold, then they may acquire some rights by virtue of their resemblance to persons. As for human non-persons, while it may be useful to distinguish between human rights and rights of persons, the former are dependent on the latter. Furthermore, although human rights are possible given the rules fashioned by the volunteers, human non-persons could not have duties since they do not have the ability to do them.

On the other hand, we have already built into the fiction of the original position the idea that the volunteers might be fooled into thinking that it is possible that they would be merely potential persons once they were removed from the original position. They might be in some state of suspended animation, they are told, to live as persons in a future generation. To thicken the veil of ignorance, they might also be given to believe that the effects of being volunteers on this committee could result in their becoming merely human non-persons. I still think that common sense would guide them to give rights primarily to persons and only in a subsidiary way to non-persons. After all, there is less point to having advantages of which one could not be aware than to having advantages which one can enjoy as a person. As a mere human, one could enjoy pleasure and suffer pain. Persons have, however, much wider scope for their enjoyment and suffering. People can anticipate a future life or an imminent death. Non-persons do not have the capacities needed for such anticipation.

Sympathy

Human rights would reflect the need for rules which can be followed by people with the sympathies we typically have. This is built into the instructions given to the volunteers. Considering our sympathies for human beings whether persons or not, we would make rules against cruelty to sentient beings. Not only would such rules be of the kind which people with typical sympathies can follow, they would be in the self-interest of the volunteers if only since what is done to sentient beings who are not people may very well be extended to people. It is also self-interest to avoid having one's own sympathies offended. People in the original position know they have human feeling. Even dead human bodies have rights since there is some behaviour toward them which would not be tolerated by people in the original position. In general, the volunteers would tend to disallow anything which undermines sympathy for those like the volunteers, whether like them only in outward form or in capacity to suffer. It is common sense to minimize cruelty in the community one must join. In this we see the dovetailing of two features of the original position: the pursuit of self-interest by the volunteers and their recognition that their rules must be acceptable to those with ordinary human sympathy.

So what should we do?

From the history of what we have believed ourselves to be, I have cobbled together a concept of a person. It is interdependent with social contracts of a moral, metaphysical, and epistemic kind. It is Byzantine in its complexity. It gives us initial answers to the questions, What is a person? and What makes a person at one time identical to a person at another time? Supposing that I am right in my speculations as to which elements of our views about what we are can be consistently and fruitfully maintained, the question now arises, What good does it do us? The pragmatists discussed in chapter 7 would want to know how such a concept would affect us if we were to take it up into our lives. That has, I hope, been partially answered by this chapter on applications. In general I would say this: as the secret to survival is knowing what to throw away and knowing what to keep,[29] one should develop one's essence, one's special capacities, to the fullest. One should cherish and preserve these individuating capacities. This is what lies behind the advice to be oneself and to live life to the fullest. One should also promote a world in which people can live well. Seen through Western eyes, this is only common sense.

Content questions

1. How is the concept of the original position used to speculate on the ideal social contract in social contract theory?
2. Describe the condition of people in the original position (the volunteers in our metaphor) with respect to power, intelligence, self-interest, and knowledge.
3. How is ablism avoided by the theory proposed here?
4. Why would people in the original position not put forward rules that would favour a few people in the hopes that they would turn out to be among the favoured few in the real world?
5. How is sexism in the ideal social contract ruled out?
6. What is the decontextualization objection and social contractarian reply?
7. Why is the allocation of health care on a first-come-first-served basis wrong from the social contractarian point of view?
8. Why is paternalism with respect to access to information not acceptable to those in the original position?
9. What, for the social contract theory sketched here, is the relevance of resemblance to persons where moral questions concerning non-persons is concerned?
10. Distinguish the various varieties of euthanasia.

11. Why would the volunteers oppose selective abortion of female fetuses to ensure male offspring?
12. Why, given that the volunteers base their decisions on self-interest, would the volunteers not devise rules that require us to equalize the wealth of nations?
13. What in general, on the view proposed here, are our obligations to future generations?
14. Why would the volunteers protect such traditional civil liberties as freedom of speech, association, religion, and movement?
15. Why would it be wrong to try to impose a religion on a foreign culture but still right to interfere with some practices like that of burning a wife on her husband's funeral pyre?
16. Why would the volunteers accept the concept of human rights that apply to non-persons?
17. What general advice is given at the end of this chapter?

Arguments for analysis

Argument 1: The moral weight objection revisited

Because the concept of a person is importantly dependent on abilities, the level of abilities of persons must determine moral worth. This is little better than the might is right doctrine. Those who are born with lesser abilities will be considered less worthy. The accidents of birth should not determine whom we respect.

Argument 2: The contractarian reply

It is now possible to reply more completely to this argument. Those in the original position would never accept discrimination based on the accidents of birth. After all, they do not know what they will have, in the way of abilities, by birth. It would not be in their interests to allow such discrimination. The veil of ignorance protects us from the unfair assigning of moral weight.

Argument 3: The ignorance objection

We cannot know what people would decide about the rules in the original position. They might choose irrationally, acting like gamblers in favour of a lopsided distribution of benefits. Who knows what their tolerance for risk would be? In any case, we cannot define persons or personal identity nor decide on moral rules using the ideal social contract since we cannot tell what it would be.

Argument 4: The common sense reply

In this version of the social contract theory, the people in the original position are assumed to exercise common sense as traditionally understood in the West. The tolerance for risk would have to be rational by this standard. This standard is not precise but is captured with sufficient clarity by Aristotle's advice to seek the mean between extremes. In taking risks we should be neither foolhardy nor timid but courageous. While this does not tell us exactly what might be decided by those in the original position, it rules out the extremes on which the ignorance objection depends. It gives us a narrow enough range of possibilities to give us some plausible ideas about what persons are, when a person survives, and what we ought to do.

Argument 5: The relativity objection

The kind of social contract described here does not help us to understand persons, personal identity, or morality but merely versions of these relative to Western culture. Instead of what we think in the West, philosophy should give us the truth about these matters.

Argument 6: The objectivity reply

Instead of chasing unattainable absolute standards, this social contract theory tries to make the standards as objective as possible. Although they are of necessity culturally relative, the standards do not simply favour that culture. Behind the veil of ignorance, the volunteers would not know what culture they will inherit. This makes it counter to their interests to simply make Western culture predominate. Tolerance of other cultures would be a value that those in the original position would be motivated to adopt. There would be clear limits on tolerance that the inhabitants of the original position would have to accept to protect themselves. Cultural behaviour such as slavery or prejudice against other cultures would be examples of things that must be contrary to rules chosen behind the veil of ignorance. Whoever does not know her own race, creed, or colour will want these things to be irrelevant to social position. The effect of such an ideal social contract is to justify rules that are probably as close as we can get to the absolutes we long for but cannot find.

Argument 7: The extreme pro-life contractarian argument

Since persons in the original position would not know if they were persons in the real world or only human beings with the potential to become persons, it would be in their interest to completely disallow abortion. From the hypothetical original position, they might be sheltering their own revivals in the real world. A corollary to this argument is that those in the original position would have to set rules that would require extreme measures for protecting future generations since they might be members of one of those generations.

Argument 8: The moderation reply

On the contrary, it is in the interests of volunteers in the original position to avoid extremes and rules that admit of no exceptions. Behind a veil of ignorance one does not know if one is a potential mother in a desperate situation. The easy cases are those where the mother's life is threatened. Those in the original position would not want to sacrifice an actual person to preserve the life of a human being who had the potential to become a person. If they allowed such sacrifice in the case of abortion, they would have to allow it for future generations. People in those generations would have the right to reduce us to abject penury now to preserve their chances to live later. This could be argued in each generation. This leads us to the absurdity that each generation must sacrifice its interests for the many people yet to come. In both the abortion and future generations arguments, the actual persons should not be sacrificed to preserve merely potential persons. These considerations, however, have minimal force when it comes to ending a healthy pregnancy in which the mother is not threatened with physical injury. That leads us to the degrees of potentiality reply.

Argument 9: The degrees of potentiality reply

In the original position, volunteers would have to ask themselves what degree of potentiality would move them to protect a future person. After all, if we allow this for any degree we get absurdities. If we confer rights on a zygote (a newly fertilized ovum) because it has the potential to form part of a process that may ultimately lead to a person, then we would have to do so for the unfertilized ovum or the sperm as well. The sperm and ovum after all do have some potential to form part of such a process. Without the idea that a soul enters the zygote at conception, conception does not form a clear dividing line. We have, instead of sharp dividing lines, a continuing process. As the process continues, the potential for this process to eventuate in a person becomes greater. In other words, the probability that the process will cause a person to exist becomes greater. In the original position we would, no doubt, think it a foolish decision to sacrifice the interests of existing persons in order to maximize the chance of each sperm to be part of such a process. The potential of the fetus just before birth, however, is much greater. At that point we would want to give it protection that could perhaps only be overridden by a very serious physical threat to the mother. At each stage of development of the fetus, there is a difficult judgment call concerning which interests of the mother are strong enough to outweigh the interests of the future person that depend on the life of the fetus. There is a gradual change and a gradual increase in the future interest of the fetus in life.

Argument 10: The sympathy reply

At the same time as the fetus is increasing its potential to become a person, it is increasing its resemblance to a newborn. With this increased resemblance comes increased sympathy of persons for the fetus. Whatever rules regarding the fetus would be chosen in the original position, they would have to be rules that could be followed by people with normal sympathies. A moral system that requires that such sympathies be ignored is probably not one that could gain a wide following. The rules of the ideal social contract could not require us to treat a zygote as we would an adult human being. By the same token, they could not require us to distinguish greatly between a fetus shortly prior to birth and a newborn baby. The result would be a varied response to the permissibility of abortion depending on the stage of development of the fetus.

Argument 11: The chance of error argument

Since death is irrevocable, euthanasia should never be used. Just as we rule out the death penalty because of the possibility of error, we should rule out euthanasia. The patient may err about the severity or degree of suffering that the patient is facing. Diagnoses can be mistaken. In the original position, it would be in our interest to protect ourselves from premature death by disallowing death as a means to treat suffering.

Argument 12: The adequate safeguards reply

Sometimes the chance of error is so minimal and the suffering so great that it would be very much in our interest to be able to choose death. People with throat cancer suffering from air starvation as the tumor chokes them slowly are in this position. This sort of circumstance is relatively rare in developed countries today as pain control has made many courses of disease bearable. In the original position, not knowing whether we might be in one of the situations where life is unbearable, we would insist on the right to euthanasia once we are adequately informed and not acting from temporary despondency. Adequate safeguards to prevent the mistaken use or abuse of euthanasia are key to its acceptance in the original position. They must be strong enough to make premature death by error much less likely than unbearable suffering would be if euthanasia were banned outright. In any case, it would be severely restricted.

Argument 13: The Frankenclass argument

If we allow genetic alteration of human beings, then we will end up with the "gen-rich" (ie, genetically rich class) and the "gen-poor" as the Princeton biologist Lee Silver calls them.[30] Those who control the means of genetic enhancement will make themselves into an oligarchy by keeping superior abilities within their class. Ultimately they will form a superior species or set of species. From the point of view of those in the original position, the chances of getting left behind in the gen-poor class or species would be great. Wealth and power will be even more concentrated than they are now.

Argument 14: The defence of necessity

Disallowing genetic alteration of human beings could condemn many to suffering and disease that might be prevented. This consideration would weigh heavily in the hypothetical original position. More importantly, now that the technology is available, some governments may well use it for nefarious purposes, even if most governments refrain from using it. It is better therefore, that research in this area continue under the strictest safeguards. If genetic alteration of human beings could be stopped entirely, it might well be best to stop it. Since it probably cannot be stopped and since non-proliferation treaties are limited in their effect, it is better that it be pursued and well understood by those who are committed to use it for the betterment of the entire human species and by those who might stop abuses. The parallels with nuclear power are disturbing. In the original position, we would be stuck with choosing the lesser of two evils. That is, we would have to accept continuation of research under governments thought to be somewhat on the side of the angels rather than leaving it to the other side entirely.

Argument 15: The imbalance argument

Social contract theories cannot work since the constraints of the original position always lead to excessive protections. For example, since nobody would want to be in a position where medical care is inadequate, moral rules from the original position would create duties to give everyone all necessary care. This could create an allocation of resources that utterly undermines the ability of a society to progress even in such areas as medical research. So much would be devoted to practical health care that cultural, economic, and scientific progress would by stymied.

Argument 16: The self-answering reply

Like many objections to social contract theory, this one contains within itself the seeds of its own reply. By pointing to possible problems with a policy that supposedly would be accepted in the original position, the objection tells us how to alter the policy within the original position. In that position, if we really did think that imbalance in the use of resources would be a consequence of a given rule, we would modify that rule to correct the imbalance. Consider two rules affecting the particular imbalance suggested:

1. Everyone must be protected from physical suffering of any kind all of the time.
2. Decisions should be biased to prevent physical suffering of persons, but some such suffering may be allowed for educational purposes, for voluntary development of the individual, or to achieve significant cultural, economic, and scientific goals. These goals and purposes must be sought within a system of benefits accessible to all and must always benefit those who suffer most.

If the imbalance objection has merit in the view of the volunteers in the original position, then they will accept rules more like the second than the first.

Notes

Chapter 1

1 G.E. Moore, *Principia Ethica* (Cambridge: Cambridge University Press, 1971), p. 13.
2 P.F. Strawson, *Individuals: An Essay in Descriptive Metaphysics* (London: Methuen, 1959).
3 Amelie Oksenberg Rorty, "A Literary Postscript: Characters, Persons, Selves and Individuals," in *The Identities of Persons* (Berkeley: University of California Press, 1976), p. 301.
4 Adolf Trendelenberg, "A Contribution to the History of the Word Person: A Posthumous Treatise by Adolf Trendelenberg," trans. Carl H. Haessler, *The Monist* 20 (1910): 353.
5 Herbert Morris, "Persons and Punishment," *The Monist* 52, 4 (October 1968), repr. in Joel Feinberg, *Philosophy of Law*, 2nd ed. (Belmont, CA: Wadsworth, 1975), p. 582.
6 Trendelenberg, p. 338.
7 Immanuel Kant, *Grundlegung der Metaphysik der Sitten* [Foundation of Metaphysical Ethics], 1785, quoted in Trendelenberg, p. 337.
8 Jeremy Bentham, *An Introduction to the Principles of Morals and Legislation*, chap. 17, n. 330. in *The Utilitarians* (New York: Anchor Books, 1973) p. 381.
9 Max Black, "The Identity of Indiscernibles," *Mind* ns 61 (1952): 153-64.
10 Warren Bourgeois, "The Identity of Indiscernibles" (doctoral thesis, University of California, Irvine, 1979), chap. 1 and pp. 33-47.

11 Milton C. Nahm, *Selections from Early Greek Philosophy*, 3rd ed. (New York: Appleton-Century-Crofts, 1947), p. 91.
12 Abraham Kaplan, *The Conduct of Inquiry: Methodology for Behavioural Science* (New York: Chandler Publishing, 1964), p. 11.
13 See, for example, the discussion on Bernard Williams and Derek Parfit in chapters 11 and 13, respectively.
14 Kathleen Wilkes, *Real People: Personal Identity without Thought Experiments* (Oxford: Clarendon Press, 1988), pp. 6-12.
15 Ayer attributes this bon mot and decisive objection to Ogden and Richards. See A.J. Ayer, "The Concept of a Person," in *The Concept of a Person and Other Essays* (London: Macmillan, 1963), p. 101. The general idea is that those who have sensations have minds; so materialists in denying their own minds deny they have sensations. Global anaesthesia deprives one of sensations.
16 Ludwig Wittgenstein, *Tractatus Logico-Philosophicus*, trans. D.F. Pears and B.F. MacGuiness (London: Routledge and Kegan Paul, 1961), 6.54, p. 74.
17 Wittgenstein, 5.64, 5.641, p. 58.
18 David Berlinski, *Philosophy: The Cutting Edge* (Port Washington, NY: Alfred Publishing, 1976), p. xi.

Chapter 2

1 Solomon Asch, "The Psychology of Relativism," in *Social Psychology* (Englewood Cliffs, NJ: Prentice Hall, 1952), repr. in Arthur J. Minton, *Philosophy: Paradox and Discovery* (New York: McGraw-Hill, 1976), pp. 215-22.
2 Asch, p.219.
3 Harry G. Frankfurt, *The Importance of What We Care About* (Cambridge: Cambridge University Press, 1988), p. 81.
4 Frankfurt, p. 81.
5 Shklar in Richard Rorty, *Contingency, Irony, and Solidarity* (Cambridge: Cambridge University Press, 1989), p. 74.
6 Rorty, chap. 4.
7 Rorty, p. 44.
8 J.N. Findlay, *Values and Intentions* (New York: George Allen and Unwin, 1961), p. 399.
9 Bernard Williams, *Ethics and the Limits of Philosophy* (Cambridge, MA: Harvard University Press, 1985), p. 114.
10 W.D. Ross, *The Right and the Good* (Oxford: Oxford University Press, 1930), p. 141.
11 Steven G. Smith, *The Concept of the Spiritual: An Essay in First Philosophy* (Philadelphia: Temple University Press, 1988), pp. 63-64.
12 Ross, p. 141.
13 Rorty, p. 44.
14 Aristotle, *De Anima*, in *The Basic Works of Aristotle*, ed. Richard McKeon (New York: Random House, 1941), pp. 535-606.

15 Blaise Pascal, quoted in Lyof N. Tolstoï, *Life* (London: Walter Scott, 1889), p. 3.
16 Daniel C. Dennett, *The Intentional Stance* (Cambridge, MA: MIT Press, 1989), p. 32.
17 Thomas Nagel, *The View from Nowhere* (Oxford: Oxford University Press, 1986), p. 16.
18 Rorty, p. 44.
19 Thomas Nagel, *Mortal Questions* (Cambridge: Cambridge University Press, 1979), p. 13.

Chapter 3

1 David Ross, *Aristotle* (London: Methuen, 1949), pp. 240-41.
2 Kathleen Wilkes, *Real People: Personal Identity without Thought Experiments* (Oxford: Oxford University Press, 1988).
3 Adolf Trendelenberg, "A Contribution to the History of the Word Person: A Posthumous Treatise By Adolf Trendelenberg," trans. Carl H. Haessler, *The Monist* 20 (1910): 338 and 342. But see also Arthur C. Danto, "Persons,"in *The Encyclopaedia of Philosophy*, vol. 6, ed. Paul Edwards (New York: Macmillan, 1967), pp. 110-14. There is an exact cognate, *purusa,* in Sanskrit, with all the ambiguity of our contemporary term "person."
4 Trendelenberg, p. 336.
5 Ross, pp. 240-41.
6 Samuel E. Stumpf, *Socrates to Sartre: A History of Philosophy*, 4th ed. (New York: McGraw-Hill, 1988), p. 11.
7 See, for instance, Milton C. Nahm, ed., *Selections from Early Greek Philosophy* 3rd ed. (New York: Appleton, Century, Crofts, 1947), p. 91.
8 Erich Fromm and Ramón Xirau, *The Nature of Man* (New York: Collier, 1968), p. 44.
9 Heraclitus, in Fromm and Xirau, p. 43.
10 Heraclitus in Stumpf, p. 13.
11 Roger Trigg, *Ideas of Human Nature* (Oxford: Basil Blackwell, 1988), p. 6.
12 Stumpf, p. 13.
13 Since I wrote this, I have heard of someone setting up in a mall and doing fairly well.
14 Protagoras in Stumpf, p. 32.
15 The following discussion is my way of reading Plato's *Republic* through the filter of my interest in persons. See Plato, *The Collected Dialogues*, ed. Edith Hamilton and Huntington Cairns (Princeton, NJ: Princeton University Press, 1961).
16 Wilkes, pp. 201-209.
17 Wilkes, p. 209.
18 See Plato's dialogue *Parmenides*, in *The Collected Dialogues.*
19 Aristotle, *De Anima*, in *The Basic Works of Aristotle*, ed. Richard McKeon (New York: Random House, 1941), pp. 402a-403a.
20 Wilkes, p. 210.
21 Wilkes, p. 212.

22 Aristotle, *De Anima*, iii 9 pp. 432a22ff. See Wilkes, p. 210.
23 Trigg, pp. 23-25.
24 Trigg, pp. 25-28.
25 Plato, *Republic*, 5, p. 456b.
26 Aristotle, p. 412b, 17.
27 Trendelenberg, p. 343.
28 Trendelenberg, p. 346.
29 Trendelenberg, p. 349.
30 Trendelenberg, p. 351.
31 Trendelenberg, p. 348.
32 Trendelenberg, p. 356.
33 Trendelenberg, pp. 342,344.
34 Stumpf, p. 119.
35 Epictetus in Fromm and Xirau, p. 69.
36 Stumpf, p. 129.
37 Trendelenberg, pp. 346 and 348.
38 Stumpf, p. 129.
39 Fromm and Xirau, p. 43.
40 Fromm and Xirau, chap. 3.

Chapter 4

1 Samuel E. Stumpf, *Socrates to Sartre: A History of Philosophy*, 4th ed. (New York: McGraw-Hill, 1988), p. 135.
2 Stumpf, pp.144-45.
3 Stumpf, p. 149.
4 Stumpf, p. 148.
5 Stumpf, p. 148.
6 Plato, *Republic*, 5, p. 456b.
7 Stumpf, p. 170.
8 Stumpf, pp. 173-74.
9 Stumpf, p. 171.
10 Roger Trigg, *Ideas of Human Nature* (Oxford: Basil Blackwell, 1988), p. 40.
11 Leslie Stevenson, *Seven Theories of Human Nature*, 2nd ed. (Oxford: Oxford University Press, 1987), p. 45.
12 Trigg, p. 53.
13 Trigg, p. 42.
14 Trigg, p. 46.
15 Mirandola in Erich Fromm and Ramón Xirau, *The Nature of Man* (New York: Collier, 1968), pp. 103-105.
16 Adolf Trendelenberg, "A Contribution to the History of the Word Person: A Posthumous Treatise By Adolf Trendelenberg," trans. Carl H. Haessler, *The Monist* 20 (1910): 352.

17 Trendelenberg, pp. 351-53.
18 Trendelenberg, p. 354.

Chapter 5

1 Montaigne in Samuel E. Stumpf, *Socrates to Sartre: A History of Philosophy*, 4th ed. (New York: McGraw-Hill, 1988), p. 215.
2 Erasmus in Erich Fromm and Ramón Xirau, *The Nature of Man* (New York: Collier, 1968), p. 108.
3 Fromm and Xirau, p. 107.
4 Fromm and Xirau, p. 109.
5 Stumpf, p. 210.
6 Mirandola in Fromm and Xirau, pp. 103-105.
7 Edward Suntz, "More, Thomas" in *The Encyclopededia of Philosophy*, vol.5, ed. Paul Edwards (New York: Macmillan, 1967), pp. 389-92.
8 Fromm and Xirau, p. 125.
9 Montaigne in Stumpf, p. 214.
10 Stumpf, p. 215.
11 Stumpf, p. 216.
12 Michel de Montaigne, *Apology for Raymond Sebond*, in Fromm and Xirau, *The Nature of Man*, p. 133.
13 Stumpf, p. 218.
14 Stumpf, p. 218.
15 Leonard Cohen, "Stories of the Street" (New York: Stranger Music, 1967).
16 Actually, according to the common view in current philosophy of science, this is impossible, as facts are dependent on theories.
17 David Gauthier, *Morals by Agreement* (Oxford: Clarendon Press, 1986), p. 268.
18 Stumpf, p. 227.
19 Gauthier, p. 268.
20 René Descartes, *Discourse on Method*, trans. John Veitch, in *The Rationalists* (Garden City, NY: Dolphin Books, 1960), part iv, p. 63.
21 Descartes, *Meditations*, in *The Rationalists*, Meditation 2, p. 42.
22 Descartes, *Discourse on Method*, in *The Rationalists*, part 4, p. 63.
23 Peter Unger, *Identity Consciousness and Value* (Oxford: Oxford University Press, 1990), p. 15.
24 Stumpf, p. 247.
25 Descartes, *Meditations*, in *The Rationalists*, Meditation 1, pp. 115-17.
26 Stumpf, p. 252.
27 Spinoza in Fromm and Xirau, p. 140.
28 Stumpf, pp. 249-53.
29 Stumpf, p. 253.
30 Harold W. Noonan, *Personal Identity* (London: Routledge, 1989), p. 30.
31 Derek Parfit, *Reasons and Persons* (Oxford: Oxford University Press, 1986, orig. pub. 1984; repr. 1985).

32 Thomas Nagel, *The View from Nowhere* (Oxford: Oxford University Press, 1986).
33 Noonan, p. 30.
34 John Locke, *An Essay Concerning Human Understanding*, II, xxvii.14. See also Noonan, p. 33.
35 Locke, II, xxvii. 17.
36 Locke, II, xxvii. 9.
37 Kathleen Wilkes, *Real People: Personal Identity without Thought Experiments* (Oxford: Oxford University Press, 1988), pp. 169-71.
38 Locke, II, xxvii. 17.
39 Stumpf, p. 269.
40 John Perry, "The Problem of Personal Identity," in *Personal Identity* (Berkeley: University of California Press, 1975), p. 21.
41 Perry, pp. 21-22.
42 Locke, II, xxvii.
43 Noonan, p. 53.
44 Noonan, p. 53.
45 Locke, II, xxvii. 20.
46 Locke, II, xxvii. 22.
47 Locke, II, xxvii. 13.
48 Noonan, p. 54.
49 Locke, II, xxvii. 6.
50 Locke, II, xxvii. 6.
51 Gary Wedeking, "Locke's Metaphysics of Personal Identity," *History of Philosophy Quarterly* 4 (January 1987): 17. Professor Wedeking tells me he does not accept the persons-as-modes interpretation of Locke.
52 Locke himself uses this way out in a related matter: II, xxvii. 13.

Chapter 6

1 George Berkeley, "Three Dialogues between Hylas and Philonous," in *Berkeley: Essay, Principles, Dialogues with Selections from Other Writings*, ed. Mary W. Calkins (New York: Charles Scribner's Sons, 1937).
2 Harold W. Noonan, *Personal Identity* (London: Routledge, 1989), pp. 63-64.
3 Noonan, p. 60.
4 Noonan, pp. 59-60.
5 G.W. Leibniz, *New Essays on Human Understanding*, trans. and ed. Peter Remnant and Jonathan Bennett (Cambridge: Cambridge University Press, 1981).
6 Ralph Walker, "Leibniz's Philosophy of Mind," in *The Oxford Companion to the Mind*, ed. Richard Gregory (Oxford: Oxford University Press, 1987), p. 433.
7 Noonan, p. 62.
8 Walker, p. 433.

9 Noonan, p. 62.
10 Noonan, pp. 63-64.
11 Warren Bourgeois, "The Identity of Indiscernibles" (doctoral thesis, University of California, Irvine, 1979), chap. 1.
12 Leibniz in Noonan, p. 61.
13 Kathleen Wilkes, *Real People: Personal Identity without Thought Experiments* (Oxford: Oxford University Press, 1988), p. 105.
14 Wilkes, p. 106.
15 Butler in Noonan, p. 65.
16 Bourgeois, pp. 13-17.
17 John Perry, "The Problem of Personal Identity," in *Personal Identity* (Berkeley: University of California Press, 1975), p. 15.
18 Reid in Noonan, pp. 66-67.
19 Noonan, p. 68.
20 Noonan, pp. 75-76.
21 Noonan, p. 71.
22 Chisholm in Noonan, p. 76.
23 Noonan, p. 76.
24 John Perry, "The Problem of Personal Identity," in *Personal Identity* (Berkeley: University of California Press, 1975) pp. 21-22.
25 David Hume, *A Treatise of Human Nature*, ed. L.A. Selby-Bigge (Oxford: Oxford University Press, 1973), I, IV, vi, p. 251.
26 Hume, p. 252.
27 Hume, p. 235.
28 Hume, p. 259.
29 Hume, p. 262.
30 Hume, p. 262.
31 Hume, p. 272.

Chapter 7

1 Samuel E. Stumpf, *Sócrates to Sartre: A History of Philosophy*, 4th ed. (New York: McGraw-Hill, 1988), p. 293.
2 Immanuel Kant, *Groundwork of the Metaphysic of Morals*, trans. H.J. Paton (New York: Harper & Row, 1964), pp. 32-33.
3 Immanuel Kant, *Critique of Pure Reason*, trans. Norman Kemp Smith (New York: St. Martin's Press, 1965), p. 342 A363.
4 Kant, *Critique of Pure Reason*, p. 343 A364.
5 S. Korner, *Kant* (Harmondsworth: Pelican Books, 1955), p. 67.
6 Kant, *Critique of Pure Reason*, pp. 469-79 B568-B586.
7 Kant, *Groundwork*, pp. 32-33.
8 Kant, *Groundwork*, p. 22.
9 Kant, *Groundwork*, p. 17.

10 Korner, p. 165.
11 Korner, p. 113.
12 Stumpf, p. 328.
13 Stumpf, p. 330.
14 G.W.F. Hegel, *The Phenomenology of Mind*, trans. J.B. Baillie (New York: Harper Colophon Books, 1967), p. 133.
15 Hegel, pp. 792-93.
16 Stumpf, p. 333.
17 Shakespeare, *Hamlet*, act V, sc. 2.
18 G.W.F. Hegel, *The Philosophy of History*, trans. J. Sibree (New York: Dover Publications, 1956), p. 70.
19 Hegel in Stumpf, p. 337.
20 Walter Kaufmann, *Hegel: A Reinterpretation* (Notre Dame: University of Notre Dame Press, 1965), p. 250.
21 Hegel, *The Philosophy of History*, p. 56.
22 Richard L. Gregory, "Hegel," in *The Oxford Companion to the Mind*, ed. Richard L. Gregory (Oxford: Oxford University Press, 1987), p. 308.
23 Stumpf, p. 341.
24 Stumpf, p. 345.
25 Stumpf, p. 349.
26 Kohlberg in Vincent Barry, *Philosophy: A Text with Readings* (Belmont, CA: Wadsworth, 1980), p. 159.
27 Bentham in Peter Singer, *Practical Ethics* (Cambridge: Cambridge University Press, 1979), pp. 49-50.
28 Roger Trigg, *Ideas of Human Nature: An Historical Introduction* (Oxford: Basil Blackwell, 1988), pp. 108-109.
29 Karl Marx in Leslie Stevenson, *Seven Theories of Human Nature*, 2nd ed. (Oxford: Oxford University Press, 1987), p. 62.
30 Barry, p. 49.
31 Marx in Stumpf, p. 442.
32 Stumpf, pp. 440-41.
33 Kierkegaard in Stumpf, p. 479.
34 Alasdair MacIntyre, "Existentialism," in *The Encyclopedia of Philosophy* (London: Macmillan and New York: Free Press, 1967), 3, p. 148.
35 MacIntyre, p. 148.
36 Thomas Nagel, *Mortal Questions* (Cambridge: Cambridge University Press, 1979), p. 15.
37 Nietzsche in Stumpf, p. 389.
38 Stumpf, p. 387.
39 Stumpf, p. 387.
40 Stumpf, p. 391.
41 Stumpf, p. 390.
42 Stumpf, p. 389.
43 James in Barry, p. 396.

44 Stumpf, p. 422.
45 Stumpf, p. 412.
46 Murray G. Murphey, "Peirce, Charles Sanders," in *The Encyclopedia of Philosophy*, vol. 6, ed. Paul Edwards (London: Macmillan and New York: Free Press, 1967), 70-78.

47 William James, "The Will to Believe" in *Reason and Responsibility*, 8th ed. Joel Feinberg, ed. (Belmont: Wadsworth, 1993) p. 109, orig. 1896.
48 William James, "The Will to Believe," p. 116.
49 John Dewey, "The Nature of Moral Philosophy," in *The Moral Writings of John Dewey*, ed. James Gounlock (New York: Hafner Press, 1976), pp. 1-22.
50 William James, "The Will to Believe," p. 109.

Chapter 8

1 Bergson in Samuel E. Stumpf, *Socrates to Sartre: A History of Philosophy*, 4th ed. (New York: McGraw-Hill, 1988), p. 397.
2 Bergson in Stumpf, p. 398.
3 Bergson in Stumpf, p. 401.
4 Bergson in Stumpf, p. 402.
5 T.A. Goudge, "Bergson, Henri," in *The Encyclopedia of Philosophy*, vol. 2, ed. Paul Edwards (London: Macmillan and New York: Free Press, 1967), pp. 288, 294.
6 Whitehead in Stumpf, p. 404.
7 Alfred North Whitehead, *Process and Reality* (New York: Free Press, 1969), p. 39.
8 Whitehead, p. 23.
9 Whitehead, p. 10.
10 Whitehead, pp. 39-40.
11 Alfred North Whitehead, *Symbolism: Its Meaning and Effect* (New York: G.P. Putnam's Sons, 1959), p. 20.
12 David Berlinski, *Philosophy: The Cutting Edge* (Port Washington, NY: Alfred Publishing, 1976), p. xi.
13 Leslie Stevenson, *Seven Theories of Human Nature*, 2nd ed. (Oxford: Oxford University Press, 1987), p. 99.
14 Jean-Paul Sartre, *Being and Nothingness: A Phenomenological Essay on Ontology*, trans. Hazel E. Barnes (New York: Washington Square Press, 1966).
15 Stumpf, p. 486.
16 Edmund Husserl, *Ideas: General Introduction to Pure Phenomenology* (London: Collier Macmillan, 1962), pp. 37-42.
17 Stumpf, p. 491.
18 Georges Thines, "Husserl," in *The Oxford Companion to the Mind*, ed. Richard L. Gregory (Oxford: Oxford University Press, 1987), pp. 326-27.
19 Husserl, p. 161.
20 Husserl, p. 156.

21 Martin Heidegger, *Being and Time* (New York: Harper & Row, 1962), pp. 78-90.
22 Stumpf, p. 499.
23 Stumpf, p. 500.
24 Victor Farias, *Heidegger and Nazism* (Philadelphia: Temple University Press, 1990).
25 Jean-Paul Sartre, *Existentialism and Humanism*, trans. Philip Mairet (London: Methuen, 1949), p. 85.
26 Sartre, p. 85.
27 Leslie Stevenson, p. 109.
28 Stevenson, pp. 100-101.
29 Stevenson, pp. 101-102.
30 Richard Rorty, *Contingency, Irony, and Solidarity* (Cambridge: Cambridge University Press, 1989), p. 44.

Chapter 9

1 Samuel E. Stumpf, *Socrates to Sartre: A History of Philosophy*, 4th ed. (New York: McGraw-Hill, 1988), p. 446.
2 Bertrand Russell, *An Outline of Philosophy* (London: George Allen and Unwin, 1970), p. 312.
3 Russell, p. 83.
4 Russell, p. 387.
5 Bertrand Russell, *An Inquiry into Meaning and Truth* (Baltimore, MD: Penguin Books, 1962), p. 93.
6 Bertrand Russell, *Human Knowledge: Its Scope and Limits* (London: George Allen and Unwin, 1948), p. 247.
7 Bertrand Russell, *The Problems of Philosophy* (Oxford: Oxford University Press, 1959), p. 4.
8 David F. Pears, "Russell's Philosophy of Mind: Dualism," in *The Oxford Companion to the Mind*, ed. Richard L. Gregory (Oxford: Oxford University Press, 1987), p. 689.
9 Willard V. Quine, "Russell's Ontological Development," in *Essays on Bertrand Russell*, ed. E.D. Klemke (Chicago: University of Illinois Press, 1970), pp. 12-13.
10 David F. Pears, "Russell's Philosophy of Mind: Neutral Monism," in *The Oxford Companion to the Mind*, ed. Richard L. Gregory (Oxford: Oxford University Press, 1987), p. 690.
11 Quine, "Russell's Ontological Development," p. 14.
12 Pears, "Russell's Philosophy of Mind: Neutral Monism," p. 690.
13 Pears, "Russell's Philosophy of Mind: Neutral Monism," p. 690.
14 Pears, "Russell's Philosophy of Mind: Neutral Monism," p. 690.
15 Pears, "Russell's Philosophy of Mind: Neutral Monism," pp. 690-91.

16 William of Ockham in Ernest A. Moody, "William of Ockham," in *The Encyclopedia of Philosophy*, vol. 8, ed. Paul Edwards (New York: Macmillan, 1967), p. 307.
17 Pears, "Russell's Philosophy of Mind: Neutral Monism," p. 691.
18 Bertrand Russell, "Science and Ethics," in *Philosophy: Paradox and Discovery*, ed. Arthur J. Minton (New York: McGraw-Hill, 1976), p. 229.
19 Bertrand Russell, quoted in Charles W. Morris, *Six Theories of Mind* (Chicago: University of Chicago Press, 1932), p. 136.
20 Russell, *Inquiry into Meaning and Truth*, p. 322.
21 Ludwig Wittgenstein, *Tractatus Logico-Philosophicus*, trans. D.F. Pears and B.F. MacGuinness (London: Routledge and Kegan Paul, 1961), para. 6.54.
22 Russell, *Inquiry into Meaning and Truth*, p. 322.
23 In the introduction to Wittgenstein, *Tractatus*, p. ix.
24 Wittgenstein, *Tractatus*, 5.631-5.632.
25 Ludwig Wittgenstein, *Philosophical Investigations*, trans. G.E.M. Anscombe (Oxford: Basil Blackwell, 1976).
26 Ludwig Wittgenstein, *The Blue and Brown Books* (New York: Harper Colophon Books, 1958).
27 Wittgenstein, *The Blue and Brown Books*, p. 63.
28 Ludwig Wittgenstein, *Philosophical Remarks*, ed. Rush Rhees, trans. Raymond Hargreaves and Roger White (Oxford: Basil Blackwell, 1975), pp. 88-89.
29 Wittgenstein, *The Blue and Brown Books*, pp. 61-62.
30 Wittgenstein, *The Blue and Brown Books*, p. 62.
31 Wittgenstein, *Philosophical Investigations*, p. 404b.
32 Kathleen Wilkes, *Real People: Personal Identity without Thought Experiments* (Oxford: Oxford University Press, 1988).
33 John Passmore, "Logical Positivism," in *The Encyclopedia of Philosophy* vol. 5, ed. Paul Edwards (London: Macmillan and New York: Free Press, 1967), p. 52.
34 Passmore, p. 56.
35 Gilbert Ryle, *The Concept of Mind* (Harmondsworth: Penguin Books, 1963).
36 Ryle, p. 17.
37 Ryle, p. 13.
38 Ryle, p. 17.
39 Ryle, pp. 17-18.
40 Ryle, p. 23.
41 Richard Rorty, *Contingency, Irony, and Solidarity* (Cambridge: Cambridge University Press, 1989), p.44.
42 Ryle, p. 180.
43 Ryle, p. 181.
44 Ryle, p. 181.
45 Ryle, p. 179.
46 Ryle, p. 180.
47 Ryle, p. 186.

48 Ryle, p. 188.
49 Ryle, p. 187.
50 Ryle, pp. 188-89.
51 Ryle, pp. 187-88.
52 Ryle, p. 59.
53 Ryle, p. 35.
54 Ryle, p. 49.
55 Ryle, p. 49.
56 Ryle, p. 60.

Chapter 10

1 P.F. Strawson, *Individuals: An Essay in Descriptive Metaphysics* (London: Methuen, 1959), p. 9.
2 Strawson, p. 10.
3 Strawson, p. 9.
4 Strawson, p. 11.
5 Strawson, p. 87.
6 Strawson, p. 89.
7 Strawson, pp. 87-88.
8 Kathleen Wilkes, *Real People: Personal Identity without Thought Experiments* (Oxford: Oxford University Press, 1988).
9 Strawson, pp. 90-94.
10 Strawson, p. 95n 1.
11 Strawson, p. 96.
12 Strawson, pp. 96-97.
13 Ludwig Wittgenstein, *Tractatus Logico-Philosophicus*, trans. D.F. Pears and B.F. MacGuinness (London: Routledge and Kegan Paul, 1961), para. 7.
14 Strawson, p. 99.
15 Strawson, pp. 99-100.
16 Strawson, p. 100.
17 Strawson, pp. 101-103.
18 Strawson, p. 104.
19 Strawson, p. 106.
20 Strawson, p. 106.
21 Strawson, p. 110.
22 Strawson, p. 112.
23 Strawson, p. 113.
24 Strawson, p. 114.
25 Thomas Hobbes, *Leviathan* (London: J.M. Dent and Sons, 1914).
26 Strawson, pp. 113-15.
27 Wilkes, pp. 200-209.
28 Strawson, p. 115.

29 Alfred J. Ayer, "The Concept of a Person," in *The Concept of a Person and Other Essays* (London: Macmillan, 1963), p. 82.
30 Ayer, p. 82.
31 Ayer, p. 116.
32 Strawson, p. 94.
33 Strawson, p. 96.
34 Strawson, pp. 96-97.
35 Ayer, p. 117.
36 Ayer, pp. 116-17.
37 Ayer, pp. 118-21.
38 Willard V. Quine, "Two Dogmas of Empiricism" in *From a Logical Point of View: Logico-philosophical Essays* (New York: Harper & Row, 1953), pp. 20-46. See also Samuel E. Stumpf, *Socrates to Sartre: A History of Philosophy*, 4th ed. (New York: McGraw-Hill, 1988), pp. 458-59.
39 Willard V. Quine, *The Roots of Reference: The Paul Carus Lectures* (Lasalle, IL: Open Court, 1973), p. 9.
40 Antony Flew, ed., *A Dictionary of Philosophy* (London: Pan Books, 1979), p. 250.
41 Quine, *The Roots of Reference*, p. 35.
42 Willard V. Quine, "Identity, Ostension and Hypostasis," in *From a Logical Point of View*, p. 65.
43 Quine, *Roots*, p. 65.
44 Quine, *Roots*, p. 65.
45 Harold W. Noonan, *Personal Identity* (London: Routledge, 1989), p. 107.
46 Willard V. Quine, *Theories and Things* (Cambridge, MA: Harvard University Press, 1981), p. 12.
47 Quine. See also Noonan, p. 107.
48 Strawson, pp. 132-33.
49 Strawson, p. 133.
50 Strawson, pp. 133-34.
51 Strawson, p.138.

Chapter 11

1 David Wiggins, *Identity and Spatio-temporal Continuity* (Oxford: Basil Blackwell, 1967). See also *Sameness and Substance* (Oxford: Basil Blackwell, 1980).
2 Wiggins, *Sameness*, p. 183.
3 Wiggins, *Identity*, pp. 24-25.
4 Wiggins, *Identity*, p. 47.
5 Wiggins, *Sameness*, p. 187.
6 Wiggins, *Identity*, p. 41.
7 Aristotle, quoted in Wiggins, *Identity* p. 47.
8 Wiggins, *Identity*, pp. 47-48.
9 Wiggins, *Identity*, p. 58.

10 Wiggins, *Sameness*, pp. 151-53.
11 Wiggins, *Sameness*, p. 155.
12 Wiggins, *Sameness*, p. 155.
13 Wiggins, *Sameness*, pp. 186-87.
14 Wiggins, *Sameness*, p. 187.
15 Wiggins, *Sameness*, pp. 180-82.
16 Wiggins, *Sameness*, p. 189.
17 Wiggins, *Sameness*, p. 169.
18 Depending on what one counts as synthetic, this can be done now. It is medically feasible to take an ovum from an aborted fetus and fertilize it with sperm preserved from a dead male human being. The fertilized ovum can then be implanted in a woman's womb and brought to term. The resulting infant may grow to be an adult.
19 Bernard Williams, *Ethics and the Limits of Philosophy* (Cambridge, MA: Harvard University Press, 1985), p. 114.
20 Bernard Williams, "Personal Identity and Individuation," in *Problems of the Self* (Cambridge: Cambridge University Press, 1973), p. 1.
21 Williams, "Personal Identity," p. 14.
22 Williams, "Personal Identity," pp. 14-15.
23 Williams, "Personal Identity," p. 13.
24 Williams, "Personal Identity," p. 14.
25 Williams, "Personal Identity," p. 13.
26 Williams, "Personal Identity," p. 14.
27 Williams, "Personal Identity," p. 14.
28 Kathleen Wilkes, *Real People: Personal Identity without Thought Experiments* (Oxford: Oxford University Press, 1988), pp. 185-86.
29 Williams, "Personal Identity," p. 17, n. 9.
30 Williams, "Personal Identity," p. 17.
31 Charles Rycroft, "Dissociation of the Personality," in *The Oxford Companion to the Mind*, ed. Richard L. Gregory (Oxford: Oxford University Press, 1987), p. 197.
32 Williams, "Personal Identity," p. 18.
33 Williams, "Personal Identity," pp. 17-18.
34 Bernard Williams, "Are Persons Bodies?" in *Problems of the Self*, pp. 64-78.
35 Williams, "Are Persons Bodies?" p. 66.
36 Williams, "Are Persons Bodies?" p. 70.
37 Williams, "Are Persons Bodies?" p. 64.
38 Williams, "Are Persons Bodies?" p. 74.
39 Williams, "Are Persons Bodies?" p. 75.
40 Williams, "Are Persons Bodies?" pp. 75-76.
41 Williams, "Are Persons Bodies?" pp. 75-76.
42 Williams, "Are Persons Bodies?" p. 79.
43 Williams, "Are Persons Bodies?" p. 80.
44 Williams, "Are Persons Bodies?" p. 81.
45 Williams, "Are Persons Bodies?" p. 81.

46 Williams, *Ethics and the Limits of Philosophy*, p. 114.
47 Williams, "Are Persons Bodies?" p. 76.

Chapter 12

1 Robert Nozick, *Philosophical Explanations* (Cambridge, MA: Harvard University Press, 1981), p. 114.
2 Nozick, p. 114.
3 Nozick, p. 33.
4 Nozick, p. 35.
5 Nozick, p. 37.
6 Nozick, p. 38.
7 Nozick, p. 38.
8 Nozick conceives of the continuer and predecessor relations as quite different from equivalence relations which must be symmetric, reflexive, and transitive. These relations have none of those properties.
9 Nozick, p. 42.
10 Nozick, p. 86.
11 Nozick, p. 108.
12 Nozick, p. 105.
13 Nozick, p. 106.
14 Nozick, p. 107.
15 Nozick, pp. 88-89.
16 Nozick, p. 74.
17 Nozick, p. 79.
18 Nozick, p. 667.
19 Nozick, p. 78.
20 Nozick, p. 78.
21 Nozick, p. 78.
22 Nozick, pp. 109-10.
23 Nozick, p. 42. See also Derek Parfit, *Reasons and Persons* (Oxford: Oxford University Press, 1986, orig. pub. 1984; repr. 1985), pp. 200-201.
24 Nozick, p. 107.
25 Nozick, p. 106.
26 Nozick, p. 38.
27 Nozick, p. 35.
28 Nozick, pp. 38-48.
29 Nozick, pp. 47-48.
30 Nozick, p. 107.
31 Nozick, p. 63.
32 Nozick, p. 63.

33 Nozick, p. 114.
34 Nozick, p. 112.

Chapter 13

1 Derek Parfit, *Reasons and Persons* (Oxford: Oxford University Press, 1986, orig. pub. 1984; repr. 1985), p. 217.
2 Parfit, p. 202.
3 Parfit, p. 202.
4 Parfit, p. 216.
5 Parfit, p. 217.
6 Parfit, p. 227.
7 Parfit, p. 228.
8 Parfit, p. 228.
9 Parfit, p. 200.
10 Parfit, pp. 231-43.
11 Parfit, p. 200.
12 Parfit, p. 217.
13 Parfit, p. 471.
14 Parfit, p. 223.
15 Perhaps what Parfit says can be compared to the following mathematical convention: a set has members but we cannot say that a set is its members; a set, moreover, is distinct from its members but cannot exist separately from them. Experiences, on this way of thinking, are just members of a set including physical events, character, and other items. It is the set which is the person. We could, however, describe the things in the set without unifying them, by convention, in such sets and calling them "persons."
16 Parfit, p. x.
17 Parfit, p. 199.
18 Parfit, p. 201.
19 Parfit, p. 201.
20 Parfit, p. ix.
21 Parfit, p. 346.
22 Parfit, p. 346.
23 Parfit, p. 216.
24 Briefly put, Parfit wants personal identity to be a transitive relation.
25 Derek Parfit, "Personal Identity," *The Philosophical Review* 80, 1 (January 1971), repr. in *Personal Identity*, ed. John Perry (Berkeley: University of California Press, 1975), p. 208.
26 Parfit, *Reasons and Persons*, p. 206.
27 Parfit, *Reasons and Persons*, p. 205.
28 Parfit, *Reasons and Persons*, p. 206.
29 Parfit, *Reasons and Persons*, p. 202.

30 John Perry, "The Importance of Being Identical," in *The Identities of Persons*, ed. Amelie O. Rorty (Berkeley: University of California Press, 1976), p. 84.
31 Parfit, *Reasons and Persons*, p. 241.
32 P. Strawson, *Individuals: An Essay in Descriptive Metaphysics* (London: Methuen, 1959), p. 133.
33 Parfit, *Reasons and Persons*, p. 247.
34 Colwyn Trevarthen, "Split Brain and the Mind," in *The Oxford Companion to the Mind*, ed. Richard L. Gregory (Oxford: Oxford University Press, 1987), p. 746.
35 Trevarthen, p. 746.
36 Parfit, *Reasons and Persons*, pp. 217 and 247.
37 Parfit, *Reasons and Persons*, p. 251.
38 Kathleen Wilkes, *Real People* (Oxford: Oxford University Press, 1988), chap. 5.
39 Wilkes, p. 156.
40 Wilkes, p. 148.
41 A comparison of the works cited for Wilkes and Parfit will show that Wilkes successfully deflates other attempts by Parfit to use real-world examples as exotic examples of division paralleling the teletransportation case.
42 Parfit, *Reasons and Persons*, p. 218.

Chapter 14

1 Thomas Nagel, *The View from Nowhere* (Oxford: Oxford University Press, 1986), p. 3.
2 Charles W. Morris, *Six Theories of Mind* (Chicago: University of Chicago Press, 1932), p. 245.
3 Nagel, p. 28.
4 Nagel, p. 5.
5 Nagel, p. 5.
6 Nagel, pp. 75-77.
7 Nagel, p. 76.
8 Nagel, pp. 3-12.
9 Nagel, pp. 5-6.
10 Nagel, p. 10.
11 Hilary Putnam, *Representation and Reality* (Cambridge, MA: MIT Press, 1989), p. xi.
12 Nagel, p. 27.
13 Nagel, p. 8.
14 Nagel, p. 9.
15 See, for example, David Lewis, "Survival and Identity" and John Perry, "The Importance of Being Identical" in *The Identities of Persons*, ed. Amelie O. Rorty (Berkeley: University of California Press, 1976), pp. 17-40 and pp. 67-90, respectively.
16 Nagel, p. 17.
17 Nagel, pp. 29-30.

18 Nagel, p. 60.
19 Nagel, p. 40.
20 Nagel, p. 41.
21 Nagel, p. 42.
22 Nagel, p. 30.
23 Nagel, p. 51.
24 Nagel, pp. 49-50.
25 Nagel, pp. 51-53.
26 Nagel, p. 45.
27 Bernard Williams, "Personal Identity and Individuation" in *Problems of the Self* (Cambridge: Cambridge University Press, 1973), pp.1-18. See also Harold W. Noonan, *Personal Identity* (London: Routledge, 1989), p. 16.
28 Nagel, p. 44.
29 Nagel, p. 45.
30 Nagel, p. 44.
31 Nagel, p. 45.
32 Nagel, p. 46. See also Saul A. Kripke, *Naming and Necessity* (Cambridge, MA: Harvard University Press, 1972), p. 155n.
33 Nagel, p. 46.
34 Nagel, p. 37.
35 Nagel, p. 33.
36 Nagel, p. 41.
37 Nagel, pp. 61, 62.
38 Nagel, pp. 65, 61.
39 Nagel, p. 66.
40 Nagel, pp. 57-60.
41 Williams, p. 14.
42 Nagel, p. 66.
43 Nagel, p. 62.
44 Nagel, p. 66.
45 Thomas Nagel, "The Absurd," in *Mortal Questions* (Cambridge: Cambridge University Press, 1979), pp. 11-23.

Chapter 15

1 Marcel Mauss in Michael Carrithers, Steven Collins, and Steven Lukes, eds., *The Category of the Person: Anthropology, Philosophy, History* (Cambridge: Cambridge University Press, 1985), p. 13.
2 Clifford Geertz, *Local Knowledge: Essays in Interpretive Anthropology* (New York: Basic Books, 1983), p. 59.

3 Kathleen Wilkes, *Real People: Personal Identity without Thought Experiments* (Oxford: Clarendon Press, 1988), p. 170.
4 David Wiggins, *Sameness and Substance* (Oxford: Basil Blackwell, 1980), p. 160.
5 Gauche as it is to explain a joke, I must say for those of my readers who are not trained in philosophy that G.E. Moore was a British philosopher who championed common sense.
6 Aristotle, *Nicomachean Ethics*, trans. W.D. Ross (Oxford: Oxford University Press), 1925.
7 Adolf Trendelenberg, "A Contribution to the History of the Word Person: A Posthumous Treatise By Adolf Trendelenberg," trans. Carl H. Haessler, *The Monist* 20 (1910): 336-63.
8 William James, "The Will to Believe," an Address to the Philosophical Club of Yale and Brown Universities in *Reason and Responsibility*, ed. J. Feinberg (Belmont, CA: Wadsworth, 1989; orig. pub. in *New World*, 1896), pp. 91-98. Blaise Pascal, *Penseés: Notes on Religion and Other Subjects*, ed. Louis Lafuma, trans. John Warrington (London: J.M. Dent and Sons, 1960).

Chapter 16

1 Derek Parfit, *Reasons and Persons* (Oxford: Oxford University Press, 1986, orig. pub. 1984; repr. 1985), pp. 254ff.
2 Kathleen Wilkes, *Real People: Personal Identity without Thought Experiments* (Oxford: Clarendon Press, 1988), pp. 38-39 and passim.
3 Jonathan Glover, *I: The Philosophy and Psychology of Personal Identity* (London: Penguin Books, 1988), p. 65.
4 W.D. Ross, *The Right and the Good* (Oxford: Clarendon Press, 1930), p. 141.
5 Wilkes, p. 210.
6 Wilkes, p. 211.
7 Adolf Trendelenberg, "A Contribution to the History of the Word Person: A Posthumous Treatise By Adolf Trendelenberg," trans. Carl H. Haessler, *The Monist* 20 (1910): 338.
8 Wilkes, p. 213.
9 Wilkes, p. 210.
10 Wilkes, pp. 210, 234.
11 Parfit, pp. 206, 216.
12 Wilkes, p. 105.
13 Note that a fetus is not a person from this perspective but may have special worth because of the potential to become a person.
14 Trendelenberg, "A Contribution."
15 Trendelenberg, p. 354.
16 David Wiggins, *Sameness and Substance* (Oxford: Basil Blackwell, 1980), p. 187. See also chapter 11, above.
17 Trendelenberg, p. 356.

Chapter 17

1 John Rawls, *A Theory of Justice* (Cambridge, MA: Harvard University Press, 1971). Rawls intends to deal only with large social questions, not interpersonal moral matters, so he might disagree with the positions I take on the basis of social contract theory. Indeed, even my positions on social questions may depart from his, though my survey owes a great debt to Rawls. I have used a very different way to that of Rawls for explaining the original position. I do not try to say what an ideal just society is nor how it would be maintained over time.

2 Rawls, pp. 12, 17.

3 Rawls, p. 8.

4 Rawls, p. 8.

5 Jane English, "Abortion and the Concept of a Person," *The Canadian Journal of Philosophy* 5, 2 (October 1970); repr. in *Biomedical Ethics*, ed. T.A. Mappes and J.S. Zembaty (New York: McGraw-Hill, 1986), pp. 479-80.

6 See for instance Marilyn Friedman, "The Social Self and the Partiality Debates," pp. 160-79 and Allison M. Jagger, "Feminist Ethics: Projects, Problems, Prospects," pp. 78-104 in Claudia Card, *Feminist Ethics* (Lawrence: University Press of Kansas, 1991). Annette Baier, *Moral Prejudices* (Cambridge Mass.: Harvard University Press, 1994), chap. 12. Lorraine Code, *What Can She Know? Feminist Theory and the Construction of Knowledge* (Ithaca: Cornell University Press, 1991), chap. 3. Virginia Held, *Feminist Morality: Transforming Culture, Society, and Politics* (Chicago: University of Chicago Press, 1993). Eve Browning Cole, *Philosophy and Feminist Criticism: An Introduction* (New York: Paragon House, 1993).

7 See for example, Eve Browning Cole, chap. 3.

8 Lorraine Code, chap. 3.

9 Eve Browning Cole, pp. 99-104.

10 For instance Lorraine Code, chap. 3.

11 Marilyn Friedman, pp. 160-79.

12 Marilyn Friedman, p. 162 and p. 164.

13 Nel Noddings, *Caring: A Feminine Approach to Ethics and Moral Education*, (Berkeley: University of California Press, 1984) pp. 149 ff.

14 James Rachels, *The Elements of Moral Philosophy*, 3rd ed. (Boston Burr Ridge, IL: McGraw-Hill College, 1999) p. 171.

15 Marilyn Friedman, p. 176.

16 David Gauthier, *Morals By Agreement* (Oxford: Clarendon Press, 1986).

17 David Gauthier, p. 268.

18 Jane English, "Abortion and the Concept of a Person."

19 John Locke, *The Second Treatise of Government*, in *Two Treatises of Government*, ed. Peter Laslett (Cambridge: Mentor, 1960), 31, p. 332.

20 Peter Singer, *Practical Ethics* (Cambridge: Cambridge University Press, 1979), pp. 128-30.

21 Jane English, pp. 479-80. English disagrees with my theses about the importance of the concept of a person, but we concur on the importance of the social contract and of sympathy.
22 English, p. 449.
23 For an interesting discussion of the concept of the differences between future interests and full rights, see Herbert Morris, "Persons and Punishment," *The Monist* 52, 4 (October 1968), repr. in Joel Feinberg and Hyman Gross, *Philosophy of Law*, 2nd ed. (Belmont: Wadsworth, 1980), p. 590.
24 Southwestern India is an example in favour of this thesis, as are most so-called developed nations.
25 Robert E. Goodin, "Ethical Principles for Environmental Protection," in *Contemporary Moral Issues*, ed. Wesley Cragg, 3rd ed. (Toronto: McGraw-Hill Ryerson, 1992), pp. 323-35.
26 A *locus classicus* of this move is Bernard Williams, *Morality: An Introduction to Ethics* (New York: Harper & Row, 1972), pp. 20-26.
27 Utilitarians try to maximize utility as the way of doing what is morally right. Utility is pleasure for the hedonistic utilitarians. Act utilitarians judge each action individually, while rule utilitarians follow a set of rules which they believe will maximize utility.
28 Sheila and George Grant, "Abortion and Rights, " in *Contemporary Moral Issues*, ed. Wesley Cragg, 3rd ed. (Toronto: McGraw-Hill Ryerson, 1992), p. 70.
29 D. Schlitz, "The Gambler," Elektra/Asylum Records, ASCAP, 1980.
30 Lee M. Silver, *Remaking Eden: Cloning and Beyond in a Brave New World* (New York: Avon Books, 1997).

Glossary

A if and only if B, for any two sentences A and B, means if A then B, and if B then A. This is standard usage in logic, mathematics, and philosophy.

Ablism is unjust discrimination against persons on grounds of abilities.

Absolute means unconditional. Absolute values are not relative to groups but good for all persons, times, and places.

Absolute idealism is the view that all things are expressions of a single non-physical reality. For Hegel this was a mind, the Absolute, of which individual persons are mere parts, not self-existent particulars.

Accidental properties are the properties that a thing or its accidents may lose without going out of existence.

Actual occasions are, according to Whitehead, events such as our experiences of which the universe is formed.

Agnosticism is the view that we cannot know whether or not God exists. This term is also used more broadly by philosophers to refer to other kinds of suspension of judgment. One who argues that there is no way to tell whether materialism, idealism, or dualism is true may be said to be an agnostic concerning the nature of reality.

Altruism is the general term to include views that require us, morally, to do what is in the interest of others at times, even if it is not in our own self-interest.

Analytic school refers to the community of philosophers prominent in Britain and North America that is fond of precise, detailed analysis of concepts with a heavy concentration on the insights to be gained by examining language. (*See* Continental school.)

Antinomy is a conflict between the conclusions of two *a priori* arguments. Two such arguments tell us that all of our choices are caused, but that we are morally responsible beings making free choices.

Ascription principle refers to Strawson's claim that "it is a necessary condition of one's ascribing states of consciousness, experiences, to oneself, in the way one does, that one should ascribe them, or be prepared to ascribe them, to others who are not oneself." (*See* chapter 10.)

Authenticity is what we have according to Sartre when we live in good faith, accepting that what we do is determined solely by our own choices and cannot be justified by appealing to authorities or standards beyond ourselves.

Automatic behaviour is behaviour that we perform when we are not conscious but seems, to others, like consciously motivated behaviour.

Axiology or value theory is a field of study in philosophy concerned with the nature of values and with the things that have value. It includes ethics and aesthetics.

Bare particulars are substances that have properties but are not themselves properties. They are individual things from which we can, theoretically, strip away all their characteristics without destroying them.

Beings-for-themselves are, in Sartre's philosophy, persons as distinct from beings-in-themselves which are mere objects.

Cartesian means having to do with Descartes.

Cartesian Ego is the non-physical part of a person that directs the body and does the thinking.

Category mistake is Ryle's term for the error of treating things as if they were in one logical category when they are actually not. (*See* chapter 9.)

Causal determinism is the view that everything has a cause, which makes it the way it is without any possibility of its being different.

CC theory *See* Closest continuer theory.

Closest Continuer is the continuer of a person who most closely resembles that person on a similarity metric chosen by the continuer within the limits described in chapter 12.

Closest Continuer Theory is Nozick's general view that persons are definable in terms of closest continuers. He offers four possible ways of doing this, as described in chapter 12.

Closest Predecessor is the predecessor of a person who most closely resembles that person on a similarity metric chosen by that person within the limits described in chapter 12.

Commissurotomy is an operation in which the commissures linking the two halves of the cerebral cortex are partially severed. In the past they were sometimes totally severed. The lower brain remains intact.

Compatibilism is the view that caused choices may still be free; freedom and determinism are compatible.

Complex is a description of persons if what is essential to persons has internal divisions such as Plato's tripartite soul, as opposed to Descartes' Ego.

Consciousness means awareness of what is going on in oneself, particularly one's mind, but Locke also uses it in a stronger sense to mean the witnessing of one's own actions.

Continental school refers to a group of philosophers much more concerned with large system building than with the precise, detailed work of the analytic school.

Contingent truths are those that are true but could have been false in contrast to necessary truths. If a claim is necessarily true, then it is not possible that it could be false.

Continuer of a person is someone whose properties are caused to exist by that person, but a continuer need not be spatio-temporally continuous with that person.

Continuous persons are those who do not have temporal gaps at any time during their lives. *See also* Psychological continuity.

Criterion of identity is a standard by which we evaluate the claim that person A at one time is the same as person B at another time. For instance, Locke gives us the memory criterion: A is identical to B if and only if B remembers doing A's actions. This is also called the continuity of consciousness criterion.

Cultural relativism is the view that philosophical truths are not absolute but are dependent on the culture in which they are accepted.

Dasein is Heidegger's word for person, roughly speaking.

Deductive arguments attempt to establish their conclusions with certainty given the premises.

Deontological theories are theories in which other things besides ends or consequences must be considered when we determine whether an action is morally right. These things might be, for instance, duties or virtues.

Descriptive metaphysics describes, according to Strawson, the structure of our thought about reality as opposed to revisionary metaphysics which tries to improve on that structure.

Determinate describes persons for whom the question of whether they are about to die has a definite answer. Determinate persons cannot just fade away. Their existence is all or nothing.

Determinism is the view that every event must happen as it does; in other words, each event could not be otherwise; usually because fate, God's foreknowledge, or prior causes predetermine it. Note, determinism implies that at any time the future is already fixed. If one is deciding whom to vote for, one's choice is already determined by antecedent events.

Determinists are those who affirm determinism.

Diachronic identity is the identity of a thing over time, of which personal identity is a particular form.

Divisibility thesis is the concept that persons are complexes of psychological or physical things that may be divided.

Dualism is the view that both material and non-material things exist.

Élan vital is, according to Bergson, the creative force that makes up the universe, a force of which we persons are expressions. (*See* chapter 8.)

Emotivism is an ethical view that moral claims are not statements of fact but merely expressions of emotion. Russell held this view as described in chapter 9.

Empiricism emphasizes the role of the five senses as the ultimate way to gain knowledge. Our mental analyses can get us nothing without sensory input. Locke, Berkeley, and Hume were empiricists. (*See* chapters 5 and 6.)

Epistemic social contract is an ideal social contract containing the rules of evidence that specify what counts as genuine knowledge. Like the ethical and metaphysical contracts it is conceived as what would be agreed to by those in the original position.

Epistemology is the field of philosophy in which we study theories of knowledge.

Epoche (or bracketing) is Husserl's device of looking at things with pure vision, not distracted by any features of the thing seen that are not immediately present to experience. For instance, if one looks at a painting and thinks of how much it cost or what pigments make up the colours, one is not bracketing things like that out. Epoche is just looking. (*See* chapter 8.)

Essential properties are the properties of a thing (or its essence) that it never loses as long as it exists; those properties that define it. They are said to be necessary properties of that thing.

Ethics is the field of philosophy in which we study moral concepts, judgments, and codes.

Euthanasia is the taking of a human life or allowing a human being to die with the intention of being merciful to that person. Euthanasia is voluntary when the patient asks to die, involuntary when the patient asks to live, and non-voluntary when the patient is not capable of expressing the choice between life and death and has left no advance directives to tell us what her or his wishes are. Active euthanasia is killing the patient. For example, giving a lethal injection to prevent a patient from dying a horrible death through bowel cancer is clearly active. Passive euthanasia is letting the patient die. For example, allowing a severely deformed newborn to die of pneumonia rather than giving antibiotics is generally called "passive."

Existentialism is a philosophical movement without any single doctrine common to all who are in the movement. There is a general emphasis on the importance and uniqueness of individual persons and their exercise of personal freedom. The rejection of essentialist doctrines concerning persons, the importance of being authentic in the sense of true to one's own chosen values, and anxiety concerning approaching death are all common themes. Many of those categorized as existentialists have rejected the label.

Experience principle is the view of empiricists that we should not affirm the existence of that which we do not experience.

Extension is possessed by objects that take up room in space. They are extended in space. The body is usually said to have this feature, while the mind is not.

Fallacy of misplaced concreteness is, by Whitehead's lights, the error of taking the abstractions of science and treating them as if they were concrete things (*See* chapter 8). Seeing persons as particular individuals commits this error.

Fission (of persons) is any process, such as duplication, in which two persons result from one person. This is still science fiction.

Forced options are, according to William James, unavoidable choices between hypotheses. (*See* chapter 7.)

Forms are for Plato the fully real universals that particular things, as they appear to us, only dimly resemble. For Aristotle they are that which imparts character or structure to matter, and a form is usually inseparable from the formed matter (*See* universal and particular). (*See* chapter 3.)

Foundationalism is the epistemological view that there are fundamental knowledge claims that need no justification on the basis of which the rest of our knowledge is justified. Descartes tried to lay a firm foundation for all knowledge with his Cogito ("I think; hence, I am.")

Free persons are those who could possibly exercise their will to do otherwise than they in fact do.

Fugues are periods of prolonged amnesia together with a flight from one's usual surroundings.

Functionalism (with respect to persons) is the view that person is a category determined by abilities; hence, it can change with convention in contrast to a natural kind. Persons are not tied to particular bodies by functional accounts.

Fundamental particulars are the basic objects of our metaphysics in terms of which other things are understood.

Fundamental value thesis is the view that psychological continuity and connectedness, not personal identity, are what is basically important about people.

Fusion (of persons) is any process, such as merging, in which one person results from two persons. Since head transplants have been medically feasible since 1972, it is debatable whether fusion is merely science fiction.

Genuine option is William James's term for a decision between two hypotheses that are living, momentous, and forced. (*See* chapter 7.)

Hard determinists are determinists who reject compatibilism. They say that the freedom of persons is an illusion. Behaviourists are often in this category.

Hoi polloi is a Greek term for the majority of people used in the sense of the common people.

Humanism is a set of themes rather than a single doctrine. It puts persons first not as things subject to the divine or mere puppets of the environment. It takes people seriously as individual free moral agents. It is opposed to those ways of seeing persons that make either the supernatural or science predominate in the explanation of human action.

Hypothesis is a supposition to be tested. Berkeley thinks that we do not need to suppose that there is any physical stuff to explain our experiences.

Ideal social contract as I use the term here refers to a set of rules governing how we are to act, what is to be considered real and what can be known. These are rules that would be chosen by persons in the purely hypothetical original position. Normally the term is used only in ethical contexts, but I extend it to metaphysics and epistemology. *See* original position.

Idealism is the view that there is no matter, just minds, ideas, and perhaps other immaterial things that give rise to the illusion of a material world.

Identity criterion is a phrase used to speak of standards that we use to determine whether things are identical. For example the bodily criterion, the brain criterion, the mind criterion, and the soul criterion are standards for saying under what conditions a person at one time is identical with a person at another time.

Identity of indiscernibles is the principle that things that cannot possibly be discerned from one another are identical. In other words, if *x* and *y* have all their properties in common, then *x* is identical to *y*.

Immanental essences are the things one sees through Husserl's epoche. Unfortunately, persons are not among these.

Immediate perception is unmediated or direct perception. When one sees something with one's own eyes, one's perception is direct while, if one sees it through the medium of television, it is mediated. Some might claim that all perception would be mediated by the senses if there were a world outside the mind and senses to perceive it.

Incorruptible things are those that cannot rot or otherwise lose their essences.

Indefinability (of persons) has two senses: (1) We cannot say what is essential for being a person in general, and (2) We cannot say, for a particular person, what makes one who one is. Persons have, in both senses, intransmissible essences.

Indeterminacy thesis is the view that the question, Am I about to die? does not always have a definite answer.

Indexical as used by Ryle is a word that indicates to the hearer the particular thing, episode, person, place, or moment referred to. "I" is an important indexical in the discussion of persons. It is also called an index word.

Indiscernibility of identicals is the principle that things cannot possibly be discerned from one another. In other words, if *x* is identical to *y*, then *x* and *y* have all their properties in common.

Individualism is the doctrine that each person is a unique individual morally responsible for her/his own choices. It is opposed to doctrines that treat human beings as varying expressions of some larger person. Most of the philosophers we discuss accept individualism, while Avicenna, Averroës, and Spinoza, for example, do not.

Individuative naturalism is Wiggins' view that person is a natural kind under which we individuate persons. Persons are in a category of things determined by nature, not by their own conventions. To tell who is who, you must distinguish each person from others in this kind or category.

Indivisible persons may exist in two senses: (1) if and only if they are not complex, and (2) if and only if their essential properties must always remain bundled together for the person to exist. Sense (2) is opposed to sense (1).

Inductive arguments attempt to establish their conclusions with some degree of probability given the premises—the higher the degree, the stronger the argument.

Inference to the best explanation (IBE) is the principle that, if a hypothesis is the best explanation of the data, then that hypothesis is true. It is a very controversial principle. Among those who accept it, there is a debate over what "best" should be taken to mean.

Interaction problem is the difficulty of saying how the mind or other non-physical part of the person interacts with the physical part, the body. How can the mind cause the body to act?

Interchangeable *salva veritate* means "substitutable for one another without changing truth-values." It is said of terms. If "John is a bachelor" is true, then "John is an unmarried male of marriageable age" is true. The terms "bachelor" and "unmarried male of marriageable age" are interchangeable *salva veritate* in this context. They would not be in the sentence, "John is a Bachelor of Arts."

Intransmissible means incommunicable. A computer program is not intransmissible, because we can transmit it from one computer to another. Essences of persons, however, were thought to be intransmissible so that a person could not move from one body to another.

Intuition is a way to acquire knowledge—according to some philosophers, for instance Spinoza and Descartes—that does not use reason, perception, memory, or even introspection. With intuition, we immediately see things to be true. Descartes thinks that each of us can intuitively know the proposition "I exist" to be true beyond the evidence of a demonstration (*See* chapter 5). Intuition is, according to Bergson, a kind of knowledge that involves seeing the universe from the perspective of the object known as if one were the object. Intuition is opposed to the usual scientific knowledge by observation that Bergson calls "analysis" (*See* chapter 8).

Irreducibility of persons is the impossibility of reducing persons to a set of parts in a certain configuration. Persons are more than the sum of their parts, if they are irreducible. *See* reductionism.

Leibniz's law is the identity of indiscernibles plus the indiscernibility of identicals, in other words, x is identical to y if and only if x and y have the same properties. *See* properties and A if and only if B.

Libertarianism is the view—in the context of the free choice debate—that persons are free in the sense that the past does not determine their future choices or actions; persons themselves determine their own choices.

Living options are, according to William James, choices between two hypotheses both of which are live, that is, both are real possibilities to the person making the choice. (*See* chapter 7.)

Logical positivism is empiricism plus the verification principle. As a philosophical movement it rejected many of the traditional claims of religion, ethics, and metaphysics. Also called logical empiricism. *See* verification principle.

Man is the measure is Protagoras' way of expressing the view that reality is relative to the observer. (*See* chapter 3.)

Materialism is the view that everything that exists is matter.

Mechanism is the view that the activities of persons can all be explained by the mechanical analysis of the motion of particles, just as we can explain the movement of billiard balls. Hobbes held this view. The word is also used more broadly for the view that persons are to be understood as complex machines.

Metaphysical social contract is a set of claims about what is real that equally powerful, equally intelligent, self-interested human beings would assent to if they were utterly ignorant about the particulars of their own lives.

Metaphysics is the field of philosophy in which we study theories about reality and existence.

Mode is Locke's word for a token of a property, for example, a particular patch of redness as opposed to that type of redness in general.

Momentous options are, according to William James, extraordinarily important decisions that we have a unique chance to make. (*See* chapter 7.)

Mono-relatedness is a relation between two people who are related as closest continuer and closest predecessor to one another. This is probably intended to rule out merging or splitting of persons.

Mutual love, as defined by Ross, is "a blend of virtuous disposition of two minds towards each other, with the knowledge which each has of the character and disposition of the other, and with the pleasure which arises from such disposition and knowledge." (*See* chapter 2.)

Natural kinds are types of things that are determined by natural laws and discovered by attending to the properties of any good specimen of that kind. Gold, for example, is a natural kind. Such kinds are discovered, not created by our conventions. If a thing *x* is a member of the natural kind *N*, then *x* is necessarily a member of *N*. Natural kinds are classifications fixed by nature. Quine thinks there are none. (*See* chapter 10.)

Neutral Monism is the view that mind and matter are both made out of one kind of thing.

Nominalism is the position with respect to universals (e.g., redness) that they are merely linguistic, and are not real entities, as the metaphysical realists hold. Nominalists say that words such as "redness" do not refer to things in the world. Realists say they pick out real things such as Forms or properties.

Non-relational properties do not stand as a relation between two things but are simply properties of a single thing. For example, the property of being bigger than relates two things. The property of being red seems to be a property that can be had by one thing in isolation, so it might be thought of as purely qualitative. This is controversial.

No-ownership view is Strawson's term for those views—for instance, Wittgenstein's and Hume's—which allow for experiences without anyone to have or own those experiences.

Noumenal describes, for Kant, the world behind the world of appearances. *See* phenomenal. (*See* chapter 7.)

Numerical identity is sameness or genuine identity as opposed to mere qualitative identity. If *x* and *y* are numerically identical, *x* is the same thing as *y*, not just completely similar to *y*.

Objective means intersubjective. A group of individuals can share objective knowledge or morality. (Unfortunately, "objective" is sometimes used to mean "absolute." This is confusing. Let us stay with the definitions given here.)

Ockham's razor is the principle that entities are not to be multiplied beyond necessity. This minimalist metaphysical principle, due to William of Ockham, is wielded by Russell and more fiercely still by Quine. (*See* chapters 9 and 10.)

Ordinary language philosophers (e.g., Ryle and Strawson), believe that fundamental philosophical concepts are determined by linguistic usage.

Original position refers to a purely imaginary position in which people find themselves equally powerful, equally intelligent, self-interested, and completely ignorant of any information particular to themselves like that would tell them what their advantages and disadvantages might be in the real world. They do understand the general human condition. *See* ideal social contract.

Particular is an individual thing as opposed to something more general such as one of its properties. It is a token, not a type.

Passional beliefs are beliefs "based on emotion and will," according to William James. (*See* chapter 7.)

Persona is a Latin term for an actor's mask meaning literally "through the sound holes" to refer to the sound holes in the mask. Masks stood for roles that the actor played, so *persona* came to mean a role that one plays. This is one sense of "person."

Phenomenal for Kant, describes the world as we know it, the set of objects of our experience. Our knowledge cannot penetrate to the noumenal world, the reality behind the appearances in the phenomenal world, the things in themselves. Things in the noumenal world, such as our freedom, are transcendental. They transcend the phenomena. We are phenomenally caused but transcendentally free. (*See* chapter 7.)

Phenomenalism is Berkeley's view of the world without God to take care of difficulties (see chapter 6). To be is to be perceived. The universe is just minds and ideas, especially perceptions. Objects are permanent possibilities of perception. When we think we see material objects, we just have perceptions in a regular sequence as if there were such objects external to our minds. Matter is an unnecessary hypothesis.

Phenomenology is the study of the world through Husserl's method of epoche. (*See* chapter 8.)

Positivism is a strict empiricism founded by Auguste Comte (1798-1857). (*See* chapter 7.) Comte believed that knowledge comes from observation and that there is no knowledge of things that cannot be observed. He opposed metaphysical speculation about unobservable things. His views were adapted by the logical positivists of the 1920s. They added the verification principle that any meaningful statement is either empirically verifiable or analytically true. Since the principle itself is neither, positivism has undergone considerable refinement since the 1920s and tends to go by names other than positivism.

Pragmatism is a philosophical movement that emphasizes actions flowing from theories. Meaning, in particular, is explained in terms of what we would do.

Predecessor (of a person) is the one who caused a person to have the properties that she/he has.

Primary qualities are the objective, quantifiable properties of things that are really in the things, as opposed to being mere artifacts of the way we perceive those things. Motion, size, position, and density have been offered as examples. (*See* Secondary qualities.)

Primitive terms are terms that are not defined but are used as the basis for defining all other terms in a given context. If "point" is primitive in Euclidean geometry, then "line" can be defined as the shortest distance between two points. Point is left undefined.

Properties of a thing are features or qualities of that thing. Properties are usually taken to be universals. Locke, however, talks about particular instantiations of properties. *See* mode.

Pseudo-questions are sentences that appear to ask a question but, through lack of meaning or some other linguistic problem, do not succeed in asking anything at all. For example, Is it hotter in the south than it is in the summer? is such a sentence. One may argue that, What is a person? is such a sentence.

Psuche was Aristotles' term for soul, self or organizing principle of a living organism. It does not have the same meaning as our term "psyche." (See chapter 3.)

Psychological connectedness is the holding of particular direct psychological connections. Parfit talks about beliefs, desires, and memories but allows any other psychological feature to be part of the chain. (*See* chapter 13.)

Psychological continuity is the holding of overlapping chains of strong connectedness.

Purely qualitative properties are non-relational.

Qualitative identity is complete similarity, the sharing of all properties, or, in other words, indiscernibility.

Question begging (or begging the question) is a fault in argument, namely, making an unproved claim that implies that one's own side of the debate is right.

Rationalism emphasizes the role of reason and the mind over the senses. Descartes, Leibniz, and Spinoza were rationalists.

Reducibility thesis is the view that is theoretically possible to describe all of reality without mentioning people.

Reductionism is the acceptance of the reducibility thesis. On this view, a person is what has experiences, as a matter of linguistic convention. A person, however, is not something over and above the body, including the brain, and the physical and mental events associated with the body. (*See* irreducibility and reducibility thesis.)

Reduplication is the term Williams uses to speak of producing exact copies of living persons.

Reflexive caring is caring for oneself as oneself.

Reflexive self-reference is the reference of a term at least in part to itself each time it is used. The term "I," for instance, refers to the producer of this token of itself.

Reflexivity (of relations) is a property relations have when they relate things to themselves. Identity is reflexive since, for any thing x, $x = x$. Similarity is reflexive, since for anything x, x is similar to x. The relation "is as old as" is also reflexive. Nozick uses the term more generally to talk about things that loop back on or feed into themselves, such as self-reference of the term "I" or caring for oneself as oneself.

Relation *R* holds between person p and a later person q if q has strong connectedness to p.

Relative means dependent. Subjective values are relative to individuals. Objective ones are relative to groups. Absolute ones are not relative to anything.

Relative identity is a kind of identity that applies to things when they are categorized in one way but not to the same things categorized in another. For example, we might say that an Alzheimer's patient is the same human being he used to be but not the same person he once was. Wiggins thinks there is no such identity.

Secondary qualities are the subjective, unquantifiable properties of things that depend on the way we see those things. Colour, taste, and sound have been offered as examples. (*See* Primary qualities.)

Self-existent things are things that are not merely parts or qualities (properties) of another thing.

Self-synthesis is self-creation through the act of choosing one's own similarity metric within the limits specified by closest continuer theory. It includes an act of reflexive caring. (*See* Closest continuer theory.)

Sense data are things immediately known in sensation. You might look at the chalkboard and see a green patch in your field of vision. The green patch is a sense datum that helps to convince you that there is a chalkboard before you. Sense data are usually thought of as mental events caused by the input through the senses from objects outside the mind.

Short path problem is the problem of who to see as the continuing person when the closest continuer is very short lived and a close runner up as closest continuer is long-lived. This is Nozick's term. (*See* Closest continuer.)

Similarity metrics are sets of properties of persons weighted with respect to their importance for the continuation of the person. These are, in part, determined by the choices of the person whose closest continuers and predecessors they are used to identify. (*See* Closest continuer theory.)

Skepticism is doubt. Cartesian skepticism is doubt that one can know anything for certain but one's own mind and the kinds of things going on in it. This epistemological view may lead to metaphysical solipsism. Humean skepticism is doubt about the existence of the self.

Soft determinists are determinists who accept compatibilism. The Stoics, Spinoza, Hobbes, Locke, and Hume are soft determinists, as were the Protestant reformers. (*See* Compatibilism.)

Solipsism is the view that one's own mind is the only existing thing.

Sortals (or sortal predicates) are terms that describe things in such a way that they imply identity conditions for those things. To say something is a gold specimen or a person is to say under what conditions that thing would be the same gold specimen or the same person. Terms for natural kinds are thought to be sortals by Wiggins and others who accept their existence. (*See* chapter 11.)

Sound arguments have both validity and true premises. (*See* validity.)

Space-time worms, (four dimensional) are objects that trace a continuous path through three dimensions of space and one of time. At any point in time they have a location at or next to the location they had at the previous point in time if they are continuous.

Spatio-temporally continuous means uninterrupted through space and time. A continuous particular draws a smooth locus through space and time without any gaps. It occupies a series of contiguous moments and locations. Think of a book-worm chewing through the pages of space and time. There is a hole in every page and it is near the same position on the page as the hole in the page before. Philosophers sometimes speak of continuous physical particulars as continuous space-time worms.

Spectra are Parfit's examples of a gradual physical spectrum of change and a gradual mental spectrum of change that a person might go through to become totally different. (*See* chapter 13.)

Strong connectedness is present in a person if, every day, that person retains at least half of the direct connections to that person's mind in the day previous. For example, if you remember half of what happened to you the day before, you are strongly connected to yourself yesterday, but memory is just one way of being connected.

Subjective means dependent on an individual.

Substance concepts are concepts that apply to things through their life span. "Person" is one according to Wiggins, but "infant" is not.

Substances (or hypostases) are the underlying things that have properties. A red ball has redness and roundness as properties. If we strip away all the properties, conceptually, then we are left with the substance in which these properties inhere.

Teleological ethical theories are theories such as utilitarianism that justify actions by appeal to their ends or consequences. The ends justify the means.

Teletransportation for Parfit is the science fiction thought experiment in which one enters a booth and presses a button, after which a machine records one's every feature. One is destroyed and the information about one is sent to a distant location. This information is then used to produce there one's exact replica who acts and thinks just as one would if one had travelled physically to that location. Parfit thinks this is just about as good as ordinary survival. (*See* chapter 13.)

Telos is the end or purpose that guides and may even determine the development of a thing. Aristotle would say that the *telos* of an acorn is an oak, which determines the development of the acorn.

Thinking substance is the underlying thing that supports the property of having ideas. It is not itself an idea or a property.

Transferability principle is my term for Strawson's claim that "only those things whose ownership is logically transferable can be owned at all." (*See* chapter 10.)

Type is a category of thing, while a token is an individual thing of that type. The token has the properties that define the type. You are one token of the type "person." You exemplify the type.

Unconditioned values are absolute values. For example, Kant would say that a person has unconditioned value, not value depending on some condition being satisfied.

Unconscious is any part of our mind of which we are not aware.

Universal is something that can be shared by many particulars such as the property of being red. It is a type, not a token.

Utilitarianism is an ethical theory that an action is morally right if and only if it creates the greatest pleasure and least suffering for the greatest number of sentient beings affected by that action.

Valid deductive arguments are those in which it is impossible for the conclusion to be false if the premises are true.

Verification principle refers to Wittgenstein's principle that the meaning of a proposition is identical with the method of verifying it. It is interpreted by early positivists as implying that a proposition is meaningful if and only if it is either analytic or empirical. (*See* Logical positivism and chapter 9.)

Viewline refers to the series of viewpoints throughout a person's life.

Viewpoints are subjectively known places from which we seem to ourselves to be getting our sensations and perceptions of the world outside of our minds.

Worldviews are systematic philosophical theories including a metaphysics, epistemology, and axiology. They cover reality, knowledge, and value, and answer the questions of what we are, what our world is, what we can know, and what we should do.

Zygote is a single fertilized cell, the union of the sperm and ovum, sometimes thought of as the beginning of the development of such organisms as human beings.

Bibliography

Aristotle. *De Anima*. In *The Basic Works of Aristotle*, edited by Richard McKeon, 535-606. New York: Random House, 1941.

———. *Nicomachean Ethics*. Translated by W.D. Ross. Oxford: Oxford University Press, 1925.

Asch, Solomon. "The Psychology of Relativism." In *Social Psychology*. Englewood Cliffs, NJ: Prentice Hall, 1952. Reprinted in *Philosophy: Paradox and Discovery*, edited by Arthur J. Minton, 215-22. New York: McGraw-Hill, 1976.

Ayer, A.J. "The Concept of a Person." In *The Concept of a Person and Other Essays*. London: Macmillan, 1963, 82-128.

Baier, Annette. *Moral Prejudices*. Cambridge MA: Harvard University Press, 1994.

Barry, Vincent. *Philosophy: A Text with Readings*. Belmont, CA: Wadsworth, 1980.

Berkeley, George. "Three Dialogues between Hylas and Philonous." In *Berkeley: Essay, Principles, Dialogues with Selections from Other Writings*, edited by Mary W. Calkins. New York: Charles Scribner's Sons, 1937, 217-344.

Berlinski, David. *Philosophy: The Cutting Edge*. Port Washington, NY: Alfred Publishing, 1976.

Black, Max. "The Identity of Indiscernibles." *Mind* ns 61 (1952): 153-64.

Bourgeois, Warren. "The Identity of Indiscernibles." PhD thesis, University of California, Irvine, 1979.

Card, Claudia. *Feminist Ethics*. Lawrence: University Press of Kansas, 1991.

Carrithers, Michael, Steven Collins, and Steven Lukes, eds. *The Category of the Person: Anthropology, Philosophy, History*. Cambridge: Cambridge University Press, 1985.

Churchland, Patricia S. and Paul M. Churchland. "Could a Machine Think?" *Scientific American*, January 1990, 32-37.

Code, Lorraine. *What Can She Know?Feminist Theory and the Construction of Knowledge.* Ithaca: Cornell University Press, 1991.

Cole, Eve Browning. *Philosophy and Feminist Criticism: An Introduction.* New York: Paragon House, 1993.

Danto, Arthur C. "Persons." In *The Encyclopedia of Philosophy.* Vol. 6, 110-14. London: Macmillan and New York: Free Press, 1967.

Dennett, Daniel C. *The Intentional Stance.* Cambridge, MA: MIT Press, 1989.

Descartes, René. *Discourse on Method.* Translated by John Veitch. In *The Rationalists.* Garden City, NY: Dolphin Books, 1960, 1-96.

———. *Meditations.* Translated by John Veitch. In *The Rationalists.* Garden City, NY: Dolphin Books, 1960, 99-175.

Deutsch, Eliot. *Personhood, Creativity, and Freedom.* Honolulu: University of Hawaii Press, 1982.

Dewey, John. "The Nature of Moral Philosophy." In *The Moral Writings of John Dewey,* edited by James Gounlock. New York: Hafner Press, 1976, 1-22.

English, Jane. "Abortion and the Concept of a Person." *The Canadian Journal of Philosophy* 5, 2 (October 1970). Reprinted in *Biomedical Ethics,* edited by T.A. Mappes and J.S. Zembaty, 479-80. New York: McGraw-Hill, 1986.

Farias, Victor. *Heidegger and Nazism.* Philadelphia: Temple University Press, 1990.

Findlay, J.N. *Values and Intentions.* New York: George Allen and Unwin, 1961.

Flew, Antony, editorial consultant. *A Dictionary of Philosophy.* London: Pan Books, 1979.

Frankfurt, Harry G. *The Importance of What We Care About.* Cambridge: Cambridge University Press, 1988.

Fromm, Erich, and Ramón Xirau. *The Nature of Man.* New York: Collier, 1968.

Geertz, Clifford. *Local Knowledge: Essays in Interpretive Anthropology.* New York: Basic Books, 1983.

Glover, Jonathan. *I: The Philosophy and Psychology of Personal Identity.* London: Penguin Books, 1988.

Goodin, Robert E. "Ethical Principles for Environmental Protection." In *Contemporary Moral Issues,* edited by Wesley Cragg, 323-35. 3rd ed. Toronto: McGraw-Hill Ryerson, 1992.

Goudge, T.A. "Bergson, Henri." In *The Encyclopedia of Philosophy.* Vol. 3, pp. 287-94. London: Macmillan and New York: Free Press, 1967.

Grant, Sheila and George Grant. "Abortion and Rights." In *Contemporary Moral Issues,* edited by Wesley Cragg, 68-74. 3rd ed. Toronto: McGraw-Hill Ryerson, 1992.

Gregory, Richard L. "Hegel." In *The Oxford Companion to the Mind,* edited by Richard L. Gregory. Oxford: Oxford University Press, 1987, 308.

Hegel, G.W.F. *The Phenomenology of Mind.* Translated by J.B. Baillie. New York: Harper Colophon Books, 1967.

Heidegger, Martin. *Being and Time.* New York: Harper & Row, 1962.

Held, Virginia. *Feminist Morality: Transforming Culture, Society, and Politics.* Chicago: University of Chicago Press, 1993.

Hobbes, Thomas. *Leviathan.* London: J.M. Dent and Sons, 1914.

Hume, David. *A Treatise of Human Nature*. Edited by L.A. Selby-Bigge. Oxford: Oxford University Press, 1973.

Husserl, Edmund. *Ideas: General Introduction to Pure Phenomenology*. London: Collier Macmillan, 1962.

Jaggar, Allison M. "Feminist Ethics: Projects, Problems, Prospects" in *Feminist Ethics*, edited by Claudia Card, 78-104. Lawrence: University Press of Kansas, 1991.

James, William. "The Will to Believe." An Address to the Philosophical Club of Yale and Brown Universities. In *Reason and Responsibility*, edited by J. Feinberg, 91-98. Belmont, CA: Wadsworth, 1989. First published in *New World* (1896).

———. *Pragmatism and Other Essays*. New York: Washington Square Press, 1963.

Kant, Immanuel. *Groundwork of the Metaphysic of Morals*. Translated by H.J. Paton. New York: Harper & Row, 1964.

———. *Critique of Pure Reason*. Translated by Norman Kemp Smith. New York: St. Martin's Press, 1965.

Kaplan, Abraham. *The Conduct of Inquiry: Methodology for Behavioural Science*. New York: Chandler Publishing, 1964.

Kaufmann, Walter. *Hegel: A Reinterpretation*. Notre Dame: University of Notre Dame Press, 1965.

Korner, S. *Kant*. Harmondsworth, England: Pelican Books, 1955.

Kripke, Saul. A. *Naming and Necessity*. Cambridge, MA: Harvard University Press, 1972.

Leibniz, G.W. *New Essays on Human Understanding*. Translated and edited by Peter Remnant and Jonathan Bennett. Cambridge: Cambridge University Press, 1981.

Lewis, David. "Survival and Identity." In *The Identities of Persons*, edited by Amelie O. Rorty, 17-40. Berkeley: University of California Press, 1976.

Locke, John. *An Essay Concerning Human Understanding*. London: J.M. Dent and Sons, 1961.

———. *The Second Treatise of Government* in *Two Treatises of Government*, edited by Peter Laslett, 299-478. New York: Mentor, 1960.

MacIntyre, Alasdair. "Existentialism." In *The Encyclopedia of Philosophy*. Vol. 3, 147-54. London: Macmillan and New York: Free Press, 1967.

Minton, Arthur J. *Philosophy: Paradox and Discovery*. New York: McGraw-Hill, 1976.

Montaigne, Michel de. *Apology for Raymond Sebond*. In Fromm and Xirau, *The Nature of Man*, 133-35.

Moore, G.E. *Principia Ethica*. Cambridge: Cambridge University Press, 1971.

Morris, Charles W. *Six Theories of Mind*. Chicago: University of Chicago Press, 1932.

Morris, Herbert. "Persons and Punishment." *The Monist* 52, 4 (October 1968). Reprinted in *Philosophy of Law*, edited by Joel Feinberg. 2nd ed. Belmont CA: Wadsworth, 1975, 582-94.

Morton, Adam. "Why There Is No Concept of the Person." In *The Person and the Human Mind: Issues in Ancient and Modern Philosophy*, edited by Christopher Gill, 39-68. Oxford: Clarendon Press, 1990.

Murphey, Murray G. "Peirce, Charles Sanders." In *The Encyclopedia of Philosophy*. Vol. 6, 70-78. London: Macmillan and New York: Free Press, 1967.

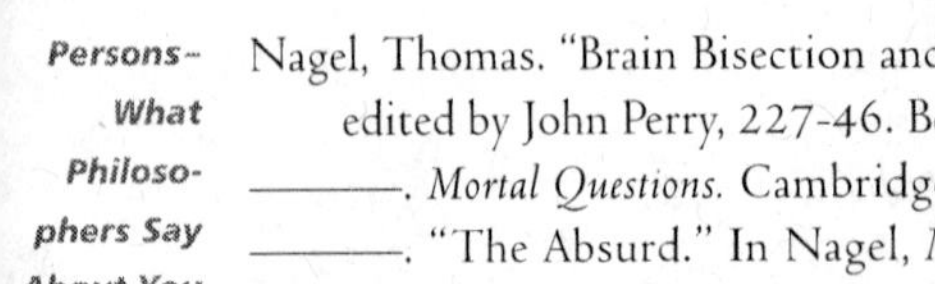

Nagel, Thomas. "Brain Bisection and the Unity of Consciousness." In *Personal Identity*, edited by John Perry, 227-46. Berkeley, CA: University of California Press, 1975.

———. *Mortal Questions.* Cambridge: Cambridge University Press, 1979.

———. "The Absurd." In Nagel, *Mortal Questions*, 11-23.

———. *The View from Nowhere.* Oxford: Oxford University Press, 1986.

Nahm, Milton C. *Selections from Early Greek Philosophy*. New York: Appleton, Century, Crofts, 1947.

Noddings, Nel. *Caring: A Feminine Approach to Ethics and Moral Education*. Berkeley: University of California Press, 1984.

Noonan, Harold W. *Personal Identity*. London: Routledge, 1989.

Nozick, Robert. *Philosophical Explanations*. Cambridge, MA: Harvard University Press, 1981.

Parfit, Derek. "Personal Identity." *The Philosophical Review* 80, 1 (January 1971). Reprinted in *Personal Identity*, edited by John Perry, 199-226. Berkeley: University of California Press, 1975.

———. *Reasons and Persons*. Oxford: Oxford University Press, 1986. Originally published 1984.

Pascal, Blaise. *Penseés: Notes on Religion and Other Subjects*. Edited by Louis Lafuma. Translated by John Warrington. London: J.M. Dent and Sons, 1960.

Passmore, John. "Logical Positivism." In *The Encyclopedia of Philosophy*. Vol. 5, 52-57. London: Macmillan and New York: Free Press, 1967.

Pears, David F. "Russell's Philosophy of Mind: Dualism." In *The Oxford Companion to the Mind*, edited by Richard L. Gregory, 688-90. Oxford: Oxford University Press, 1987.

———. "Russell's Philosophy of Mind: Neutral Monism." In *The Oxford Companion to the Mind*, edited by Richard L. Gregory, 690-91. Oxford: Oxford University Press, 1987.

Perry, John. "The Problem of Personal Identity." In *Personal Identity*. Berkeley: University of California Press, 1975.

———. "The Importance of Being Identical." In *The Identities of Persons*, edited by Amelie O. Rorty. Berkeley: University of California Press, 1976.

Plato. *The Collected Dialogues*. Edited by Edith Hamilton and Huntington Cairns. Princeton, NJ: Princeton University Press, 1961.

Puccetti, R. "Brain Bisection and Personal Identity." *British Journal for the Philosophy of Science* 24: 339-55.

Putnam, Hilary. *Representation and Reality*. Cambridge, MA: MIT Press, 1989.

Quine, Willard V. "Two Dogmas of Empiricism." In *From a Logical Point of View: Logico-philosophical Essays*, pp. 20-46. New York: Harper & Row, 1953.

———. "Identity, Ostension and Hypostasis." In *From a Logical Point of View: Logico-philosophical Essays*, pp. 65-69.

———. "Russell's Ontological Development." In *Essays on Bertrand Russell*, edited by E.D. Klemke, 3-14. Chicago: University of Illinois Press, 1970.

———. *The Roots of Reference: The Paul Carus Lectures*. Lasalle, IL: Open Court Publishing, 1973.

______. *Theories and Things*. Cambridge, MA: Harvard University Press, 1981.

Rawls, John. *A Theory of Justice*. Cambridge, MA: Harvard University Press, 1971.

Rorty, Amelie Oksenberg, ed. *The Identities of Persons*. Berkeley: University of California Press, 1976.

———. "A Literary Postscript: Characters, Persons, Selves and Individuals." In *The Identities of Persons*, 301-24.

______. "Persons and Persona." In *The Person and the Human Mind: Issues in Ancient and Modern Philosophy*, edited by Christopher Gill, 21-38. Oxford: Clarendon Press, 1990.

Rorty, Richard. *Contingency, Irony, and Solidarity*. Cambridge: Cambridge University Press, 1989.

Ross, David. *Aristotle*. London: Methuen, 1949.

Ross, W.D. *The Right and the Good*. Oxford: Oxford University Press, 1930.

Russell, Bertrand. *Human Knowledge: Its Scope and Limits*. London: George Allen and Unwin, 1948.

———. *The Problems of Philosophy*. Oxford: Oxford University Press, 1959.

———. *An Inquiry into Meaning and Truth*. Baltimore, MD: Penguin Books, 1962.

———. *An Outline of Philosophy*. London: George Allen and Unwin, 1970.

———. "Science and Ethics." In *Philosophy: Paradox and Discovery*, edited by Arthur J. Minton. New York: McGraw-Hill, 1976, 223-38.

Rycroft, Charles. "Dissociation of the Personality." In *The Oxford Companion to the Mind*, edited by Richard L. Gregory, 197-98. Oxford: Oxford University Press, 1987.

Ryle, Gilbert. *The Concept of Mind*. Harmondsworth, Middlesex: Penguin Books, 1963.

Sartre, Jean-Paul. *Existentialism and Humanism*. Translated by Philip Mairet. London: Methuen, 1949.

———. *Being and Nothingness: A Phenomenological Essay on Ontology*. Translated by Hazel E. Barnes. New York: Washington Square Press, 1966.

Schlitz, D. *The Gambler.* Elektra/Asylum Records, ASCAP, 1980.

Silver, Lee M. *Remaking Eden: Cloning and Beyond in a Brave New World*. New York: Avon Books, 1997.

Singer, Peter. *Practical Ethics*. Cambridge: Cambridge University Press, 1979.

Smith, Steven G. *The Concept of the Spiritual: An Essay in First Philosophy*. Philadelphia: Temple University Press, 1988.

Stevenson, Leslie. *Seven Theories of Human Nature*. 2nd ed. Oxford: Oxford University Press, 1987.

Stone, Jim. "Parfit and the Buddha: Why There Are No People." *Philosophy and Phenomenological Research* 68, 3 (March 1988): 519-32.

Strawson, P.F. *Individuals: An Essay in Descriptive Metaphysics*. London: Methuen, 1959.

Stumpf, Samuel E. *Socrates to Sartre: A History of Philosophy*. 4th ed. New York: McGraw-Hill, 1988.

Thines, Georges. "Husserl." In *The Oxford Companion to the Mind*, edited by Richard L. Gregory, 326-27. Oxford: Oxford University Press, 1987.

Tolstoï, Lyof N. *Life*. London: Walter Scott, 1889.

Trendelenberg, Adolf. "A Contribution to the History of the Word Person: A Posthumous Treatise by Adolf Trendelenberg." Translated by Carl H. Haessler. *Monist* 20 (1910): 336-63.

Trevarthen, Colwyn. "Split Brain and the Mind." In *The Oxford Companion to the Mind*, edited by Richard L. Gregory, 741-46. Oxford: Oxford University Press, 1987.

Trigg, Roger. *Ideas of Human Nature*. Oxford: Basil Blackwell, 1988.

Unger, Peter. *Identity Consciousness and Value*. Oxford: Oxford University Press, 1990.

Walker, Ralph. "Leibniz's Philosophy of Mind." In *The Oxford Companion to the Mind*, edited by Richard Gregory, 433. Oxford: Oxford University Press, 1987.

Wedeking, Gary. "Locke's Metaphysics of Personal Identity." *History of Philosophy Quarterly* 4 (January 1987): 17-31.

Whitehead, Alfred North. *Symbolism: Its Meaning and Effect*. New York: G.P. Putnam's Sons, 1959.

———. *Process and Reality*. New York: Free Press, 1969.

Wiggins, David. *Identity and Spatio-temporal Continuity*. Oxford: Basil Blackwell, 1967.

———. *Sameness and Substance*. Oxford: Basil Blackwell, 1980.

Wilkes, Kathleen. *Real People: Personal Identity without Thought Experiments*. Oxford: Oxford University Press, 1988.

Williams, Bernard. *Morality: An Introduction to Ethics*. New York: Harper & Row, 1972.

———. *Problems of the Self*. Cambridge: Cambridge University Press, 1973.

———. "Personal Identity and Individuation." In *Problems of the Self*, 1-18.

———. "Are Persons Bodies?" In *Problems of the Self*, 64-81.

———. *Ethics and the Limits of Philosophy*. Cambridge, MA: Harvard University Press, 1985.

Wittgenstein, Ludwig. *The Blue and Brown Books*. New York: Harper Colophon Books, 1958.

———. *Tractatus Logico-Philosophicus*. Translated by D.F. Pears and B.F. MacGuinness. London: Routledge and Kegan Paul, 1961.

———. *Philosophical Remarks*. Edited by Rush Rhees. Translated by Raymond Hargreaves and Roger White. Oxford: Basil Blackwell, 1975.

———. *Philosophical Investigations*. Translated by G.E.M. Anscombe. Oxford: Basil Blackwell, 1976.

Index